DATE DUE

The Meaning of Modern Business

THE MEANING OF

Modern

Business

AN INTRODUCTION TO

THE PHILOSOPHY OF

LARGE CORPORATE ENTERPRISE

By Richard Eells

COLUMBIA UNIVERSITY PRESS

NEW YORK 1960

HⅡ2731
E26m

Preface

THIS BOOK has been written as an introduction to the philosophy of a great institution—the modern business corporation. Such a philosophy, when finally matured, will make the corporation more comprehensible and provide norms for corporate performance in a society that relies so heavily upon this remarkable organizational instrument.

At some future time, when the task of formulating a philosophy of the corporation will have been completed, many disciplines will have made their contributions, including some disciplines which do not now exist. This task will also require deep insight into the mystery of human organization. I pretend to no such sweep of knowledge. Making use of such tools as are now available, I have tried to organize my thoughts around the elementary problems of corporate adjustment and survival, dealing with relatively simple situations for illustrative purposes.

Though the findings at this stage of the inquiry are necessarily tentative, they do represent the collaborative efforts of many people; and it has been one of the most rewarding experiences of my life to find that busy men with a lifetime of success within the corporation and men of learning with heavy commitments within the academy were so generously cooperative in the development of this study.

A work of this sort must build upon the experience and scholarship of a great many persons. The published sources from which I have derived help are recorded in the Notes, which must take the place of a bibliography. My obligations to individuals are extensive. Some have worked with me on conceptual foundations, others on the organization of materials, others have read the manuscript, and others have been important sources of encouragement. I wish to acknowledge my debt and express my gratitude to the following, though mine is the responsibility for any errors or deficiencies: John W. Ackley, Claire Baldwin, Joseph M. Bertotti, Virgil B. Day, Henry Du Flon, Libert Ehrman, Alvin C. Eurich, Eli Ginzberg, Covington Hardee, Clifford J. Jenks, Hans H. Jenny, Robert A. Kavesh, Joseph T. Klapper, Katherine Foster Kennedy, Chester H. Lang, William H. Long, Vincent L. Marsilia, Kenneth G. Patrick, Mildred Frye Reid, Ross Reid, O. Glenn Saxon, Jr., Leonard R. Sayles, Eustace Seligman, Kathryn W. Sewny, John F. Sly, Harold F. Smiddy, John M. Stalnaker, Hoyt P. Steele, George A. Steiner, Frank Tannenbaum, Jane Belo Tannenbaum, W. Homer Turner, Clarence C. Walton, Arnold J. Zurcher. In particular I wish to thank James J. Robbins and Ithiel de Sola Pool, teachers and friends, who contributed unstintingly of their knowledge and insight.

During the past three years I have had the special pleasure of discussing the ideas in this book with Courtney C. Brown, dean of the Graduate School of Business at Columbia University. The Dean's suggestions have helped me avoid pitfalls and the lines of investigation undertaken here have in large part followed the tenor of our many rewarding discussions.

I have tried to present major problems and varying points of view that make up the current intellectual climate of the business corporation. I have tried to fit these many ideas together into a comprehensible framework. Some of the ideas reviewed in this book I agree with personally, some I most warmly disagree with, and there are some positions where I have not made up my own mind. My purpose has been to present all these ideas objectively on a large tapestry, as it were, and not to make a case or brief for any particular school of thought. While I have not hesitated in some instances to evaluate some of these ideas, many are presented without evaluation simply because they exist. The necessary antecedent to wise advocacy is understanding. And the better understanding of this remarkable phenomenon—the business institution—has been my objective.

This book was made possible by a research grant from the Alfred P. Sloan Foundation to the Graduate School of Business at Columbia, and by permission given me by the General Electric Company to pursue this study periodically, on a leave basis, and to publish its results as an independent personal project. Obviously, therefore, the views expressed here are my own, and do not necessarily reflect, indicate, nor suggest the official views or policies of any company, foundation, institution, or other organization.

RICHARD EELLS

New York City
February, 1960

Contents

INTRODUCTION   1

The Quest

I. THE SEARCH FOR A PHILOSOPHY OF BUSINESS   17
Lag in Economic and Corporate Theory, 20; Strands of the Business Creed, 22; Needs for Further Study, 25; Concept of the Corporation, 26; Social Significance of the Corporation, 29; Power and Authority over People and Things, 30; Alternatives for the Future, 35.

II. THE TRADITIONAL CORPORATION   38
The Traditional Corporation and Stockholders, 41; The Traditional Corporation and the Public, 43; Ethics of the Traditional Corporation, 45.

III. THE METROCORPORATION   50
Traditional vs. Metrocorporate Polity, 52; Corporate Polity and Public Governments, 56; The Metrocorporation and Labor Relations, 57; A Metrocorporate Feudalism? 62; The Uses of Corporate Power, 63; The Metrocorporate Pattern, 66.

IV. THE DILEMMA OF CORPORATE RESPONSIBILITY   69
Nature of Responsibility, 70; The Climate Nurturing Social Responsibility, 72; Depth of the Dilemma, 75; The Case against Social Responsibilities, 77.

V. FIVE SCIENTIFIC PROBLEMS   95
Corporate Goals, 97; Corporate Ecology, 99; The Policy Process, 103; The Strategic Decisions, 106; Corporate Governance, 108.

Corporate Realities

VI.   CORPORATE GOALS   115
The Need for a System of Goal-Values, 115; The Entrepreneurial Objective, 117; The Reach for Noneconomic Objectives, 122; Goal-Values of Men and Corporations, 123.

VII.   RATIONALITY AND REALITY IN DECISION MAKING   138
The Decision Process, 138; Concept of Rationality, 141; Business Policy and Game Theory, 143; Of Time and the Multitude of Things, 145; Operational Codes, 152; Operational Codes of Corporation Executives, 154; The Imaginary Audiences of the Corporate Decision Maker, 155; Executive Assessment of Motives, 158; Executive Perceptions of the Instruments of Policy, 159; The Executive's View of His Role, 159.

VIII.   POLICY STEPS AND POLICY INSTRUMENTS   166
Stages in the Decision Process, 167; The Instruments of Corporate Policy, 185.

IX.   STRATEGIC DECISION AREAS   189
First Approach: Corporate Policy in Terms of Competitive Business, 192; Second Approach: "Business Statesmanship" as the Key, 196; Third Approach: Corporate Enterprise as Public Business, 199; Operational vs. Subjective Selection of Key Policy Areas, 204.

Corporate Responsibilities

X.   CLAIMANTS ON THE CORPORATION   211
Direct Contributor-Claimants, 211; Indirect Claimants, 214.

XI.   SECURITY HOLDERS AND CUSTOMERS   217

XII.   EMPLOYEES AND SUPPLIERS   236

XIII.   COMPETITORS, LOCAL COMMUNITIES, THE GENERAL PUBLIC AND GOVERNMENTS   248

XIV.   PUBLIC RELATIONS AND CORPORATE INTERESTS   273
The Public Relations Function, 274; The Central Purpose, 276; Public Relations and Corporate Goals, 278; Whose Public Relations? 280; Problem of Perceiving and Communicating the Corporate Image, 283; The Related Publics, 287; The Communicational Relationship, 292; Building the Corporate Reputation, 296; Public Relationships in the Foreseeable Future, 300.

The Future Course

XV. THE WELL-TEMPERED CORPORATION 307
Counterposed Corporate Models, 307; Requirements of a Better
Corporate Model, 309; The Economic Process of a Free Society,
310; Control of the Economic Process in a Free Society, 313;
Coordinate Economic Functions of the Corporation, 316; Co-
ordinate Political Functions of the Corporation, 319; Coordinate
Social and Cultural Functions of the Corporation, 326; Toward
a More Tenable Model, 329; Ecology of the Well-Tempered Cor-
poration, 330; Corporate Adaptation of a Global Ecosystem, 333;
The Well-Tempered Corporation, 335.

NOTES 341

INDEX 405

The Meaning of Modern Business

Introduction

THE SURVIVAL of human institutions depends not upon heaven but upon man. Yet there appears to be something in the nature of man that takes what he has constructed not merely for granted but as guaranteed for all eternity. The greatest hazard to institutions is not the problem of survival through the earliest years of their inception but survival after they have become established. At this point, the patterns of the past are preserved without thought of what they signify—merely because they are there.

In large organizations of an institutional character this process amounts to stratification—a species of hierarchical sedimentation. This is often dismissed as bureaucracy, but it is generally accepted as being in the nature of things. Yet organizations grow old and die when their vital functions deteriorate, just as men do. Governments fall, established social patterns disintegrate, businesses fail. Are these the whim of a mischief in the universe which we call bad luck, or are they the result of an inability to cope with change? Nature is no certain friend of man's. The most he can hope for on that score is neutrality. And, if the artifacts and institutions of our civilization are destroyed, it will be according to a familiar pattern.

Man's long struggle to master his environment through intellect and plan has been marked by curious lapses both in effort and judgment. When he rests from his labors, confiding in the sure thing, the found solution, he is merely shoring up the ruins on which the generations that follow must rebuild. With a dynamic

plan the future might have been his doing, without one it becomes his undoing.

Civilizations, to survive, must be willing to adapt to the changes
which their very development brings into being. Yet their tendency seems rather to be to perpetuate what they have achieved.
Organizing, on any level, adds an ingredient to the present which
alters the potential future. The problem of institutions today is
not very different from what it has always been, save for the
change in the nature of modern man's perception of Time.

The secrets of nature explored in laboratories bring into being
new technologies which, in their turn, are dedicated to exploiting
these secrets further. The microscope, the telescope, and now the
computer have added to human senses and to memory an acuity
never dreamed of by the scholar and technician of the past. Information media developed by science and engineering have cut dis-
tance down to units of minutes rather than units of miles. And
time, once slow and reckoned traditionally in terms of ages, centuries, scores, or decades is now as speeded up as is modern transportation by comparison with the carts and coaches that rumbled
over our highways less than a hundred years ago. It has been a
cliché of experience in any generation to observe that "times
change," but it is safe to say today that time as a factor in human
affairs must be viewed in a totally new context. It is no longer a
type of conveyor belt but a medium in which we are suspended.

For human organizations this is an important truth. The
future thus becomes the present for most of our important decisions and those decisions tend to alter its outlines. The changes
to come are not just random aspects of time but, rather, aspects of
the creative planning of men. And this makes it necessary for the
administrator to think of the consequences of his planning not
just in terms of his own life-span. He must consider instead the
goals and the outspan of the organization which he serves and
must decide for it in those terms.

Closely related to the time speed-up is that other distinctive
alteration in twentieth-century human affairs, the development of
massive organization. Our ardor for organizing resembles that
passion for building which characterized several earlier civilizations. The medieval church fostered the cathedral; the Ptolemies

preferred pyramids; even the Druids achieved Stonehenge. True, none of these great monuments could have been built without organization of some kind. But the monument of organization today appears to be organization itself—the slow evolution of human association into human institutions. Technology, which is behind the time speed-up, has also made it possible to control organizations of any size, in any sector of society. Without new organizational techniques, information and communication devices, office machines, computers, and of course electricity and electronic techniques, architectonic organization would be no more practicable now than it was in the past.

But contingent to the emergence of modern organization and its larger-than-lifetime calculus is the question of whether the large corporation will really serve society or whether society is being reconstructed to serve it. This problem has created considerable stir in the last few years. There is an increasing, restless inquiry into the administration of big business corporations and big labor unions. Government has been asked to take a hand in controlling their growth and influence, but government itself is now so large that people are uncertain whether it is wise to extend its influence further. Government is deterred by law from doing much to settle people's minds in this matter and is usually unwilling to ask for new legislation lest it impair substantive guarantees such as freedom of association.

Traditional organizations, like the State, the Church, the Army, have the advantage in this dilemma of an established rationale for their activities and functions. Government has its prerogatives and responsibilities under a constitution or a charter; the Church has its theology; and the Army has a science of war as well as its code of military justice. For all these institutions, there are rules by which they live or let live, and they have further an authority over their particular sectors of society which is conceded, held in some deference, and can if necessary be used coercively. If there is wisdom in their leadership, they are equipped to foresee, to correct, to change and to progress, and to continue to survive.

The case of the economic organization is quite different. It is a newcomer to the organizational hierarchy, and it has reached its present status far too fast to have had time to do much theorizing either about its ends or its means. Both corporations and unions are now being recognized as complex systems of private government, yet there is no body of theory either to direct or to account for their function in society.

This book proposes two kinds of questions about the business corporation that might clarify its nature and objectives as a human institution. One is a scientific question, answerable only by definition of what the corporation is and what functions it actually performs. The other is a normative one, answerable only in terms of preferred values, and it asks what the corporation should be.

The most sustained effort hitherto toward an objective evaluation of corporate ends and means has been the movement called "scientific management." It is attempting today to establish some rationale of business practice, though this was not the original intent of its founder, F. W. Taylor. He described his system initially as "task management" and intended that it speed up production through rewards to the worker both in wages and in the simplification of his often tedious employment. The "science" behind this undertaking was the essential objectivity of the time and motion study. Its purpose was not just to produce more but to expedite production through minimum waste of time, motion, and materials, and so a way was paved for mass organization for mass production. But no such scientific approach has yet been made to the nature of the resultant economic organization.

Nor have the human values challenged by the necessity both for specialized skills and anonymity, which characterized the assembly line, been analyzed in more than random fashion. The businessman is not typically aware, as he expands product lines and extends services, of the ancient philosophical opinion that "a certain amount of goods is necessary to a man to lead a good life." For him the benefits attendant upon the possession of goods are implicit in their very manufacture and marketing, and probably neither the administrator of a business nor his employees see themselves as benefactors to society in terms of the goods they offer. Initially, they understood merely the task of supplying at a profit artifacts that would meet a demand and create through their own merits an even larger demand. Out of this simple and matter-of-fact principle the large modern business enterprise has evolved.

This evolution from the simple supplier of artifacts to the great industrial enterprise, with organization on a large scale, has brought with it some new and thorny problems. The transition from individual to corporate ownership has not been accompanied by adequate attention to the principles of internal governance in the corporate enterprise. The entrepreneur's lot in a small organization remains relatively simple. But when his business grows to the size where it employs hundreds of thousands of people he has a silent problem of government on his hands and few policy guides for the administration of justice. He must go it alone, whether he is really alone or whether he is a member of a board of directors. He has no handbook of theory, and as a result, though he has power, he has no rationalization of that power.

The fact is that our economic organizations, like many of our children, have reached an early and overgrown maturity without benefit of traditional conscience, and they often betray an ignorance of many of the principles on which American society was raised. The phrase "business is business" set up a hierarchy of relative values for business which, for want of any other, has had to do. But any responsible firm today knows that, whatever this means in the way of practice, it is too little and has been invoked too long. In a society that lives by a simple but uncompromising code of values whose basis is freedom and equality, the results have been at times embarrassing and will continue to be if business becomes the government's business.

The remedy lies within the framework of what we call philosophy, the science which investigates the facts and principles of reality and of human nature and conduct. A careful examination of the relationships between business and its deeper social foundations could lead to a philosophy of business that might be of inestimable value as one approaches specialized issues of business policy. The need for a mature philosophy of business is now generally recognized, but it has become increasingly urgent for several reasons. The global struggle between free and "open" societies tied strongly to the liberal traditions of Western culture, on the one hand, and the collectivist and totalitarian way of the Communist bloc, on the other, has sharpened the conflict about the meaning of private enterprise.

Hence, we are in the middle of a sociopolitical debate as to the proper scope and objectives of business in our society, especially those of the business corporation. There are two "models" of the modern corporation that stand at opposite poles, though there are modified views that lie between them.

At one extreme is the position that the corporation is nothing but the organizational arm of its stockholders as private-property owners. Profit maximization for the owners is sometimes urged as the sole legitimate function of corporate enterprise. In this traditional view of the corporation, austerity in the use of its resources is the keynote, with enhancement of the equity of owners as the single purpose.

At the other extreme is the model of the social corporation with a wide range of social purposes and objectives. From this point of view, it is a kind of "metrocorporation"—a mother corporation—with a host of interest groups under its protection. Its professional managers maintain a balance of interest among competing claimants; but more than this, they become "socially responsible" for the welfare of these claimants in numerous ways. The traditional corporation was concerned only with the "economic man"; but the metrocorporation thinks of the "whole man" in much the same way as the all-embracing political community is *parens patriae* and the guardian of the welfare of citizens.

This last attitude results from today's fact that, since there are so many different groups that contribute to the success of a business, so likewise are there many different claimants on the valuable things it produces. These products are not entirely—and perhaps not even mainly—economic in the classical sense. Indeed, the twentieth-century business enterprise has become more than a specialized agency of society's economic function. The large corporation is therefore seen by some as a smaller model of the greater society catering to a wide range of noneconomic needs of those associated with it.

In between these extreme views of the *traditional* corporation, on the one hand, and the *metrocorporation,* on the other, are many variant models or pictures in the minds of men as to what the business unit is and should be. There are, for example, many businessmen who lean strongly to the older view that " business is business " in a strict sense but concede nonetheless that a corporation has certain more or less well-defined "social responsibilities." Others insist upon the precedence of claims by one or more of the constellation of interests in a corporate enterprise—the customers, the share owners, the employees, the suppliers, the competitors, and the general public. The emphasis put upon one or the other of these claims will to a large extent determine one's philosophy of business.

We live in an age of large-scale enterprise which is but one aspect of the "organizational revolution" of the past century. The interrelationships among business and other large organizations are so complex and so far-reaching that the "community" which sustains a business unit is no longer parochial. Today's top executives must focus only upon the *strategic* decision areas, leaving the *tactics* to others. Their time and energies must be saved for the important issues and the wise use of the instruments of policy.

What these strategic decision areas are and how the instruments of policy are to be used in these areas are questions that yield various answers depending upon how one estimates the goals of business in relation to more general social goals. Although, as has been frequently pointed out, the strategic decisions of the businessman were once relatively limited in scope and number—what to produce, how to produce, and how to market—the emergence of large-scale enterprise in a dynamic society has forced him to concentrate upon decision areas that have wide social and political dimensions. In addition to the traditional techniques of market operation, he has also to consider such instruments of policy as political action, negotiations of a quasi-diplomatic sort with other organized groups, and communication relationships that demand much beyond limited "public relations" techniques. The community that a business serves, and on which it depends, is regional, national, and even international in scope. Nor can that community be defined adequately in territorial dimensions. The functions of business and the businessman are thus to be seen in the framework of the greater society and not as isolated functions. Their new significance can be understood only by relating these functions to some of the basic ideas and institutions that have endured, and will continue to endure, through the short-run ups-and-downs of social change.

Business is not the only field in which "creative destruction"—to use Schumpeter's term—presses ahead, in free societies, to break the bonds of the past and open new opportunities for human achievement. But business is one of the most dynamic forces in this process, and with it are allied the forces of free enquiry and freedom of expression in intellectual, political, and cultural pursuits. The student of business, whether he is an untried youth in a university lecture-room or a mature man behind an executive desk in a great corporation, will move toward a developed philosophy of business, and a better understanding of his role in a free society, only if he gives careful attention to these interrelationships with the other liberating forces at work in our society.

The ever-changing pattern of social relationships poses for business leaders the problem of cleaving to those ideas and institutions that free men have cherished, while adjusting to new environmental conditions created by the dynamics of technological, scientific, and economic growth. Freedom of association and the principles of constitutionalism, for example, have long been and will continue to be of fundamental importance to freedom of private enterprise.

Yet both these ideas, and the practices and procedures through which they are expressed, lead to new and still inadequately explored terrain for the businessman. The right of association, applied universally, leads not only to business combinations that come under the watchful eye of public officials concerned with maintaining a competitive market and preserving a "balance of power" in society. It leads also to large labor unions and other kinds of voluntary associations which, though basic to a "free society," generate power that is different in degree and perhaps in kind from the more or less atomized power residual in society as conceived in the older liberal views of politics and economics.

In our evolving capitalism, with its emphasis still on freedom of men to choose, the role of labor is not to be understood alone through the philosophy of unionism. The so-called managerial revolution has reared a new "laboring" class of professional managers whose stake in a business is basically different from that of the owner-manager of former times. This, so some have said, creates a "power elite," which tends toward neofeudalism and a return to the idea of vassalage, with its guarantees of security in exchange for service. In this light, collective bargaining becomes something distinguishable from a "labor-market" operation; it tends to resemble negotiation among sovereign powers, accompanied by the use of all the instruments of state policy—pressures of an economic, legal, and ideological kind to bring the other collective party to terms, followed by agreements (treaties) that constitute a sort of fundamental law for ordering the rights and duties of the parties' respective members. Constitutionalism, as a doctrine of limited government, then becomes relevant not only to public governments but also to the private governments of corporations and labor unions, as well as to professional and business associations generally.

With respect to the "factors of production" in any business enterprise, the problem of mobilizing the requisite human resources also involves an appreciation of the historic and comparative role of labor—not only the labor of wage earners but also of all those who contribute their time and energies to the maintenance of the business system in all of its aspects. Private property and labor—in this broad sense, which includes managerial competence—are two indispensable factors of production in any economic system.

The role of labor in a business system is thus intimately related to the issues of profit and profitability, and more broadly to the issue of distribution of the fruits of enterprise or the distribution of earnings. How can labor unions, professional managers, the stockholders, and the public as customers and protectors of the public interest, come to terms as to how the earnings and losses of industry are to be shared? What are the justifiable claims of each of these groups in the distribution of earnings, and what are their appropriate burdens in sharing the losses? Here, again, one needs to have a historical and functional view of the concept of profits before one formulates a sound business philosophy.

Though I have not pursued in this book all the elements

basic to a sound business philosophy, I have been acutely aware of several that should be mentioned here. There are, for example, such deep-rooted ideas and institutions as private property and contract, not so much in terms of the specific rules of law that a well-informed business practitioner ought to be aware of but rather in terms of the background out of which these rules have grown, and the philosophical principles that underlie them. That society is in a constant state of change is a platitude, but it is sometimes forgotten that change also occurs in such basic concepts as private property and contract. The modern corporation and private property, for example, are not mutually incompatible concepts, but the corporate form of business has brought with it important changes in the relations between property owners and property managers. Contract, similarly, assumes a different meaning when the contracting parties are collectivities like labor unions and corporate entities.

The roles of credit and money in the past development and continued survival of a business system such as ours are likewise of direct concern to the formulator of a sound business philosophy. Credit institutions and mechanisms, and monetary policy, play an indispensable part in any modern economic system; but under the changing capitalism of our time their functions become increasingly issues of public policy toward which the businessman must have a reasoned position. Here, again, historical perspective and comparative analysis become indispensable to an understanding of current problems.

The increasing demand for greater "social responsibility" for those who exercise power over these private governments raises new and difficult problems—or perhaps very old problems in new forms—for the businessman.

When the corporation became a constitutional person, it took title to the rights and assurances due to a citizen under procedural and substantive guarantees. But along with these rights it acquired duties and responsibilities not merely to individuals but to the public interest. The deeper historic roots of constitutionalism are found in ancient philosophic principles expounded by the stoics of ancient Greece and developed continuously through ages of Judaic, Early Christian, medieval, and modern thought. These principles, together with more general doctrines about the relationship between power and authority, were implemented in recent centuries as specialized procedural safeguards against irresponsible exercise of power by any official group. And today when, despite strong socialist trends in more modern states, we still maintain much of the older view that under capitalism the economic process is largely entrusted to the private businessmen, the pressure for procedural safeguards to ensure responsible exercise of this trust is constantly growing. Only an awareness of the constitutional and philosophical background of his freedom can prepare the businessman for responses that will be pragmatically sound and idealistically justifiable.

There are still other basic ideas, concepts, and institutions, that one should approach in the same way in formulating a viable philosophy of business. The idea of the market for example, has far-reaching implications for a free society, since the market is an organizer of society alongside the state and other institutions. The business unit's market operations thus signify more than "higgling" for private advantage; the preservation of the market itself as a basic social institution of a free society becomes more and more a matter of direct concern to every businessman in an age of encroaching statism. The prospect for the survival of liberty in an "organizational economy"—as distinguished from the individual-enterprise, laissez-faire, private-property economics of "old-style capitalism"—may depend heavily upon an operational business philosophy with a new and different focus—a focus of the executive on acceptable relations between the economy, liberty, and the state—and not exclusively on the success of the single enterprise unit in isolation.

All of these factors have prompted me to try to discern the nature of modern business and to survey its realities and implications with impartiality. It is for this reason that material I have quoted ranges from the sound and scholarly to outbursts of an obviously polemical variety. But the book itself attempts to preserve the neutrality necessary to the philosophical end it pursues. It presents the modern business in terms of "models," though I am aware that models are denigrated by some as creatures of the imagination, however scientific they may appear to be. Yet in reflecting on the *traditional* model, and then on the model of the *metrocorporation* the knowledgeable reader will be reminded of companies whose names could be cited as specific cases.

Further, the book proposes as a model of corporate business what is here called the *well-tempered corporation*. Students of the history of music will recall that the term "well-tempered" was first used to describe the equal temperament system which is now in universal use for keyed instruments. The piano is an early example of technology adapted to the needs of a sensitive art form. One can perhaps concede that as an instrument it is, in its way, as complex as a modern business, when one realizes that of the seventy-eight intervals that lie within the range of a single octave on the keyboard, not a single one is in perfect tune, though every interval could be improved if there were not others to think about.

The institution of corporate enterprise, by analogy, voicing as it does many of the goal-values of men, is but one theme in the complex structure of the social order. To remain in harmony with modern growth and perennial human aspiration it too must adjust and be in tune. In short, to survive, it must become, and remain, well tempered.

How can the corporation achieve this end? As I have suggested, it must first know what it is. While much has been said and written about specific aspects of its economic function, the corporation as a largely self-governing unit with certain internal power and authority relationships is little understood.

Further, the corporation must perceive itself in the social fabric. Corporations, like other associations in the private sector, perform important, quasi-governmental functions; and the significance of these voluntarily assumed functions of private government in a free society has yet to be explored systematically and empirically.

The idea of corporate "social responsibility" is the force that is transforming the corporation into something less wedded to the private property interests of the primary owners than is the case with the traditional model, yet into something far less "socialized" than the metrocorporation. What this entity is to be depends on the wisdom of the men who transact business and on the men who describe these transactions. It also depends on the evolution of an economic "theory of the firm" into a business philosophy which will include the private theory and values of the men who run it and the men everywhere who have come to depend upon it.

Recent research on current business education sponsored by the Carnegie Corporation[1] and the Ford Foundation[2] points to the need for reappraisal of the total relationships of business as an institution of modern society. This reappraisal is going on in many fields other than business. The pressure of change necessitates it.

The quest for a philosophy of business, though it is pursued here through a study of the nature and responsibilities of the large corporation, must be undertaken from many points of view. The book's audience, therefore, should include such diverse groups as social psychologists, social anthropologists and other social scientists, executive managers, individual staff members concerned with top policy, and public relations and advertising firms whose business it is to concern themselves with the corporate image. Each of these groups has something to contribute to a philosophy of modern business.

Perhaps the point of view of a participant in corporate life is only a first step toward full definition of the nature and function of the corporation. Still, most Americans participate in corporate life at some level. It is said that over eighty percent of all wage earners not on farms work for corporations. It is an economic fact that the child with one share of stock is a corporate owner. The family with no particular brand loyalty may share its home with a dozen products of corporate effort and know-how. Most families have cars, and the family car is a composite of corporate contributions. The food we eat is largely corporation processed and packaged. Electric current and the telephone also are processed into the home by corporate organization. And so on. There is almost universal participation in corporate life today.

We live, as a result, in the most comfortable material surroundings, home for home, that time has ever witnessed. But the pervading climate of our spirit remains uneasy. And doubtless there is a reason for this. I have tried to understand what it might be. The monuments of far less well-organized cultures than ours still stand. The cathedrals are there, the pyramids are there, and Stonehenge is there, perhaps not *as* they were erected but *where* they were erected. Can we be sure that the corporation will have, for future centuries, a significance as monumental?

Great organizations, the monuments of our time, differ from the structural achievements of the past in one important respect. They lack a dimension common to the others. They have no geographical location. They exist less concretely in space than in time. They have entity in law. But they are, in fact, more than legal abstractions. They are built not so much with human hands as with human intellects, compounded not of stones and mortar but of human hopes, and human ambitions.

And this abstraction is marvelous, in the case of corporate organization, because it can produce material goods. Yet no one is amazed. And not everyone is pleased. In spite of its production, the corporation as an organization has been found wanting. What seems to be demanded of it by society is not that which it has traditionally demanded of itself—greater goods for a greater number of people—but some frame of reference that defines more clearly its commitment to the greater society.

The Quest

A great society is a society in which its men of business think greatly of their functions.

Alfred North Whitehead, "Foresight," the introduction to Wallace Brett Donham, *Business Adrift.*

CHAPTER I

The Search for a Philosophy of Business

THE MODERN CORPORATION is an institution in search of a philosophy.[1] The Church and the State are examples of institutions that possess well-developed philosophies and are sustained by them. Each has a vast literature that expounds its origin and its purposes. Each has a rationale that makes it comprehensible, if not universally acceptable. For the seeker after truth, there is no standard treatise which fully explains the role of the modern corporation[2] in society. For the moral philosopher, there is no set of ethical standards, widely accepted and generally applied, by which corporate behavior can be judged.

A philosophy of the corporation would have a two-fold objective. First, it would set forth scientifically the necessary and sufficient conditions for the rise of the corporation to a position of dominance in the economy, its continuance in that position, and its eventual demise—if that is what its destiny may be. Second, it would set forth the standards of conduct that should govern the internal and external relationships of this new institution.

A philosophy of the corporation will thus have two distinguishable elements. One will be descriptive, analytical, predictive, and nonnormative in that it will involve no ethical evaluation. The other will be normative, evaluative, and prescriptive in that it will assert and defend canons of right conduct and preferred goals for the corporation as an institution. Because these two elements of business philosophy are commonly merged in a

single body of ideas, there is a resultant confusion of thought.
Though both are relevant to a philosophy of the corporation, any
systematic study finds it necessary to separate them for investiga-
tory purposes.

Such a philosophy of corporate business even in an age of
great industrial enterprise has yet to be formulated. Only when
this is achieved will there be a systematic view of the multifunctional corporation in its total environment. The purpose of
this study is to contribute toward the formulation of such a
philosophy. The focus is upon certain selected problems that
confront students of this elusive subject as well as responsible
managers and interested observers.

The first of these problems revolves around an ethical
dilemma: whether the corporation should become—as it is in fact
becoming—a multifunctional institution that takes on more and
more of the comprehensive responsibilities of man in his society
or whether it should somehow return to the limited role of a
strictly economic instrument concerned almost exclusively with
the production of goods and services. The first alternative suggests staggering implications which involve the whole of life. At
what point does an institution become a lesser society—a society
within the greater society? Is it in the interests of the good life
that the corporation should become a lesser society which, by
nature, must be identified with the whole of life?

It would seem that, to be so concerned, the corporation must
reach for the whole man. If so, there is the recurrent and haunt-
ing question: Can a corporation, or any institution, expect to
attain such a status of total involvement without making a total
claim? So far, in the history of Western civilization, only two
institutions have assumed this role of majesty and of burden—the
Church and the State. Although this dilemma has long been a
matter of serious debate among those concerned with social
theory, the issue is rapidly assuming major importance and may
well, within the coming decade, become the central social issue
for business corporations.

A second problem involves corporate objectives. A disparity
arises between the operational goals of the business institution,
the aims actually pursued, on the one hand, and, on the other

hand, the picture in men's minds of what the corporation ought to be in terms of idealized goals or some preconceived corporate model. What would be the goals of a corporation that might confine its activities to narrowly defined economic functions, in contrast with a corporation that has become a multifunctional institution of society? Closely related to this inquiry is the fact that the goals and the values of men are multiple—and that the modern corporation tends to mirror this multiplicity of goal-values, aims, and drives of men.

A third problem concerns corporate policy. Central to the problem is the gap that exists between the policy process as it actually occurs and the idealized dream world of policy making as envisaged by otherwise practical men. An understanding of the policy process involves an examination of the realities of decision making in all large organizations, the steps leading to policy, and the various instruments necessary to policy execution.

A fourth problem arises from the interdependence between the modern corporation and many other sectors of society, both public and private. Many sectors contribute to the survival and success of a business corporation; many lay claim to the fruits of corporate enterprise; many are concerned with the common life which is lived within the corporate body. The nature of a corporation's obligation toward those who contribute and those who claim requires the most careful examination. Undoubtedly, this inquiry will persist in our time.

Finally, interwoven with each of these great problems is the little-understood matter of corporate governance—the structure and functioning of the corporate polity. The development of a science of corporate polity, like the development of a science of politics or like the study of any field of social interaction, means the penetration of a little-explored territory. But it is likely that within our generation we will see considerable penetration into the workings of private governments generally. The development of a theory of business polity will constitute a new and important chapter in the history of political science itself.

It should not be forgotten that political science was enriched, in the later middle ages and in the early modern period, by profound studies of the polity of the Church—a dominant social institution of the time. The bases of ecclesiastical polity greatly influenced the theory of modern constitutionalism. We may be living at a time when we are on the brink of important new developments in political theory. For, just as the great councils of the past introduced patterns of theory and practice that profoundly influenced the development of Western parliamentary institutions, so the modern corporation may bring forth theory and practice that will shape many social patterns of the future. It already influences the patterns of law and order in the market place of the world community. It could influence our basic ways of adjusting conflicting interests within nations. It could help to crystallize meaningful and working concepts of human freedom.

Only through detailed consideration of issues of this magnitude can one hope to gain new angles of insight into an old and vast terrain of which we still know much too little. In the end, our travels and our charting of this terrain have an ethical goal. For just beyond the horizons of the problems here outlined looms the transcending question: How shall we design the patterns of our institutional systems so that we can preserve the values of our constitutional heritage of freedom?

LAG IN ECONOMIC AND CORPORATE THEORY

There is some evidence that the modern corporation is becoming comprehensible as a social institution, that we know why we have it and what its chief functions are. But comprehension comes slowly, partly because of the multiplicity of these functions. To describe them accurately, one must call upon many disciplines, such as anthropology, history, economics, law, political science, sociology. But there is another reason why comprehension comes slowly: the persistence of stereotyped models in our thinking. Social thinking rarely keeps pace with the march of events; usually it lags far behind. So it is with the theory of the modern corporation.

Large-scale industrial enterprise, as we know it today, is scarcely a hundred years old. It is characterized by (1) the rise of a new type of entrepreneur, (2) changes in economic mentality, and (3) radically new conditions of production and marketing that have exerted enormous pressures on the social and economic policies of governments.[3] Adjustments to these new conditions are made, as a rule, without any deep insight into epochal trends. At best, the legislator and the corporate executive discern only a secular trend of limited time-span, so rapid is technological change and so pressing the immediate problem of adjustment to its imperatives. There is little time to place the decision of the moment within a broad frame of reference or to theorize on institutional development.

As a result, anachronistic theory is perpetuated, not only in the writings of academicians but especially in the inarticulate major premises of many business and governmental policy makers. Those who denigrate the merit of theory are often the most stubborn exponents of outworn theory. Simplistic explanations of our economy abound. But skeptics like Walton Hamilton have denied that it is possible to produce a map of our economy through facile use of words. "A glib term," he wrote, "such as capitalism or free enterprise belies the variety of the phenomena it professes to sum up. As the prevailing order has come into being, the new has come, yet the old has lingered." [4]

In the same vein, shortly after the Second World War, Oswald Knauth, a writer with long experience as a corporate executive, decried the tenacity with which people cling to the philosophy of free competitive enterprise in the face of the newer form of economy—managerial enterprise—that businessmen have fashioned in meeting the exigencies of the modern world.[5] It was this newer form of economy which had not yet been recognized in economic or legal theory. Yet it had embraced half the industry of the United States, the other half operating under free enterprise or collectivism.

Managerial enterprise under the aegis of the large corporation was, at that time—and for the most part is still—evolving so fast that its methods were not understood, codes for it were lacking, and adequate laws had yet to be worked out. No blueprint of American business had been drawn up. A new philosophy had yet to be evolved. If managerial enterprise continued to be regarded as a variant of free enterprise or of monopoly, Knauth reasoned, little progress would be made in realistic assessments of its true nature.[6] Almost a decade later he declared that businessmen engaged in the management of large enterprises had long since rejected the classical theory, that is, of Adam Smith and David Ricardo, as an explanation of their actions and methods.[7]

STRANDS OF THE BUSINESS CREED

On closer examination, the ideology[8] of American business reveals an interesting duality in business thinking. An analysis of the period of the 1940s demonstrates a remarkable verbalized persistence of the classical theory. The authors of *The American Business Creed*[9] found a "basic stability, indeed almost a stubborn intellectual conservatism" in the many business pronouncements they studied. There was repeated confirmation of the classical picture of a society in which business firms compete freely with one another under the inflexible rule of *simple* economic laws. While economic reality had undergone profound changes, economic ideology had not kept pace.

Businessmen in this period exhibited a marked distrust of abstract theory, indeed paid little explicit honor even to Adam Smith and other classical economists. Nevertheless, they thought of themselves as rational, cold, and practical. A general tone of austerity appeared in their conviction that certain fundamental economic laws govern the affairs of men. These laws were similar to those stated in the earlier works of the "dismal science." There were inexorable market forces of which the businessman was merely the agent. His pursuit of profit automatically served the welfare of society and was indeed the prerequisite of economic efficiency.

The business organization was defined in the prevailing business creed in terms of property rights and contractual relationships: management was responsible to the owners of the business, and its responsibilities to others—employees, customers, and suppliers, who were outsiders—were confined to the fulfillment of contractual obligations. The doctrine of self-reliance relieved the businessman of responsibility for the effects of his actions on other people. The virtues of practicality and hardheadedness were extolled as universal values, applicable to all alike. What might appear to the sentimental as unfriendly or unjust action by businessmen intent upon rational conformity to economic laws was more properly thought of as a strengthening of the moral fiber of society generally.[10]

Two different strands of business ideology appeared, however, in the period these authors explored. The "classical strand"— along the lines just described—was to some extent counterbalanced by a "managerial strand." The investigators found, for example, that, in many statements of businessmen, excessive profits were held to be unfair and sinful. The firm was not just a network of property rights, contractual relationships, and lines of authority. It was, rather, a family of human beings cooperating in a common purpose. Neutrality, hardheadedness, lack of concern for warm human relationships—virtues in the classical strand of business ideology—gave way in the managerial strand to real concern for these and other relationships.

The businessman, in fact, had moral responsibilities. A manager had indeed to assume responsibilities toward his employees, his customers, the general public, as well as stockholders. He must balance their competing claims against the fruits of the enterprise. He had to make decisions as to *fair* wages, *fair* prices, *fair* dividends, and prudent reserves. Business management was to be judged by much more than its stewardship of stockholders' property rights. The human satisfactions of employees, the degree of progressiveness in scientific and technological research, contributions to the local communities—all were significant. Management was a profession with social status, dedicated to service and committed to the general interest. Attaining maximum profits was no longer its sole objective.

Proponents of the managerial strand had thus faced "the facts of business size and concentration and of separation of business ownership and control, which the logical exigencies of its argument compel the classical creed to dodge in one way or another" —so the authors of *The American Business Creed* reasoned. They pointed out a "discrepancy between the classical model of small and weak business proprietorships and the real world of the great corporate enterprises." [11]

Yet, according to these investigators, the classical creed persisted and they regarded the managerial strand as really no more than a variant of the more basic classical theme. It was not a parallel alternative, and there were several reasons why. In the first place, the managerial strand had nothing like the logical completeness of the classical theme. This, however, was not the chief difficulty. The managerial definition of business responsibility left businessmen at sea without a compass. Their responsibilities were too numerous, conflicting, and incommensurable. The proposed codes of managerial behavior were extremely vague. There were no operationally meaningful norms by which business performance could be measured when responsibilities became so diffused; the classical test of profitability was far simpler. If the manager had to balance a multitude of interests, rather than to serve the single interest of property rights of stockholders, he became a judge rather than a businessman.

The managerial creed, it was argued, assigned far too much discretion and left far too much power at the disposal of the businessman; it opened the way to disturbing questions about the legitimacy of that power and the mechanisms by which abusers of power could be replaced.

In the classical creed, by contrast, the businessman could insist that he was simply the agent and victim of impersonal market forces. It was more comfortable to assume that competition [12] and "consumer sovereignty" were the regulators of managerial conduct. Abandoning the classical creed on the subject of competition, indeed, may expose corporate managers to the charge that price and other policies are "administered" by them and not subject to external forces over which they have no control. And whereas the classical creed had placed its main emphasis upon the Economic System as the great regulator, the managerial creed focused upon the individual business enterprise as a social system in itself, in which employees, customers, and suppliers are no longer outsiders but integral parts of the organization. Moreover, the modern corporation was an organization in which managers were assigned a highly important and nearly autonomous role. Theirs was "the statesman's function of mediating among the groups dependent on the enterprise, satisfying their just claims, and preserving the continuity of the organization—while always remembering that private office is a public trust and keeping the interest of the general public paramount." [13]

The classical creed placed no such awe-inspiring responsibilities upon the businessman—nor did it arouse concern about the way in which such responsibilities should be enforced. The managerial creed had to face the fact of bigness. It responded by emphasizing the humble beginnings of the large, successful corporations, the extent to which authority is decentralized in them, the wide dispersion of ownership, the increasing emphasis upon the human relations approach to management. All this, concluded the authors of *The American Business Creed,* proved inadequate in the forties to counter the much stronger influence of the classical creed with its more disciplined and ingrained theory and its more comfortable philosophy explaining the working of the whole economic system.

The study reviewed above has been justly criticized for the brevity of the period covered—a limitation readily conceded by its authors. They attempted nothing more ambitious. Yet these questions remains: Would the contours of the image alter if the authors had been able to extend the time-span to the present? Is it true that so different an implicit philosophy of business prevails today as to antiquate the conclusions of their study? Is there now a widely accepted body of ideas which makes the modern corporation truly and accurately comprehensible as a major social institution? Are there clearly established norms of corporate behavior which are indisputable? The answers to these questions must obviously be in the negative.

NEED FOR FURTHER STUDY

It is because there are still no clear answers to these questions that Dean Courtney C. Brown of the Columbia University Graduate School of Business has recently expressed the need for two new professorships in this field. The appointee to one of these would analyze the evolutionary development of business institutions and provide a close functional inquiry into the reason why the institution of business has evolved as it has, the hope being that research would disclose why attitudes, both internal and external to business, have changed from decade to decade. The other appointee, a philosopher rather than a scholar trained in business disciplines, would take the ideas of the great social, political, and ethical philosophers and relate them to the world of modern business. Modern professional management, the Dean recognizes, has new responsibilities and is aware of them; but it has no clear-cut criteria to apply in meeting these responsibilities. Corporate law has not provided such criteria, nor has economic theory.

The great debates of the past on liberty and authority were focused upon religious and political institutions. In our time they are coming to focus increasingly upon business institutions and especially the corporation, with its profound influence on all phases of contemporary life. Its "extra-business" functions are expanding, and new dimensions have developed in the affairs of the corporation. Basically a voluntary organization depending for its effectiveness upon consent of great numbers of people, the modern corporation is, in fact, a highly democratic instrument; but there are dangers to be watched. If the corporation, with its broadened role, comes to represent "little more than a yearning for a return to static feudalism . . . [and] if we ever permit a high degree of conformity and the other characteristics of bureaucracy to begin to dominate our corporations, they will again change their nature and will lose much of the opportunity they have now to achieve great good for increasing numbers." [14] On the other hand, ways may have to be sought to preserve and increase the voluntary and democratic nature of the business organization without losing its present effectiveness and efficiency.[15]

CONCEPT OF THE CORPORATION

The search for a philosophy of business, as we have said, moves at two levels: the level of scientific understanding and the level of ethical norms. This search has deep historical roots. Begin-

ning with Maitland's seminal studies of the origins of corporation theory at the turn of the century,[16] English and American
students of jurisprudence and political science have probed with
increased interest the nature of the corporation, both as an evolving institution and as a social concept.

The concept of the corporation is an ancient one. Its continuous usefulness [17] is apparent to anyone who follows the development of political and economic thought from the Roman
Republic through the Middle Ages to modern times. Corporateness, as a central idea in the growth of modern business, has been
the subject of many exploratory studies by legal historians.[18] In
1932, Berle and Means [19] set off a train of inquiry on the subject
that took a new direction. They declared that a new concept of
business enterprise, as concentrated in the corporate organization,
was emerging.

Like Rathenau,[20] they saw the corporate enterprise assuming
a life of its own, independent of its owners, with an objective
existence comparable only to that of the State or, in earlier days,
of the Church, the borough, the craftsman's guild, and the religious order. This meant that the analysis of the corporation
had to be not in terms of business enterprise but in terms of social
organization.

For Berle and Means, the corporation involved a concentration of power in the economic field comparable to the concentration of religious power in the medieval Church or of political
power in the national state. They saw an increasing demand that
the men controlling the great economic organisms be made to
accept responsibility for the well-being of those who are subject
to the organization, whether workers, investors, or consumers.
"The law of corporations," they concluded, "might well be considered as a potential constitutional law for the new economic
state, while business practice is increasingly assuming the aspect
of economic statesmanship." [21]

A new concept of the corporation could well be emerging,
they thought, because the traditional doctrine that the corporation "belongs" to its security holders, to be managed in their
interests alone, had become untenable, while the recent trend
toward control of its affairs by a "corporate oligarchy" had be-

come increasingly unacceptable. They foresaw the possible development of a third corporate pattern: one in which the managers of corporations would have to be responsible to a group far
wider than either the "passive owners" or the non-owner "control
groups." Neither the claims of ownership nor those of control
could probably stand against "the paramount interests of the community." It remained only for the claims of the community to
be put forward with clarity and force.

Some of the ways in which these community claims have been
expressed in the years since *The Modern Corporation and Private
Property* was published, are spelled out in a recent article [22] by
Mr. Berle. He speaks of the "inchoate law" of the "system of industrial concentrates," a body of law which will meet two kinds
of community requirements: first, "a requirement that the collectivized organisms essential to the economic life of the modern
state shall be so handled that they can and do acceptably perform
their functions of supply and growth" and, secondly, "that within
them, and as an offset to their necessary organization and power,
the basic rights of individuals shall be as scrupulously protected
against them as they were against the erstwhile state"—as shown
in the development of due process of law.

During the past half-century, this constitutionalist approach
to the study of the corporation has been given more and more
emphasis. By 1946, Peter Drucker was saying that the social and
political analysis of the corporation had to proceed on three levels: the autonomous institution; the beliefs and promises of the
society it serves; and the institution in its relationship to the functional requirements of the society of which the corporate institution is a part.

At the first level, Drucker emphasized the problems of corporate policy and corporate leadership and the need for "an objective yardstick by which to measure the success of its policies
and its leaders." At the second level, he asked whether the corporation was fulfilling its role in meeting the aspirations and beliefs of the American people. At the third level, the central problem, as he saw it, lay in "the relationship between profit, which
is the purpose of the corporation as an autonomous unit, and the
maximum production of cheap goods, which is the purpose of
the corporation from the point of view of society." [23]

SOCIAL SIGNIFICANCE OF THE CORPORATION

The social significance of the large corporation has now become the subject of numerous penetrating studies. Nor is this, as Carl Kaysen [24] has pointed out, merely because it is big, though bigness in itself has greatly concerned lawyers and economists as they debate antitrust policies.

Quite aside from corporate bigness, an imposing list of other considerations must be taken into account: the complexity of a structure characterized by many components that are widely spread geographically, the marketing of a variety of products, the operating of diverse industries, and the crossing of boundaries of industrial divisions so that it is simultaneously engaging in primary production, manufacture, and trade; the corporation's innovating and marketing methods in an age of mass production; its reliance on complex technologies; the rapidity of its growth as a timeless entity designed to endure through the decay of particular markets and sources of supply; the wider and wider dispersion of share ownership; and the professionalization of management, with the attendant development of bureaucratic characteristics; the recruitment of a labor force that becomes in effect a "corps of lifetime employees"; and the augmentation of market power through domination of major markets by one or a few large corporate enterprises.

Kaysen further points to some other characteristic features of corporate behavior as being socially significant. The modern corporation emphasizes "scientific management" with a high degree of rationality in the managerial function. "Flying by the seat of the pants" is passé. There is gradual invasion of decision areas hitherto reserved for intuitive "business judgment" by the tools and techniques of academic science.[25] Corporate managers put great weight on growth and technical progress as measures of achievement, with increased emphasis upon long-range planning as well as short-run stability. Management assumes wideranging responsibilities, not only to stockholders, but also to customers, employees, the general public, and—as Kaysen thinks—most importantly to the firm itself as an institution, thereby qualifying in significant respects the older assumptions of maximizing profits as the overriding motivation in corporate enterprise.

Appraisal of the social significance of the modern corporation leads Kaysen to many questions: Is it used as a device for maintaining and enhancing power, especially market power, and what is the effect of this on the competitive system? Are decisions that are made within the corporation about the allocation of scarce resources relatively insulated from the processes of the market? How wide is the range of choice open to managers of the large corporation as to investment and development? Are these decisions rational or efficient for the whole economy? Does the modern corporation, with its "characteristic style of behavior" have a considerable impact on "the style of social processes in general"? Does it so rationalize the economic process within its own corporate boundaries that the relevance of its activity to the basic notions of economic rationality and the economizing process generally becomes doubtful? Are the values implicit in corporate policy destined to spread widely throughout society? What are these values, and are they consistent with the scale of values which we as Americans have cherished and will want to preserve? [26]

Thus, the search for corporate social significance is not simply a search for a viable economic theory which will explain the behavior of the economic system, although this is certainly an important and unresolved issue.[27] Perhaps, more important, the quest is for ethical standards that managers can rely upon to guide business policy. To some, this is more than merely a tremor of corporate bliss and a wink of heaven. It is the burden of Berle's plea for "Lords Spiritual" to guide the collective corporate conscience, of Whyte's concern about the "organization man," and of a great stream of current literature reflecting the attack on Big Business.[28]

POWER AND AUTHORITY OVER PEOPLE AND THINGS

There are certain areas of American life, wrote Margaret Mead [29] during the last World War, "in which all ideals have been sacrificed to a limbo of cynical grabbing—politics being the most notable example; business ethics often another." In whole areas of life, she thought, Americans had ceased to see any element of moral responsibility. But is not this "cynical grabbing" simply a struggle for power, whether political or economic, and a part of the game of life? As Geoffrey Gorer sees us, the struggle for power in the United States is condoned so long as power means power over things—over natural resources, goods, services, money, chattels. Power in this sense seems to him to be morally neutral in the eyes of most Americans, and even highly praiseworthy "within certain ill-defined limits." [30]

Gorer, in commenting further upon American attitudes toward power and authority, distinguishes interestingly between *power* over things and *authority* over people. The modern corporation, like the modern state, is an effective device for collectivizing power over *things;* and in politics and business, those who seek such power by struggling to the seats of the mighty are not necessarily condemned. According to Gorer, it is when the holders of position begin to exercise authority over people—as distinguished from power over things—that our dander rises.

The American attitude, says Gorer, is that "authority [is] always morally bad." The powerful, in American culture, always have to accept an "unauthoritarian role" if they wish to avoid the condemnation of the crowd. Authority is traditionally suspect with us.[31] And it is

imperative for those in positions of great power to manifest in their persons the absence of authority . . . . [They must be] conspicuously plain citizens, with the interests and mannerisms of their fellows; whatever their private temperament, they must act as "one of the boys," glad-handed, mindful of first names, seeing their subordinates in their shirt-sleeves and with their feet on the desk, democratically obscene in their language, with private interests, if any, simple and within the reach of all . . . . If the powerful will not accept this unauthoritarian role, they may well have it thrust upon them . . . for respect and awe are the usual emotional responses to personified authority, and are among the most painful emotions that Americans recognize, and are as carefully avoided by them as the feeling of shame-facedness is by the Japanese.[32]

These perceptive comments serve to remind that perhaps the real reason for the vast amount of attention given to the modern corporation is not that it represents a vast aggregate of private

funds in the hands of a corporate person, be he soulful or soul-
less, but that this fictitious person acts in fact through the agency
of flesh-and-blood people who exercise authority in Gorer's sense
—the control over people as a matter of right.   In the Organization Man one sees an imposed conformity that is resented not
less than conformity imposed by authority of the State.   Indeed,
it is the State-like authority of corporations (and labor unions)
over the lives of men that arouses public criticism and leads contemporary observers to talk more and more in terms of the internal governments and politics of these and other organizations
in the private sector.   One passes here from a focus upon economic analysis of the subject matter to political analysis.   Power,
in the political scientist's sense, not Gorer's, is the issue.   And
where power resides, there responsibility arises.

The growing literature on "human relations" in business at-
tests to the weightiness of this problem as a moral problem, quite
aside from the issue of efficient management.   The power of Big
Business, Big Labor, and Big Government—so long as it is power
over things without danger of undue control over persons—is
thought tolerable and even necessary in an age of mass production and international conflict.   But when these large organizations begin to assume vast claims of authority, in Gorer's sense—
control of people's lives, over human beings within and outside
these great organizations—the old American suspicion of authority
begins to assert itself.   One result is the demand for justification
for such authority, for limitations upon its exercise, for mechanisms to enforce responsibility on the part of the authority wielders.

So it is with the modern corporation.   As long as it was simply
a system for collective use of private capital to do business, to
produce more and better things and to get these things widely
distributed at a reasonable profit, the corporation as a symbol of
power was not too threatening and, indeed, was regarded with
some pride as an example of American ingenuity in subduing the
nonhuman environment to man's beneficent uses.   This was an
ideal example of power over things.   It was the growing sense of
managerial authority over people that gradually precipitated the
moral issue.   Was that authority being exercised with neutrality,

or did it favor the few at the expense of the many, the elite at the expense of the masses? Was it an authority that more and more resembled the power of government with its coercive connotations? What were the moral standards that governed the top managements of these large corporations in their exercise of this authority over people? Were there adequate safeguards in the natural and human laws regulating the market? Could the Protestant ethic or, more broadly, the traditions of our Judaeo-Christian society, internalized in corporate managers, be depended upon alone to channel the authority of corporate executives?

These are some of the philosophic issues that have arisen in the past few decades. And, one must add, the same issues affect all large aggregates of private power within our society, as witness the recent public concern over the authority of labor-union leaders. It had long been established in our political tradition that constitutional restraints were indispensable in the exercise of power by public government, and this conviction had been implemented by intricate mechanisms embodied in the laws and conventions of our constitutional system. The private sectors, on the other hand, were generally left to their own devices: some were extremely authoritarian in character, others were either patterned on the public model or went to the other extreme of completely democratic private government. In any event, these private governmental systems were not a subject of general public debate, nor were the ethical standards of their leaders the business of the public electorate. Great debates on such issues might rage within the private domains of churches, companies, labor unions, professional associations, and universities. But essentially they were not public issues.

Today a different picture exists. Political leaders in Washington demand more democracy in labor unions and urge legislative proposals with teeth, to assure high ethical standards for authority wielders within these private sectors. No comparable legislative proposals have yet appeared with respect to the internal governance of business corporations. But there is more and more emphasis everywhere upon the so-called "public and social responsibilities" of the businessman and especially of large corporations. Enlightened self-interest, some say, is not enough.

Some would even say the corporation must "have a heart"; it must be "soulful."

No one can follow the public and private utterances of responsible businessmen today without coming away with a feeling of deep concern—concern about the role they should play, not only as entrepreneurs but also as entrepreneurial citizens. Especially since the Second World War, thoughtful and perceptive business leaders have become acutely aware of the frightening weaknesses in the social and political structures—national and international—within which they must operate as managers of large, successful business organizations. No matter how well and efficiently they are able to organize the internal affairs of the firms for which they are immediately responsible, they see grave pathologies in the wider social environment. Their public and social responsibilities are, in part, simply the logical consequence of the more immediate responsibility for preserving their businesses in the midst of constantly threatening external forces.

There is considerable evidence that American management generally has a deep sense of social responsibility. To a degree, they are indoctrinated with the Judaeo-Christian ideals of our civilization, with its sense of community among all men of good will and its respect for the dignity of man. The search for a philosophy of business is a search for workable principles in the business world that will maintain the necessary autonomy of the entrepreneurial unit in accordance with classical concepts of economic theory and pay prudent attention to the necessary and sufficient social conditions for guarding this autonomy. But this is not enough. High-minded regard for the basic rights of one's fellow human beings is also a necessary ingredient.

The form of words for a philosophy of business varies greatly from decade to decade. At the moment, it tends to take the form of statements about the public and social responsibilities of the businessman—statements which would probably seem anathema to the classical economic theorist and indeed are anathema to a good many modern theorists. It would be premature to say that by common consent we have arrived at a durable statement of business philosophy. The present shortcomings of economic analysis, with the attendant difficulty of describing with accuracy just what goes on in the economic system, are only one reason for this caution. Not only do we lack adequate economic [33] analysis for stating clearly and unequivocally the actual role of the modern corporation in the dynamics of the business world, but we also lack adequate analysis of the surrounding social and political dynamics.

The very dynamism of society renders it doubtful that any generalizations of today, however accurate, would be applicable in the world of tomorrow. In addition to these difficulties, we face a world of conflicting ideologies: we do not know what doctrines will influence the minds of men even in the next decade, and the prevailing philosophy of business in any age will be strongly influenced by the prevailing ideology.

ALTERNATIVES FOR THE FUTURE

The idea of the corporation is undoubtedly "the most dynamic and serviceable concept in the portfolio of modern business." [34] But serviceable to what end? What the corporation is and where it is going remains a basic question of public—as well as corporate —policy. The conduct of its affairs can be self-centered and parochial. But it can also be, as Louis D. Brandeis once remarked, "great in service and grand in manner." [35] It can subordinate our culture to an economy in which we have no other choice, in Niebuhr's phrase, but to "live luxuriously to keep our productive enterprise from stalling." [36] Or it can be a major source of order and freedom. "A great society is a society in which its men of business think greatly of their function." [37]

Whether the corporate leaders of tomorrow will measure up to a standard of greatness depends not alone upon their own measure of their obligations. It depends quite as much upon a tenable concept of the corporation that is widely and earnestly upheld. It is not enough that a broad-gauged philosophy of business be accepted and acted upon by corporate executives themselves. They cannot achieve their larger goals without general acceptance of the corporation as an instrument of a free society. In molding the essential patterns of thought and action for the Great Society, the corporation of tomorrow will probably

figure far more significantly than is commonly supposed.[38]   Indeed, the philosophy of tomorrow's business has a teleology that
is already discernible in these larger terms.

We have passed the time when the science of corporate polity
can be left in the hands of "amateur political theorists" [39] or be
dealt with in passing while the focus of attention is elsewhere. A
mature philosophy of business awaits, more than anything else, a
careful analysis of the functions and governance of business. An
examination of corporate realities will aid in determining the
nature of corporate governance, but the central problem on the
normative side is to establish the ideal purpose of the business
corporation. Whose instrument is it? Is it the instrument only
of its owners, or an instrument of society? Or is its purpose
ideally the service of only selected interests in society, of which
the stockholder interest is the primary one?

The argument over the functions of the corporation rises out
of the conflict between the tenets of the classical economic creed
and those of the modern managerial creed, which we have discussed. We can, therefore, distinguish two broad categories of
corporations: those which conform more nearly to the *traditional*
patterns of economic behavior and serve the traditionally conceived purposes of the business corporation; and those which can
be regarded as *derivative,* with modifications of the original purpose of the corporate instrument in response to changed social
and economic conditions, revisions of corporate objectives as envisaged especially by professional managers and public policy
makers, and new skills and techniques in organization.

In the *traditional* corporation, considered simply as a heuristic
model and not necessarily the prototype of any one observable
company, we can discern an original or primitive type of corporate instrument. It is an instrumentality of a single group, the
stockholders. It has a single purpose: the conduct of a business
enterprise for maximal profits to its owners, collectively and individually. In the next chapter this model of the traditional, or
austere, corporation will be elaborated in some detail, and following it we shall spell out one of two different models of the
derivative type of business corporation. One of these derivative
types—simplified again for expository purposes—is the *metro-*

corporation, an instrumentality of many interests with a multiplicity of purposes, becoming, as it were, a society in microcosm, a lesser society circumscribed by a greater, and no longer an organizational means of achieving the single goal of profitable return to its original owners.

At the end of this book the other derivative type of corporation is conceived of as a means between the two extremes of the traditional and the metrocorporation. We shall designate this as the *well-tempered* corporation, a model for investigative purposes, though obviously with normative assumptions, since the model is drawn with a deliberate intention to find a *via media* between traditional standards of corporate behavior and modified standards that are quite unacceptable to the traditionalists.

All three models—the traditional corporation, the metrocorporation, and the well-tempered corporation—can be important points of departure for both the critique of corporate policy and the analysis of corporate trends.

CHAPTER II

The Traditional Corporation

IN THE TRADITIONAL CORPORATION there is a simple answer to the basic ethical question that confronts every director and every executive officer. The central question—what is my station and what are its duties? [1]—has an answer that is fortified by law and custom: to serve the property interests of the company's stockholders. There are secondary responsibilities to creditors, to employees, to customers, and others; but the primary responsibility is to the group of persons who are investors in the enterprise.

Nor does the grant of corporate privilege by a public act in itself effect any conversion of the traditional corporation into an instrument or society or a "social institution." For rhetorical purposes it may often be proclaimed that a business corporation has public responsibilities because it owes its very life as a corporate "person" to the State. But for practical purposes, the responsible officers of a business corporation look to the body of share owners as their real principal and not to the State nor to society.

One seeks in vain in contemporary corporate statutes for any theory of corporate social responsibility that places the share-owner interest in a subordinate role, as though the use of the corporate form required them to transform a private business operation into a quasi-public agency. On the contrary, the authorizing of incorporation of a business with limited liability is regarded in the traditional model as an enabling act that leaves the promoters relatively free to set up an organization in which business decision making can be transferred to executive management. The purpose of incorporation in other words, from the public's point of view, is not to create a *public* instrumentality; it is rather to implement a *private* enterprise through an effective means of merging private resources.

That this traditional view of corporate purpose and corporate responsibility is the prevailing philosophy reflected in contemporary corporation law can be substantiated by a review of the statutes.[2] There are variations on the theme from state to state, to be sure. Legislators have not generally accepted the view that promoters should be completely free to define the scope of the enterprise and to allocate risk, control, and profit through the corporation's security structure. Restrictions on this allocative authority, in particular, have been laid down in many statutes designed to protect other property interests such as those of creditors and nonvoting security holders. Corporation law, in short, is mainly designed to carry out the purpose of the traditional corporation—a business instrument of its owners—with only such restraints on managerial freedom as appear to be necessary to protect the owners' interests and those of certain other contributors of factors of production.

But the theory of the traditional corporation by no means rests on such legalistic grounds alone. The philosophy which corporation statutes reflect is a far more pervasive one. It is at once an economic and a political philosophy. On the economic side it is a philosophy that relies heavily on the market mechanism as the chief means of making the optimum use of a society's resources. On the political side, it is a philosophy that circumscribes the authority of public government or of any private collectivity to meddle with this self-regulating mechanism. And since it is presumed to be an automatic process, the market mechanism when left relatively free is expected to achieve the beneficent results in public welfare that "socially responsible" corporations would erroneously try to achieve by making the business corporation a quasi-public instrumentality.

Thus the model of the traditional corporation rests essentially on a social theory that has variously been described as economic liberalism, "the conventional wisdom," and the doctrine of "intact" or "old-style capitalism." The managers of the traditional corporation think of their business as an entrepreneurial unit operating essentially as an individually owned and managed business unit would operate in a "free enterprise system," with a minimum of intervention by any outside force except the forces of the market.

"Business is business" for managers of the traditional corporation, and this does not include any such objective as the promotion of the general welfare. That the general welfare of society will be advanced by those who pursue the profit motive is certainly one of the articles of faith of the American business creed. But by this view the general welfare is held to be the automatic net result of the system as a whole and not the motivating force that impels the individual businessman to do what he does as a businessman. There is, in fact, a general suspicion that when he dilutes business with altruism the net result for all concerned will be neither businesslike nor altruistic. And the business corporation, under this traditional theory, is but the businessman writ large. It is simply a specialized instrument for the kind of competitive drive that has presumably brought our way of life to the high level of affluence of which we are so proud.

It may perhaps be objected that this view of the corporation is antiquated and has been superseded everywhere by the more "modern" view that the corporation has substantial social responsibilities even if it is not a public instrumentality in any proper sense. Our purpose here is to construct a heuristic model for clarity of exposition and not to describe the median type of corporate theory and practice. But even if we were to attempt such an empirical task—which is beyond the scope of this book— it is safe to say that the doctrine of social responsibility has neither been reflected in the law of corporations (with some notable exceptions) [3] nor in managerial practice.

But it is sometimes held that the theory of social responsibility is reflected in corporate practice, particularly with reference to corporate giving, better community relations, employee benefit programs, plant safety programs, the new emphasis in management techniques on "human relations," the lending of selected personnel to educational institutions and public service, and the development of a "corporate conscience."

It is equally arguable that social responsibility stops at the pocketbook. The figures for total corporate giving in the United

States would tend to support this view, for while they are large in dollars they are minuscule in percentages of corporate net income. The most generous corporate givers are not the large but the middle-sized corporations, and for the country as a whole the percentage has usually been around one fifth or less of what a corporation is allowed to deduct for tax purposes. As for non-deductible expenditures, it is questionable whether many corporations can justify such expense for the fulfillment of social responsibility. Costly programs for employee benefits, as another example, are the result of irresistible pressures on management or are undertaken simply as inevitable costs of doing business.

If one studies the usual statements on behalf of the new doctrine of social responsibility, it is found that its justification generally lies in the *quid pro quo* argument: social responsibility pays off, even if the pay-off has to be long-run rather than of immediate advantage to the corporation. There are exceptions. But it is fair to say that for most advocates of the socially responsible corporation their rationale is hardly more than a gloss on the theory of the traditional corporation, despite statements which might seem to indicate otherwise.

Language that proclaims the doctrine of social responsibility is usually little more than a verbal commitment to abstract principles of justice. In the traditional corporation one is especially careful not to specify concrete applications, particularly as to who has responsibility for what and to whom, and how these responsibilities are to be implemented in practice. We shall turn shortly to this matter as it applies to the metrocorporation but here it is pertinent to inquire, in the same way, what the theory of the traditionally austere corporation entails. The kinds of action required by that theory may look very like what most of the proponents of the theory of social responsibilities advocate; but the rational basis for them is entirely different.

THE TRADITIONAL CORPORATION AND STOCKHOLDERS

The traditional corporation as a model tends to its owners' business and its managers are not diverted by irrelevant activities. They function in the strictly limited role of profit makers [4] and subordinate every functional kind of work within the organization to the goal of profitability for stockholders, who are entitled to one hundred percent of net earnings after taxes.

Austerity will be the governing principle in allocation from gross earnings to every factor of production with the exception of equity capital represented by common stock. There is no "balancing of interests" by management in distributing the corporate usufruct since the prior claim of stockholders on earnings after taxes is unquestionable and cannot be subjected to any kind of arbitration by directors, who are collectively the share owners' *alter ego*. Competing claims on the corporate usufruct from the suppliers of labor and borrowed capital and from customers demanding lower prices are satisfied by means of minimal diversions of funds that might otherwise be siphoned off into dividends. Retention of earnings for capital expansion, research and development, and other justifiable costs of doing business "progressively" is by no means inconsistent with the objective of the traditional corporation; but every distribution of funds from gross earnings will be watched with care to make sure that extraneous functions are not introduced by accident or design.

Thus the traditional corporation rigorously excludes the idea that corporate growth and company prestige *in itself* justifies any additional costs. The doctrine that a corporation has an independent life of its own worth preserving, independent of the share owners' interest in it as a profit-maker, is regarded as insidious and ridiculous. Similarly, there is no place for corporate philanthropy. The traditional corporation has nothing to give away. Its managers are expected always to insist upon the *quid pro quo* in every deal with the suppliers of material and services and the buyers of its products. To protect the owners' interests they must be hard bargainers. A reputation for fair dealing will be regarded in the traditional corporation as a good-will asset, but its executive officers will be careful not to arouse any stockholder's skepticism about their capacity as shrewd negotiators in every market.

Corporate austerity in the traditional corporation does not necessarily mean shortsighted frugality, however. If the business need not run on forever with a costly reputation for opulence and generosity, it will still require some well-rationed expenditures to provide the necessary innovations, the expected gestures of good will, and adequate evidence of stability to assure its standing as a "sound" and profitable enterprise. Otherwise, it cannot maintain its status as a clearinghouse of skills and materials—an organization useful to its owners. But its managers must never forget that they are there primarily to serve the property interests of those owners.

THE TRADITIONAL CORPORATION AND THE PUBLIC

The traditional corporation clearly has no general *public* responsibility. As to its wage policies, for example, it is argued that neither industry nor labor should be expected to "exercise voluntary restraint" in the public interest. Labor unions and traditional corporations are, by function, the stewards of special interests; their obligation is to their own organizations; and their duty is to face the community in the name of their members and not their members in the name of the community. The argument in the case of labor-management relations is said to apply with equal force to all market operations of the corporation. Each must look out for his own; and when a leader of business (or of labor) goes over to the "public interest" his associates may suspect that he ceases to function in accordance with the ground rules of a free, capitalist society.

This traditional position, which leaves the public interest to the care of the State or to the automatic operations of the market, has been attacked as being ultimately destructive of the foundations of a free society. Bertrand de Jouvenel, for instance, warns that the body politic as a whole will not be well served by "the untrammelled clash of special interests within it." [5] De Jouvenel urges further that concern for the public interest is not the business of public officials alone but of everyone and, not least, of the large and powerful organizations in the private sector. For it is a fundamental assumption of liberal defenders of the free society that the public interest is well served by the clash of opinions about the public interests.

But managers of the traditional corporation feel no compunction to exercise voluntary restraint on such matters as wage and price policy, guided by zealous concern for the public interest. In the austere view, managers are responsible for the operation of a competitive enterprise and will not, in this role, concern themselves unduly with "the general welfare." As citizens and as members of associations devoted to social melioration, they can and should be concerned with advancing the public interest. But they will insist that the business corporation is not designed for such a task. Rather, they would say, the traditional corporation is designed to supply goods and services to those who assert a market demand for them, and to supply these only at a profit to the risk taker.

Managers of the traditional corporation do not have to answer the question: What goods and what services? That question will be answered by the votes of consumers as they register their choices in the free market. Nor do they have to ask the questions: How much profit? At what just price? These, too, are questions that will be answered automatically in the market place.

Nor do managers of the traditional corporation have to ask about the "correct" formula for the distribution of gross income. This, too, is left to the working of economic laws or to what are thought to be "laws." Risk capital will flow to those enterprises which offer the best opportunities for profitable return on investment. The best opportunities will be found in those corporations which make the most prudent allocation of corporate resources among the factors of production; and companies which permit imprudent allocations will sooner or later fade out, while those which survive and prosper will demonstrably have the best allocation formulas.

In its allocation of costs, the traditional corporation naturally will try to avoid charges of social irresponsibility not by undertaking any altruistic ventures but simply by making the irreducible concessions to pressure groups. Pressures for corporate giving, for more humane labor relations, for better community relations, and so on, will be carefully weighed against the prime necessity of maximizing profit for the owners of the business.

Therefore, the strategic areas of corporate decision will center about those functions directly concerned with corporate profit making.

In the great public debates on necessary measures for protecting and extending the system of free and competitive enterprise, for securing law and order in the global market place, and for assuring the survival of a free society against the threat of totalitarianism, managers of the traditional corporation will avoid "controversial issues" that seem to them to have only a remote bearing on their immediate business operations. They will define the institution of "business" in quite restricted terms and thus their conception of the relevant corporate environment will be limited.[6]

Those who believe in corporate austerity, as represented in this heuristic model, will as a rule adhere to the tenets of social Darwinism. Their traditional corporation is incessantly involved in a struggle for survival. They will fear the expansion of public government for the same reasons that they fear the expansion of corporate social responsibilities. Both will seem to undermine the self-reliance of the enterprising unit and to dilute dangerously the responsibility of the individual to those most nearly associated with him. Only with the greatest reluctance will the manager of the traditional corporation concede that his responsibilities—or those of his corporation—extend beyond this immediate group. The struggle for survival will seem too intense; the dangers of extinction in the race for survival in a highly competitive environment will be too obvious.

ETHICS OF THE TRADITIONAL CORPORATION

The traditional corporation thus gives the impression of being parochial, self-centered, materialistic, and imbued with a fundamental pessimism characteristic of the older classical economists. It is true that the classical tradition in economic thought was intimately tied in with the ethics of utilitarianism. The ethics of the traditional corporation are related historically to the liberal-utilitarian tradition. The traditional corporate executive not only insists upon the conventional proprieties and meticulous obedience to law; he may subscribe wholeheartedly to doctrines of progress and of the greatest good for the greatest number. But his faith is identified with the older liberalism and not the revised liberalism [7] that began to be developed in England toward the end of the nineteenth century and emerged on this side of the Atlantic in Square Deal, New Deal, and Fair Deal political-economic programs.

In the traditional corporation, corporate policy reflects a brand of theory about political economy that is seldom articulated by corporate executives in examinable form. This theory is often incorrectly described as stubborn reactionary dogma or pure negativism toward the great issues of public policy. The theory may be untenable. But implicit in it is the moral conviction that progress depends upon everyone's minding his own business. With respect to issues of public policy this means that the executive of the traditional corporation has no *moral* obligation nor *social* responsibility for any kind of joint management of a nation's resources.

In the recent flurry of pronouncements about the social responsibilities of the businessman, the positive aspects of the traditional point of view are apt to be overlooked. The traditionalist does not merely avoid corporate involvement in the larger issues of resource management for the economy as a whole; he denounces the very idea of "planning" in this larger political-economic arena as a dangerous heresy, in which the traditional corporation must play no part at all.

The idea that a nation's economy must somehow be controlled as to the development of material and human resources, the deliberate allocation of available resources to the "best" uses, the establishment of public policy for the equitable disposition of conflicting claims on resources, and the establishment of methods for preserving the widest possible latitude of consumer choice—this whole approach to planned solutions of a nation's economic problems is anathema to the executives of the traditional corporation, and they resist involvement of their companies in such planning.

When the Committee on Economic Development—a group representing many companies that would regard themselves as

socially responsible and nontraditionalist—focuses the businessman's attention on urgent national issues like those listed below,
the executive of the traditional corporation will say that these
are matters for each man to ponder as a citizen but not as the
manager of a business enterprise. Here is the list as drawn up
by a spokesman [8] for the Committee:

How can we make adequate economic provision for national
   defense?

What internal economic adjustments to international developments?

How insure economic growth, i.e., increase in efficiency, or the
   "maximum production of wanted goods, services and leisure
   with the resources available"?

How can we meet the major hazards [9] of a severe depression?

How are we to deal with cost-inflation and, more especially, wage-
   inflation?

What are we to do about the concentration of economic power in
   business and labor?

How achieve a proper balance between public services financed
   by taxation and private services paid for by consumers in the
   market?

How adapt the economy to population growth and population
   movements?

How can we preserve those economic institutions (above all, the
   free market) that support our freedoms?

What kind of education do we need and how is it to be financed?

That these are important problems, no responsible corporate
executive would deny; but in the traditional corporation they are
problems for the owners of the property which executives manage
and not problems for the executives. The stockholders must give
corporate managers the cue about any position they want their
corporation to take on such problems, if indeed they want any
position taken at all.

Here the traditional corporation is confronted with a
dilemma. The dilemma concerns the respective rules of public
and private polities in the governance of the economy as a whole.
Public polities are designed, in traditional theory, for the gov-

ernance of the public sector, while corporate polities are designed for the management of highly specialized business operations carried on in corporate form. If corporate polities are to be designed strictly as organizations for the management of market operations of the stockholders' enterprises, the inevitable result will be the continuing expansion of economic activities by public polities—with progressive encroachment of public government on the free market area. If, on the other hand, corporate polities are to be redesigned to assume some of the responsibility for solving the big problems confronting the economy as a whole, these corporate polities will lose their traditional character. They will cease to be traditional corporate enterprises and will be gradually transformed into quasi-public institutions.

There is an incipient revolt against this transformation of the business corporation into a nontraditional institution. The outlines of this revolt can be seen in the growing literature in opposition to social responsibilities for business organizations. Yet the proponents of social responsibilities are becoming more articulate and more insistent, too, for they see in the model of the traditional corporation a moribund form of business organization. They see the traditional corporation moving dangerously away from the mainstream of human affairs toward innocuous desuetude. They want the corporation to become a major energizer of a society with naturally entropic tendencies.[10]

It would be inaccurate to predict either the immediate demise of the traditional idea or the universal adoption of the idea of the socially responsible, quasi-public business corporation. In our highly pluralistic society, with its tolerance for a great variety of private associations, the traditional corporation will persist alongside new and emergent forms. The nascent forms have yet to prove themselves viable and to provide themselves with an acceptable rationale.

The traditional corporation has been a characteristically voluntary response of free men to ecological stimuli that were both material and ideological. An untrammeled continent had to be tamed to man's purposes, and these purposes were by no means entirely materialistic and mundane. But in the development and exploitation of our natural resources, the traditional corporation was an extraordinarily effective instrument of an unplanned economic system. The development and exploitation of our natural resources could not have been carried out either by agencies of public government—for the modern administrative state had not yet been created—nor by individual enterprise alone. In these circumstances, the traditional corporation, guided by measures of business performance in profit and loss, and by the discipline of the balance sheet, undoubtedly proved its social usefulness. And it will continue to do so, provided that we hold to our basic tenets about the market mechanism as a powerful means of preserving liberty.

As every sector of society becomes more and more highly organized, however, and as the business unit itself grows in size and influence, there is increasing demand upon all organizations to become instrumentalities of the commonweal. One of the responses to this demand is the idea of the metrocorporation.

CHAPTER III

The Metrocorporation

ONE RESPONSE to a crescendo of demand for more "socially responsible" business enterprises has been the conception of a business corporation that is far more socially oriented, more gregarious, more civic-minded and more cosmopolitan than the austere traditional corporation. We shall call this conceptualized model of a nascent corporate form the *metrocorporation,* thereby underlining its maternal concern for a numerous brood.

As a heuristic model, the metrocorporation is more difficult to describe than the traditional corporation, and not merely because it is still an inchoate form of business organization. The traditional corporation is better known in legal and economic theory. Since we are outlining only the most simplified models, it will be conceded that there are many variations on the traditional type; but it stands in decided contrast, even with modification, to the idea of a metrocorporation.

In their search for a new pattern of corporate behavior that avoids the extremes of privatization and statization, business leaders have tried to preserve a high degree of corporate autonomy while at the same time steering the corporate ship into the main streams of public policy. Privatization—or acute withdrawal into the corporate shell—is characteristic of corporate behavior in the traditional corporation. Statization—or surrender of business decision making to public governments—is the other extreme, and one of grave danger to individual liberty as well as to freedom of enterprise for the businessman. To steer a course between these treacherous shoals has been a matter of concern not only for the corporate executive but for the public policy maker as well. The metrocorporate idea is one answer to this problem.

The metrocorporation lays emphasis upon the rights and duties of the corporation as a citizen and upon its relationships to society. Its managers undertake a dual role as individual citizens in their political communities and as representatives of the "corporate citizen." The metrocorporation is more a quasi-public than a private association as indicated by the general use of the term "public corporation" to designate a company with widely dispersed stockholding. Technically, it is a private corporation with constitutional protections not available to public corporations such as municipalities and government corporations. It is also clearly a part of the private sector of the economy and not within the public sector as an administrative unit of public government. It has a private or, at the most, a quasi-public polity or governmental system of its own with a considerable degree of autonomy vis-à-vis the public governmental system and other private polities. Yet one can regard the metrocorporation as consociate with these other polities in the sense that its affairs, though self-governed, have much in common with public affairs and the affairs of consociated groups in the greater society of which it is an organic part. The concept of consociation, implying alliance or confederacy, is not entirely inappropriate in describing the metrocorporation because of the pluralistic theory that pervades our political and economic thought—a pluralism that underlines not only the autonomy of private associations but also their interdependence and their community of interest.

The metrocorporation, as a model, is premised more on the similarity of Government and Business than on their disparity. The range of corporate policy is not so narrowly defined as to exclude large issues of public policy. The strategic decision areas of corporate policy in the metrocorporation are not limited to its own economic problems. It has concern for the larger economic problems of the economy as a whole, as well as for those problems that concern managers of single enterprises which must perform as efficient and profitable producers of goods and services.

But the metrocorporation also has many noneconomic goals. It tends to become a society in microcosm, with concern about human relations and human aspirations, not only among those immediately associated with the enterprise but among its neighboring social groups.

Its critics deplore this tendency because they assert that it is feudalistic and retrogressive. The metrocorporation is charged with egregious attempts to claim the whole man, giving him protection and security in return for lifetime loyalty to the Organization. It is further charged with retrogressing from a society characterized by division of labor into a centralized, collectivized, and bureaucratic institution with overweening ambitions to become a lesser society in its own right.

Seen in a more favorable light, the metrocorporation is high-minded, philanthropic, and socially responsible. It strives to avoid the labels of excessive materialism, of cynical disregard for moral and religious standards, and of undemocratic values. With this ethical perspective there is a strong tendency to develop a theory of corporate governance consistent with the ideals of a democratic society.

TRADITIONAL VS. METROCORPORATE POLITY

The issue of corporate power, its legitimacy and its impact on the freedom of men, arises with respect to the traditional as well as the metrocorporation. All organizations exercise power in some degree, and the organizational revolution of our time has brought this problem home to many quarters where it had been little noticed before. Power, in private as well as in public governments, presents inescapable ethical issues. Nor can we escape them by wishing away the organizational revolution. Big business, big unions, and big government are here to stay. But it is often argued, and with some cogency, that the traditional corporation gives small cause for worry on the score of serious encroachment on men's fundamental liberties.

The traditional corporation, it is sometimes argued, is commendably limited in the nature and scope of its powers. Some of the powers are legally defined and hedged about with enforceable fiduciary responsibilities on the part of corporate boards; other powers are of a strictly economic kind with no taint of the political and no coercive sanctions to back them up. This certainly does not state the case completely. As we shall see, one of the instruments of corporate policy—and an indispensable instrument in fact—is the force of public government, invoked by due process of law, to be sure, but nonetheless in the background when it is needed. And public government relies on *ultima ratio* as well as consent. But corporations are hardly the unique beneficiaries of this sanction; and the corporation that sticks to the business of profit making for its owners can be said to enjoy precisely the same power as the individual enjoys in seeking public protection of his property rights.

The traditional corporation, moreover, despite its collective economic power, is presumably subject to workable restraints on that power: in the operations of the market and in the special kinds of legislation enacted to curb the abuse of economic power. There may be cases in which a species of despotic internal corporate regime bears heavily upon the ordinary liberties of its employees. But, in a free and competitive economy, an abused employee can always escape to the more liberal atmosphere of another business corporation or go into business for himself. The traditional corporation, in other words, is to a degree self-corrective as to excessive power which might endanger human freedom. And the powers it exercises are functionally limited to the operations of a competitive business.

The metrocorporation, on the other hand, presents a very different situation. It does not confine its activities to business purposes in any narrowly defined sense. It has broad social goals and assumes large social responsibilities. It holds itself accountable to many different sectors of society. Its managers regard themselves as arbiters, adjusters, or balancers of many diverse interests. With such heavy and extensive responsibilities it would be natural to expect the organization to claim and to wield large powers.

The new function of umpirage at the top managerial level is but one of the problems of metrocorporate polity. With its representation of diverse interests in a complex system of corporate governance, the metrocorporation not only departs from the simple formula of managerial representation of stockholders' interest alone; it goes on to the assumption by management of a wide variety of responsibilities that would be quite alien to regimes following the principle of corporate austerity and privatization. When so many diverse responsibilities are assumed, it becomes far more difficult to assess the costs of doing business, the formulas for distribution of earnings, and the measures of accountability of management to the several contributor-claimants. The measures of business performance alone are necessarily complicated; but the metrocorporation is far more than a business in the traditional sense.

Managers of the metrocorporation face difficulty in obtaining the legal powers needed to sustain the multiple purposes of this model. Aside from the recent court decisions and state statutes authorizing corporate giving, there is little evidence that the law sanctions the general proposition that corporate powers are available for the assumption of broad social responsibilities. When corporate powers begin to expand, there will be more insistent demand for adequate controls to prevent the abuse of these widened powers.

Businessmen are already disturbed by proposals for ensuring due process of law within the corporation—one aspect of a growing insistence on some form of corporate constitutionalism. The prospect of patterning corporate governance after the norms of democratic constitutionalism, as we know it in public government, is not attractive to most professional managers. Separation of powers, checks and balances, judicial review of rule-making powers, periodic elections and the party system, representative assemblies and legislative investigations—these and many other devices to get public accountability for public servants, if translated into proposed patterns of corporate governance, would arouse vigorous antagonism in most business circles.

But even if we were to assume realistically that corporate constitutionalism could grow by gradual stages, in many different ways within many different companies, with successive adaptations to the peculiar needs and conditions of those companies rather than by a rapid mechanical transfer of public law doctrines to private sectors, there would still be resistance to change. And perhaps rightly so. It can be argued persuasively that a direct transfer of constitutional concepts from public government to the corporate polity could result in transforming the corporation into a less effective and a more bureaucratic organization than it is now. Managerial authority could become so dispersed that managers would lack the authority for rapid decision making. Under these circumstances corporate constitutionalism, though it might serve to protect the freedom of employees, would possibly make the corporation an unacceptably costly instrument for producing goods and services, thus defeating one of its primary reasons for existence. Even the metrocorporation, with all of its new responsibilities, is still an economic instrument primarily. And one of the dangers inherent in the model is that this primary economic function could be subordinated to secondary considerations.

The metrocorporation, while attractive on general principles, is likely to look far less attractive when one begins to get down to cases. The ethics of the metrocorporation, when spelled out in the large letters of corporate polity, may in the long run prove too burdensome in the multifarious obligations thrust onto the corporate entity. Yet a modified form of the metrocorporation is already beginning to put in an appearance here and there and conceivably could gain wide acceptance. The transition from the traditional corporation to the metrocorporation may be going on more rapidly than management suspects. The stockholder no longer holds the center of the stage. In some corporations the board includes representatives of nonstockholder interests. Labor unions, to some extent, have already moved into many corporate decision centers. The public, through official agencies, increasingly specifies conditions for the formulation of corporate policy.

These are but some of the factors which management must consider in deciding how to fashion the corporate polity in the transition from the traditional corporation to a newer form of business organization.

CORPORATE POLITY AND PUBLIC GOVERNMENTS

Quite aside from the question of its internal polity, the corporation must give systematic attention to the relationships between corporate and public polities. These relationships are not peculiar to the metrocorporation. They do take on different dimensions when a business corporation becomes a "corporate citizen" in more than a rhetorical sense.

The traditional corporation conscientiously avoids any general involvement in political action at any level—local, state, national, or international. On occasion it will intervene in the governmental process by lobbying or giving direct testimony before congressional committees charged with writing new legislation of direct business concern. Behind the scenes, it will use protective measures against governmental encroachments. The metrocorporation, on the other hand, will systematically, actively, and openly involve itself in political affairs at all levels and in all branches of public government. It will consider that its moral obligation is to maintain a free and open pluralistic society by giving the corporation a political voice in the governance of society. The metrocorporation represents a significant private sector with its own system of private government; but it also assumes a right—and a responsibility to its own constituencies— to help shape the economic, social, and political environment to its own ends, as well as to what it considers to be society's ends.

The metrocorporation thus becomes an instrument for achieving broad political goals. It takes an active part in such matters as government reorganization, foreign affairs, and policies on the uses of natural resources and manpower. It becomes concerned with, and attempts to influence, the over-all impact and the broad trends of legislation generally. And not least, it is actively concerned with the electorate at all levels of public government in order to insure representation that favors the multiple goals of a great enterprise. In short, the metrocorporation is concerned with the whole sweep of the governmental process.

The metrocorporation regards public governments at local, state, national and international levels as important suppliers of services. Public governments supply the indispensable minimum of law and order in the market place; they protect private property; they apply the ultimate sanctions for the enforcement of contractual obligations, without which all business enterprise would be impossible. All these services are of course recognized by the traditional corporation. But the metrocorporation sees in public government a supplier of services far broader in scope.

Through public education, for example, public governments ensure the continuous supply of manpower without which important technological advances could not be brought to bear in the production process and they prepare the consumer public to receive and use the fruits of this technology through education. Nor is it overlooked that public governments protect savings from which a large portion of equity capital is supplied to business.

Public governments, in addition to being suppliers, are also important customers of business. In some instances, large corporations are heavily dependent upon government orders. When a considerable part of private enterprise depends vitally upon the allocation of public funds for its survival, a singular danger arises for the metrocorporation. The danger is that it may completely lose its autonomy for decision making. The metrocorporation tends to identify its goals with the goals of society; and when it depends almost exclusively upon the allocation of public funds for its survival, it becomes enmeshed in the public governmental structure.

In the metrocorporation this danger leads to an even greater insistence upon the independent way of life that characterizes enclaved private sectors. Private pension and welfare systems are developed; an *esprit de corps* is encouraged by innumerable plans and policies to take care of those associated with the enterprise; and the Organization Man appears on the corporate scene.

THE METROCORPORATION AND LABOR RELATIONS

For the metrocorporation, relations with other private organizations become quasi-political and are far more complex than the contractual relationships by which the traditional corporation assembles the factors of production. This subtler type of relationship with external polities raises problems of strategic significance in corporate policy and can be illustrated in the field of labor relations.

Labor relations are more than internal employee relations; they involve external relations with unions. For the traditional corporation the problem of labor is statable as a problem of business management: the efficient use of labor as a factor of profitable production. But for the metrocorporation it has larger dimensions.

Labor relations in the metrocorporation are frankly regarded as political as well as economic in character. The employee group, in the first place, is a group interest to be brought into a stable working relation to other interests. In the second place, there has to be a policy with respect to unions and the labor movement in general. The metrocorporation has a responsibility with respect to its employees that is difficult to formulate because of their dual roles as members of both corporate and labor organizations. The search for the right formula necessitates some tenable theory of the labor movement.

A recent review [1] of the past decade of industrial relations research suggests that while much reliable knowledge is available on this subject, much is still lacking. Wage determination, collective bargaining, union government and union leadership, employee benefit plans, and the political as well as the economic effects of unionism are all subjects on which bitterness of dispute arises, partly from the absence of consensus about the significance of the labor movement and its long-range relations to corporate policy.

Is the labor movement, as John R. Commons once insisted, "always a reaction and a protest against capitalism" [2] implying the existence of a wage-earning group that has developed a consciousness of the separateness of its interests as opposed to those of its employers? Or is it a movement within and compatible with a capitalist system, a reformist rather than a revolutionary movement? Does it indicate an attitude on the part of workers and their leaders that is essentially divisive and anomic? Or is it rather the contemporary manifestation of man's age-old yearning for recognition and status, in this case a demand for workers' rights as producers and as respected members of society? Did the rise of the American labor movement bring in a new philosophy of "constitutionalism in the relations between labor and capitalism," as Selig Perlman [3] once remarked about the advent of joint agreements between unions and management?

Perlman saw in the ideology of the American Federation of Labor an industrial democracy "of unionized workers and of associated employer-managers, jointly conducting an industrial government with 'laws' mandatory upon the individual." [4] Its leaders had adapted the American labor movement to American conditions, "exchanging their class-consciousness for a job-consciousness." This job-conscious unionism was allied with a lively interest on the part of workers in problems of business management, intent as they were upon job opportunities, and this meant for the rank and file of the American labor movement a kind of "lower idealism" that stood in contrast to the more transcendental and abstract thinking of the Marxians.

But collective bargaining was not just a means of raising wages and improving conditions of employment; nor was its goal merely democratic government in industry. It was above all "a technique whereby an inferior social class or group carries on a never slackening pressure for a bigger share in the social sovereignty as well as for more welfare, security and liberty for its individual members." The emotional impetus behind collective bargaining was not the desire to displace the "old ruling class." Workers wanted rather to bring their own class abreast of the superior class, to gain "equal rights" as a class, and to assure equal consideration for the worker as an individual person. Beyond this they sought "an exclusive jurisdiction in that sphere where the most immediate interests, both material and spiritual, are determined, and a shared jurisdiction with the older class or classes in all the other spheres." [5]

This is but one of many different explanations of the labor union movement.[6] One of the significant but highly controversial explanations is Frank Tannenbaum's view of unionism as a reaction of workers to the consequences of the Industrial Revolution. The Industrial Revolution "destroyed the solid moorings of an older way of life, and cast the helpless workers adrift in a strange and difficult world." The "symbolic universe that had patterned the ways of men across the ages in village, manor or guild had disappeared." [7] The individual worker no longer had any recognized status, nor any "society" of his own, which he belonged to and looked to for the values that could guide his life.

The labor union was a response to the basic need of men for solidarity in this deeper-than-economic sense.[8] But for Tannenbaum the labor union is not simply a new model of the old guild. It is one of the manifestations of our modern attempt to recreate the community on nonfeudal patterns. The atomized society that followed the passing of the guilds was an unstable compound. There is historically "a persistent grouping of men about their tools"; and this natural grouping was bound to reappear in new forms not just because workers want higher wages, shorter hours, better conditions of labor, music in the shops, and baby clinics. For, "work must fill a social and moral as well as an economic role." [9]

Tannenbaum's philosophy of labor interprets the growing participation of the unions in managerial responsibility as a hopeful sign and not a dangerous "encroachment" on managerial "prerogatives."

The union, with all its faults, may yet save the corporation and its great efficiencies by incorporating it into its own natural 'society,' its own cohesive labor force, and by endowing it with the meanings that all real societies possess, meanings that give some substance of idealism to man in his journey between the cradle and the grave . . . . If the corporation is to survive, it will have to be endowed with a moral role in the world, not merely an economic one. From this point of view, the challenge to management by the trade-union is salutary and hopeful. It is a route, perhaps the only available one, for saving the values of our democratic society, and the contemporary industrial system as well. In some way the corporation and its labor force must become one corporate group and cease to be a house divided and seemingly at war.[10]

Tannenbaum's position would be completely unacceptable in the traditional corporation. Even in the metrocorporation it would be generally suspect and unacceptable. For, if it is conceded that managers and union should "merge in common owner-ship" and "common identity," what becomes of the other constit-uent interests that merge in the metrocorporation?

Yet the moral problems of labor relations have to be faced by the metrocorporation because of its concern with broad social re-sponsibility toward labor organizations as external private polities. How will its managers find a solution for imbuing the corpora-tion with moral purpose in its labor policy? By expanding the present programs of "human relations"? By spreading the owner-ship of corporations to more and more employee shareholders? By further developing our industrial jurisprudence based upon collective bargaining agreements arrived at by arm's-length strug-gle for power between professional managers and labor leaders?

These are issues which the metrocorporation must somehow resolve. They are issues that take on no such ethical dimensions in the traditional corporation, which rejects the premise that the corporation has any special moral obligation in dealing with organized labor. The traditional corporation deals with unions for the supply of labor as a factor of production. Such a position on labor relations will not fit the model of the metrocorporation at all, and it is hardly the preferred position even for the tradi-tional corporation.

Labor policy in most corporations today is the result of bilat-eral or multilateral negotiations among influential organizations, of which the corporation is only one of the interested parties. There are frequently many different unions which purport to speak and act on behalf of the corporation's employees, and con-tract negotiations often involve public agencies as well. This is a trend that goes against the grain of the corporate traditionalist. He would prefer to deal with the corporation's employees on an individual basis, but the pervasive organizational structure of the economy has left him no choice in the matter. The bilateral and multilateral formulation of labor policy is quite out of key with the model of the traditional corporation.

It is equally out of key with the model of the metrocorpora-tion, which would prefer to absorb all external groups that pur-port to speak for the interests of its employees. Such extreme paternalism is, of course, completely at odds with the trend toward voluntary associations for the representation of interest groups in every sector of society. But while the metrocorporation could not hope to turn the clock back, it is not inconceivable that it might achieve nearly the same result by other means than the absorption of unions.

A METROCORPORATE FEUDALISM?

During the past few decades the whole conception of industrial employment has undergone dramatic change.[11] Labor is no longer regarded as a commodity. In place of the commodity concept there is the more recent "welfare concept" of employment, especially in the case of large industrial organizations, though not limited to them. All large organizations become increasingly responsible for the welfare of their personnel. A persistently expressed goal is security for all workers in the organization. Without pursuing an ostensibly paternalistic labor policy, the metrocorporation could embrace this trend with alacrity.

What is now the striving of the worker for status, recognition, and dignity, along with material reward, could tomorrow ossify into a tenacious hold upon a species of neofeudal privilege, but with corresponding loyalties. The liegemen of the metrocorporation, although eminently secure, may quite possibly not be freemen. They may have security, even down to the grave. But they would be tied to their overlords by pension trusts and a complex network of employee benefit agreements. The metrocorporation could become a kind of feudal entity.

Whether a free and open society is consistent with a social system in which modern versions of the guild flourish will be an increasingly disturbing issue for the makers of corporate policy. Management will not be alone in its thoughts about this. For some decades the reverse movement from contract to status has been at work in the trades and the professions of this country, with progressive encroachment upon the freedom of unassociated persons to pursue the calling of their choice.[12] The prospect of a corporative society, based historically upon liberal capitalism but crystallizing into an illiberal restrictive system, is not alluring to anyone who cherishes a philosophy of individualism.

If security is attained through the loss of human freedom and if this security is linked with corporate responsibility for the individual, this would pose a fundamental ethical problem for the metrocorporation.

THE USES OF CORPORATE POWER

The traditional corporation, with its single-minded devotion to profit, has been maligned as amoral or even immoral. But its proponents are certainly moralists in their own right and their ethical principles are directly related to their economic theory. It is a liberal theory in the classical sense of that term, emphasizing liberty above equality and fraternity, and liberty not for the group but for the man. Freedom of association, for the worker and the capitalist, has become an important element in that view of liberty. Freedom of association, on the other hand, has led to the big union and the big corporation. And freedom, when men act in bodies, as Burke observed, is power.

The classical liberal answer to the problem of group power is both political and economic. Politically, it is an insistence upon constitutional limitations in the form of enforceable restraints upon those who necessarily have power in their hands. These limitations are of many kinds. Written constitutions embody specific rights of persons and their property which are enforceable against public governments by judicial officers who are sworn to uphold the constitution—not merely as a grant of public powers but, just as importantly, as a charter of private rights. In addition to the system of judicial review, political liberalism in this country has traditionally urged other kinds of restraints upon the abuse of public power.

The diffusion of power units is one of the most important of these restraints. Public governmental agencies are distributed geographically in the federal system and functionally within the several geographic units. Thus three separate types of public powers have always been carefully distinguished in our political and constitutional theory; and it has generally been assumed that political liberty would be endangered were these separate powers to be merged in the same persons or official bodies. While there are those who carefully point out that no such clear-cut distinctions between legislative, executive, and judicial power exist in practice as the theory requires, the fact remains that Americans would look with the greatest suspicion—and rightly so—on any attempt to make basic revision of our constitutional structure to abolish the separation of powers.

There is also the important restraint of periodic election of public officials, together with the whole complex apparatus of the electoral system (including the party system) through which this periodic review of official conduct is carried out.

But this is not the whole of the story of liberal theory as protective of private rights. Quite as important is the market system itself. In the classical liberal tradition, reliance is placed not only upon restraints of the powerful through political constitutions but equally upon the balance of power throughout society and especially throughout the economic sectors. The powers of corporations and of labor unions, in the liberal tradition, are to be held in check by the market. That is why the preservation of the competitive system is so important. And that is also why it may be of vital importance to hold the market units to their economic purposes.

The proponents of the traditional corporation would keep the corporation to its strictly economic functions within a free and competitive market economy, not because they defend profit seeking as the Ultimate Good, but because they believe this to be a necessary condition for the preservation of human freedom. The traditional corporation, under this view, will make no pretense of being a true "society" that serves the "whole man." Nor will any other private group, for that matter. The only true society that can serve the whole man is a political community that includes special-function organizations of many kinds: economic, educational, religious, and so on. When any of these special-function organizations try to make the enormous claim that their Organization Men should be wholly absorbed in the affairs of these enclaved groups, the result can be divisive and ruinous to the health of the community as a whole. Such absorption is avoidable so long as every private organization, corporations included, limits its functions to a reasonable division of effort.

In the traditional model, the corporate employee is employed to do economic work, specifically; he is not expected to become an initiate into an exclusive society, an enclaved guild. This greatly reduces the corporate obligation toward him, since its claim upon him is diminished. This does not mean that the employee is reduced to the status of a commodity. The enlightened employment policies of the traditional corporation will prescribe humane treatment because it will not otherwise be able to recruit and hold the human resources needed for successful operation. This, in our time, is an irreducible cost of doing business. But it is a business operation and not a welfare project.

The proponents of the traditional corporation thus resist every attempt to saddle the business with welfare functions that bear no demonstrable relation to profitable production. To assess such resistance as merely reactionary and antithetical to the responsible metrocorporation would be inaccurate. It would be a negative posture only if accompanied by a complete denial of all social welfare measures. But one who simultaneously rejects the idea of the metrocorporation and the idea of the welfare state is in a seemingly untenable position today. For if the traditional corporation is not to shoulder the burden of costs for cradle-to-the-grave security, the public philosophy of our times will demand that these costs be distributed by governmental action throughout the population.

The inevitable alternative to the metrocorporation, then, may not be the austere corporation operating under laissez faire with a public governmental system strictly limited to policing functions; it may be some modified form of the traditional corporation operating within a political system characterized by extensive social legislation. The price that might have to be paid in order to preserve the price system and to keep the business corporation within its market-oriented sphere could be at least as much social legislation as we have today and probably a good deal more.

Whether this price is too high depends upon a consideration of the consequences of the alternative: a deliberate pursuit of the welfare goals of the metrocorporation. Critics may have overdrawn the picture somewhat in conjuring up the rise of a new feudal system. But, there is more than a grain of truth in this prospect. When the corporation of tomorrow and its employees begin to face candidly a possible regime of status and all that it implies, they may well recoil from the demands it will make upon free men. Employment as lifetime attachment to a firm, buttressed by all kinds of security for the employee, has its other side: fealty to the organization. Nor will this fealty be any the less absorptive of a man's freedom if we "progress" toward Tannenbaum's predicted merging of the trade union with the corporation. The ties that may bind a man to the corporation of the future could be powerful indeed, leaving him little freedom of action in any other sphere than that prescribed by corporate policy.

THE METROCORPORATE PATTERN

In sum, the metrocorporation, even with its wide range of social responsibilities that are alien to the traditional, austere corporation, is engaged in business as its major objective. But its meaning of "business" is vastly different from any that would be acceptable in the traditional corporation. Business becomes a socially definable term and the corporate environment widens.

The business of the metrocorporation is more than profitability for the share owners. Metrocorporate managers see numbers of contributor-claimant groups, including the general public, to which they owe obligations in return for special kinds of contributions. These obligations are the corporation's "social responsibilities." Like the managers of the traditional corporation they insist upon the privateness of the sectors of business. But it becomes more and more difficult for them to draw the line between public and private affairs precisely because the metrocorporation has so many "publics" to serve.

With so many interests converging upon the corporate enterprise, it ceases to be the private domain of its stockholders. It looks more and more like a public polity. When the manager of the traditional corporation asks himself, "What is my station and what are its duties?" his answer is fairly clear. He is responsible to the property-owners who put up the risk capital; he is the guardian of a specific property interest. But the manager of the metrocorporation has no such clear-cut answer. He acts in a representative capacity in relation to many different groups of interests, but he has no theory of representation to guide him.

As a result, the corporate polity inherited from the pattern of the traditional corporation will not suffice. The ethics of the metrocorporation seem to require new patterns of corporate polity, new conceptions of corporate relations with public governments, and new forms of labor relations. In this chapter attention has been focused on these strategic policy areas. There are others of equal importance.

The metrocorporation, whose managers are sensitive to corporate ecology, will be concerned with decisions about public policy "in the large" as well as with corporate policy more narrowly defined. Productivity, for example, is always a matter of concern to the traditional corporation; but it is the productivity of the individual enterprise that counts. In the metrocorporation there is deep concern about the productivity rate of the national economy as well.

Managers of the metrocorporation may ask themselves whether we can find a way in our system to direct a higher proportion of our resources to national policy purposes without destroying freedom of enterprise, and what responsibility private companies have for finding the way. They are inclined to take the position that the game of politics is not a spectator's sport for the corporate executive when the national security is at stake. Corporate policy will have to embrace questions about the most efficient use of resources, for the nation as a whole, and indeed for the nations with whom we are allied, and not just for the single enterprise as a closed system.

The ethics of the metrocorporation, thus expanded, have an international reach and will include propositions about world politics. The metrocorporation becomes the instrument of a complex of interest groups of which the stockholders constitute but one set of interests; and it pursues multiple goals, of which profit-maximization for the owners is but one and not necessarily the primary one. Like the metropolis or "mother city," the metrocorporation is a center of authority with many satellites. It has not only diversification in the sense of products, but also in its corporate goals. It becomes a kind of lesser society within the greater society, a civicism in its own right, with its own standards of intracorporate citizenship to which the Organization Man is expected to conform, and with certain obligations of "corporate citizenship" toward the community and toward other private organizations in its vicinity.

The metrocorporation thus appears as the instrumentality of a functionally defined social unit to be equated neither with society as a whole—and certainly not a territorially defined part of society, such as a state or a nation—nor the clearly restricted stockholder group, as in the traditional corporation. In the metrocorporation there is a constellation of interests that converge in "the firm" in the sense in which one speaks of a theory of the firm. And the responsibilities of that functionally defined entity tend to be focused on its professional managers, who are in fact if not in theory its real governors.

The metrocorporate model, as a heuristic device for explaining the modern corporation in action and for deriving an acceptable code of corporate responsibilities, has many advantages over the traditional model. It does attempt to take into account the multiplicity of interests and functions clearly observable in any large industrial company. It helps to dispel the miasma of unrealism that permeates so much of the debate about business policy when the traditional model is doggedly adhered to.

There are nevertheless serious drawbacks to the metrocorporate model, particularly with respect to normative issues when one probes more deeply into the question of social responsibilities.

CHAPTER IV

The Dilemma of

Corporate Responsibility

THE ANTINOMY of doctrine as between the proponents of the metrocorporation and the traditional type of corporation is not by any means as clear-cut as might appear from the models presented in these last two chapters.

If the modern corporation is to be regarded strictly as a business institution in the neoclassical sense, its broad social responsibilities must be minimized toward zero in order to hold it within the proper bounds of its predicated functions in an economy characterized by near-perfect competition. But then it must also reject many of the responsibilities urgently pressed upon it from within and from without.

An orderly market place is essential to the survival of the traditional corporation; and its view of the area in which law and order must be preserved is comparatively parochial. The metrocorporation by contrast will be directly involved in a political economy of global proportions. Critics of the idea of the metrocorporation attack such broad concerns as being destructive of the elementary responsibilities of the managers of a business enterprise in a competitive economy.

This raises a dilemma that may well develop into the central ethical issue for business within the next decade. For in rejecting social responsibility the corporation may be in danger of eclipse, even as a business institution in the traditional sense, because of

failure to safeguard the environmental conditions of the free society which makes its existence possible.   And it is perhaps as a
result of this uneasy conviction that, in the last few decades, business has taken on responsibilities that go well beyond not only
its primary functions as responsible producer but well beyond its
legal obligations.   Company after company is moving into such
socially oriented orbits as political participation, corporate giving,
support of education, employee welfare, community relations—
all activities which many critics still insist are tangential to their
original economic functions: the protection and enhancement of
owners' interests.

NATURE OF RESPONSIBILITY

The proposition that the modern corporation is amoral, without any ethical rights or duties, must be rejected at the outset.
Few indeed would attempt to defend such a position.   As a matter
of fact, practically every business leader today hastens to affirm
the contrary.   At the least there are basic legal rights and privileges that all prudent corporate executives recognize in their capacity as fiduciaries of the property they administer.   The institution they preside over is itself a thing of value to be preserved
and protected as surely as the physical properties of the corporation.   In the older phraseology, it was a "body corporate and
politic," indicating that in some way the peculiar integration of
human resources authorized by the corporate charter bore a close
and intimate relation to society as a political entity.   The act of
incorporating was and is, in legal theory at least, a public act, and
an incorporated body clearly has certain obligations toward the
incorporating authority: the State.

But this leaves us far from an answer to the broader issue of
social responsibilities.   If the corporation is responsible to society,
there must exist some claim, or series of claims, on society's part
which requires the corporation to perform and deliver.   A responsibility entails obligation, and the existence of an obligation
is likely to raise issues concerning enforceability upon the obligor.
Is the modern corporation obligated to society to do or not to do
certain things?   And if so, what remedies lie at hand, or ought to

be prescribed, to permit society to get specific performance from the modern corporation?

Some inquiry into the nature of responsibility is essential. Are we talking about the specific legal duties of the corporation which are strictly correlated [1] to the rights others enjoy, and the specific legal liabilities to which it is subject because of the specific legal powers others may use against it? Or are we talking about something else? [2]

It is not these specifically legalistic concepts that most people have in mind when they talk broadly of the public responsibilities of the corporation. They are thinking, rather, of the ethical principles that ought to govern the relationships between the corporation and society, the economic problems that arise when corporate enterprise dominates the business scene, and the political issues that have to be faced when public policy must deal with "corporate power." They are concerned about the impact of the corporation upon the individual and the possibilities of reconciling Big Business, Big Labor, and Big Government with the integrity of the human personality and other values so deeply rooted in our culture. [3]

The legal responsibilities or duties of a company are enforceable in courts and administrative agencies. Economic responsibilities, on the other hand, are often thought of as automatically enforceable through the market system. Some would limit the company's social responsibilities to areas of expedient action alone. [4] The legal counselor may occasionally sense incipient restrictive law in prevailing public opinions and attitudes. He may even advise that legally nonenforceable obligations be assumed on a voluntary basis to forestall public legislative action. The public relations counselor may sense the need for certain actions on the part of a company—or forbearance in contemplated action—to garner valuable good will. Social responsibilities of this order are simply a case of enlightened self-interest.

But there are other kinds of public and social responsibility. The conviction that this is so appears within the corporation itself. Many business leaders are motivated by the desire to undertake corporate burdens of a truly altruistic character. It can be argued that decisions of this nature, made by corporate officers, actually divert the corporate usufruct to purposes which favor the "public" at the expense of specific contributor-claimant groups whose interests may have priority. Who is to say, for example, whether a corporate contribution to a college is an altruistic or an expedient act—and if the latter, in whose interest? Is it in the interest of the corporation in the long run, or in the interest of the security holder who hopes to send his children to college next year on earnings from dividends? In the opinion of many, both the share owner and the corporation as an entity have social responsibilities that demand from wealth accumulators such as the business corporation, contributions both of knowledge and money to society generally. Not a few business leaders themselves share this opinion.

THE CLIMATE NURTURING
SOCIAL RESPONSIBILITY

One reason for this is that the corporation has become an institution with pervasive influence on its members. As Frank Tannenbaum has so persuasively argued, "institutions tend to stake out a unique role for themselves. They each tend to make an imperative and undeniable claim upon the social body. They each take captive a given section of the population, and set their stamp upon it, and hold onto it . . . institutions quite unconsciously create orders of men." [5] Undoubtedly, every institution tends to mold the ideas, shape the characters, and determine the status of its members. The modern corporation is no exception to these general observations. It is this institutional tendency that has launched the Organization Man literature and created the current notion that to identify with a big economic organization is ultimately to lose identity altogether.

But what has been forgotten in the heat of the discussion is that the man makes an impact on the organization, else the social responsibility question might never have been raised at all. A corporation has no human values, save those which are vested in the men who administer it. And it might well be argued that it is as a result of the professionalization of management that the corporation is asked to render to society in value terms something of what society has contributed in the way of human energy and human know-how.

Many today see in the corporation a nucleus of "power" and demand that it use that power "justly." The corporation has, in this sense, a social responsibility to conform to the dominant ethical code, even though to do so may be expensive. Many declare that there are corporate obligations that have nothing to do with the expediencies of good will or the profit position of a company. Managers often share this belief. Businessmen thus internalize society's dominant values as premises for policy decisions which cannot correctly be called ego-oriented in any narrow entrepreneurial sense.

Thus, there would seem to exist a category of social responsibilities which is clearly distinguishable from the ordinary legal and economic obligations of the firm. That there is a widely felt sense of these broader responsibilities of the corporation is undeniable. The causes of this feeling are not easy to determine. Perhaps it is because the social leadership of business has been challenged in so many parts of the Western world, and businessmen sense an increased urge for public approval.[6] Managers of large corporations, it is often alleged, are anxious to prove to the public that their enterprises are socially useful, above and beyond an exclusive profit-making function.

There is said to be a widespread managerial fear of hostility toward big business, especially among some intellectual leaders. The managerial class, it is pointed out, has become defensive in the face of gradual encroachments upon its role as the responsible director of enterprise. Labor unions have moved in from one side, and government from the other. Not least, the examples of totalitarianism abroad challenge businessmen to assume leadership in fields which might otherwise be taken over by public government.

Whatever the complex of forces and causes, we have a milieu that favors socially responsible business institutions. This climate of social responsibility is sensed by corporate management. It is real and pervasive, and it is central to the emergent philosophy of business in this country.

Yet when one comes to the practical problem of describing

these responsibilities in day-to-day operational terms that managers can grasp, difficulties arise. This is because current statements of social responsibilities consistently lack substance. In its relations with customers, including dealers and distributors, the corporation is bound by specific legal obligations; beyond these it is assumed that certain undefined principles of fair dealing apply even though they are not enforceable by any court. In its relations with plant communities, there is no legal standard by which one may judge the decisions of management to reduce its payrolls or to leave the community; yet the failure to take into account the economic health of the community as a whole in such decisions is often regarded as a failure to meet unspecified community responsibilities. One could go on through the list of those groups with which a corporation maintains working relations and point to a great variety of things that a company perhaps ought to do, or ought not do. Agreement on specifics, however, is painfully difficult.

These examples are nonetheless indicative of sensed responsibilities to which a corporation is not bound by contract or the rule of law. They arise in other ways and will be taken into account by management regardless of their source, simply because they are palpable demands upon the corporation as an entity. No responsible executive can draw a hard line around such demands on the ground merely that they are extralegal or that the corporation has never explicitly agreed to recognize them. The art of managing cannot be practiced mechanically. The rapidity of social change is such that managers of large corporations must anticipate new social situations and adjust the scope of corporate responsibilities accordingly.

To assess properly the nature of such responsibilities as these is obviously one of the functions of management. It is a difficult assignment, and one which requires imaginative thought and perceptive awareness of the future. Two things we can be reasonably sure of: this is not a static age, and the modern corporation is not a static institution. Nor are the responsibilities of the corporation unalterable. They are in constant change. The obligations of the large managerial enterprise already have altered so much that they bear little resemblance to those of the individual entrepreneur of the earlier free enterprise economy. Gradually they have taken on characteristics of the responsibilities of all comprehensive institutions. Yet the large industrial corporation is still a *private institution* and not at this point in time a microcosm of the Great Society. It is a pooling medium of a mixed economy but certainly not the agency of a collectivistic national regime. It represents, however, a great diversity of interests in the community, and the scope of these interests seems to be expanding.

The trend of change is in the direction of acquiring more and more responsibility toward larger and more diverse sectors of the community.[7] The corporation, as an institution, develops an intricate maze of interrelationships with other institutions. As this change occurs, there is a strong tendency to move away from older concepts of the business firm, with primary responsibility to its owners, and toward the concept of a multifunctional institution with diffused responsibilities. Here the need for a philosophy becomes apparent. At this juncture the decisions become critical.

DEPTH OF THE DILEMMA

It would be comfortable to cling to the simpler model of economic and legal theory which described the business corporation as the instrument of private property, serving single-mindedly the property interests of its share owners. But if we do this, we lose touch with reality. For, as we shall see, the kinds of decisions that corporate boards and officers have to make today are not at all describable in these simple terms. If they were to interpret their duty as the single one of returning maximum profits to stockholders, their companies would soon face estrangement from society—which exacts other duties from them. Continuity of the corporation as such, now one of the chief objectives of management, would become impossible, and firms with such circumscribed goals might eventually disappear from the scene.

Perceptive managers of leading companies are aware of this situation. Consequently, many strive to bring the objectives of their companies into line with the broad social goals of the con-

temporary world. But in so doing, they face the determined opposition of traditionalists. Management must be prepared to
meet the charge of traditionalists that the modern corporation is
headed for transmutation into an incongruous thing: a dangerously mutable instrument for limitless groups of interests and no
longer functioning simply as the efficient and profitable producer
of goods and services in a competitive economy.

The dilemma of corporate responsibilities in our dynamic
social environment is in one sense a choice between resistance and
receptivity. To resist the many new claims made upon the corporation is to assume an eminently respectable position grounded
upon the logic of property; but rationality here may not turn out
to be reasonableness. Reasonable regard for the public interest
is a practical necessity. To accept indiscriminately the many
claims pressed upon the corporation is the path of short-run expediency, and no business leader with integrity will choose this
path. But even the discriminating choice, the weighing of these
diverse claims on their merits, will be suspect to those who stand
on the traditional rights of stockholders. As a result, every move
of corporate boards and officers to "balance the interests" of the
competing claimants is interpretable by the traditionalists as a
dilution of the primary purpose of economic enterprise, namely,
legitimate profit seeking for the owners of venture capital. The
talk about social responsibilities of a corporate enterprise, in other
words, teems with inconsistencies and is fraught with danger not
only for the share owners but for the whole economy.

The cogency of this argument is little appreciated in many
business circles today, and indeed to many it may seem to have a
"reactionary" ring. But labels for the bearers of ideas are highly
misleading. In considering the various points of view about the
scope of corporate responsibilities one can easily slip into error by
classifying men as "liberal," "conservative," or "reactionary" on
this question.

Was the New Dealer who pressed for federal regulation of
security markets, and the alignment of governmental power on
the side of the stockholder against "irresponsible" corporate
management, a radical or a conservative—or perhaps something

less printable? Is the labor union leader who denounces "fat profits" and sizable dividends and demands a bigger piece of the pie for employees taking a progressive or a reactionary stand—or merely a selfish one? And what about the management which diverts a part of the net earnings of a company to corporate giving—is this a conservative, a liberal, or a reactionary policy?

The usual clichés have no useful meaning in the context of our inquiry. They fail to get at the heart of the question. To arrive there we are obliged to give careful and detailed consideration to the case against corporate assumption of social responsibilities.

THE CASE AGAINST SOCIAL RESPONSIBILITIES

A case can be made for the proposition that there are *no* social responsibilities of the corporation at all other than the sum of its established legal, contractual, and conventional obligations to specific groups of contributor-claimants.

These obligations alone make a formidable list. The corporate managers who see to it that their companies fulfill these clear obligations in every detail, it can be argued, have their hands full without reaching out into unmapped and treacherous territory for new and undefined social responsibilities. To the importunings of outsiders who have no real responsibility for keeping the concern going or for yielding a reasonable return to those who have substantial interests in it, one should listen respectfully when they urge larger social responsibilities upon the modern corporation. But the prudent manager will not rush to ill-considered conclusions on the matter. He will have to consider carefully any possible encroachments upon outstanding obligations that the alleged social responsibilities entail. The established contributor-claimants deserve at least full opportunity to be heard before these newer demands upon the corporation are satisfied. Sweeping generalizations about the broad "social responsibilities of the modern corporation" are to be regarded with great caution.

This view of the matter can hardly be dismissed as a defensive and conservative position assumed only by businessmen who are determined to resist all change. Corporations today are under enormous pressure from all sides to undertake an infinite number of tasks simply because the corporation exists, because it is superbly organized, and because it has vast wealth at its command. Frequently, corporations are regarded as a soft touch for any "worthy" cause, especially when their actions can be interpreted as springing from guilt feelings in the face of the attacks on Big Business. In fact, businessmen as individuals are not less aware of their ethical responsibilities toward their fellow men than others. But as corporate managers they have not only responsibilities of a specific character toward specific claimant groups associated with the corporation; they also have definite responsibilities toward the corporation itself.

Though the nature of the corporation is undoubtedly changing, there is at least room for doubt that it should suddenly be transformed into a protean organism readily adaptable to any and all functions that anyone desires to thrust upon it. One may concede that any large corporate complex is more than an economic enterprise without drawing the conclusion that it is destined to take over, as an arm of society, innumerable functions now assigned to other kinds of institutions.

Faithful to our pluralistic social structure, we may well be expected to guard the autonomy of the decision-making process within all private sectors and, indeed, their very existence as vital nonpublic sectors in a society struggling to maintain large areas of freedom from state intervention. The corporation's capacity to contribute, to society at large, increments of wealth, skill, and knowledge may be seriously undermined if its managers allow it to become overloaded with irrelevant responsibilities that crowd out the essential jobs it has to do. The end result can only be the demise of the business corporation as a specialized and indispensable instrument of civilized society, so the case runs.

At this point it will be useful to examine the arguments of some contemporary critics of the doctrine that corporations have social responsibilities. Among the more persuasive arguments are those of Milton Friedman, Mortimer J. Adler and Louis A. Kelso, J. A. Livingston, and Theodore Levitt.

The Friedman Position

Milton Friedman has argued that there is one and only one social responsibility of business. That responsibility is "to use its resources and engage in activities designed to increase its profits so long as it stays within the rules of the game, within the area of free, open, and honest competition and striving for gain." [8] The view that management has a broader social responsibility is, in his opinion, "simply a particular manifestation of the general social trend toward collectivism that we have observed during the last half-century and more," even though some strong proponents of free enterprise unwittingly throw their support toward this collectivistic trend. Friedman declares: "If anything is certain to destroy our free society, to undermine its very foundations, it would be a widespread acceptance by management of social responsibilities in some sense other than to make as much money as possible . . . [and] this is a fundamentally subversive doctrine."

The danger, Friedman asserts, in assuming that businessmen have a social responsibility other than making maximum profits for stockholders, is that the State will, of necessity, have to assist in fulfilling it, for you cannot leave the exercise of social responsibility to private individuals self-chosen. "It is intolerable that public functions be performed by self-designated private officials" and to the degree that business managers assume the role of civil servants, they will sooner or later be chosen in terms of the public techniques of election and appointment. Friedman is extremely critical of corporate giving: it prevents the individual stockholder from deciding for himself how he should dispose of his funds— the corporation being "the instrument of the stockholders who own it." The corporation is not, he believes, as critics had erroneously charged, "a social institution, a law unto itself, with irresponsible management which, as a result of an alleged separation of ownership and control, does not serve the interests of its stockholders." Friedman nevertheless believes the current trend of corporate giving policy is a step in this direction and toward "undermining the basic nature and character of our society." Likewise, he condemns the President's plea for restraint in raising prices on the part of business and raising wages on the part of labor. These are not, he argues, the social responsibilities of business and labor at all.

The Kelso-Adler Position

Friedman's position against wider corporate responsibilities is not unique, by any means. The case is made at great length in *The Capitalist Manifesto,* by Kelso and Adler. Their argument is a conservative one, despite their call for a "Capitalist Revolution," in that they urge the basic importance of the rights of property. It is revolutionary only in the sense that it proposes the demise of our present-day *"mixed capitalism"* in favor of a "completely capitalist society." But the "revolution" they want would work far-reaching changes in the business corporation as we know it today. In a chapter on "The Modern Corporation and the Capitalist Revolution" they make a respectful bow toward this "matchless form for associating together the productive powers of workers (including technicians and managers) and the productive power of capital." For, "the corporation is an ideal instrument for assembling the capital owned by many households in aggregations of such size as to permit production to be carried on in the most efficient and least toil-consuming manner."

But "mixed capitalism"—their label for our present economic structure—misuses the corporation, according to Kelso and Adler. Instead of using this great instrumentality "to diffuse the private ownership of capital among the households of society, it diffuses the wealth produced by capital to those who should, but *do not,* own capital," and "its method of doing this is governed by principles of charity and expediency." Some of the wealth produced by capital in the large corporations "goes to supplement the wages labor really earns; some, to pay the double tax on wealth produced by capital; some to provide a major portion of new capital formation," while only "a trickle is returned to the nominal owners—the stockholders." [9]

What we have, they argue, is essentially a "laboristic distribution of wealth," [10] and this distribution is made partly through the instrumentality of the corporation. Their argument continues: the corporate income tax of federal and state governments is levied only upon the wealth produced by capital, and the revenues are redistributed to subsidize government-operated programs; there is a diversion of far too much of the corporate income to organized labor rather than to the share owners; there is "involuntary investment by stockholders" in the form of large plow-backs of corporate earnings into corporate investments to avoid the effects of the steeply graduated personal income tax. The result is that "the modern corporation has . . . become an instrument for a distribution of wealth that is primarily laboristic." It "has served as a device for attenuating the property rights in capital, and for almost alienating that property from its owners." The mixed economy has "brought about the erosion of private property in concentrated holdings of capital through the diversion of the wealth such capital produces, from the stockholders who own it to the mass of workers who need it and whose use of it provides a mass market." [11]

Kelso and Adler would by no means dispense with the modern corporation. They would make it instead, under the coming Capitalism, *"the instrument of private property and completely responsible to private property."* Their theory of Capitalism, in fact, calls for "a radical reformation of the relation of the owners of capital to operating management." For them, the problem of the corporation becomes largely one of "restoring shareholders to their full powers and rights as the owners of capital and the employers of management." [12]

The Capitalist Revolution would encompass the following points [13] in Kelso and Adler's plan to "reform and reconstitute" business corporations:

(1). Restoration of "effective ownership of capital to the stockholders." This means the return to the stockholders of *all* the wealth produced by their corporate capital.

(2) Greatly expanded use of present corporate income taxes in order to diffuse private ownership of capital, primarily through equity-sharing plans.

(3) Eventual elimination of corporate income taxes as transition is made to a purely capitalistic economy, and use only of personal income taxes.

(4) Government regulation of business corporations to encourage the broadest diffusion of private ownership in capital, and to give full effectiveness to private property in capital (at the same time restricting government itself from owning capital except where private ownership is technically impossible, *e.g.*, public roads).

(5) Government regulation of business corporations (*a*) to permit growth to optimum size required for use of most advanced techniques of production, but (*b*) not so large as to impair free competition in the markets affected by them.

(6) Use of government power "reasonable and proper" to effect a transition to capitalism. Underlying principles: (*a*) the protection of property; (*b*) the maintenance of free competition in all markets; (*c*) the discharge of the obligation of government to assure all households the opportunity to participate in production to an extent sufficient to provide them with a viable income.

The purpose of their reform program, let it be remembered, is to return to basic principles about the property rights of stockholders, to spell out the implications of corporate responsibility to share owners, and to them alone. Their program can hardly be attractive even to those corporate executives who have resisted the trend toward wider social responsibilities for the corporation. The alternative to such responsibilities—if one follows the logic of Kelso and Adler—could lead to greatly diminished managerial authority and to considerably augmented managerial accountability to share owners and to government.

If Kelso and Adler are on the right track, there will have to be much backing down on the case for management as an arbiter of interests, and adjuster of diverse claims on the corporate usufruct. There is no managerial balancing of interests at all in the Kelso-Adler plan. For them, management has only *one* interest to protect and preserve: the private property interest of the stockholder; corporate management is the *alter ego* of the owner, and of no one else. It performs none of that quasi-judicial function that Gossett described in his lectures on corporate citizenship. It has no broad social responsibilities to many groups of contributor-claimants that can be put on a par with the primary responsibility of management to return to the stock-holder *all* of the wealth produced by the corporate capital that is entrusted to management.

On this point, Kelso and Adler are quite specific:

The essence of property in productive wealth is the right to receive its product. Legal recognition of this right would consist in the legal requirement that the entire net income of a mature corporation during or immediately after the close of each financial period be paid out in dividends to its stockholders. Some allowances would have to be made for the need of relatively undeveloped new corporations to plough in capital in order to survive, as well as for the needs of any business for working capital and contingent reserves. Failure to apply the laws of private property to the capital owned by stockholders permits corporate managers in effect to hire capital at a price dictated by themselves.[14]

Their argument continues: Unless the net income of the corporation is thus distributed directly to the stockholders, they have no effective voice in deciding whether they want any of their earnings on their capital to be reinvested by the corporation. "No other conceivable arrangement can force corporate management to justify its performance from time to time before stockholders, *just as holders of political office must justify theirs from time to time before the electorate.*" [15]

The ultimate control of the corporation, they insist, "should rest with those who own it, not with those who merely run it"; [16] and as in public government, where the consent of the governed is the accepted defense against despotism, so in the corporation not even a benevolent or paternalistic despotism is thinkable. "For the management of a corporate enterprise to dispose of what rightfully belongs to its stockholders without their free, present, and affirmatively expressed consent is despotism, and it remains despotism no matter how benevolent or wise management is in acting for what it thinks to be the 'best interests' of its stock-holders." [17]

Harsh words, these, for corporate managers who see their function as the balancing of the best interests of all the contributor-claimants to the enterprise, including the interests of the share owners, whose interests are sometimes regarded as secondary to those of "King Customer." Harsh words, too, for those who envisage corporate managers as the rightful ultimate arbiters of the social responsibilities of the modern corporation.

To conclude the Kelso-Adler argument: Although they would not have the stockholders "invade the professional or technical sphere of management," they would make "management responsible to their principals, the owners, as the officers of government are responsible to their masters, the citizens." They would "reconstitute the corporation by creating it in the image of constitutional government," thus barring the way "to all dictatorial usurpations of power" in the form of "usurping alienations of property." They would have "the stockholder's hand restored to the economic throttle of the corporation." Their "proposed reconstitution of the corporation" seems to them to be "indispensable to the restoration of the rights of private property held in corporate form" and even during the transition to Capitalism the reform would "cauterize the dangerous concentrations of irresponsible power that are now uncontrollable growths in our economy. . . . A society of capitalists without an effective franchise vested in the rights of property would be as much a hollow mockery as a society in which all men are citizens but without the rights of suffrage."

The Livingston Position

It is a mistake to assume that the only antagonists of corporate responsibilities toward society are a few academic writers like Friedman and Adler, or Kelso, who is a lawyer. Consider the recent popular book on *The American Stockholder* by the financial commentator, J. A. Livingston. He denies that his is "a championing book, egging the stockholder on to fight for his legal and political rights in the corporation," or "a legalistic book, telling him how to use the law to protect himself in corporate infighting." He offers it as an "expository book." Nevertheless, he pulls no punches in attacking what he believes to be questionable corporate practice as it affects the stockholders' interests.

Like W. Z. Ripley in his day, Livingston in ours is forthrightly against what he calls "insider privilege" in corporations. And just as Ripley had condemned the Dodge plan in 1925 as bearing "every appearance of a bald and outrageous theft of the last title of responsibility for management from the actual owners," so does Livingston in 1958 condemn the Ford stock sale as a case of "Management *über alles*," carried out through a shrewd legal device with the silent blessing of "institutional Wall Street." He commends the New York Stock Exchange for its efforts to obtain fuller disclosure of corporate finance to share owners. He sees great value in the federal securities laws, too; the result has been much more self-searching by management. But he still sees a good many dragons to be slain. The stockholder still, in his opinion, "gets the last bite on the apple core."

Executives, in administering the affairs of the company, look to the perpetuation of the enterprise. They are more immediately concerned with maintaining "sound relations" with customers, suppliers, workers and the government and community than with shareholders whom they dangle on proxy strings. And so it becomes insistently important for those to whom investing is a business—the institutional investor, the professionals—to see that officers and directors do not, in their zeal to perpetuate the corporation as an institution, slight the shareholders financially, and, more significantly, morally.[18]

Livingston turns to Drucker's *Concept of the Corporation* and finds that the words "dividend" and "stockholder" are not in the index, though words like "worker," "labor unions," "taxation," "public relations," and "consumer" are there. "Worry about the shareholder?" comments the author acidly. "Hardly. The persnickety problem is how much to let the union have, how much to keep for the corporation." He does not blame Drucker, who is only describing the corporation as it operates, though he is obviously annoyed when Drucker dismisses "the old crude fiction" which "regards the corporation as the sum of the property rights of the individual shareholders."

Drucker is quoted as saying, "In this conventional formula, the corporation is transitory . . . the shareholder is regarded as permanent and actual. In the social reality, the corporation is permanent, the shareholder is transitory." To Livingston, these are fighting words. Nor is he pleased when a former chairman of Standard Oil (N.J.) says that corporations can "achieve their greatest social usefulness . . . when management succeeds in finding harmonious balance among the claims of stockholders, employees, customers, and public at large," with the added comment that "management's responsibility, in the broadest sense . . . [is to be] a good citizen." [19]

"A good citizen!" is Livingston's explosive rejoinder. "The corporation now has a new identity apart from profit making, apart from its charter, by-laws, and legal trappings, apart from its shareholders. It is Good Citizen, Inc.! And the corporation executive comports himself to reflect that corporate citizenship. He wears his church clothes every day, not just on Sundays. In his paneled office, in his travels about the country, in his community relations, he represents, not himself, but The Corporation. He represents not the stockholders, but The Corporation." Livingston says the status of the stockholder is that of "residuary beneficiary of Good Citizen, Inc." He continues, the consequence is a "two-toned morality—one set of morals with which executives, corporations, greet the outside world, and another set of morals with which they treat the shareholders." For him, the stockholders are unhappily "transitory" while the corporation's "permanent relatives"—the unions, customers, and suppliers—have to be cultivated in order to retain their good will; corporate executives can and do cultivate them with "the power of the corporate purse" and projection of the corporate conscience.[20]

Livingston wants "to look behind this façade of Good Citizenship." He is determined to "examine the social consequences of the erosion of shareholder power—how the incapacity to correct and restrain corporation executives has become a grant of excess freedom." To him, "executives have become an overprivileged class in a democratic society"; they have the "power to overpay themselves"; they are a "Tax-Sheltered Elite." Livingston argues further that unless this power is checked, mainly through active assumption by institutional investors and the financial press of their obligation to lift "the moral tone of industry and of finance above the dollar sign," then "corporate power could become synonymous with grab-bag morality." [21]

The significance of this recent attack upon alleged abuses of managerial power is difficult to assess. Livingston may or may not speak for a considerable sector of public opinion. In view of the apathy of stockholders generally—of which Livingston himself complains—it is doubtful that the shareholder public itself is very much disturbed by the uses of corporate powers which are lodged in the officers and directors of the large corporations. There seems to be no general stockholder resistance, for example, to the idea of corporate citizenship against which Livingston directs some bitter shafts of criticism. To say that stockholders affirmatively embrace the idea of corporate social responsibility, however, is to go farther than the facts warrant. Security holders are satisfied if a company does well financially; they seem to be willing to leave it to the discretion of managers to decide what the company ought to do—or not to do—in meeting the demands of various claimant groups—so long as its securities are a sound investment.

The Levitt Position

One of the more recent attacks on the idea of social responsibility appeared as a leading article in the *Harvard Business Review*. It was written by a marketing and economic consultant in Chicago. In this article,[22] which has been widely discussed in the business community, Theodore Levitt comes out bluntly against what he calls the contemporary school of business morality with its "series of strategic retreats masquerading as industrial statesmanship." Businessmen, he declares, have given in dangerously before strident attacks on big corporations and the moral efficacy of the profit system. Instead of meeting these attacks in truly bellicose fashion, businessmen have intoned "the pious declarations of Christian brotherhood," uttered *mea culpa,* searched their souls, and settled down into "the social responsibility syndrome." This is no longer just an attitudinizing pose for the sake of good public relations; it has become an occupational disease. Businessmen, he insists, "must fight as if it were a war. And, like a good war, it should be fought gallantly, daringly, and, above all, *not* morally." The trouble is that they have begun to believe their own propaganda about the corporation as a great public benefactor which exists "to serve the public."

"The function of business," writes Levitt, "is to produce sustained high-level profits." The essence of free enterprise is "to go after profit in any way that is consistent with its own survival as an economic system." The way that is consistent, he adds, is the way of the pluralistic society: "division, not centralization, of power; variety, not unanimity, of opinion; separation, not unification, of workaday economic, political, social and spiritual functions." Businessmen must fight tooth and claw against the unitary state and the monolithic society. Yet what is apt to happen is that "business statesmanship" will end up with the corporate equivalent of the all-embracing welfare state, or "the twentieth-century equivalent of the medieval Church." The doctrine of social responsibility, he fears, is leading us down the road to a new feudalism. The corporation has become endlessly involved in community, governmental, charitable, and educational affairs, and in hundreds of peripheral occupations with which it has no legitimate concern whatever. Nor is the danger in this trend only that the corporation will fail to carry out its primary function, profit seeking. The greater danger is that it may "eventually invest itself with all-embracing duties, obligations, and finally, powers—ministering to the whole man and molding him and society in the image of the corporation's narrow ambitions and its essentially unsocial needs."

Levitt's case against corporate social responsibilities is not to be classed with diatribes by the injured stockholder against uncontrolled professional managers who divert profits to other claimants. He has nothing to say about this problem, although, of course, this does not mean that he is unconcerned with it. His interest is of a different order. He attacks severely what are, to him, preposterous pretensions of some of the leaders of Big Business. If he had his way, they would confine themselves to "the corporation's narrow ambitions and needs" as seekers after material gain, pure and simple. And of the purity of this ambition, he has no doubt. There is nothing wrong, he insists, with such a narrowing of corporate purposes. "Indeed, if there is anything wrong today, it is that the corporation conceives its ambitions and needs much too broadly"; it is not narrowly profit-oriented enough. And "in its guilt-driven urge to transcend the narrow limits of derived standards, the modern corporation is reshaping not simply the economic but also the institutional, social, cultural, and political topography of society." The result of all this will be "a monolithic society in which the essentially narrow ethos of the business corporation is malignantly extended over everyone and everything."

So it turns out that Levitt, in urging businessmen to fight "gallantly, and *not* morally" for the survival of the corporation as a business enterprise in the narrowest sense, really has a moral purpose after all. That purpose is in part to preserve a balance of power in our social system as a whole, in which business, labor, and agriculture "fight each other so that none becomes or remains dominant for long." It is also his purpose to maintain a functional separation of powers among "the four main groups in our economy—government, business, labor, and agriculture." For, "as soon as they become amalgamated and indistinguishable, they likewise become monstrous and restrictive." It would be especially dangerous if business and government were to coalesce into a single power, unopposed and unopposable: the pattern of fascism.

Lest it be concluded that Levitt opposes any and all forms of corporate obligation to society, one must note that he allows for certain "sensible welfare obligations" that businessmen must assume. He even concedes that business has been guilty of certain "social delinquencies" in the past and some regrettable "short-sightedness in fighting practically all of Washington's efforts to provide security." Corporate welfare makes good sense to him only if it makes good economic sense, without the corrupting and debilitating influence of sentiment and idealism. The acid test is that "something is good only if it pays." Otherwise, he states "it is alien and impermissible" under capitalism. Standing on this ground, Levitt rejects the growing constellation of employee welfare programs and stock purchase plans unless they are clearly within the profit-making scheme of a company. And he thinks they seldom are. Let people run to the government or their unions, he says, if they want protection against the uneven consequences of all-out capitalism—national mass insurance being a case in point as "far cheaper and more efficient" than company welfare measures. Business, on its part, would fight its own causes openly "on the front of economic and political pressures." But "altruism, self-denial, charity and similar values," however vital they are in other walks of life, are for the most part virtues that he regards as "alien to competitive economics."

How is Levitt's position to be appraised, and to what extent does it state significant trends in the function of the modern corporation?

It would be inaccurate to label Levitt as a hardshell defender of *laissez-aller*. This would, in fact, amount to a gross misreading of his text, which is by no means a contemporary restatement of Herbert Spencer's *Social Statics*. If he objects strenuously to corporate assumption of social responsibilities, it is partly because he so firmly asserts the necessity of governmental assumption of welfare activities. One example, already noted, is national insurance in place of company welfare measures. But he goes much farther than this. He upbraids those businessmen who oppose slum clearance, urban renewal, health insurance, school construction, and other measures for what he regards as social and economic progress. "Businessmen will simply have to accept the fact that the state can be a powerful auxiliary to the attainment of the good life." And indeed some of these measures, he asserts, are necessary curatives for the "enormous social and economic cancers" which American capitalism "creates, fosters and acquiesces in." Yet business too often "adopts a placid air of indifference or a vapid neutrality" in the face of these and other evils, when it does not actually fight against the public interest. He cites as "the most shameful indifference" the failure of business to act aggressively on behalf of civil rights—the bedrock of its own effective existence. Not the rights of free enterprise alone, but the rights, for example, of some Joe Doakes who is being pilloried by some Congressional kangaroo court under the guise of eliciting information for legislative purposes.

But what Levitt's argument amounts to is a sweeping rejection of the whole "canonistic exposition of a new orthodoxy—the era of 'socially responsible enterprise.'" In its place he would instill in the businessman a single-minded devotion to profit, pursued with a decent respect for the elementary canons of honesty, good faith and other civilities, but pursued nonetheless without any apologies to anyone. Only in this way, as he sees it, can we hope to preserve our freedom in an open and balanced social order.

Whether Levitt's analysis of the situation reflects with accuracy the facts as they are or may be in future is a pertinent question. Is it true, for example, that we are surely headed for neofascism unless the corporation divests itself of the "peripheral" activities in which he sees so much potentiality for danger? Or is it more probable that all this recent talk of businessmen about their social responsibilities stops—as he suggests at one point in his argument—at the pocketbook? Is it, in other words, merely talk for public consumption and not for operational purposes? He fears that what men say so often they will come to believe and then to act upon. This is possible; but one needs to bear in mind the fact that the talk about corporate purposes today cannot be easily dichotomized into the neat categories of profit seeking and social responsibilities.

As we shall see in the next chapter, the aims of the modern corporation are multiple. They also change from decade to decade. And they vary from company to company and from time to time within the same company, depending in part upon the motives of its policy makers. It might possibly be a good thing if every corporation executive at all times were to cling relentlessly to a single purpose such as profit making and refuse to deviate one iota from the model of a well-run enterprise in a model economy enclosed in a model society, perfectly balanced and governed with single-minded devotion to the principles of human freedom. That obviously does not describe the kind of society we live in, nor the kinds of business corporations we see about us, nor the quite human managers who run them. Levitt and the other writers we have been considering also have model corporations in mind and ideal goals which they would like to have corporate policy makers pursue.

But the dilemma is not merely academic, as such a context would seem to indicate. It strikes deep at the roots of managerial authority, its scope and uses, and raises grave doubts about the place of the corporation in a free society—whether it hews to the old lines or undertakes to follow the new trends. How appropriate are the old lines to the new times? How legitimate and inevitable are the new trends?

The arguments presented in this chapter may seem to run against the tide, to represent countercurrents to the drift of law, opinion, and corporate practice. But is this really so?

It is highly doubtful that corporation law betrays any strong trend toward the theory that corporations have social responsibilities or that corporate powers have been noticeably strengthened for the purpose of enabling corporate managers to meet these larger responsibilities.[23]   Many lawyers would argue that the wider discretion allowed corporate boards, under recent statutes and judicial decisions, to engage in corporate giving is the exception that highlights the rule: the rule of fiduciary responsibility to security holders. There is nevertheless another point of view that contends increasingly for adoption.

It is of more than passing interest that repeated reference is made in recent literature to the now famous debate between Professors Berle and Dodd two decades ago about the appropriate uses of corporate powers.

Berle himself referred to this debate in his book on *The 20th Century Capitalist Revolution* in this passage, which has been widely quoted:

Twenty years ago, the writer had a controversy with the late Professor E. Merrick Dodd, of Harvard Law School, the writer holding that corporate powers were powers in trust for share holders while Professor Dodd argued that these powers were held in trust for the entire community. The argument has been settled (at least for the time being) squarely in favor of Professor Dodd's contention.[24]

It will be noted that Berle has carefully inserted a parenthetical qualification—"at least for the time being." This qualification is rarely given much emphasis in current commentary upon the scope and purpose of corporate powers. In the long run, it may assume some importance for the student of trends in the social responsibilities of the corporation.

If we turn back to Dodd's argument, we shall find that he was talking about the trends of public opinion of that period as they affected the law of corporations. He stated that lawyers had commonly assumed that corporate managers must conduct the corporate institution with single-minded devotion to stockholder profit. That assumption, he said, was based upon "a particular view of the nature of business as a purely private enterprise." He then went on to say that:

If we recognize that the attitude of law and public opinion toward business is changing, we may then properly modify our ideas as to the nature of such a business institution as the corporation and hence as to the considerations which may properly influence the conduct of those who direct its activities . . . . [Public opinion] which ultimately makes law, has made and is making today, substantial strides in the direction of a view of the business corporation as an economic institution which has a social service as well as a profit-making function . . . business is permitted and encouraged by the law primarily because it is of service to the community rather than because it is a source of profit to the owners.[25]

Dodd's argument, as can be seen, was not that the social responsibilities of the corporation had replaced its responsibilities to the share owners. It was not an either/or issue. The trend of opinion, as he saw it, was against the exclusivity of stockholders' claims upon the enterprise and toward the view that profit making and social service should go hand in hand. There is no intimation here that the share owners should move out in favor of either the community or the officers and directors of the institution. Nor, indeed, that the officers and directors of a corporation are the sole judges of what "social service" entails.

The future trend of the law may be toward strengthening the "social service function" of the business corporation as an institution. The law has always been responsive, though tardily, to public opinion; and corporate executives will be responsive to both in their conduct of corporate affairs. If the law still leaves corporate social responsibilities undefined, is it not possible that the pendulum may swing in another direction in the future? Is it not too soon to conclude that both law and public opinion have settled once and for all the debate about the social responsibilities of the corporation? Is it not more probable that the scope and uses of corporate powers will be continuously redefined by courts and legislatures in response to public opinion and that public opinion in this respect is not easily predictable?

It is plain that the debate itself rises out of evolution and trend in corporate relationships, rather than out of any practical understanding of the nature of the modern corporation. It is not to be wondered at, therefore, that statements about the norms of business behavior can be made only in terms of models or of ideal goals. Before meeting the issue of what the corporation *ought* to be and to do, an objective analysis of what it now *is* should be undertaken.

"Ought" is after all an ethical question, answerable not in pragmatic terms but rather in terms of preferred values. Yet what we want the corporation of the future to be and to do will depend no little upon an understanding of its present nature and function. And here one discovers that beyond the conflict over ethical norms, there is no generally accepted theory on which corporations operate. Beyond the law, the economic theory, and the only hazily defined theory of management of corporate enterprise, there appears to be a still unexplored field which might be called the "polity" of the corporation.

The contemporary search for a philosophy of business is in large part a search for a theory of corporate enterprise. Unlike the normative aspect of the quest, this can be handled in an objective and analytical way. The chapter which follows designates five areas in which a scientific type of research is both possible and necessary.

CHAPTER V

Five Scientific Problems

WHENEVER A GROUP of human beings, actuated by common interests, common purposes, and common objectives, creates an organized institution for the furtherance of these aims, it is polity which provides for the adjustment and control of the relationships of the institution.

An examination of these internal and external relationships should help provide a basis for understanding the actual role of the corporation as a constructive force. But such a study of relationships must be scientific to the extent that it requires an impartial confrontation of the facts. Before we begin to talk about the "reform" of a polity, we would be well advised to study closely how it functions. I do not presume to say that this avenue alone will bring us to complete understanding of the corporation, but it should guide toward a more realistic appraisal of the way in which the modern corporation does *in fact* operate.

More than one set of calipers is required to measure the total significance of the corporation. Jurists and economists have developed invaluable tools of analysis, and these have been used to great advantage for rendering more comprehensible many activities of the corporation. Other disciplines, too, have been useful. Sociologists, psychologists, anthropologists, and political scientists have increasingly turned their attention to corporate phenomena. The result has been a voluminous literature on the modern corporation; only some of it is rigorously scientific.

It is understandable that there is no synthesis at hand that provides a reliably comprehensive map of the whole terrain. The brain of man, which can comprehend the structure of the atom and of outer space, should be able eventually to comprehend the structure and functions of such an institution as the corporation. For the scientist, as Robert Frost says, is the "lock-picker" of nature's secrets; and so long as freedom of inquiry prevails, there will be those who, given time, cannot rest until they have knowledge of our social institutions and processes in their possession similar to that which savants now have of many hitherto unknown aspects of the physical universe.

The motives for inquiry into the corporation are not always disinterested. Corporate lore is heavily veined with apologetics and polemics. But even those who spend most of their energy attacking or defending business corporations, frequently—if unintentionally—throw new light on the subject. Still, there is real need for systematic, empirical studies of the corporate institution, as it exists, by those who are single-mindedly devoted to the task of "picking locks." This does not necessarily exclude the businessman.

The business executive, though usually drawn from the breed of men who spurn theory, is not always immune to it and may even embrace it when it helps him to solve his problems. But then it must be theory of the instrumental kind, as distinguished from plausible justification for preferences. It is not improbable, in fact, that in the long run, many of the elements of corporate theory will be stated most effectively by the practitioners of the corporate art. Just as executives have found that their engineering problems yield most readily to those who have a mastery of advanced knowledge in the physical sciences and technological theory, so are they finding that human problems yield only to those who acquire and develop advanced knowledge in the behavioral sciences.

Few of even the largest corporations today, it is true, are pulling their weight in the boat on either score. Basic research in either the physical or the behavioral sciences is not adequately supported by business enterprises that use the fruits of this knowledge.[1] But the picture is undergoing change. Basic research is gradually getting more support, both within the corporate structure and through corporate support payments to educational and scientific institutions on the outside. The need is obvious enough in disciplines which contribute directly to functional work such as engineering, manufacture, finance, and marketing. Now that the ferment of social change has lifted to prominence the whole problem of corporate survival, the need for a mature philosophy of corporate enterprise has become clearer.

Recognition of this problem as one of basic research may be expected among the more astute leaders of large corporations. But for the time being such research will have to be conducted mainly by scientific and educational institutions.

There are at least five major areas of inquiry that need to be examined in any basic research on the nature of the corporation. Each of these is summarized below.

CORPORATE GOALS

The "lock-picker" of the modern corporation, in the first place, will have to explain—not justify, nor bemoan—just where its managers think it is going. In other words, the observer will have to state as realistically as possible the operational goals of those who make the strategic decisions of corporate policy. Still another way of saying this is to describe the goal-values of those who make the important decisions in most business corporations today.

It should be emphasized that the discussion here does not concern what these values should be, but what they, in fact, are. The question of good or bad standards of corporate conduct belongs to the normative side of a corporate philosophy. And while this question is not only legitimate but unavoidable, it can be deferred until we have looked at the facts. The goals that men pursue may seem unworthy and mean, or utopian and ephemeral. But even if a man's method is the method of madness, an acute observer can often detect it; and presumably the business enter-priser, of all persons, is the least irrational of men. A weakness of the classical model of economic theory is that it assumes too complete rationality of entrepreneurial behavior and rational purpose along too narrowly defined lines. So much can readily be conceded. Yet none will deny, surely, that the major goal of managers of business corporations is the accumulation of wealth. Normative judgment may approve or disapprove of this goal. That it is a major goal of business is undisputed.

But the "lock-picker" cannot stop there. A little probing reveals other goal-values. Corporate managers are only human, after all. And although, to paraphrase Emerson, a man can be metamorphosed into a thing by his occupation and a manager may seem to be only an Organization Man, it also works the other way round. The bloodless and fictional corporation, limited by the dry legalistic phrases of its charter and the neat syllogism of economic theory to materialistic purposes, turns out to be a most lifelike person. It has a character all its own, and it does things and exhibits purposes that cannot be explicated from the legal and economic texts. The corporate person acts only through its agents, and these real persons are more than Organization Men. They may not always be the ideal "whole men" of Emerson's fable. But they are moved by the same purposes. They seek wealth; but they also value physical well-being and security, skill in the practice of their professions, knowledge and insight into the world they live in and their place in that world, respect for themselves as individuals and for the status of the organizations of which they are a part, moral standards as they conceive them, the sense of belonging, and the fellowship of others in their community, and, not least, the sense of influence and power.

These are some of the representative values that one would expect to find not only in the men who run corporations but also in the policies of the corporations they manage. The range of corporate goals is wide, and one does not have to look far to find many examples of this multiplicity. Nor is it difficult to observe that from company to company the emphasis will vary. Power and prestige may be more important to some than a reputation for rectitude or for any substantial contribution to the general welfare of the community. For others, security and maximization of profit may be the exclusive goals. Those who deride the idea of social responsibilities for the corporation may be right in predicting the evil consequences of such a course of corporate policy; again, this is a matter of normative judgment which we are not for the moment concerned with. But if such derision has any basis in fact and if business corporations in any considerable number are really pursuing these allegedly dangerous goals, our thesis is to that extent sustained: corporate goals are, at least in some instances, not exclusively in the wealth-accumulating category.

The point is clearly that the modern corporation is not one thing but many things. It is not just an entrepreneurial unit, nor simply a more or less efficient producer of goods and services, confined to that specialized function in a society characterized by strict division of labor. The modern corporation is, in part, an economic institution, part educational institution, part fraternal organization, part contestant in the political process. It is all these things and probably much more. More accurately, some corporations are more one thing than the other and no simple explanation will suffice to describe all of them at the same time or any one of them for all time. They change as society changes; there is a constant interaction between the corporate institution and its environment. A corporate theory must deal with corporate dynamics as well as corporate statics. And it must always have a firm base in corporate ecology, a second and undeveloped aspect of business philosophy.

CORPORATE ECOLOGY

Corporate ecology is that branch of the corporate discipline which deals with the relations between the corporation and its environment.

The ecological aspects of the emerging theory of the corporation will be of more than scientific interest. A sound understanding of corporate ecology is a prime requisite of the successful executive. This has always been so. Classical economic theory is mainly concerned with that stern ecological fact—the market. Every businessman will continue to be concerned with it so long as we maintain a relatively free and competitive economic system. But there are other things in the corporate environment that command the attention of the corporate policy maker if he expects to see his organization survive and prosper. More broadly, bearing in mind the multiplicity of goal-values which men and corporations pursue, the corporate environment is full of dangers and opportunities of a nonmarket variety that the policy maker must consider.

The political environment is by all odds the most important source of these dangers and opportunities. A corporation enjoys immortality only in a comparative sense; but it is usually one of the goals of corporate policy to assure longevity of the organization beyond the natural lives of those who man its executive posts. Consider a company which aims at viability until at least the year 2000 A.D. How will this company's managers steer a safe course through the political shoals of the next half-century? What will be the necessary and sufficient political conditions for such survival? Can they count on the preservation of the current patterns of government as the necessary basis for an orderly market place in which the business can survive? What are the geographical boundaries of the market within which the company can hope to continue in business? Are they national, hemispheric, global? What kind of political structures will be required to sustain such a market?

The nation-state pattern of law and order, despite its signal failure to preserve orderly global (or even regional and hemispheric) marketing areas, has persisted for about four centuries. Businessmen have done quite well within this faulty structure, some of them because of it, but most of them in the face of it. Most American businessmen have prospered, when they have prospered, because they enjoyed an unusually wide geographic expanse of market within our own nation. Here law and order, thanks to the designers and sustainers of our federal system, have long prevailed throughout the larger part of a big continent.

European businessmen have prospered similarly because of the maintenance of law and order by their metropolitan governments in large parts of a colonial world. The era of these colonial empires has practically come to an end. Necessity has mothered the invention, on the European continent, of radically new political patterns, as in the case of the functional unity of the Coal and Steel Community and the Common Market.

The rise of two great new empires in the East, together with the long-delayed nationalistic movements in southern and eastern Asia and in Africa, presents us in this hemisphere with the probability—indeed the certainty—of epochal changes in the boundaries of our market places. The network of Western alliances that we have developed since the last war, the system of alliances among the Communist countries, the United Nations, the Organization of American States—these are all portents of yet unknown political patterns for the world of 2000 A.D. when our hypothetical company is still supposed to be around.

Whether the corporation of today can hope to realize even the limited "immortality" of five more decades will depend first and foremost upon the kind of political environment it works within. The prospects of law and order on a global scale are none too good; but what about the prospects of an orderly regime for the next half-century within our own hemispheric and continental area? Our immediate neighbors to the north and the south have achieved degrees of political stability without which we would be in great difficulty. So much cannot be said of all the governments of the Organization of American States. Nor have we, in the United States, done all that we might do to secure this general continental political stability. What are the prospects that we shall do better during the next few decades? Will the situation worsen, or will it gradually improve? Can it be expected that the government of the United States, in the near future, will be able to command the support of the electorate in designing and carrying out the necessary political and economic policies for assuring continental political stability?

On the domestic scene, too, there are problems of political ecology which are of profound concern to our hypothetical corporation, and some of these problems have no direct relation to the broader problem of global political stability. The federal system itself, although it was put to the test a century ago and came through the dreadful fire of a civil war, is not necessarily immune, for all time to come, to other tests of a different kind. The problem of racial relations remains unsolved and is again putting enormous strain upon the constitutional structure. Business enterprises will be caught up in the toils of this struggle and in contests over other basic issues. Some companies will founder because of failure to steer a wise course.

Even now, some of these other issues present managers with almost insurmountable problems; others can be discerned on the horizon. Our difficulty in establishing and maintaining the orderly government of labor relations is perhaps the most acute problem of today. Although this issue might have been kept mainly in the realm of private government (that is to say, in the hands of the private contesting parties) had there been wise foresight on both sides early in this century, both parties have long since resorted to the invocation of public power to support their respective causes, and now there is no turning back. Union-corporate relations are now a major issue of public policy, and we have yet to see whether the governmental structure is adequate to cope with it.

The same holds true for the financing of public services. No return to the narrowly circumscribed policing functions of public governments under laissez faire is predictable. On the contrary, rapid expansion of governmental functions is fairly certain when one contemplates population gains and the attendant demands for more public education, land-use planning, water supply, sewage disposal, housing, highways, parking space, airports, social security, medical care, and so on. One cannot foresee the explosive political fission that may accompany future attempts to solve such problems, but our hypothetical corporation will not enjoy any aloof asylum from the successive detonations.

The corporation of the future will, in fact, be more and more drawn into the political fray as an active and open participant. It is too early to say whether the current moves toward corporate political action provide any sound clue to the future role of business in politics. But we know enough of the history of group action in American political life to conclude with some degree of certainty that our hypothetical corporation, if it continues long to survive, will have a corps of specialists in politics just as it now takes for granted the necessity of specialists in marketing.

A theory of the corporation will embrace the element of political ecology: it will describe the necessary and sufficient political conditions for the survival of a business enterprise in corporate form. And it will describe systematically the interactions between the corporation and its political climate. It will also take into account other factors: economic, demographic, ideological, and so forth. If such a theory is scientific, it will not scold; it will not deplore; it will not rejoice; it will state the facts of life.

Such a discipline is almost nonexistent today as a unified body of knowledge, although some parts of it—economic, mainly—have already become the subject of scientific study.

THE POLICY PROCESS

The ecological approach to corporations, if it is not to be overcast with the pall of Social Darwinism, must be balanced with other approaches to the subject. So we come to a third problem for the scientific "lock-picker" seeking a usable theory of the corporation. Any such theory must describe with accuracy how human beings make decisions on behalf of a company, and human will plays a large part in corporate decisions.

While this may seem elementary, there is considerable confusion about what actually happens when corporate policies are made. As a result, there is equal confusion about what the policies ought to be. Again, we confine ourselves for the moment to the question of fact, leaving the normative judgments for later consideration.

A corporation makes no decisions. Men make decisions. And in a corporation, the strategic decisions are not all made by the men at the top. Nor are they made at any level by men who act with complete rationality. Yet the goal is to minimize the irrational and to fix responsibility where the authority lies. This last statement is itself in part normative: it seems to say that one *ought* to be rational in his decision making and that in the well-ordered corporation those who make the important decisions *ought* to be authorized, responsible, and informed. But for scientific purposes we take such a statement as a point of departure, an operative norm, and then go on to ask whether it is, in fact, a correct description of the policy-making process.

Considerable light can be thrown on the policy process by examining the deviating influences that make it difficult for corporate policy makers to live up to the norm. Such analysis has its uses beyond scientific understanding of the corporation as a going concern; it can also provide clues for the student of corporate ethics. One difficulty with much of the polemical and the apologetic literature in the great corpus of corporate lore is that it often makes simplistic assumptions about corporate policy processes. On the polemical side, for example, there is the complaint that corporations are pyramids of power governed by self-perpetuating and irresponsible boards, or by professional managers, whose power is "separated" from ownership. The apologists of the modern corporation, on the other hand, may dismiss the whole problem of power and decision as irrelevant in view of automatic operation of market forces, there being implicit assumptions about the exclusively economic ecology of the corporation. Or, power may even be dismissed as power per se and labeled as "leadership."

Before one can take a tenable position on the ethical norms that should guide the corporate policy maker, one needs to know much more than is known about the decision process in real-life corporations. What are the larger issues that present managers with choices? In choosing one path of action as against another, what are the elements that enter into the final decision? What are the various stages through which the policy process can be traced? What are the various instruments of policy that have to be considered in making the ultimate plans of action? And are the instruments chosen compatible with the goal-values implicit in policy objectives?

These questions will be explored in the later pages; they have yet to be applied in empirical studies of representative companies. When that is done, the ground work certainly will have been laid for better scientific understanding of the corporate policy process. Moreover, there will then be some guideposts for future managers as they seek to improve corporate structure and procedure for more effective decision making.

But effective for what ends? It may well be asked. The answer is: for whatever ends one sets for oneself. One contemporary goal is the preservation of corporate autonomy and, more broadly, the maintenance of a pluralistic society in which there will continue to be a multiplicity of private decision-making sectors. If the corporation is to retain decisive autonomy, its managers must be able to exercise the power of choice impressively, demonstrating that the business corporation is a reliable center of decision making in a society which encourages diffusion of the decision process.

Failure to so exercise the power will lead most probably to its shift to other centers, possibly to those of public government. In static periods of history, such shifts may be long delayed even though functionally indicated. In our time, with its peculiar dynamism, these shifts are frequently abrupt and are sometimes accompanied by political revolution. Impressive corporate performance in the decision process can do much to forestall such disruptive shifts in the decision centers in the United States.

One notable trend in recent years has been the progressive decentralization of decision making in some large companies. It remains to be seen whether this alone will suffice. A few careful analysts of the problem have pointed out certain correlative requirements. Thus, Harold F. Smiddy, one such corporate executive, says:

The determinant level for responsibility, and authority to make a particular decision should be the lowest organizational level where both the needed skills and *competence,* on the one hand, and the needed *information*—embracing understanding of both direct and environmental probable *impacts* of the decision—on the other hand, *can reasonably be* brought to exist; so such information and understanding can be brought to bear in choosing wisely from among possible alternatives, or risks, as responsibility and need for decision arise.[2]

The emphasis here upon information indicates the importance of the intelligence-gathering stage of the policy process. While corporate intelligence may be well understood in such fields as marketing, engineering, law, and finance, it seems doubtful that it is adequate in respect to the political ecology of the corporation.

In certain other respects, the decision process in contemporary corporations merits closer study. There is probably too little understanding of the instruments of policy, for example. It is all too often assumed that economic means are the chief or only reliance of the policy maker in a business corporation.   The fact is that negotiation of a quasi-diplomatic character, the use of force through the invocation of governmental sanctions, and the ideological instrument of symbolic manipulation are all important instruments of corporate policy.   Some are used wisely and effectively, given certain goals of corporate managers.   Others are used unwisely and ineffectively.   And seldom is there a center of command in which the balanced use of these instruments is made the subject of careful strategic planning.

A sober and objective analysis of the actual uses of such instruments of policy in contemporary companies will be hard to carry out, partly because there will be resistance to any acceptance of the theoretic frame of reference here proposed.   But this is not the only reason.   Men are not disposed to disclose their strategy and tactics, even after the fact.   The researcher into corporate strategy and tactics will find few open doors for his investigations. One will have to rely here mainly upon memoirs and other documentary evidence, drawn from sources close to the heat of battle. And these sources must be the actors in the drama—the executives, that is to say, who have insight into the nature of the policy process and the urge to write.

THE STRATEGIC DECISIONS

Another problem that needs careful scientific work concerns the substantive areas of policy making.   What are the *strategic* areas of corporate policy?   Understanding of the corporation as an institution will be advanced if we can study the policy process in deciding the larger issues that confront executive managers. There is likely to be much difference of opinion about the identification of such issues.   The diversity of opinion is in itself a clue to the multiplicity of corporate goals and the pluralism of business as it is practiced today.

For many executives the most important issues of policy have to do with such matters as pricing, levels and costs of production, and the allocation of their financial resources among the factors of production. For example, what and how to spend for plant expansion, for research and development, for merchandising promotion, may frequently be regarded by some as strategic policy issues.

Others will question whether such issues as these have not become more the tactical and less the strategic decisions of the modern business enterprise. The modern *strategic* decisions, Smiddy suggests, are "those which set the initial and continuing scope of objective of the business; determine what products or services it will have for sale; elect what markets and what channels to reach them will be served; and resolve how much direct and supporting work to do on the company payroll and how much to purchase from others outside the business." [3]

The difference between strategy and tactics will depend upon the position of the observer and the scope of the field he is observing. It will also depend upon how he defines the protagonists and the nature of the contest. The corporation, viewed essentially as a private entrepreneurial unit, is engaged in a contest with its competitors.

But how different the strategic areas can be for one who is concerned mainly with problems of "business statesmanship," or one who looks upon corporate enterprise as public business carried on in private sectors. We have called these points of view normative, since they assume some proposition about the role that the corporation *ought* to perform in society.

The nonnormative, or operational, approach to the strategic policy areas disregards such norms and asks only this: What are in fact the questions that occupy the attention of executive managers? One cannot know what these questions are without making actual surveys, over periods of time, of the attention span of many executives. The table of corporate policy areas (Chapter IX) could be used as a primary schedule for such an investigation. This list is based upon comprehensive analyses of the theory of the firm. The investigator would probably find, after reliable surveys of the time actually spent by a sample of leading executives on the various items on this list, that few indeed of the items were at the focus of their attention much of the time. The items on which they do spend most of their time would be reliable indicators of the strategic policy areas as these executives assess their importance.

One could hazard a guess that Smiddy's strategic decision areas, referred to above, would be fairly close to the list of strategic areas as many corporate executives see them. But it might also be found to exclude some surprising items. The public, and more especially the political, relationships of the corporation might in some cases head the list. In other instances, executives might be wholly occupied with financial issues.

Obviously, no sweeping generalizations about "the corporation executive" and his attention to what he regards as strategic policy issues will have any validity in the absence of empirical investigation. And no sweeping generalizations about the modern corporation and whither it is bound will be very useful without such inquiry. This, then, is a further clue to the scientific understanding of the modern corporation.

CORPORATE GOVERNANCE

One of the least understood aspects of the corporate discipline has to do with corporate governance—the structure and functioning of the corporate polity. Of "business administration" we know much, or pretend to. Of the governmental processes within the corporate polity and in the external relations of that polity with other kinds of polity, public and private, we know far too little.

The lack is due partly to inadequate theoretical constructs and partly to paucity of empirical work. Governance is too generally thought of as a matter of a public government exclusively. Political theory, in so far as it is a scientific instrument and not ethics, has been developed too narrowly (with notable exceptions in recent literature) as the instrument for understanding states in their domestic and international aspects. There is today little political theory that is applicable directly to the governments of the private sectors, including business corporations. But in addition to this, we have nothing to compare with the elaborate descriptive materials on public government.

This is not only because many of the internal affairs of business corporations are normally hidden from the public eye or from the eyes of prying scholars. Few scholars seem to have been interested in the corporation as a system of government and politics worthy of serious scientific study. Were those few to approach the average corporation executive for permission to study the governmental system of his organization, they would probably encounter a mixture of anxiety and bewilderment. What would they want to know? Would their investigations disrupt the business operation? Are not politics and business disparate fields, they would ask, and are you not on the wrong track studying government in a business organization?

The time will soon arrive, if indeed it is not already here, when business leaders should welcome scholarly inquiry into corporate governance. For this will provide one of the most useful keys to an understanding of the future of the corporation. It will also offer the soundest possible basis for dispelling many of the myths that now permeate corporate lore. Are corporate boards "self-perpetuating oligarchies"? Is the hierarchical structure of corporate administration inconsistent with the ethos of our constitutional system? Are the "Corporate Democrats" on the right or the wrong track? Is the "People's Capitalism" the golden key to economic democracy? Does the free enterprise system require corporate autonomy, or will the enclaved private governments of the business world eat away the foundations of an individualistic economy?

These are to a large extent ethical questions, or at least questions that are heavily weighted with tacit value-judgments. Before one can begin to assess the rightness or the wrongness of corporate behavior, one needs to know more than is now known—as scientific fact—about the uses of power in business corporations. Charges are made and defenses are prepared on this issue without much hard information. The whole debate tends to take on a most unrealistic tone. More heat than light is generated. What the corporate managers of tomorrow will need is more enlightenment.

This is not the place to outline the science of corporate polity. Some of the subject headings of that science can be foreseen, how-

ever: the constitutional bases of corporate governance; the kinds
of power that are needed to govern the corporation; the kinds of
limitations on power that have been developed and are in the
process of development in response to the need to protect various
interests, including the private rights of those affected by the
exercise of corporate power; the types of governmental process
found in the corporate polity; the "foreign relations" of the corporation and its place in the totality of public and private political institutions; interrelationship between public and corporate
policy; and the optimum patterns of diffusion and concentration
of decision-making centers (public and private) in a free and
democratic society.

In a notable essay by John Maurice Clark a plea was made for
interpenetration of the disciplines of political science and economics. "At the nominally private level," he wrote in 1957,
"trade unions and large business corporations not only are affected
by the actions of official government, they exhibit governmental
qualities in their own structure and motivation." He asked
whether large economic organizations were constrained to act in
their collective interest by outside pressures—whether of competition, supply and demand, or the power of bargaining adversaries—which left them no alternative; or whether their economic behavior did not "depend on how well or how ill their
internal quasi-political and administrative organization operates
to make them represent the interests of their members." [4]   The
latter, he thought, was more nearly the correct statement of the
case.

"Business as a rule-maker stands high in responsibility among
human institutions, as a source of goods and services, to be sure,
but also as a source of order and freedom."   So wrote Beardsley
Ruml in 1945, in his book, *Tomorrow's Business*.   Tomorrow
has now arrived and the pertinence of the observation must be
even clearer today.

The fact is that our free society has grown up as a dispersed
and diffused power structure, with many decision-making centers,
both public and private.   This system provides for a sufficient
concentration of authority over many things, at many points, to
get things done.   For example, a regime of law for the nation as

a whole makes necessary a strong federal structure. Provision for strong corporate structures makes possible the collective use of capital to accomplish industrial objectives. Other such centers of authority exist throughout the whole fabric of our society.

Yet we have always been interested—within the American Constitutional tradition—in trying to achieve a proper balance between adequate powers in public and private sectors, and also in maintaining effective restraints of those powers. The reason for these restraints in our constitutional heritage has always been the preferred position of respect for the private rights of persons and their property. These private rights form the cornerstone not only of the polity of the State but also of the polity of business corporations, labor unions, professional associations, churches, or universities. Thus, we find that the private rights of persons and property constitute a common denominator in the genesis of polity in all of these institutions.

And indeed, if we reflect on it further, the traditional corporation would argue that the newer corporate variants have no respect for private property, while the metrocorporation replies that the classical model has no respect for personal values and private needs. And it, in its turn, is condemned by those who say it is destroying both private property and private persons by collectivizing.

It is plain that animadversions on what one faction interprets to be the intention of the other will continue merely to generate heat. Any light on the actual nature of the modern corporation will come only from a detached analysis of the realities as we have outlined them here.

We shall attempt to discern first the true objectives, the goal-values of the economic institution as it administers, through private persons, its share of private property.

Corporate Realities

The outstanding practical problem confronting our economy . . . is not how to check excessive concentration of power, but how to improve the decision-making processes of the economy so that the economy may better develop policies and institutions which reflect interests common to most of the population.

Sumner H. Slichter, "The Power Holders in the American Economy," *Saturday Evening Post,* December 13, 1958.

CHAPTER VI

Corporate Goals

CORPORATE POLICY [1] projects into the future those plans of action which are designed to achieve the major objectives of a corporation. These major objectives can be understood only in terms of the basic value systems, here called "goal-values," of the men who preside over the institution. These goal-values lend themselves to analysis. They shape the major plans of corporate action—plans formulated at decision centers—which determine the progress, indeed, the very survival, of the institution. What are these goal-values?

THE NEED FOR A SYSTEM OF GOAL-VALUES

Current theories of the firm are conflicting and inadequate in the statements of the operational objectives of large industrial corporations. Economic and legal conceptions of the corporation, for example, usually present ideal goals which may or may not be the actual objectives that govern the acts of decision makers. In order to comprehend the corporation as a living institution, it is essential to comprehend the principles that guide corporate decision makers.

The search for these guiding principles, or springs of action underlying corporate policy, necessitates both extensive empirical work and a construct of theoretical propositions that will be sufficiently comprehensive to account for the complexity of observed practices. Objectively, what are large companies doing, not exclusively in terms of a preconceived economic or legal model of "the corporation," but rather as a complex of actions which decision makers in those companies actually undertake? The inhibiting influence of a too narrowly conceived theory of the firm may obliterate new viewpoints that probe the nature and social function of the large corporation. A new perspective may provide significant clues to the goals toward which action is pointed.

Realistic appraisal of these corporate functions thus demands both open-minded observation and new hypotheses. In particular, what is most needed are new hypotheses about the range of corporate objectives. For this purpose, a general schema of goal-values is introduced later in this chapter as one possible approach to the problem of making the modern corporation comprehensible. With a wider range of possible objectives of corporate policy in mind, it should be possible to pursue the purely inductive work of investigating corporate practices more efficiently.

The wide range of corporate objectives is evident enough—as will be shown later—in the published policy statements of certain firms. But, of course, policy may be implicit and never formulated explicitly for public consumption, and corporate objectives may show up at any stage of policy making.

As in any large organization, policy making in the modern corporation is complex. Comparatively few salient objectives are kept in the mind's eye of the board of directors as a basis for review and approval of proposals brought before them by executive management. In selecting a course of business action, or measuring performance, the board will weigh proposals and adopt standards in terms of its own norms, whether the norms are implicit or explicit. Executive officers, in turn, are guided by certain norms and objectives that shape the proposals they bring before the board. Down the line of the managerial hierarchy decisions are made, to a large extent, in the light of these standards set by the board and executive management. But decisions at each level do not necessarily reflect a one-to-one correspondence of doctrine laid down by superior authority. Recommendation is itself a form of decision making. While those at lower echelons who formulate recommendations for top policy action often get their cues from the operational goals at the top, the process by which they formulate corporate goals in accordance with their own norms is frequently hidden from view. Thus, there is danger of oversimplification in describing the complex of forces which play upon the "real" goal determiners in the lower layers of management.

It might be taken *a priori,* for example, that all the way up and down the line of goal setting in a competitive firm, the key consideration in everybody's mind is always the making of superior products and services and their efficient marketing as the major prerequisite to a single company objective—profitability. This may, in fact, be the stated objective of the firm, its publicly announced aim as a business enterprise.

But the available evidence would hardly support this conclusion for any of the larger companies. Not only are their *stated* objectives far more numerous than profit seeking; their *implicit* goals are also far more complex. It is inviting to anthropomorphise "the corporation" as the rational and calculating man of classical theory; but corporations in action bear little resemblance to the "economic man," or even to the reconstructed post-Freudian man of unconscious and irrational, as well as ratiocinating, components. It is a complex association of men whose actions are only to some—and varying—degree polarized around the profit motive.

The position taken in this study is that although the objectives of a business corporation are primarily economic, an attempt must be made to understand the totality of the aims of this institution and to place them in a reasoned perspective.

THE ENTREPRENEURIAL OBJECTIVE

"Economists," it has been said, "have thus far handled the question of managerial motivation primarily by establishing simple assumptions. Thus most economic theory . . . and much public policy merely assumes profit maximization to be the paramount if not the sole goal of business and businessmen." [2] There is wide acceptance, even today, of the Ricardian view of entrepreneurial motivation: the "economic man" seeking to maximize his profits and, as such, contributing indirectly to the general welfare. This approach, as has been indicated, is not a safe guide in an empirical investigation of the objectives of corporation policy; its view of managerial motivation is too circumscribed.

Other elements are needed to complete the picture. Survival of the corporate enterprise, continuity of operations, maintenance of "reasonable profits" over the long pull, physical growth, prestige—all these are also on the canvas. The need for social approval ("people *like* our company"), the desire to improve the well-being of the community, the love of power, the urge to enlighten, pride in innovation—these too show up in empirical, as distinguished from armchair, investigation of managerial motivation.

Awareness of these factors suggests that the "cold" corporation is not so inhuman after all. The modern corporation is managed and carried on by people whose goal-values are hardly distinguishable from those of their fellow-citizens. Yet the roles men undertake, as members of the corporate institution, do seem to effect some restructuring of their goal-values as individual persons.

The corporation as an economic institution has, in a sense, a life of its own which is said to mold a member of the corporate family into the Organization Man. If so, it is hazardous to conclude that the goals of corporate policy reflect the goals of the "whole man," especially in the Emersonian sense.[3] For Emerson, "you must take the whole society to find the whole man." Perhaps the organization or corporate man represents only a specific economic function in our age of specialization. In the Emersonian phrase, man is but part of the whole man "metamorphosed into a thing . . . [just as] the priest becomes a form; the attorney a statute book; the mechanic a machine; the sailor a rope of the ship." The corporation is not a whole society; it is not an epitome of the great world; nor is the Organization Man a whole man.

The search for corporate goals in the broadest range of human goals may thus be as misleading as the narrowly circumscribed Ricardian view of entrepreneurial motivation. But if the first is too sweeping, the second is too confined. The institutional economists and the sociologists have searched for realities by looking at the actual practices of business institutions without doctrinal preconceptions. The business corporation, from this point of view, is not seen as performing a simple function; it is studied in all its multiform aspects as a cluster of activities, the meaning of which has to be understood inductively. For, if the corporation is too doctrinally regarded as the instrument of a single function—such as the entrepreneurial—there remain many phenomena in the whole picture of the modern corporation that are quite unexplainable.

Nor is the difficulty overcome by revision of the earlier and stricter definitions of the entrepreneurial function.[4] In 1775, Cantillon [5] spoke of entrepreneurs as dealers who "buy the wares of the country—give them for a fixed price, to sell them again wholesale and retail at an uncertain price." Certainly the large industrial corporation of our day is more than an entrepreneur in this sense. More than one hundred fifty years ago, objections were raised by J. B. Say [6] to the practice of the earlier English economists in failing to distinguish between the capitalist, as a passive investor with income from interest, and the entrepreneur, whose income derived from "profit."

But even with Say's correction, the classical view helps little in discerning the characteristic economic goals of the modern corporation, including, as these goals do, far more than profit maximization. Nor is risk-bearing the essential function of the entrepreneur, either in the owner-managed form or in the large corporation of many shareholders.[7] F. A. Walker,[8] toward the close of the nineteenth century, came closer to the mark in defining the entrepreneur's function as furnishing technical skill, commercial knowledge, and powers of administration; as assuming responsibilities and providing against contingencies; as shaping and directing production; and as organizing and controlling the industrial machine. By 1911, with Joseph Schumpeter's accent on the carrying out of new combinations [9] as the distinctive work of the entrepreneur, we move nearer to a comprehension of the set of functions that a modern corporation actually performs.

Schumpeter, in his last work, published in 1954,[10] reviewed the development of the idea of "enterprise" since 1870. The major theories of entrepreneurial activity and entrepreneurial gains were analyzed as theories of a specific function. He concluded that Maurice Dobbs' characterization of entrepreneurs as people "who take the ruling decisions" of economic life would have served as "a common motto" for all of these writers.[11] They started "by attributing to entrepreneurs *an essential function in the productive process*", and they all "went on to explain entrepreneurial gains by success in filling that function." [12] Clark's contribution, for example, connected "entrepreneurial profits, considered as a surplus over interest (and rent), with the successful introduction into the economic process of technological, commercial, or organizational improvements." [13]

In current usage, the entrepreneur is one who "assembles the various means of production, and by mobilizing them, renders them operative and useful," [14] thereby earning a profit. He is an industrial organizer who causes land, capital, and labor to function. By organizing the use of these to advantage, he seeks to make his own remuneration. Enterprise has been defined as "that factor in the productive process which is responsible for adjusting a business organization to a dynamic world through innovation and adaptation," a factor which "historically and currently, in the large corporation . . . is identified with general executives and directors." [15] The dynamic element is of great importance. The corporation does not exist in a static world, free from unpredictable change. In such a world, as Knight has observed, no managerial decisions would be called for and there would be no scope for enterprise.[16]

The analysis of the corporation as an enterprise certainly leads to one of the most important objectives of the large industrial company. This objective is not the technical direction and operation of productive processes. It is, rather, in a private enterprise economy, the making of wise business decisions in performing two kinds of tasks: (1) keeping the corporation in continuous operation as a profitable private enterprise; and (2) performing adequately the regulatory functions of private and decentralized decision centers in a "mixed economy." It is a nonhomogeneous economy, a part of which is "small business" operating to some extent under conditions described in classical economic theory, another part operated by government or under its control, and the remainder—perhaps two-thirds—under the conditions of mass production within the ambit of corporate decision making.

The basic issues in such a mixed economy—allocating resources to the best advantage of everyone and maintaining a proper balance between stability and growth—are not resolved by a central planning board but by a large number of public and private decision centers. The business corporation, as an important decision center, thus has social as well as private functions of an economic nature to fulfil. But as an entrepreneur it performs both functions simultaneously through its operations in the market.

Oswald Knauth, after surveying the complexity of business practices as they exist today, found "a theoretical unity . . . in the universal urge for protection against the chaotic fluctuation of the untamed market place." [17] The chief goal sought by large managerial enterprises, in his view, is an advantageous trade position. Their search for a trade position of an appropriate degree of strength and durability, moreover, is made under conditions that differ radically from those which were assumed to have prevailed in classical economic theory. In a "natural" economy it was assumed that "an automatic response brought relationships to an equilibrium which was the 'natural' condition of all human relationships, including the economic." In an era of mass production, business practices that are necessary for survival "are the complete antithesis of those governing small-scale competition." [18] Knauth reasoned that in order to build up a trade position assuring survival and success for a company, to protect it from "the vagaries of the market place," corporate managers must be free to "create and coordinate all the elements that enter into the process" [19] of survival.

That an advantageous trade position constitutes the *major* goal of the modern corporation would be rejected as a generalization by many observers. In Knauth's work [20] the advocacy of change in antitrust policy overshadows to some extent his descriptive and analytical contributions. But when he lists what might be called his catalog of errors in current theories of business practice,[21] he provides useful clues to other goals besides those of an advantageous trade position.

THE REACH FOR NONECONOMIC OBJECTIVES

From other points of view, especially those of the critics of Big Business, the *actual* objectives of the modern corporation will seem more complicated than they do to those who focus upon the entrepreneurial function.

The goal of advantageous trade position is rendered by some critics more bluntly as monopoly and more generally as a struggle for power. Nor is it only economic power that the critics of the modern corporation see as a major objective of corporate policy. There are said to be social and political aims inconsistent with democracy.[22] The themes of "harmony" and "business trusteeship" or "stewardship" in the public statements of some companies' labor relations and public relations policies have been criticized because these ideas are associated with the corporative regimes of totalitarian, status-bound, and hierarchical societies.[23] The country is said to be run by a "power elite" of the corporate rich and the military brass functioning in and through "the political directorate," [24] implying that the political objectives of large corporations are quite as significant as its entrepreneurial functions.

The polemical literature ordinarily gives no balanced picture of the actual policies and practices of enough specific corporations to yield representative and reliable samples for the country as a whole. Like the literature in defense of business, it emphasizes and illustrates what it sets out to prove. If the polemical writers concentrate too much on extraentrepreneurial goals of an allegedly sinister kind, as though these were the "real" aims of corporate policy, the apologists tend to expand the range of corporate objectives, perhaps unduly, in order to prove corporate benevolence. Together, these two streams of thought add up to a much wider scope of corporate objectives than Knauth, for example, finds. How many of the alleged aims of corporate policy are operational in most firms remains an open question. The problem cannot be solved by advocacy. It requires empirical studies probing into the case histories of numerous companies. An adequate accumulation of such objective studies has yet to be made.

It is reasonably certain, however, before such exhaustive research, that the large corporation today is a multipurpose institution. It performs many kinds of functions and has many objectives. Its economic functions and goals are doubtless primary, and its noneconomic functions and goals secondary; but this distinction does not enable us to make a simple classification of the roles that the modern corporation plays in society. What do we mean by the "economic" function? Are we talking about the entrepreneurial role? Do we mean, for example, profit making? Production of goods and services, the efficient use of scarce resources? Efficient from what point of view, that of the "enterprise," or of the industry, or of the community generally? If the community, what community? Is an economic function served when the corporation adjures its employees to participate in public affairs and to make the company a "good corporate citizen," or is this a noneconomic function? Is corporate giving for charitable purposes an economic function? Or is it an example of the pursuit of a wide range of extraeconomic objectives?

For the purpose of arriving at some systematic view of the whole range of corporate objectives, it is useful to turn to the schema suggested at the beginning of this chapter. The schema provides a broad framework for understanding the goals and values of man in the modern corporation. With such a generalized view of human motivation before us we may ask the question whether any or all of the goal-values of man find their counterparts in corporate policy.

GOAL-VALUES OF MEN AND CORPORATIONS

The "corporation" is frequently spoken of as though it were a person. In the legal sense, of course, it is. But the policies of a corporation are made by flesh-and-blood persons whose personal value systems enter into the decisions they make on behalf of the company.

These goal-values are affected, moreover, by the various roles a man assumes in society. The corporate manager, for example, has a definite role to perform which underlines the goal-value of wealth, for profitability is certainly a standard of business performance that stands high on the list of criteria by which a manager's role is assessed. Certainly it is not the only one. In the largest companies, business performance is held to be measurable in such other terms as market position, productivity, product leadership, personnel development, employee attitudes, and public responsibility. Even as a business manager, a man's goals are multiple.

But these measures of business performance, numerous as they may be, are not nearly so comprehensive as the value system which underlies a manager's own personal decision making. There are, for example, types of values [25] that are related to one's search for physical security and welfare such as *well-being* (one's health, and physical safety); *wealth* (in terms of economic income); *skill* (proficiency in the practice of one's trade or profession); *enlightenment* (knowledge, insight, and information concerning one's relations with others and the world one lives in); and *survival* (security, both for oneself and for one's business). There are also certain "deference values" that refer to the consideration given to a person by others. These include *respect* (status recognition, prestige, repute); *rectitude* (the moral values of law-abiding, good and righteous men); *solidarity* (belongingness, friendship, affection); and *influence* or *power* (capacity to influence the decisions of others). Such a list is, perhaps, representative of values that men hold universally, though with considerable variation in priorities from person to person, from place to place, from culture to culture, and from one point of time to another.

The goal-values of persons, acting on behalf of the organizations they identify themselves with, tend to be projected into the organization itself; and the result is a value system for the corporation. One seeks, in his decision making as a manager, to achieve maximum performance for the corporation against these standards of value. For example, he wants it to be a company with a well-deserved reputation for profitability and growth (wealth); influence in the industry (power); leadership in the fields in which it operates (respect); a force for good in the community and a sense of well-being among its employees (rectitude); a contributor to knowledge in scientific, technological and other fields (enlightenment); a high degree of competence in its chosen field (skill); and solidarity with the society in which it operates (affection).

These are far from hypothetical assumptions. An examination of the published objectives of numerous corporations shows that such goal-values as indicated have indeed been projected onto the corporation and have become stated corporate objectives.[26] Some of these are presented below, indicating the wide range of goal-values with which company officials believe they must be identified.

Profitability and Economic Growth

In no company statement is the profit-motive the sole objective, and in some published statements it does not appear at all. Below are some examples of how the goal-value of wealth is phrased:

To be the most successful company in relation to our profit potential (a textile manufacturer)

To conduct our business so that we earn a reasonable profit and are enabled to provide shareholders with a fair return on the money they have invested in our company (a meat-packing company)

To operate a successful and profitable business for shareholders and obtain the highest possible return on their investment; to afford employees the opportunity to earn wages equal to or better than the average for the community (an optical goods manufacturer)

To generate adequate profits at least equivalent to those of similar enterprises (an industrial materials producer)

Leadership

Every corporation seeks the value of status, which is not the same as power and influence. Managers want their company to be recognized for certain reputable qualities. They give deliberate attention to its prestige.

So, a major goal-value in corporate policy is to arrive at a reputation for leadership: in supplying worth-while services and

products to its customers; in establishing wages, working conditions, benefits, job security, opportunity and personal recognition
in such combination as to "make our company the best in our
industry in which to work" (a rubber manufacturer); in demonstrating through every field that it is outstanding. Since the
modern corporation is a large organization, with many diversified
functions, there is a deliberate aim to achieve leadership in all
these functions: manufacturing, marketing, research and development, public relations, employee relations, legal and financial
operations, and the work of professional managing.

The specific skills in each of these fields are of course important; but it is the *reputation* for leadership in these skills that
becomes a separate aim in itself. A company that is respected for
these attributes is in a better position generally—and not merely
in profit position—than one which has no such reputation. So it
becomes an aim of corporate policy to generate that reputation,
not alone by advertising the fact, but more especially, by constant
attempts to measure up to and above one's competitors in the
effort to achieve status. To be associated with a respected company is to increase the respect one wants for himself as a person.

Integrity

Integrity is a goal-value that gathers increasing attention today as concern develops in the matter of the social responsibilities
of the corporation. The company tries to be a "good neighbor
and citizen," tries to be active in the support of good government, tries to contribute to charities, to education, and to other
worthy causes—in many instances succeeding admirably.

A meat-packing firm sets as its first objective "to conduct all
of our affairs according to the highest standards of ethics and
business integrity." An industrial materials company declares
that it will "adapt promptly and smoothly the company's activities as an essential industry to emergency conditions in the event
of mobilization or war." One air-conditioner manufacturer "encourages all its men and women to take a working interest in the
well-being of their communities and the nation." In the phar-
maceuticals field, one company states its "ethical policy" as
follows:

The ethical policy demands that there be no secrets from the medical profession. The full and complete formula is always given for every . . . product. No extravagant therapeutic claims are made. Therapeutic statements are based upon the observation and experience of the medical profession and the Company's own scientific staff. Furthermore . . . medicinal products are offered only to the medical profession, which means that the Company does not advertise or promote its products to the general public.

And the above company's policy is said to be based upon well established economic and ethical laws and upon the "fair deal." No one man in the organization is entirely responsible for policy formulation but, rather, it is the outgrowth of contributions of several men.

In a major electrical goods manufacturing company, it is one of the general company objectives to:

adapt Company policies, products, services, facilities, plans, and schedules to meet continuously, progressively, foresightedly, imaginatively, and voluntarily the social, civic and economic responsibilities commensurate with the opportunities afforded by the size, success, and nature of the business and of public confidence in it as a corporate enterprise.

Integrity, for the large corporation, means more than observance of the law and living up to general ethical expectations of the public at large. It involves "doing right" by the specific contributor-claimant groups immediately associated with the enterprise. A smaller electrical manufacturing company, for example, states that "in all decisions affecting the conduct of the business it will consider always what is right and best for the customers, shareholders, and employees, as a whole, rather than what may be expedient in dealing with a single situation."

The professional manager must dedicate himself, in the words of the president of one of the largest diversified industrial companies,

not only to the owners of the business through his Board of Directors, but also as a steward to the Company's customers, its industry, its employees and to the community at large. The professional manager must consciously place the balanced best interests of these ahead of his own personal interests.[27]

"Every company," he believes, "should be managed in accord-ance with some workable, ethically responsible philosophy of management"—a view expressed among many industrial leaders.

Knowledge and Skill

The necessity for adapting basic and applied research to per-fect products is not the exclusive reason for making enlighten-ment an aim of corporate policy. Product development certainly depends heavily upon adequate research programs; but the pur-suit of knowledge, insight, and information permeates all func-tional fields in the large corporate organization.

Intelligence operations have to be planned and executed for financial, manufacturing, legal, marketing, employee and public relations, engineering, and managerial work. A company must assure itself of a continual inflow of data in these several areas, followed by analysis and synthesis of the information for opera-tional uses. Thus, enlightenment becomes a major aim of corpo-rate policy.

A pharmaceutical company's scientific policy, for example:

is based upon the profound conviction that medicine is a science as well as an art; that only scientific pharmacy can properly serve it; and that the problems of pharmacy can only be met and solved by scientific means. Hence, the scientific laboratories and staff are dominating fac-tors in production and progress.

A building materials corporation declares:

We believe that we should stimulate the genius of science and utilize the methods of research to improve our products and to create new ones so as to continuously provide new fields of employment for the present and coming generations.

One surgical goods manufacturer states in its "Credo":

Our executives must be persons of talent, education, experience and ability. They must be persons of common sense and full understanding.

A steel producer "believes in training for its personnel" and that

only by developing the capabilities of the individual employee can we obtain that teamwork which is essential to efficient production.

In the field of food processing, one manufacturer is dedicated to a program of research and expansion. We believe that future growth, future employment, and national prosperity depend upon increased output of products. Scientific research raises the general standard of living in two ways: by making it possible for us to buy new and better things, and by providing more jobs.

In industries where a high degree of technological competence is obviously necessary in order to meet competition and assure growth, one would expect to find an emphasis upon scientific research on products and marketing. Many large companies today also put increasing emphasis upon scientific approaches in other fields, such as the work of managing, and public and employee relations. Efforts are also being made to marshal the current findings of the social and behavioral sciences. Almost inevitably, these sciences have lagged behind the natural sciences; consequently management often makes a special effort to encourage basic and applied research in the human sciences in universities and other centers of learning.

Conflicting aims of corporate policy may develop here, as in the fields of the natural sciences. Should a company attempt to establish proprietary claims to new knowledge in order to maximize the goal of profitability? Or should a company pursue a policy of general enlightenment? An industrial corporation is first of all a business enterprise, not a scientific or educational institution. Enlightenment is not the major goal, but a subsidiary one. But without a constant inflow of new knowledge in every area of work done by personnel of greatly diversified skills, the future position of the company is jeopardized. From the point of view of total environment, it is to the long-range advantage of a company that new knowledge in all fields of human inquiry be developed within and outside the organization.

Yet the decisive factor in attaining an advantageous market position may be exclusive possession of certain kinds of knowledge through patents and copyrights. A balance must be struck between exclusivity and sharing of knowledge, not only out of respect for the "public interest" but more especially because undue emphasis upon secrecy may frustrate the business aims of the company in the long run. There is a close parallel here between the problem of secrecy in the individual company and the analogous problems of sovereign states.

For example, leading American scientists have begun to raise basic issues of national policy by pointing out that barriers to scientific progress are thrown up by wholesale classification of public documents regarding atomic energy. Some believe that overclassification not only blocks scientific advance, but in the long run hurts us more than it hurts our potential enemies. Similarly, the large corporation in its search for enlightenment as a means of attaining business objectives may take too narrow a view of its own interests by tightening its grip upon knowledge that could be usefully shared.

Integrity—in the form of conformity with the patent and copyright laws and concern for prevailing concepts of the national interest—is, of course, a corporate policy aim that will vie with the aim of profitability and market position. But ethics aside, it is questionable whether a company properly balances its long-term with its short-term objectives when it grasps new knowledge too exclusively.

The importance of enlightenment as a major aim of corporate policy has received little attention in the contemporary literature of the theory of the firm. Nor has sufficient attention been given to the problem as an aspect of the work of managing. It is doubtful that many large corporations have developed a well-reasoned policy on the subject. Perhaps this is not so remarkable, since the role of science is still too little understood in our culture. Yet the corporation may conceivably forge ahead of political government in recognition of the need for enlightenment—a need that impresses itself upon the competitive businessman for reasons of sheer survival.

Amity

As with the individual person who values the sense of belonging and has a need for affection, the corporation exhibits a need for solidarity with the society in which it operates.

"We must be a good citizen" is a theme that recurs in statements of company objectives. This may be dismissed by the thoughtless as public relations pap or a vacuous expression of high moral purpose, applicable on Sundays but not on weekdays. But it reveals more than the values of respect and rectitude—both of which are operative in all large organizations. It reveals a desire to be liked, quite aside from one's power and influence or one's righteousness as a member of the business community.

To say that a corporation wants to be loved would seem to reify a fictitious person, the corporate entity. Yet managers, in their roles as representatives of large concerns, are extremely sensitive to the charges of cynicism in big business. They react vigorously to the taunt that businessmen are men without culture, without deep human feelings for their fellow creatures.

Big companies spend large sums in polling public opinion about attitudes toward the *symbols* of company neighborliness. It is not enough for them to know that their products are getting wider recognition, that their securities are eagerly sought by potential investors, that their profits are rising. They want to sense the feeling that they are an integral part of the community, a built-in institution that is just as important to people as churches and schools and fraternal organizations. Affectionate regard may smooth the way toward easier recruitment of capital, personnel, and other resources, and it may be an invaluable aid toward a better market position. But there is a plus value in the sense of amity that cannot be measured in any of these terms, and it is entirely probable that decision making in many large corporations is considerably influenced by this policy aim.

It would be unbecoming a large industrial corporation, in our culture and given our standards of public behavior, to come out openly with a statement that it needs affection. The modern corporation cannot say, "We want to be loved." Some have held that Americans, as compared with Europeans, are more prone to insecurity with respect to the degree to which they are held in affection. They feel that other Westerners who are managers and entrepreneurs are less concerned with attitudes of affection on the part of their workers and the community in which their companies are located. In any event, no such statement is to be found in any available list of company objectives in America. But it can easily be inferred from the public pronouncements of businessmen and can be read between the lines in pleas for recognition of social responsibilities and the reputation for good corporate citizenship. To stamp these concepts as expedient devices of a protective sort intended to combat antagonism toward Big Business is to overlook the fact that corporate policy is made by human beings and the further fact that all human beings hold affection to be a major value. Many executives identify so strongly with their organizations that the goal-value of affection cannot be satisfied in extraorganizational activities.

Influence and Power

For Hobbes, "the Power of a Man (to take it Universally) is his present means, to obtain some future apparent Good." Power, in Hobbes' philosophy, was amoral in itself, and all men struggled to get it. A corporation seeks power in Tawney's [28] sense: "the capacity of an individual, or a group of individuals, to modify the conduct of other individuals or groups in the manner which he desires." Power is sometimes regarded as a means to an end. But power, as Lasswell and Kaplan have pointed out, is itself a value, "a deference value: to have power is to be taken into account in others' acts (policies)." [29]

Power, in this sense, is indispensable to a company. The power (more generally, the influence) of the organization—in the industry, in the community, and internally with respect to its members—may be regarded with suspicion, with approval, with respect or with fear, depending upon a point of view. Whether a corporation has real power and influence is a question that can be answered without attendant ethical judgment. We may assume that "good" managers will use that power for "good" purposes and "bad" managers for "bad' purposes. But this is irrelevant to the fact of power. Certainly it may be set down as elementary that a goal-value in every large corporation is the establishment and maintenance of an influential position for the company.

Power, as a corporate goal, is never stated explicitly and baldly as an aim of corporate policy. Moreover, it is rarely explored with complete objectivity by social scientists. Nor is there objectivity with regard to it in corporate statements on the subject. In many companies there is an expressed growth objective. There are also objectives stated in terms of strong market position, leadership in civic affairs, and so forth, but these statements of aims always have an ethical coloration. A strong market position is never represented as a threat to one's competitors. "Leadership" carries the connotation of rectitude. It would be quite a different thing to come right out and say to the world: "We intend to be powerful, and stronger than any other company, at least in our own field," or, "We are a lot stronger than the unions that press claims on us, and we intend to assert our power in a trial of strength if necessary," or, "Government may be pretty strong, but we intend to pit our strength against it and you will see who comes out on top." Power, as power, is not a popular goal-value for the business corporation, and to flaunt power would be an invitation to countermoves by other power-wielding entities.

That power *is* a major goal-value for corporate policy, however, is undeniable. Certainly a manager who dismisses it as inconsequential would find himself in an untenable position. Stockholders expect their companies to take a stiff position at the bargaining table with unions, to offer hard competition in the market, to meet the encroachments of government with firm and defensible positions. Boards expect managers to exercise power within the organization in dealing with subordinates, whether disciplinary authority is maintained by command or persuasion. Consumers and customers do not applaud power per se in the companies that supply the goods and services they want; on the other hand, they would not willingly see a breakdown in the discipline of organizations that produce these goods.

Many citizens see in the power of corporations a useful counterpoise to the power of other corporations, government, and the unions. Mass production necessitates aggregates of manufacturing power. Businessmen are perhaps averse to admitting this publicly, but, without the operational goal of power and influence for the organization, corporate policy would be spineless. Certainly, the decision process in the large corporation cannot be comprehensively understood without assuming that power is a major goal-value.

Survival

The use of the term "institution" to describe the corporation
is familiar enough so that the idea of survival as a goal of business should need little qualifying. In general, that which follows a repetitive and predictable pattern is described as an institution. Baseball is an American institution, marriage is a
cultural institution. But on another level the word is applied to
buildings or plants in which activity of a particular kind goes on
regularly, and ostensibly interminably. The use of the word to
describe the nature of the corporation implies that it is in the
category of those organizations, like church and state, which are
both influential enough and indispensable enough to the social
complex so that their disappearance would create major alterations in the nature of the society which fosters them.

An institution, in the strict sense, therefore is a quasi-perm-
anent organization which is vital enough in the whole context of
human needs and human drives, to be maintained by the common
consent of many generations. It is at such a point in organizational evolution that the corporation now finds itself. Its time
span is already longer, in many cases, than that of its founders,
and the process of change to which it contributes so great an impetus, has now accelerated to the point where its plans for the
future bypass, by a number of years, the ambitions of all but the
youngest of its employees.

While its individual operating components anticipate the
obsolescence and "death" of new products, as a part of their in-
novative planning, there are no plans among today's corporation goals for self-liquidation. There are several good reasons for
this.

In the first place, the size of the corporation alone, and the
number of people whose economic lives depend upon it, make
any schemes for quick dissolution look virtually immoral. In
addition, the lifetime employee, who is encouraged by health
benefits and pension plans to stay with the company during his
productive years cannot conceive of an even gradual cancellation
of the promise of security toward which his efforts are pointed.

But the goal of survival is encouraged further by the rise of a
managerial class, a corps of professionals who resemble their

counterparts in an army general staff, career diplomats of the department of state, or the hierarchy of a church. They are imbued with the same organizational loyalties and have the same pride in its prestige and in their identification with it as one observes in any big university stadium on Homecoming week-end. They share an ethos, an esprit de corps which excludes the possibility that its rallying point will not be there forever.

Survival, therefore, though it may never be listed among organizational objectives, is one of those tacit aims which characterize all institutions, and, like some of those which are clearly formulated, it is a projection of one of the most basic drives of the human nature which animates the corporation.

In sum: the modern corporation becomes more comprehensible when the diverse aims of corporate policy are examined. By the aims of corporate policy we do not mean the ideal aims. The pictures in men's minds of what the modern corporation *ought* to be in terms of some preconceived corporate model will be of limited usefulness in answering the question: What, in fact, *is* the corporation?   Economists' models, reformers' invectives, and businessmen's credos are apt to be misleading charts for identifying the value systems that *actually operate* in the making of corporate policy. They all offer useful hints, but none is a proper substitute for empirical investigation.[30]

The goals of corporate policy are primarily economic. But the economic functions of the modern corporation are not statable with anything like the comparative simplicity of principle that one encounters in earlier theories about the role of the entrepreneur. The corporation as we know it today is not simply a larger model of the owner-entrepreneur. The attainment of maximum profits is no longer posited as the sole motivation for managerial decision making in the large corporation, if indeed it was ever the sole motivation for the owner-entrepreneur.

For some purposes of economic analysis it is undoubtedly useful to posit this sole motivation. But does it give us much of a clue to the emergent role of large corporations as major institutions in our whole social structure? There is room for doubt when one observes the corporate executive in action. A theory of the firm, complete with hypothetical constructs so designed as to accommodate the vast complex of corporate behavior, observed objectively, would be a sound guide to the actual objectives of corporate policy. There is no such theory of the firm available. When a theory eventually appears, it will take into account more than the wealth-producing aspects of corporate behavior, and will include a wide range of goal-values commonly held in contemporary society.

A schematic view of the range of values which men hold includes, besides the desire for wealth, a number of goal-events that cannot accurately be described in economic terms exclusively. Wealth or income alone will not assure one of the conditions of physical well-being; knowledge and skills are values of equal rank and we find that great emphasis is put upon them in statements of company objectives. Men, as individuals and in their roles as corporate executives, hold other values as well: they value influence and power, respect, rectitude, and affection. For the corporation, policy aims can be expected to include, beyond the accumulation of wealth and the distribution of earnings, status for the company, influence in the industry and in the community generally, good corporate citizenship, and other qualities associated with rectitude, solidarity, or a sense of belonging and of being the recipient of the affectionate regard of others, and the will to carry on forever.

We should expect to find, upon close examination of corporate policy in action, that all of these values play some part in the decision process. The empirical study of the modern corporation will be greatly hampered if one approaches the decision process with blinders. The right questions have to be uppermost in our minds, lest we overlook some of the pertinent facts. One cannot assume, for example, that decision making at the managerial level is confined to issues of the acquisition of wealth and its distribution. Otherwise data will be brushed aside which might throw light upon the noneconomic functions of large corporate organizations.

The concept of the multifunctional role of the modern corporation would seem to offer the more rewarding hypothesis; but in adopting such an hypothesis one does not make any preferential assumptions. One does not assume, that is to say, that it is either proper or improper for a large industrial company to pursue policy aims that depart from the classical model of economic theory. The scope of an institution's activities is a question of fact. If new theoretical models are necessary to explain these activities, then by all means let us have new models. But we should beware of an attempt to fit inescapable facts into a theory that cannot possibly account for them.

The system of values introduced here for the purpose of widening the scope of inquiry into the aims of corporate policy need not be defended as the only possible one. But it will serve the purpose of departing from more restrictive analyses of the general problem. Furthermore, it will help point the way toward a better understanding of the kinds of decisions that corporate leaders are asked to make and toward a more realistic assessment of the scope of corporate responsibilities in our time.

With a wider and more realistic span of corporate purposes in mind, management is in a more advantageous position to examine the whole span of corporate policy and to appreciate the variety of strategies required to reach multiple objectives. There are several strategies or, what is called here, instruments of corporate policy, by which a company strives to better its position with respect to the whole range of values. The instruments of policy, properly used, prevent a corporation from slipping into an unfavorable position—unfavorable as measured by any of these values.

The ultimate test of effective policy making for the corporation, as an institution, is more than the test of profitability or the production of wealth. The test is rather the degree of realism and rationality that is used, first, in establishing the basic goals of policy and, then, in planning all the acceptable avenues of achieving these goals. We turn now to this question of minimizing the distorting influences which tend to prevent the application of realism and reason to the policy process, in which goal setting and implementation both occur.

CHAPTER VII

Rationality and Reality

in Decision Making

THE MULTIFUNCTIONAL CHARACTER of the modern corporation becomes more understandable when the process of corporate policy
making is analyzed. Are the key decisions in large corporations
made by the highly rational processes assumed in the central
tradition of economic analysis? Or, is it necessary to modify our
concepts of the corporate decision process in the light of newer
models, such as, for example, those provided by recent game
theory? What is the corporate executive's mental picture of the
world "out there"? Is it one that conforms fairly closely to reality? How does the corporate policy maker see himself in relation
to the company and the company in relation to society, and with
what consequent effects on corporate policy?

THE DECISION PROCESS

Recent developments in the policy sciences [1] indicate that a
considerable gap exists between cliché and reality in describing
decision processes in large organizations. The unrealistic character of many prevalent notions about decision making in general,
whether in government, in business, in military organizations, or
in games, arises in part from unsupported assumptions concerning the rationality of decisive acts.

For many reasons one does not, and cannot, make everyday

decisions according to prescribed patterns of formal logic. There is not enough time. We do not expose all the premises to thorough examination. We fail to explore all the alternatives. We are unable to foresee all the consequences of each conceivable alternative. Nor do we always proceed logically even when we do have the premises, the alternatives, and the probable consequences before us. Our choices, in short, are frequently not the hardheaded decisions we would like to imagine ourselves capable of. They are the result of an admixture of rational and irrational choices among alternatives, the pressure of time, and a host of other pressures existing at the moment of decision. If this is the situation for decision making in general, it is not less true of the corporate decision process in particular.

Perhaps the decision process in love and war—to illustrate the point with an example from other realms of human activity—cannot and should not be a strictly logical and rational one. The universe has no mechanism for creating our lovers. This we do ourselves with decisions based on a turmoil of emotion, prejudice, and desire. The heads of state have devised no instruments for predicting with certainty the actions of the enemy nor even the actions and reactions of their own populace. Frequently, in both instances, improvisation rather than rationality wins the moment. The successful policy maker uses intuition, insight, good judgment, and his instinct for the jugular.

Is business fundamentally different from love and war and politics in its decision processes? Why do we need to be so concerned about business decisions? Business results are impressive, are they not? But decision makers do not remain fully satisfied with their decisions, particularly as events change. Therefore, there have long been compelling reasons for maximum rationality in business decisions, and for getting at the gremlins which war upon rational means of dealing with the buzzing universe around the enterprise.

One important approach to the study of policy making is to consider it by stages and to examine closely the subprocesses involved in the decision process as a whole. These stages in policy making have to some extent been the subject of study with respect to governmental systems but not apparently with respect to corporate policies. Seven such stages have been proposed in a recent study: [2] *intelligence* (information, prediction, planning); *recommendation* (promotion of policy alternatives); *prescription* (the enactment of general rules and regulations); *invocation* (provisional characterizations of conduct according to prescriptions, including "demand" for application, bearing in mind that the intensity of the demand may be very mild or very severe); *application* (the final characterization of conduct according to prescriptions); *appraisal* (the assessment of the success or failure of the policy) and *termination* (the ending of prescriptions and of arrangements entered into within their framework). The social aspects of corporate policy not separately mentioned above will become clearer as business decision making is examined from the point of view of the governmental internal structure and operational characteristics of the corporation—its polity.

Still another useful approach to corporate policy making is in terms of the instruments of policy. Policy goals were mentioned earlier. How are these goals attained? All large organizations pursue their aims by means of various instrumentalities, none of which alone would be adequate to implement policy. Crude force theories, for example, make the assumption that states enforce the sovereign will by mere command backed up by bailiffs and armies. The truth is that even the state, with its alleged monopoly of coercive power, relies heavily upon other means to implement policy: negotiation (diplomacy), economics, and ideological weapons. A corporation has no armies, but it may call upon the judicial and executive powers of states to enforce its rights.

Economic instruments alone ordinarily come to mind when one considers the instruments of corporate policy; and it is true that there is a certain "discipline of the market place" which governs much of corporate decision making. But corporations, like other institutions, also make use of negotiatory techniques that fall outside the realm of economic bargaining. Corporations make use of ideological means to win and maintain an advantageous position—advertising, public relations, communication of ideas, the projection of symbols through diverse media—and to influence the minds of men. In the decision process within large corporations, basic questions are raised concerning the effectiveness, the appropriateness, and the ethical justification for the relative emphasis that will be given to the instruments of policy.

Certain "overt actions," [3] still another approach, can lead to policy formulation. These open and observable stands, as it were, can be classified into major substantive policy areas that are commonly found in all large businesses. To inventory these substantive policy areas is to chart the span of business operations; and the span is broad indeed. Policy decisions project plans of action that corporate managers can undertake, given (*a*) the internal conditions that prevail within the corporation itself and (*b*) external conditions over which managers have very little control but which exert an influence upon the nature of the decision. The patterns and trends of social, political, and economic institutions in the corporate environment, for example, must be understood by the wise policy maker; and his assessment of this external world will strongly affect the success or failure of his decisions.

While the three mentioned approaches (viz., by stages, by instruments, and by overt actions) aid in analyzing the decision process, still another merits attention.

This last approach calls on game theory. However, in discussing game theory in relation to the decision process, it is essential to bear in mind a basic assumption. Game theory does *not* become an *instrument* for policy making, but rather produces models from which to view the policy-making process with greater insight. In other words, the value of game theory lies in the fact that it *is* a model of what rational decision making would be in an idealized world where the logic of game theory would apply exclusively. It can be argued that game theory could present a base line from which to examine the pragmatic nature of the decision-making process. In sum, game theory may possibly aid in spotlighting some of the factors and conditions that limit rationality in policy making.

CONCEPT OF RATIONALITY

Historically, the notion of the rationally calculating businessman goes back well before the word "rationality" became popular. It underlay the development of classical economics and its popularity may be identified with such writers as Adam Smith and Ricardo. Their theories explored what would happen if each businessman sought to maximize his own profit, and their findings were that the results would be laudable. This value judgment was coupled with a notion, widespread at the time, that businessmen actually do behave single-mindedly as profit maximizers. This self-seeking view of business had usually been held in condemnation. In eighteenth-century England the merchant and manufacturer were still denied the respect and prestige accorded the landed gentry, public officers, and clergymen. There is no English counterpart as famous as Moliere's *Bourgeois Gentilhomme,* but the image, though milder, was the same. The literature of the time is replete with deprecatory remarks about the money-grubbing trader.

But, in the same period, the eighteenth century, defense of the businessman could be heard. The defenses did not then talk of social responsibility; the individual businessman was too small to see himself as having a social impact such as the modern corporation has. Instead, the defense rested upon the moral qualities of individual diligence, thrift, and industry, which the tradesman possessed in conspicuously greater degree than some of his supposed betters. Simultaneous with publication of these moralistic arguments, however, a few people were to be found who took the bull by the horns and, instead of denying the charge of money-love leveled at businessmen, praised it. Outstanding was a poem by Bernard Mandeville, *The Fable of the Bees; or, Private Vices Public Benefits.* His argument was that which came to be known as laissez-faire—that if each follows his own profit, then social welfare will result. As Mandeville's *Fable* described it, "Thus every part was filled of vice, yet the whole mass a paradise."

This shocking poem, banned and condemned, horrified among others a professor of moral philosophy named Adam Smith. He set out to refute it. He was too wise simply to dismiss the argument. He saw that it contained some merit. But he was not a man to accept it in such simple form. He recognized the importance of the altruistic sentiment of sympathy in human behavior and wrote a book to refute Mandeville by expounding the importance of that side of man's nature.[4] He later penned his masterwork, *The Wealth of Nations,* in which he explored to the limit the large element of truth in the thesis that men do act to maximize their wealth and that the result can in the proper circumstances be beneficial. From this recognition arose the great tradition of economic analysis of rational business policy.

Looking back at this tradition from the perspective of the twentieth century, some sociologists, outstanding among them Max Weber, recognized that the emphasis on rational calculation was characteristic of our times. They developed the concept of rationality as a social science category. They analyzed the processes of calculation involved in decision making, not only in the business firm but also in bureaucratic bodies. Indeed, Max Weber's works remain the classic studies of the ethos of rational decision making.[5]

BUSINESS POLICY AND GAME THEORY

While Weber extended the concept of rationality into a broader and more sophisticated one than simply profit maximizing, it remained for contemporary scholars to introduce a broader concept into the long established body of quantitative economic theory. The leading name connected with that development was von Neumann. He presented an analysis of rational strategy in reaching given goals, regardless of how the goals may be defined, whether they be profit or anything else.[6]

The relevance of game theory to corporate policy making can be illustrated by contrasting two kinds of environment in which decisions are made. In one kind of environment, *nature* is the only adversary of the policy maker. A navigator, for example, may choose to follow a southerly course at certain seasons of the year because of storms and winds. In business, however, policy decisions have to be made by the corporate manager in situations in which other *persons* are also making policies that are designed for the purpose of frustrating him, or that at least will have the effect inadvertently of impinging upon what he is doing. Game theory, which concerns itself with the latter of these two types of situations, may come to play a useful part as a model for understanding all competitive strategy, whether, as one author has put it, in poker, business, or war.

This is not the place to outline game theory in more than the most superficial way. But let us at least try to spell out its assumptions as a basis for a general understanding that may shed light on its relevance to business decisions. Suppose we enumerate the strategies available to each player in a game. These matched against each other give us a certain number of combinations. For each possible combination the "pay-off" is estimated, that is, which player wins and how much he gets. With this information at hand, game theory will tell us how each player should play. With so much information available the solution may sound obvious, but it is not, for the same strategy may result in big gains if another player plays in a certain way, and big losses if he plays differently. Thus a corporation expanding its share of the market may gain if government does not move against it in antitrust proceedings, and could lose if government does. The complexity of game theory arises from the fact that it seeks to define the best move for a player in the light of the possible moves of other players each of whom is seeking his best move in the light of the possible moves of the first, and so on *ad infinitum.*

Note that the outcome is defined in terms of a pay-off. Such a pay-off need not be in money or profit. Game analysis can be carried out in terms of any desired goal that is capable of precise specification and measurement, whether it be military advance, profit, share of the market, prestige, or votes. Rationality implies use of appropriate means toward some defined end. Without such an end no strategy can be judged. On the other hand, given such a measurable end, game theory seeks to determine the optimum strategies. How well does it succeed?

Modern game theory does indeed succeed in adding a good deal to our understanding of the decision-making process in many fields, including that of the corporation, but only within the limits of its strict assumptions.[7] As used by mathematicians, formal game theory is probably only of conceptual interest to the rest of us, but various game models are finding increasing use in practical strategy analysis at the business level. Whether it be in the guise of *management science* or of *operations research,* the theory of games and decisions in conjunction with other new and powerful scientific techniques and tools (such as: linear, nonlinear, and dynamic programming, and the developments in organization, information, and general systems theories, etc.) yields crucial insights into the process of corporate decision making. More important, however, is that the rapidly accumulating knowledge in this area may in turn bring about a marked change in business practice, bringing the latter in line with the norms of decision models designed for optimum results, be the latter defined in terms of profit or some other agreed-upon goal.

OF TIME AND THE MULTITUDE OF THINGS

The social science study of decision making is for the most part a study of deviations, the regularity in these deviations, and the reasons for them. In other words, if decision making were done under perfectly logical conditions, it would be a matter for applied mathematicians to evaluate the outcome. Fortunately, or unfortunately, man is not this kind of rational animal. Thus, the social scientist studies those deforming aspects of reality for the purpose of approaching it.

The first of these deforming aspects to be considered is "time and the multitude of things"—important types of pressures upon the corporate decision maker that tend to minimize the ingredient of rationality in business decisions, when action cannot always wait for thorough analysis; and when, even if this were possible, the outside world of reality refuses to be disciplined into the neat context of the theory of games. Next to be examined is "the mind's eye"—a further distorting element that interferes with rationality in corporate decision making because of the "operational codes" of executives.

These distorting pressures, upon examination, may serve to indicate some of the ways in which corporate policy making can be improved in order to enhance any given value, whether it be the pay-off of profit or the strengthening of the corporation as a major social institution with other objectives.

Corporation executives are busy men. That is a banal observation—so banal, in fact, that the full implications of it have seldom been looked into. Some studies of decision making, as previously noted, have been made in terms of the "values," aspirations, and ideology of such men. Other studies have focused on the communications process—what reaches them through the formal and informal organization. Yet one of the most important and unnoticed determinants of what happens is that there are just too many things to do in a day, so some of them must be selected for attention or priority.

There are few studies that take this fact as a point of departure. Lewis Dexter's study of Congressmen [8] is one of them. Another is Sune Carlson's *Executive Behaviour*.[9] Further, Professors Leonard Sayles and Eliot Chapple of the Graduate School of Business at Columbia University have initiated research in this relatively unexplored area.

Dexter describes how the very busyness of Congressmen reduces to a vague haze most of the pressures to which they are subjected. Instead of being able to keep accurate track of who wants what, often all they can acquire is a vague perception of unease among groups of constituents. Letters are skimmed, briefings are hurried. Many decisions have to be guesswork. His busyness both decreases and increases the Congressman's freedom. It decreases it by giving him so many options of activity that he is forced to select, but the selection process is a place in which his own preferences can come into play.

To date, probably nothing comparable to Lewis Dexter's study exists for business. There are, of course, many time, motion, and flow studies. These are mechanical in conception and generally concern lower echelon jobs. How long a piece of paper sits on which desks is not unimportant, but it is not the issue before us here. The most nearly appropriate published study is by Tom Burns writing from the University of Edinburgh in 1957. Here, too, the data are minimal, but we get some clues as to how company officials [10] distribute their time.

The literature here provides little information and leaves room to speculate on the meaning of time as an element of policy making. First of all, there is never enough time to be rational. Considered policy decisions take time. They may require the writing of staff reports. Once written, the staff reports have to be read. Often that is impossible and decisions have to be reached before a deadline by the quickest advice available. A company may stay out of a particular market because the responsible executives feel it unlikely that the returns would justify the time spent examining the situation to make the decision. Another company may oppose a piece of legislation, even though it might help one branch of that business, because there was no time to investigate that fact, whereas the fact may already have been clearly established that the legislation would hurt a different branch. The executive is like a chess player in a sixty-second-per-move game. He must move. He tries his best to use judgment. But he cannot allow himself the time to reach conviction.

Not that this is the corporate ideal. The doctrine of almost all top managers and management theorists is that the top man's job is to be free of day-to-day routine in order to have the time to plan and to think. Long-range planning and long-range thinking may indeed be the test of the top executive, but to protect time for these purposes is a struggle against odds. Time cannot be allocated in an optimum way to solve operating problems. The priorities of access to the executive's time cannot correspond to the scale of priorities of his job, for he is operating in a context. There are claimants to time who cannot be denied. These include his superiors. They include those to whom he has personal ties—his wife, his children, his close friends. They include those who are part of his team. His secretary's or assistant's problem becomes his own. These team members whose job was originally to protect him become, in a sense, extensions of his own self, and all their vulnerabilities become his. Thus, the executive's time budget becomes controlled by the web of his interpersonal relations as well as by the ostensible goals of his job.

All the adventitious claims on the executive's time may be perfectly proper, for the aim of the organization may require interferences with any one man's job. The point to be made here is not that a given man's job is more important than a given interruption; the point is, rather, that the nature of the system may result in placing intraorganizational functioning ahead of the operational task to which a given man is assigned.

Suppose a man's job is to sell; the one set of things which systematically take priority over that in his day's time budget are the interruptions imposed by the administrative functioning of the organization: answering a superior's questions, filling out auditing forms, keeping peace in the office. This may well be as it should be, but if these concrete priorities are overlooked in distributing minutes of working time, one is apt to fall into the cliché of reversing the priorities and to consider organizational life as a mere service function to doing the real job. The time priorities suggest that the most important thing to the organization is its long-range viability, the stability of the system, and not the doing of any one job.

In a different sense the pressure of time produces an emphasis on the short run. Deadlines must be met. The less important task due tomorrow takes priority over the more important one due months hence. One of our largest corporations, with a highly developed overseas program and a highly developed public relations program, has virtually no public relations program in its area of foreign operations. It is clear to everyone that this situation should be corrected, but it is far from clear just how to act. For years some officials have been seeking action, but there are no deadlines and confusion prevails as to a solution. As one exasperated official said, "Our company thinks in twenty-year terms. They don't get excited. If we have to wait two or three years to decide on the right thing to do, they feel we'll still be there." But all companies have some deadlines, and it is on meeting them that time will be spent at any given moment.

The example above illustrates another point. It shows how the pressure of time acts as a brake on innovation and expansion. How big should a firm get? Executive time is often the limiting factor. The one-man-leader company faces the choice of becoming a different sort of company with a bureaucratic structure, or of not growing. And often the man who is good as a personal leader is not good as a staff head. If his gifts lie in productive creativity (e.g., as a designer or mechanical engineer), he must, if his company has the opportunity to grow, either yield his leadership to an administrator, do uncongenial administrative jobs, or reject the opportunity to let his firm grow.

This may be illustrated with the case of an enterprise in which the top men are all professionals working at their profes-

sional field. They do not choose involvement in more entrepreneurial efforts than they now make, and they never think about
the alternative of placing themselves under administrators as superiors.

Farther up the ladder of size there are corporations which
have carved a unique place for themselves in a field. To grow
they would have to expand into more competitive fields at the
cost of much time and effort for the corporate managers—time
and effort that would not be proportionately well paid as compared with the present easier tasks. And even among corporations committed to growth, the innovations and aggressive de-
velopmental ideas of executives down the line run into the bottle-
neck of having to be reviewed, acted on, and supported by other
officers beset by the feeling that they are already doing all they
can and are thus particularly resistant to any new idea that will
take another chunk of their time.

Yet the pressure of time not only restricts the policy maker;
in some sense it also frees him. The pressure of time is, after all,
nothing but the obverse of the multitude of alternative things
available for the executive to do. The top corporate executive
is obliged to supervise and inspect operations, develop his staff,
build company morale, engage in long-range planning, review
finances, negotiate major deals, concern himself with government
policy, assume public relations functions, and carry out a host of
additional company responsibilities and duties. The very fact
that he cannot do all these things to the full, forces him to make
choices, and in making these choices he is expressing his own individuality as a leader. True, the pressure of time makes him
feel unfree; he feels driven. The policy maker is driven by the
tyranny of choice, and that is perhaps one of the best definitions
of freedom. He can define his own job. For reasons soon to be
examined, he may not realize this. He may think of himself as
responding to pressures, but, in so doing, he chooses his pressures.
For example, an invitation is received to give a speech. The most
common reply is that Mr. X does not have the time. Clearly this
answer hides an important choice, the choice of what things are
worth doing; and what things seem worth doing are not unrelated

to what things one enjoys doing. Lack of time is a euphemism behind which hides the value system of corporate executives and corporate entities.

So far, consideration has been given to one major aspect of time in relation to corporate policy, namely, its scarcity. We have noted that, to paraphrase Robert Louis Stevenson, the world is so full of a number of things that I think we should all be as busy as prime ministers. And as a result, decisions reached can never represent the perfect expression of corporate policy.

Time confounds rationality in another way, too. There is the problem of time-perspective as one looks out into the future. A pay-off tomorrow has greater value than a pay-off five years hence, and that more than a pay-off fifty years hence. It is argued that this is good sense both because of the impatience built into the psychology of human beings and because of the cumulation of uncertainty as we move into the future. This is a familiar economic and business concept, and it finds its expression in what economists call a time-discount or, in its most familiar form, in the interest rate, which may be viewed as a reward for waiting. If rewards for waiting were all that was involved in time-perspective there would be very little problem; interest rates would simply balance out the bird-in-the-hand with x birds-in-the-bush. But there are other problems involved in time-perspective. Among these is the question of how to apply a time discount to our own effectiveness in regard to what happens at different points in the future.

The complexities of this matter can be illustrated by reference to a piece of research conducted during 1957 at the Massachusetts Institute of Technology. It concerned the differences in the values and perspectives ("operational codes") of pure science (mathematics and physics) students and industrial management students. A questionnaire full of hypothetical questions was distributed. One involved putting a sum of money away in an untouchable account at high interest for a period of years, and the student indicated for how long he would tie up the money. Another question involved how long one would stick with a position pending a promotion. In replying to both these questions the pure science students showed a shorter time-perspective, in the sense that they would settle for smaller rewards sooner and let the future take care of itself.

Other questions dealt with long-range policy planning. For example, one question gave projected school population figures through the next century. Given that the later estimates were decreasingly reliable, the students were to act as school board members in making plans. Here it was found that the industrial management students had the shorter time-perspective. They based their decisions on what was likely to happen in the next twenty years and tended to treat the rest as too remote and speculative to consider. They would let the future take care of itself. The science students had a shorter time-discount for personal rewards, but a longer time-perspective for abstract speculation. Thus we see that time-perspective is partly a matter of what one pays attention to, partly a matter of what one thinks one can influence by present actions, partly a matter of what one cares about regarding the future, and only partly a matter of one's time-discount on rewards.

It is one of the characteristics of our culture that Americans tend to focus on the middle-range future. In contrast to some present-oriented cultures, we do not insist on immediate satisfaction. In the political sphere, for example, we may urge on colonial peoples the view that they ought to be satisfied if things are moving in the right direction and that they can hope for substantial improvement in the next five years. In business we may be satisfied to take small profits, delayed for a while, and regard as exploitative the capitalist who wants to recover his capital in eighteen months. On the other hand, in contrast to the Communists, we are not satisfied with a generation or two of deadlock. In short, we spend most of our planning time working on schemes which should be paying off in the range of five to ten years. Practically all our planning time is devoted to schemes for the next two to twenty years. Serious planning for a longer period than that seems largely visionary to us.[11] It is of some interest to compare such time-motivation on the part of managers with their long-term responsibilities toward the corporation, which, presumably, has perpetual life, unrelated to the life span of an individual.

Yet even within the range of normal American business planning there is room for variation. Some men and some firms take a longer perspective than others. In general, larger corporate entities have to take a longer time-perspective. This results partly from the fact that corporations have masses of immobile capital sunk in such things as manufacturing plants, railroad tracks, or a telephone system, but partly also because of the impact which changes in such great units can have. A large corporate entity cannot afford to be irresponsible regarding such things as fluctuations in the level of its production, employment, and profits. Otherwise, it may find itself penalized for such irresponsibility by adverse public reactions or by public authorities. Thus, large corporate entities need to take a long time-perspective, to think, for example, about continuing activities for fifty years hence. Yet the individual executives in a corporation may have difficulty assuming such a time-perspective. It is not the perspective of his own activities or of his own punishments and rewards. It is also not the attitude toward time that men of action are used to. Accordingly, there may be a conflict between rationality for the human beings who constitute corporate management as individuals and rationality for a long-continuing corporate entity, since they operate in different time-spans.

Thus, time enters the process of decision making in various ways. The fact that decision making takes place in vessels buffeted by the rushing stream of time, precludes their conforming to the model of rational action in a world of perfect knowledge and unlimited leisure which all extant theories of business tend to assume.

OPERATIONAL CODES

A man's time-perspective is but one of a series of deeply embedded habits of thought and action which affect the way in which he will handle any decision situation. The totality of these habits may be described by the term "operational code"—a concept developed mostly in connection with political behavior. It evolved in the attempt to understand Communist behavior and was influenced by earlier studies of national character.

All through the Second World War, American planners were conscious of the fact that, faced with the same set of data, or the same situation, the Japanese would see the data or the situation differently. They would react differently from the way our men reacted to such things as hara-kiri, kamikaze attacks, and jungle warfare. The nature of the attack on Pearl Harbor itself made us conscious of a mysterious quality in the enemy. The usual processes of empathy by introspection (i.e., figuring out what the other chap would do by asking what I would do in the same situation) did not work. And so our High Command called on anthropologists and psychologists to tell us about the ways of thought and patterns of behavior of the enemy. The result was a large literature on national character dealing mostly with the Japanese but also with other peoples.[12]

When, after the war, social scientists turned their attention to Communist behavior, they faced a more complex problem. It was obvious that Communist behavior was just as mysterious to us as Japanese behavior had been. Churchill's phrase, "an enigma wrapped in a mystery," expressed the reactions of most Western negotiators who had come to grips with Russian perceptions of facts and Russian diplomatic behavior. The Soviet representatives seemed firmly to believe in fantastic myths, to react with incredible suspicion to the rest of the world, and to show incredible gullibility and subservience to their own leaders and to their leaders' crimes. The problem was to understand and predict this behavior. National character alone seemed an inadequate basis for explanation, for non-Bolshevik Russians in many respects do not act in the same way as do Bolsheviks. Geoffrey Gorer made an analysis of Russian national character in 1950,[13] but a more fruitful approach seemed to be to study the assumptions about the world and reality involved in the mental processes of those particular Russians who have controlled the Bolshevik movement, and that was the source of operational code studies.

The major work in this field is Nathan Leites's study.[14] He attempted to spell out in a coherent system the way the world looks through the mind's eye of the Bolshevik. An example of the kinds of postulates involved may be helpful here. One postulate is that nothing ever happens by accident; one is surrounded by malevolent and powerful enemies, and whenever anything happens one assumes that it is produced in some way by their plotting. It is clear how very different will be the behavior of a man who sees an enemy plot in every event from that of a man who tends to think of the world as a great confusion of events which nobody really controls. And so it is with various habits of thought. If one can identify them, one can say something about how a man will behave.[15]

OPERATIONAL CODES OF CORPORATE EXECUTIVES

To date no one has attempted to study systematically the operational code of the American corporate executive or, more accurately, their variety of operational codes and the implications of these for policy.[16] Furthermore, various current plays, novels, and overtly hostile nonfiction works on the corporation are even less adequate representations of executive thinking. This deficiency cannot be repaired here. That would be a major undertaking requiring years of intensive interviewing and observation in the business milieu by persons of great perceptivity and detachment. However, it is possible to present briefly a few of the major dimensions encompassed by any such operational code and to discuss each briefly.

An operational code deals with several things. It includes *value systems,* i.e., what a man wants, what he believes is good and what he wants to achieve.[17] It is also concerned, and even more importantly, with *perceptions:* how the world is seen through the mind's eye. About perceptions one can ask a whole series of subsidiary questions.

How is time perceived? This is the matter of time-perspective already mentioned.

What is the cast of characters perceived in the situation? What persons does a given policy maker think about when he considers the consequences of a given course of action?

How does he perceive their motives? The illustration of the Bolshevik code given above is an example.

How does he perceive the usefulness of different instrumentalities; e.g., knowledge, money, political power? What, for example, does he think of the usefulness of basic research?

How does he perceive himself? Whom does he think of as "we" and whom does he think of as "they"? Who does he think he is? How does he define his own job?

Corporate policy may, and perhaps should, give a clear answer to some of these questions. Already noted has been the long time-perspective which the modern corporation requires. Correspondingly, the modern corporation must be concerned with a wider range of human motivations than those expressed in monetary bargaining. Public relations, advertising, and human relations activities all attest to an awareness in contemporary corporations of other responses than those which can be bought for cash. Similarly, the modern corporation has become increasingly aware of ends and means with which business was not much concerned in the past. Today, personal fulfillment, security, recognition, achievement, and pure research are among them. How will these ends and means fare? A persistent and revealing question for the future will be: How will the corporation perceive its own identity?

One way of arriving at a realistic perception of corporate identity is to understand the operational codes of corporate executives. A preliminary analysis would seem to indicate that four major elements exist: (1) the imaginary audiences of the corporate decision maker; (2) executive assessment of motives; (3) executive perceptions of the instruments of policy; and (4) the executive's view of his role. Each of these elements warrant consideration here.

THE IMAGINARY AUDIENCES OF THE CORPORATE DECISION MAKER

In analyzing the imaginary audiences which the corporate decision maker faces, the matter of reference groups comes to mind first. As in the matter of time-perspective, the cast of characters to which any given executive responds is apt to be considerably narrower than that which corporate policy would seem to call for. Let us cite a previous example, i.e., that the pressure of time, coupled with the accessibility of one's immediate staff, coupled, additionally, with the primacy of the smooth running of the organization, gives to the needs and desires of the immediate staff a saliency in the thinking of the executive which does not necessarily correspond to its role in general corporate policy. Similarly, power figures represent a key group for anyone; one's superior is always watching. Studies of newsmen suggest that they are often writing for their editors as the main audience rather than for the reading public. Certainly more than a small amount of irrational activity occurs in corporations because of the *supposed* prejudices and preferences of the president, the directors, and the department heads.

Beyond these obvious distortions there are the distortions which come from the limited range of imagination of executives in thinking about other people. This type of problem is magnified in departments which have a major responsibility for relations with people, such as in advertising and public relations. While market and audience research have some effect in correcting the image that executives hold, a large proportion of decisions in these fields is based on a process of forced empathy in which the decision maker tries to put himself in the shoes of "the average man." This average man is an imaginary interlocutor to whom the decision maker, in his mind, submits the new policy or text for a reaction. Many writers and other creative persons have a clear image of their imaginary interlocutor. It may be a friend or neighbor who has somehow come to represent the average, or it may be a critic he admires or fears. Others have no clear image, but a vague and varying one. Whoever this imaginary interlocutor is, he has been shown to have a profound impact on the thinking of the writer or other decision maker.[18]

While advertising and public relations provide the clearest illustration of the impact of the imaginary audience on policy action, the process is taking place in all fields. Every executive conducts a large part of his deliberations in imaginary conversations. With whom he holds these imaginary conversations in large part determines the pressures he feels upon him. The people he thinks of are the people who matter to him. They are his major reference groups. They are the "real" people in his own world of fantasy, and the rest slip into an indistinguishable blur. The important reference persons may be people he likes or people he fears; they may be people he knows or people he only imagines; they may be truly relevant people, such as customers, or they may be the people with whom he grew up. But people who are not thought of, not visualized, do not influence decisions.

It is important to know who the imaginary audiences of corporate decision makers are, but they are not generally known. However, one can speculate about the matter. The social milieu of top management is generally top management. In so far as top management as a whole is one of the most important audiences for any single corporation, this is all to the good. There is probably a highly sensitive perception by top managers of the reactions which the leadership of the business community will have to their actions. But this sensitivity is not matched by their perceptions of other audiences. Executive perceptions of such important audiences as scientists, professionals, government policy makers, journalists, writers, labor leaders, labor, consumers, and stockholders are sufficiently second-hand and inaccurate as to require systematic correction by research. Indeed, it is often necessary to remind executive management of the very existence and importance of some of these audiences. The population of images in the world of the executive's head is far from identical with the population of the world in which his corporation functions.

In short, the salient audiences of an executive may be:

(1) the power figures over him;

(2) his immediate colleagues and office entourage;

(3) the people for whom he is functionally responsible (e.g., customers for a sales executive, labor for a personnel man, etc.);

(4) his personal associates (e.g., the kind of persons with whom he plays golf, has lunch, and has intimate discussions, and to whom he goes to for personal advice);

(5) persons he fears and/or respects from conflict experiences in life (e.g., competitors, an older brother, the law).

EXECUTIVE ASSESSMENT OF MOTIVES

The motives which the American corporation executive assumes to be operative are perhaps not far from the full range of
which the corporation must be aware. In short, distortions of
policy arising from the policy maker's limited perceptions of
motives may be less severe than some other distortions. True,
there is a tradition of the hard-boiled businessman who projects
his own guilt with the assertion that everyone is out for himself.
This image of the businessman has some residual support from
the ideology of classical economics. The fact is, however, that
American business practice reflects a far more sophisticated awareness of motives than that with which it is usually credited. The
corporation does not neglect the appeals of institutional loyalty,
prestige, good fellowship, creativity, unconscious instinctual grati-
fications, and fear—along with the profit motive. The development of services to the corporate family and the development of
the arts of advertising and human relations give ample evidence.
It is a poor executive who is not aware of all sorts of devices to
tap such human emotions as loyalty and pride as means for solving
a problem.

If, in fact, the executive's operational code overstresses the
significance of certain possible motives and understresses others,
it is perhaps in the direction of overstressing the external recognition motives and understressing the internalized motivations towards creative action. This notion to some extent reaffirms the
familiar Riesman thesis about the other-directedness of our society as against inner-directedness.

The modern corporate entity is a stable, continuing institution, in which many persons may serve for their entire career.
That kind of life-long involvement exists in a small noncorpo-
rate enterprise only for the entrepreneur himself or else it is con-
founded with personal loyalty by and to the faithful retainer.
The employee of the corporation, on the other hand, may see in
the company a complex milieu providing all the facilities for the
working out of his entire career. For this reason it is essential,
in the long term, for the corporation to give full scope to the
human need for a sense of creativity, a sense of purpose, and a

sense of usefulness. To the extent that the executive's operational code fails to be sensitive to these needs, it simultaneously undermines morale and destroys valuable resources of creativity which the corporation requires.

Just as evidence of audience sensitivity may be seen in the advertising and public relations departments, so the conflict between the typical and easily recognized business motivations and creative motivations that may be concurrently present may be found in research laboratories.[19] But the conflict between the motivational system of the executive and the scientist is but an exaggerated form of a problem which pervades the whole corporate structure. It may be summarized as the projection by the administrator of his own motivational patterns onto the creation-oriented persons within the organization.

EXECUTIVE PERCEPTIONS OF THE INSTRUMENTS OF POLICY

Almost all the things mentioned so far about perceptions of motivations may be said also about perceptions of the usefulness of different instrumentalities. Here, too, the executive freely considers a wide range of possible instrumentalities ranging from legislation to pricing policy. Here, too, he is apt to be confined by an administrative penchant for stressing stability and experience and to hesitate about trying more daring ideas. These penchants may indeed serve him well. They may protect the basic orientation of the corporate entity toward stability and persistence. It is worth noting that responsible corporations in recent years have acquired an increasingly long list of taboos on what methods they, as particularly powerful entities, can use. No modern corporation could expect to survive if its executives had the operational codes of the robber barons of a former day.[20]

THE EXECUTIVE'S VIEW OF HIS ROLE

The final, all-important question is how, in his mind's eye, the executive sees himself. What is his job? Who is "we"? Whom is he serving? Whose gain is he trying to maximize? Of course, he is there to earn money for the stockholders, but the corporate community which he is serving is much wider than that. And even in the area of serving the stockholders there is room for much difference in interpretation of the manager's role.

For example, the officers of one American corporation which is largely British-owned took a protectionist stand on certain legislation which, if passed, would have increased their profits and dividends. In so doing they were acting on behalf of their stockholders viewed solely as a set of pieces of paper, namely as stock certificates. On the other hand, the British owners, if viewed as live men, might have been better off accepting slightly lower dividends and thus maintaining the unbroken structure of a low tariff policy in the United States, with all that may signify for the state of the British economy.[21] How broadly is the American corporation president justified in considering such matters? How far has he a right to sacrifice the interests of the American minority stockholders to the broader interests of the majority stockholders? Should he serve the interests of the stockholders only in the fictitious legalistic sense that he is trying to maximize a certain figure on the company books?

The question of who is "we" brings us also to the great issues of social responsibility and national interest. At some point every corporation subordinates its narrower interests to serve these broader ones. The sensing of the proper point is part of the operational code.

The executive's image of himself and his role also determines what he thinks his job is and thus determines what he makes it. The definition of the job is in part an outcome of the shortage of time. There is never enough time to do everything a job calls for. As previously noted, while this makes the executive feel unfree, it actually frees him to define his own job by forcing him to choose what he will do. The head of one firm does public relations and simply has no time personally to consider the technical aspects of research and development. Another does the latter and has no time for the former or for the supervision of current production. Another sees such inspection and control as a major part of his job and neglects other aspects.

The public-relations-conscious executive shudders when his

corporation is attacked and feels that he is experiencing the pressure to behave. Another executive will say, as Vanderbilt is reported to have exclaimed, "The public be damned." The latter view has greatly diminished in the last half century, while the critics have been growing in influence. In the future, it is more likely that to damn the critics out of hand will have the effect of casting aspersion on the public, a practice that will be avoided increasingly.

But sensitivity to pressures which are actually there, while varying between executives, is a far less important matter than variations in the pressures which an executive produces. The man who goes to industry meetings, gives speeches, and does public relations work draws into his orbit persons concerned with broad external issues and brings their demands upon himself. He gets to know public officials and active citizens. He creates opportunities for himself and his firm to gain public recognition and stature through civic affairs. When opportunities are offered in the form of requests to assume such responsibilities, he cannot well evade acceptance. He sees these as pressures of the job, but does not see that he has created and selected them.

So it is with the executive who chooses to concern himself with his research laboratory. By that nurture he will draw into the laboratory energetic, creative, ambitious men and will energize those already there. By thus drawing innovators to him he will soon find himself under pressure for development, innovation, and expansion. He will see his job as trying to keep his firm abreast of burgeoning technology and will feel that it is the external reality of modern science which makes the great challenge in his job.

So, too, the man oriented to advertising or sales builds up a sales organization which is constantly demanding that he move into this market or that, that he undertake some big promotion.

To build a dynamic organization a man must invent issues, goals, or causes in the name of which he can energize people. He must make himself a spokesman for them and make them seem important to others. Thus, to do his job well, a man must stimulate followers in ways which, in turn, generate pressure on himself.

As he does so, he both builds his job and defines it. He creates symbols to justify his own and his followers' perspectives and activities. A policy is such a symbol. The corporation or large organization stands for certain policies, and each component of the organization stands for policies that flow out of the over-all policy. Primary importance may be assigned to obeying the law by one, to saving money by another, to increased production by a third. These are all worthy goals, and executive management has to decide how much of each to do and when. It has to define the company's emphasis. In so doing, in deciding what things to do most of, and thereby selecting the pressures which will impinge upon him, the executive is expressing his own operational code. In his mind's eye he sees it as the demands of the world upon him, but in fact his own unanalyzed—and often irrational—penchants determine what he sees of what the world offers, and how he thinks such things may be coped with. That is why it is essential to understand the executive's operational code if one wants to understand how he will play the business game.

We have considered thus far two major aspects of corporate policy as a decision process: first, the extent to which rationality may be maximized in this decision process, using game theory as an idealized model; and, second, the deforming aspects of reality, especially in executives' operational codes, as these affect corporate policy making.

Game theory helps to illumine the role of rationality in corporate decision making. Two points need to be stressed.

Game theory, it will be recalled, assumed perfect knowledge of the available strategies and their outcomes but complete ignorance about which would actually be chosen. No player or manager ever knows all the alternative strategies available nor all of the outcomes. On the other hand, knowledge of the plans and characters of our opponents often enables us to guess what they will do. Thus various methods are used for gaining intelligence. This either brings us closer to the knowledge which the game model assumes that we have initially or permits us to "cheat" by giving us knowledge which, in its framework, we should not have. Intelligence and research operations of all sorts being useful to the players and, their knowledge being variable, their behavior can be understood and predicted by the scientist only if one adds to a game analysis some sort of analysis of the information flows reaching them.

Little research exists on information flows.[22] There is, however, unpublished research by Alexander Bavelas on the amounts of information which persons can use, in which he shows that full information may often slow down problem solving since persons can only cope with a limited amount of information. All of this suggests a large and unexplored group of factors which operate in the real business situation in a way considerably at variance with the game model. This suggests that the executive's knowledge or ignorance may deform rationality in decision making and indicates that corporate action in reality is quite different from an idealized model of corporate policy formulation. Among the examples cited earlier was avoidance by businessmen of fields of endeavor which would require expenditure of scarce time to gain a full understanding of them.

Game theory, in assuming rational behavior, is useful as a model in reaching or maximizing some goal-value. In real life, time does not permit this, and irrational penchants embodied in a man's operational code impel him to one strategy or another. Some businessmen, for example, will have nothing to do with government even when it is demonstrably important to their business for them to do so. Others with chips on their shoulders are aggressive when the soft word would help. The enjoyment of the contest, satisfaction with what they have, the hope for the big killing, all affect strategy choices by way of the value system of the individual. That is why intelligence operations, as previously noted, are important, for the strategies a given player will use are highly predictable. Intelligence operations consist in part of determining who is making the key decisions, what kinds of decisions he has made in similar situations in the past and, from that, guessing what he is likely to do regardless of what is rational.

As to certain deforming aspects of reality, as revealed in the analysis of operational codes, an attempt has been made to distinguish several different aspects of these partly objective, partly subjective views of the world in the executive's mind's eye: the imaginary audiences of the decision maker, his assessment of motives, his perceptions of the instruments of policy, and his view of his own role as a corporate decision maker. His goal-values as a person and as a representative of his company are a part of his operational code. The objectives of the enterprise, as seen and acted upon by him, may be not at all the same as the hypothesized goals of an abstract firm conceived by an economist or the "corporation" as conceived by the lawyer. We have already seen that the range of goal-values, as operative factors in actual policy formation, is far wider than one might assume on the basis of some current concepts of the corporation. The complexity of influences exerted upon the policy maker's mind, as we have tried to indicate, makes it even more obvious that a philosophy of corporate enterprise, realistically constructed, may have to be far more eclectic than was formerly supposed.

The policy *process* is infinitely complex. The instability, the unpredictability, and the intricacy of human affairs, might perhaps be measurably reduced if men in every important decision center —business, government, labor, churches, universities, professional societies—better understood how to introduce into their policies a higher degree of rationality and reality. Corporate executives are probably no less and no more rational and reality-oriented than leaders in other large organizations. But whether the decisions are rational, irrational, or a mysterious combination of both, they are not without effect. It is difficult to foresee the long-range consequences of the acts of men. The corporate policy maker is hardly an exception to the rule.

One might ask whether or not a relatively high degree of rationality and reality-orientation in the modern corporation would substantially affect its role in society: Would it become a more powerful force, a more "constructive" element in the total social structure, or perhaps a disturber of "social balance"? It might be hypothesized that optimum rationality and reality-orientation in all important decision centers is a prerequisite to human mastery of the problems of social disorder, as well as the beginning of accord on the goal-values of society. Thus, men might communicate more easily and thereby diminish the anomie that besets so many societies. Yet there are dangers, too. For the diminution of the deforming aspects of reality in decision makers' minds, together with highly rational processes in reaching decisions, could vastly increase the manipulative potentialities of leaders everywhere. These are, to be sure, speculative issues that are probably academic, in view of the paucity of available evidence concerning the corporate decision process in actual practice.

If corporate policy were simply and exclusively entrepreneurial policy, the maximization of rationality in the process would be measurably less difficult; but the objectives of the large so-called corporate enterprise are, in fact, multiple. And because there is a large organization to steer, the decision process necessarily involves a multiplicity of considerations and interests that have somehow to be brought into unity of action. This complicates the decision process. A comprehensible "theory of the firm" has to take into account the various steps in this process and the instruments of policy available to corporate decision makers.

CHAPTER VIII

Policy Steps and Policy Instruments

A BRIEF REVIEW of the preceding chapters is in order before we proceed on to a further examination of corporate policy as a process.

An observer of the modern corporation, seeking comprehension of so complex a phenomenon, has to cast off certain intellectual blinders inherited from the past. Restrictive concepts of the corporation drawn from economic and legal theory tend to conceal many things that are relevant to the whole picture.

The large corporate enterprise, as we have seen, is a multifunctional institution and its goals embrace more than entrepreneurial aims. In resolving the great issues of corporate policy, managers cannot assume the role merely of the classically conceived owner-entrepreneur maximizing profits in a coldly rational way in a market of the economists' model. They have many roles and many responsibilities; and their own perspectives of these roles and responsibilities are influenced by nonrational as well as rational factors in the entire situation of which they are a part. These operational codes are far more the determinants of the actual functions of the modern corporation than are the preconceived managerial motivations drawn from simplified models [1] of either economic or juristic theory. And when the decision process in corporations is examined in terms of game theory, it is obvious that there are many influences that impair or deform the neat model of complete rationality so frequently assumed to be the pattern of corporate policy formulation.

The ideal method of policy making, whether in poker, war, or business, is to maximize rationality and to minimize the deforming influence of irrational processes. As the game theorists have shown, however, strategy is a matter of probabilities and not of complete certainty. And the effort to achieve complete reality-orientation on the part of the decision maker can only be partially, and never wholly, successful. Corporate policy processes, from these points of view, become more understandable, and the corporation as an institution more comprehensible.

Additional light is thrown upon the institutional aspects of the modern corporation when careful consideration is given both to the various stages through which policy making proceeds and to the diverse instruments available to those who are responsible for carrying out the policies they adopt.

STAGES IN THE DECISION PROCESS

Corporate policy, viewed as a continuous process, is a succession of stages in decision making. At each stage in the process a special function is performed as a necessary element of the process as a whole. For purposes of exploring the decision process in the large industrial corporation some recent functional analyses [2] may be used as a point of departure. In this way one may distinguish seven different functions or stages in the process: intelligence, recommendation, prescription, invocation, application, appraisal, and termination. Our task here is to consider each of these stages in turn.

Intelligence — M B H , Ph D   Business

Intelligence is the functional stage in corporate policy in which information is gathered and processed, predictions are made, and planning is done.

In theory, before any corporate policy can be formulated, a minimum of factual information has to be gathered, analyzed, and the results synthesized as a basis for setting up alternative plans of action. The choice of one plan as against another, if made with maximum rationality, would involve the fullest use of all available data and analyses. Perfection, as in all things, is unattainable here as well, for reasons that have been mentioned: the pressure of time, the "multitude of things" that refuse to be reduced to usable premises despite our best efforts, the operational codes that limit our perspectives. There are, however, degrees of imperfection, and it is pertinent to ask what attention modern corporations give to this stage of the decision process. It is useful to take an example drawn from a particular policy area to illustrate the possible role of intelligence, as a data-generating tool, in helping to guide decision making.

With respect to a policy on the disposal of a company's net income, for example, there are a number of questions that one might ask about the intelligence function. What are the pertinent types of data? From what sources are they sought? To what persons and components of the company are the data routed? What is done with the data when they are received? Who analyzes them and how, and with what questions in mind? To whom are the results sent? Do they want the information they get, or are they unconcerned; that is, is their decision (chosen plan of action) unaffected by information supplied by their operational codes? Does their appraisal of the success or failure of a previous policy on the subject determine whether attention is focused upon certain kinds of information while other kinds are dismissed as irrelevant?

Most critical in determining which data are to be gathered is the question of the scope of information needed by the board of directors as a basis for formulating policy for the assignment of the net profits.

The disposition of profits may constitute, after the making of profits, the most important financial policy during the year-to-year operation of a company. "Provided the accounting methods are sound," writes Dewing, "and all the adjustments have been made, and provided the dividend disbursements do not infringe on the stated capital, the entire net profits of the business, after the payments of corporate taxes, may be appropriated as the directors see fit." [3] Except for certain limitations imposed by state statutes, and barring fraud, it is up to the directors as representatives of the stockholders to "determine what amounts, if any, of the surplus earnings after all charges shall be distributed to the stock-holders as dividends." And this is not a question "of the theory of accounts nor of business law nor even of universally applicable financial principles . . . it is purely one of individual business expediency," for directors, he maintains, are not *required* to de-clare a dividend merely because it is legally permissible. Henry Ford was once forced by other stockholders to declare a dividend, however, and similar successful stockholder efforts might be cited. Yet it is certainly true that directors generally enjoy wide discre-tion in this area. One alternative before the directors is to vote to retain earnings for the purpose of maintaining an adequate ratio of current capital. They might thus reduce appropriations for dividends accordingly. In making such decisions they "must be fully conscious of the great fluctuations in general economic activity . . . they must have insight into the multifarious ways these fluctuations affect their particular enterprise . . . otherwise they court disaster."

But this is not all. Dividend action, Dewing continues, must not be based upon misrepresentation, as by overstatement of earnings in order to present an accounting justification for the payment of unearned dividends. Understatement of earnings, on the other hand, may err on the side of "overmaintenance," he says, leaving a margin of profit too low for payment of earned dividends. If the board, in its dividend action, is to preserve a balance between overmaintenance and undermaintenance of the corporate property—a policy which he thinks the great majority of stockholders prefer—directors must determine that the statements of earnings will "express as accurately as accounting procedure permits the true condition of the company—neither better nor worse. . . . They want the cow properly fed and housed, but they also want all of her milk."

Not all stockholders, however, want the milk to flow. Those in the ninety-percent tax bracket may never want to see a dividend at all. They may prefer to take their profit in capital gain. When ninety percent of the milk goes to the government, the better alternative may be to make the cow much fatter and take no milk. Here there is obviously conflict of interest among the stockholders themselves.

What kind of information does a board of directors need in order to keep the milk flowing to investors while they make certain that the cow maintains her full productivity? Or, alternatively, to fatten her?

To the layman, it may appear that this is an area in which the intelligence function within the corporation operates with a high degree of precision. Accounting is a fairly rigorous discipline; [4] financial specialists can supply the board with accurate figures; net earnings can be computed to the last cent after production costs have been deducted from gross, and sufficient reserves have been set aside for depreciation, obsolescence, and contingencies. The fact that in this area of corporate intelligence one works with quantified data under legal standards that minimize the opportunity for fraud, may mislead the outsider to the conclusion that here, at least, rationality in the decision process can be maximized. The conclusion would be illusory.

That net earnings can be computed with precision after "sufficient reserves" have been set aside is a proposition that raises many issues about calculating reserves. Directors can go all over the lot in their judgment on reserves; the precision presented by the figures in many balance sheets is more apparent than real. So many intangibles and judgment factors enter into the determination of reserves that they can be hotly debated in most cases, and are in many. Also there are many techniques that have been developed for distorting earnings. A sales promotion in November, for example, can actually bring the succeeding year's sales into this year and make this year look much better; and this is likely to be done where a management wants to show a good record for a particular year. Management has not thereby improved its performance; it has merely sold something a few months earlier to make the annual report look good.

How, furthermore, does one maintain a "proper balance" between dividend disbursements, on the one hand, and the amount of yearly earnings that should be set aside and reinvested in the business, on the other? Economists have observed that directors must take into consideration a number of important factors. They must have a sense of confidence in the accounting methods by which the net earnings are computed. They must look closely at the methods by which figures for reserves were calculated. The part of net earnings to be set aside for reinvestment in the business must be properly balanced as between plant investment and current capital. They need to weigh the strength of the feeling that a dividend rate once commenced should be adhered to—a policy which requires that reserves be set aside in years of affluence to be used to pay dividends during the years of deficient earnings. All these are considerations that require the judgment type of decision rather than straight financial analysis from undisputed and clear premises to obvious conclusions.

The question of contingencies arises. For example, how can one predict economic events with precision so as to be certain of the amount to be set aside for reserve under this heading? As to reinvestment of earnings, directors face several responsibilities: one, to the corporation to insure its permanent welfare; another, to stockholders to invest their money properly or to return it to them; still another, "to society," as Dewing puts it, "to conserve and to employ, with farsighted wisdom, the slow accumulations of social capital." The guideposts for board decision on such matters are not facts and figures but qualitative norms. These cannot be derived from financial reports and production figures alone. They rest as well upon inflow of information from widespread social, political, and economic sources; and in part upon the values held by the directors themselves.

As to the regularity of dividend payments, here again there arises a basic issue that requires judgment that is grounded upon wide knowledge of comparative earnings in different kinds of industries, perceptions of business trends generally, and value considerations concerning the relationship between the company and its stockholders.

Dewing's observations on the intelligence function (not so called by him) in arriving at such decisions are pertinent.

Accounting methods are efforts to state precisely—or rather with that degree of precision according to which figures may express economic values—a set of varying, and in many cases intangible, economic values. So long as these estimates serve only as checks to actual conditions, errors in them are not vital. But should they mislead the judgment in distributing as net profits what was, in truth, capital, the misinterpretation becomes more serious. To prevent such an overestimation of earnings . . . allowances should be set aside for various unpredictable contingencies. But the majority of corporation officials do not insist on any such sophisticated precision. They prefer merely to keep some of the earnings in the business, so that if "something comes up" the corporation shall have an unappropriated reserve to fall back upon.[5]

As to reinvestment of earnings, however, he thinks that directors are apt to err in balancing their respective responsibilities to the corporation, to the stockholders and to society.

A director likes to participate in the growth of his corporation. He easily encourages in himself the belief that the surplus earnings of his business can be invested wisely in the business in order to carry out a policy of expansion; he convinces himself that, in forcing the stockholders to dedicate the surplus earnings to a policy of expansion of which they are only dimly conscious, he is acting for their best interests. Directors easily assume that they can invest the stockholders' money better than the stockholders themselves can. For this assumption they have no evidence . . . . Rather than to force the stockholders to invest their money in an expanding business by withholding earnings, it is more fair, more honest, for the directors to distribute the surplus earnings, not needed in the business, and then to appeal to the stockholders for the new capital required to carry out a policy of expansion.[6]

Whether or not one concurs with Dewing, the passages above serve to illustrate the main point: corporate intelligence involves a high degree of judgment in addition to the collection of "hard information." The predictions, the assessments of trends, the inclusion and exclusion of data that are thought relevant to the problem in hand and the values held by directors when they approach the problem and select the relevant data—all these enter into the picture. Many of the determinants upon which directors base decisions are imbedded in "insight" and "experience." Moreover, the values they hold—with reference, for example, to such points as maintaining adequate reserves as against letting the stockholders decide for themselves what they want to do with their earnings—are a part of their operational codes, the premises of which rarely are made explicit either to themselves or to others.

However, spectacular events in the corporate environment sometimes have the effect of bringing these unspoken premises to the surface for review and public examination. War and depression have the effect of fixing public attention upon overexpansion of fixed assets and underinvestment or overinvestment in certain industries. Crises in politics and economics increase the need for inflow of intelligence to corporate decision makers in every kind of work—financial, legal, public relations, manufacturing, research, and engineering. In such circumstances, the interrelations between governmental and corporate intelligence become more intimate and expose unsolved problems that may have been less acute in normal times.

Government secrecy and security regulations, for example, raise issues of open and closed sources of vital data without which the business cannot be carried on or expanded by rational planning. Moreover, pressing demands upon industry to contribute in the public interest to the strength (military and economic) of the nation and even of the whole free world, force upon policy makers increased attention to global trends as distinguished from domestic economic fluctuations and the status of particular industries.

In the end, the effect of these crucial policy demands is to bring about a reassessment by corporate managements of the adequacy of their intelligence operations. Research becomes an inseparable subfunction of every functional kind of work. The education and training of personnel gets greater emphasis, particularly at the managerial level. "Horse sense" proves to be insufficient. Executives find they need, above and beyond specialized training for the functional work, a broad background of knowledge about the world they live in. They discover they must become planners of corporate strategy and tactics in an economic, political, and social situation that is dynamic.

Recommendation

Recommendation is the functional stage in the corporate decision process in which policy alternatives are set up preparatory to the prescriptive stage, when general principles of action are laid down. Recommendation is thus a kind of decision making in itself that depends upon intelligence but precedes "final" action on the proposals drawn from intelligence. How are recommendation functions carried out in some typical areas of corporate policy?

Decision on a policy of earnings distribution rests with the board of directors. But the formulation of policy alternatives for the board's consideration is largely a job for professional managers at top levels. The board will expect, for example, that before it sits down to arrive at a formula for the distribution of net earnings, professional managers will have worked out in detail a recommended plan. Ideally, a board may rightly expect the executive officers of the corporation to have worked out policy alternatives together with calculations of the probable consequences of each alternative. All of the considerations previously mentioned will have to be taken into account by management in setting up these alternatives. In addition, they must be prepared to defend the budgets for production costs, since these costs will affect the amount of net earnings. Here, the cost of labor could well be one of the dominant items. Since this cost is the result, in large part, of union negotiations, it becomes involved with the entire question of union relations. Against such considerations will be balanced the relative importance of research and development, and other major matters upon which the board may express divergent views.

Policy alternatives as to labor costs may require thorough review of strategies proposed by management and others for dealing with unions at collective bargaining periods. The proposal made in January, 1958, for example, by Walter Reuther as head of the United Auto Workers union, presented fundamental issues for the auto makers that reached much farther than wage adjustments. Reuther proposed that through collective bargaining, earnings of the auto companies should be split among stockholders, employees, and car buyers. Here the Big Three were not faced by a simple demand for a wage boost. They regarded the proposed method as a radical threat to the free enterprise system and to the balanced interests corporations seek to serve. Because the Reuther letter opened up a number of key questions about corporate policy alternatives, both sides of the issue will be examined in some detail.

In an open letter to the auto companies, Reuther referred to the growing problem of inflation and the need for full acceptance by both labor and management of their social and moral responsibilities toward the public as a whole in setting wages and prices. The UAW recognized, he said, that management was obligated to obtain a reasonable return on its stockholders' investments, just as the union had an obligation to obtain for its members a fair share of the fruits of their labor. But, he went on, "neither stockholders nor workers . . . have a right to insist on levels of income obtained through inflationary prices that deny to other citizens their full and proper equity in the national product." Specifically, he expressed his union's concern over the plight of the millions of Americans without the protection of cost-of-living escalator clauses to shield them from the ravages of a rising price level, and especially of the people with fixed incomes who were the greatest sufferers from inflation.

He reminded the automobile companies of President Eisenhower's plea for private restraint in setting prices and wages and stated his union's acceptance of the validity of the principle underlying this plea. Although he discredited any contentions that past automobile price increases could legitimately be blamed on labor, he supported the idea that particular economic interests must be subordinated to the general social good and that "free management and free labor cannot for long remain free if they abuse their power."

The UAW, Reuther continued, was therefore prepared to enter into a cooperative effort with the automobile companies in an attempt to stop and reverse the inflationary trend. Specifically, he proposed that the automobile companies reduce prices on 1958 models to levels averaging at least $100 below the prices for comparable 1957 models. If they agreed to this, Reuther promised that "full consideration" would be given to the effect the price cut had on the companies' financial positions when the union's 1958 contract demands were being drafted, and during the contract negotiations.

Reuther's further comment indicated, however, that he was assuming that such a price cut would not put the companies in a financial position that would make his currently planned contract demands unreasonable. He reasoned that the price cut would increase sales of automobiles by about a million units a year for the industry. After such an increase in sales, he argued, the companies would still be receiving a return on their investments that would be well above the 12.1 percent average for all manufacturing industries.

Nevertheless, Reuther agreed that if the companies could prove, to the satisfaction of an impartial review panel, that their resultant financial position could not support the granting of UAW's contract demands without a price increase, the union would lower its demands accordingly. "In other words," he said, "we are not asking you to take any risk that we are not prepared to share."

Finally, he argued, the union's proposal for "supplementary economic demands" was "based upon the earning position of each company or corporation using the plans, in effect in General Motors and the Ford Motor Company, under which corporation executives share the profits of the company, as the basis for computing the equity which workers and consumers should share." The "workers and consumers" had been "short-changed" while the "fantastic profits" of "many of America's giant corporations have been shared in by the high-paid executives." He proposed that after "basic wage costs" and "basic salary costs" had been met, and after setting aside "basic dividends" for stockholders, the "excess profits" should be shared as follows: one-half to the stockholders and executives; one-fourth to wage and salary workers; and one-fourth to consumers through a year-end rebate.

To the automobile manufacturers the Reuther proposal was an outrageous "publicity-maneuvering" attempt to shift the blame for the inflationary spiral from unions, where they insisted it properly belonged, to management. It was evident, however, that they had been sharply stung by the effectiveness of the maneuver. They recognized that Reuther's suggestion had a great deal of popular appeal. It created the impression that Reuther, by offering to forego wage increases for his members if the automobile companies would forego some of their profits by reducing prices, was demonstrating the kind of public-spirited statesmanship that President Eisenhower had appealed for. A closer examination shows that his offer was not quite such a *quid pro quo* arrangement. The manufacturers were quick to point out, in fact, that it was "all *quid* and no *quo*." Nevertheless, the automobile companies were as sensitive as Reuther had been about the danger of being labeled as culprit in the "whodunit" debate over inflation. The President's repeated appeals to both business and labor to exercise restraint, the wide public attention then being given to Senator Estes Kefauver's investigations of "administered pricing" in large industry, and the fact that the three automobile companies involved had already made plans to raise 1958 car prices—all contributed significantly to this sensitivity.

It was obvious that acceptance of the Reuther proposal would have given the automobile manufacturers little in return other than Reuther's promise to "consider the companies' positions" after they had cut their prices. Even to secure such "consideration" the companies would have had to open their books to the suggested impartial review panel which would then decide whether the companies could grant the UAW's demands and still make a "reasonable" rate of return on their investments. In facing this prospect the companies were well aware that Reuther had been attempting for years to obtain detailed cost data from them in order to "prove" that their profits were excessive.

The three automobile companies all replied to Reuther within the week. General Motors replied first. This led Reuther to charge that GM had "in effect dictated the policy, as it has in every such major policy decision for the last twenty years." Chrysler's answer was forthcoming the following day, and Ford responded two days later. Although their letters varied somewhat in severity of tone, the points made for the most part were identical.

Points made in common by all three companies through open letters in the press included a number of important economic and policy issues.

(1) Inflation is a grave national problem from which everyone ultimately suffers.

(2) Costs for materials in auto manufacture have increased greatly in recent years chiefly as a result of increased labor costs in the companies supplying these materials.

(3) Increases in wages and benefits must be based upon in-

creased productivity. This has not been the case in American industry generally and in the automobile business specifically, and this is the principal source of inflation.

(4) All three companies called attention to the paradox represented by Reuther's professed public-spirited concern over inflation and his announced intention to obtain the "largest package we've ever demanded in the 1958 contract negotiations."

(5) Each of the companies maintained that it had already exhibited considerable restraint in holding prices as low as it had in the face of skyrocketing costs. General Motors called attention to the period following the Second World War when the shortage of automobiles and the enormous demand for them would have permitted prices "several hundred dollars" higher than those actually set by the manufacturers. "We kept our list prices at the lower levels," said General Motors president Harlow H. Curtice, "rather than take advantage of an abnormal market situation." Ford and Chrysler both offered statistics to illustrate the degree to which wage increases had far outpaced increases in the price of automobiles.

(6) All three companies emphasized their intention to keep price policy out of the area of union negotiation.

(7) All of the replies pointed out the one-sidedness of Reuther's proposal for a "cooperative effort." Both the Ford and Chrysler replies employed a "turnabout" analogy to illustrate their reaction to the proposal. As Henry Ford put it, "Suppose I were to say to you: 'If you will accept an immediate reduction in wages to the levels prevailing at the introduction of our 1957 models, we will take this into consideration in determining how much we will increase prices of our 1958 models.' " Curtice of General Motors suggested as a counter-proposal that the UAW announce its intention to extend the current agreement with General Motors for a period of two years beyond its expiration date of May 29, 1958. This, he argued, would continue to give workers the protection of the cost-of-living allowance, continue to provide an Annual Improvement Factor wage increase, and make "a real contribution to economic stability in our country."

(8) The union proposed, according to Harlow H. Curtice, speaking for General Motors, to "bargain not only for employees

they represent but also for salaried employees, shareholders, and customers over the distribution of earnings of the business." According to Ernest R. Breech, board chairman of the Ford Motor Company, it was a "kill-the-profits plan" that "strikes at the very roots of the economic system that has made and kept American strong—and is a plan under which Mr. Reuther demands the power not only to bargain for his union's members but also to negotiate dividends for stockholders, compensation for management, and prices for customers." To L. L. Colbert, president of the Chrysler Corporation, it appeared that Mr. Reuther was insisting "that part of a management's job" was to be "turned over to him, so that he can increase still further the already dangerous degree of monopoly power he possesses." [7]

Aside from the many implications of this episode for the internal structure of the corporate policy, involving as it does "radical" revision of the methods of balancing interests, it raises hard questions about the meaning of loaded terms like "excess profits." Calculations of the size of profits to be divided depends upon many debatable factors. Do you start off with profits before taxes? Or are the "basic dividends" computed only after the taxes have been paid? What is an appropriate figure for return on the investment of the corporation? Is it ten percent, as Reuther stated it on a nation-wide television program? And does he refer to net after taxes, reserves, and reinvestment of a part of the earnings?

Clearly, here is a case in which recommendation, as a stage in the decision process, occurs in a wide social area. The policy alternatives take their root not only within the ranks of professional managers alone but in far wider circles. The publication of his demands at an early stage in the bargaining proceedings indicated that Reuther hoped to mobilize large sectors of public opinion behind his proposal. Coming as it did at a time when there was concern about a recession, he was able to link his proposal with argument that it would stimulate purchasing power and thus set the wheels of industry in motion on a higher level.

The counterargument was that the proposal, joined with specific demands for higher wages, welfare, pension, and unemployment benefits, would push employment costs up far faster than any foreseeable rise in productivity could support without more inflation. A writer for the New York *Times* declared that despite "such obvious objections" to the proposal, "the Big Three's complaint that it represents a 'radical' threat to the free enterprise system has a weary sound inconsistent with the auto industry's own record of inventiveness and imagination in labor relations." [8] And although many commentators saw in the Reuther plan an attempt to carry out "a major invasion of the sphere of corporate management," with results that might cripple company expansion and undermine managerial responsibility, it was clear enough that the whole issue had been brought into the public domain.

Policy alternatives in such a situation are not formulated entirely *in camera*. Professional managers and board directors cannot resolve the issues on the basis of internal intelligence and internal operational codes alone. They have to assume a quasi-legislative function. They hold no public hearings; but they must have their ears to the ground. Certain policy considerations are thrust upon them. The alternatives of policy that they formulate will be profoundly affected by their assessments not only of union demands but of the prevailing pressures of opinion in many sectors: financial, customer, stockholder, and government.

At this recommendation stage of the decision process, then, one has to take note of the fact that there are many changes and events in the political arena that can affect policy making in the large corporation.

Prescription, Invocation and Application

Turning now to the stages of prescription (the authoritative adoption of general rules governing policy), of invocation (spelling out provisionally who is to do what in accordance with these general rules) and application (implementing the policy in specific cases through designated components of the company organization), brief mention can be made of the kinds of issues that arise at each stage.

Who prescribes the general rules which spell out the content of high policy in the corporation? On whom are these general rules binding, both within and without the organization? Are there superior rules that bind the organization itself and narrow the limits of its decision authority? What is the source of these external rules—are they entirely governmental, or do they arise in other quarters? Are there discernible changes, with time, of the locus of the prescriptive authority? These questions are unanswerable in general terms. The answers will vary from company to company and will frequently depend upon the internal polity of the individual corporation.[9]

Legally, the board prescribes general rules and sets general policy within the corporation. Yet the prescribing function at the board level is usually carried out only in broad terms and with respect only to certain kinds of issues. Much is left to professional managers; and the shift away from board to managerial "control" is constantly referred to in contemporary comment on corporate organization. The generalization is misleading. Boards still give careful attention to what some might regard as matters of detail in running the business. A proper assessment of the emergent role of the corporation in society generally will require one to find out what typically comes to the focus of a board's attention and why.

The invocation of the general rules and broad policies adopted by the board is usually the function of management at the executive level. One can distinguish invocation of rules from their application. Decisions have to be made at both stages, but they are different kinds of decisions. One invokes a rule of policy when he characterizes in a preliminary way certain patterns of conduct as falling in or outside of the four walls of the policy. He applies the rule when he makes the final determination that a person or group of persons shall or shall not follow the rule.

It is one thing for the president of a corporation to hand down a policy that budgeted costs must be cut by fifteen percent throughout the company; it is another for the manager of a particular component to specify the ways in which costs will be reduced; and still another, to make the actual cuts in specific instances. Different decision processes are involved at every level. Little is known, in fact, about the norms that people use in applying policy in the specific event, although it is generally assumed—probably incorrectly—that the norms used are those laid down in policy as originally issued. But men interpret words differently, and policies are notoriously vague. The operational codes that govern the top policy maker may not be at all the same as the operational codes of those who do the invoking and the applying. They have not the same grasp of the background of fact that moved the policy maker to act in the first place; and even if they do, they may interpret it in a different way. Budget cuts on "frills" imply various things, depending on one's outlook.

There is also no clear-cut understanding in most organizations as to who is to do the final applying of policy. The percentage of noncompliance is often very high. Those who are supposed to make the final application of a rule of policy may not have the means at their command to enforce the rule, despite brave attempts to establish the principle throughout the organization that "authority is commensurate with responsibility" at every level. Even in public government, with relatively higher degrees of visibility of those who invoke and apply policy, there are still large areas of invisibility with resultant failure to detect whether the policy is really effective or not. Corporate policies operate typically out of view of the press, the stockholders (their ultimate constituency, legally speaking) and even of boards. In labor unions, recent publicity stimulated by congressional investigations has thrown the spotlight upon the internal workings of union governments. It has become quite obvious that the broad democratic policies enunciated in their constitutions and declared by their leaders are neither invoked nor applied in practice in many locals.

Appraisal and Termination

The assessment of the success or failure of a policy is the stage of appraisal. This involves decision making in the form of measuring performance against the standards and goals set up by policy. "Control" is the word that is often used in management language, but in some companies the term "measurement" is preferred because it emphasizes the principle of "authority of knowledge" as distinguished from "authority of command." One who knows in advance what he is trying to do, and why, should be in a position to measure the results of his own work. If his policy planning (projection of plans of action to achieve stated goals) has been well done, he should be able to see at the end of the period under review whether the plan worked in terms of the goals set. Termination of unrealistic plans would normally follow negative measurement results. Subsequently, new plans would be formulated if the objectives were still worthy of achievement.

Appraisal, in this sense, is a stage in corporate policy making that may be entered into systematically only with respect to certain kinds of policies. Pricing policies, for example, will yield directly measurable performance in a competitive industry and will always be followed by careful appraisal because of the impact upon the market position of the business and upon its profitability. Policies of corporate giving, on the other hand, have rarely been followed up by systematic attempts to appraise the results, partly because of the difficulties inherent in such appraisals and partly because no ascertainable standards have been prescribed as goals. The result is that many companies may go on year after year with contributions programs without knowing whether these are yielding optimum returns to the company. Nobody knows, and few care, so long as the legal requirements are met and tax advantages observed. Similarly, the policy of maximizing employee satisfactions may be invoked and applied without adequate appraisal of the results in terms of clearly stated objectives.

Trends in the focus of attention given to appraisal in various fields of company operations have never been charted, but it is notable that in recent years some companies have at least tried to move toward measurement of business performance in areas other than profitability. One reason for this is that the multifunctional character of the modern corporation is more widely recognized than it used to be. The emphasis upon community relations is a case in point. But even in terms of business performance, as such, separate standards can be set for market position, product development and leadership, productivity, personnel development, employee attitudes, and balance between the long- and short-term goals of the company.

The locus of components having primary responsibility for the appraisal function is an important matter. In a highly centralized organization, appraisal will be reserved to a few highly placed officials; in decentralized companies, the function will be delegated down the line. Little has been done to determine empirically which method works best, and the test of what is "best" once again involves the question of goal-values.

Where democratic values prevail, the appraisal function will be more widely shared than in organizations which operate on the principle of a benevolent autocracy. From the standpoint of society as a whole, it is hard to know whether one system is better than the other. There seems to be a general trend toward the establishment by law of standards of performance for business corporations. This tends to remove some aspects of the appraisal function from the internal policy and organization and to place them in organs of public government. The rise of unions has been accompanied, as some see it, by the transfer of appraisal functions, in some areas, from management to the bargaining table. It has become clear that sectors of society external to the corporation are beginning to assert an interest in corporate performance, with resultant "encroachment" upon managerial prerogatives.

All of these considerations indicate that the decision process in the modern corporation, at the stage of appraisal and termination or revision of policy, calls for far more extensive empirical research than has yet been undertaken. Until it has been accomplished, discussion will remain speculative.

The decision process, then, can be studied in terms of the different stages of policy making: intelligence, recommendation, prescription, invocation, application, appraisal, and termination of policies. At every stage, questions can be raised about the maximization of rationality at that stage, about the goal-values [10] that become operative, and the ways in which decision makers assess the world about them and their identity in it. If one assumes that managers always act on behalf of "the company," one still needs to know how they perceive the company and its interests as against other and competing interests. If they act on behalf of other than company interests, what are these interests, and with whom are they identified? What are the value systems that enter into decision making at the respective stages? What are the "facts" that form the basis of the decisions made—the pictures in the executive's mind as to the past, present, and future patterns and trends of events that presumably impinge upon each stage of the decision process?

These are some of the relevant questions that call for answers when comprehension of a large industrial corporation is sought in terms of the over-all decision process within the organization.

THE INSTRUMENTS OF CORPORATE POLICY

At every stage of the decision process consideration should be given to the available means for carrying out the actions planned. The fullest use of all appropriate instruments for realizing the plans of action is one indispensable attribute of the successful decision maker. The question of appropriateness can be answered in both naturalistic and ethical terms: some instruments of corporate policy will be effective but frowned upon; others will be noble but impractical. What are the chief instruments?

First and foremost is the category of economic means of implementing policy. Economic means refer to cooperation and exchange in the "market" where, in Cournot's words, "every one seeks to derive the greatest possible value from his goods and labors." In the "perfect market" of Jevons "all traders have perfect knowledge of the conditions of supply and demand and the consequent ratio of exchange." The value pursued in the market is wealth, not power in the political sense, and economic means are at least theoretically noncoercive. Businessmen, of course, are engaged—like everybody else—in the pursuit of power as a deference value; but this is not the primary value they seek as free enterprisers, and for the purposes of analysis it can be assumed that any instruments of corporate policy used for the purpose of invoking coercive forces are distinguishable from purely economic means.

Competition in the market place is distinguishable from competition in the political arena. One never encounters free trade in the purest form, with no coercive force anywhere in the situation—government at least intervenes to preserve "law and order," to enforce contracts, and to protect the property rights of owners. The minimization of coercion is the test of a comparatively free, competitive society. Goods and services are offered at the most advantageous prices in order to win a favorable market position by attracting the most takers who voluntarily exchange things of economic value for the products offered. To invoke the coercive powers of government (through legislation, administrative action, and judicial proceedings) in order to limit choices of consumers or to weaken the position of one's competitors, is to make use of noneconomic instruments of corporate policy. This may be legitimate and necessary, given the prevailing legal norms and mores of the community; but one must distinguish the use of such instruments of policy from noncoercive methods.

A second instrument of corporate policy, then, is force, invoked indirectly and by due process of law through the agencies of public government. Businessmen will usually deny that force is an important instrument of corporate policy. But few corporate boards act without legal counsel; and legal counsel are specialists in the invocation of the coercive sanctions of the state, both for defensive and offensive action on behalf of the corporation.[11] It must be assumed, then, that the decision process in corporations necessarily involves consideration of the propriety, the timeliness, and the probable effectiveness of the use of this instrument, along with the other instruments of corporate policy.

Third, there is the negotiatory instrument. Transactions in the market are the outcome of production and exchange. But many corporate acts resulting from policy decisions are not in this category, nor are they invocations of the coercive power of the state. Many of the agreements reached between corporations and other organizations and persons are not classifiable as economic agreements but appear to be rather like diplomatic arrangements between sovereign states. They establish a working relationship, a *modus vivendi,* an understanding as to respective spheres of interest. Thus, collective bargaining agreements cover much more than wages and working hours, benefits; they also cover grievance procedures and mutual understandings as to the respective spheres of union and company responsibilities and authority. Trade associations, especially under rigorous public enforcement of antitrust policy, shy away from economic agreements among the member companies; but they lay special emphasis upon market development, exchange of information, and mutual aid in production processes. Standardization is a movement that has been based largely upon negotiation among companies, and between companies, on the one hand, and governments, on the other. Neither coercion nor economic exchange is involved.

Finally, there is the ideological instrument of corporate policy: the use of ideas, argument, propaganda, education, advertising, to win men's minds without coercion and short of actual market operations. The enormous growth of public relations as a profession underlines the significance of this instrument of policy, not only in business but in all other fields of human activity. The effective use of ideological means to achieve value-goals has a very long past but only a very recent history; it is only within the past few decades that a scientific literature on the subject has begun to appear. Corporate enterprise, viewed strictly as an economic activity, makes use of the ideological instrument only as an accessory to market operations. When account is taken of the multifunctional character of the modern corporation, however, it becomes clear that the projection of symbols, the interchange of ideas, the use of persuasion, the enunciation of doctrine, all play an important part in corporate effort to attain the various goals set forth in company objectives.

It may be concluded that in the making of important decisions corporate policy makers necessarily consider the possible use of all four of these major instruments of policy. The significance of the modern corporation as a social institution, alongside other major institutions such as the churches, public governments, labor unions, and others, will be better understood if the fact is faced frankly that *all* large organizations rely upon *all* these instruments in order to reach their objectives. Churches and universities rely heavily upon the ideological instrument; but they cannot avoid the use of force (indirectly through the agencies of public government), of economics, and of negotiation, though their apologists sometimes pretend that this is not so. Business corporations make use primarily of economic instrumentalities; but they simply would not be able to operate as business firms outside the framework of government, despite the fact that negotiatory and ideological means obviously constitute normal ways of getting business done.

At every stage in the decision process, then, the corporate policy maker who is reality-oriented will survey the possibilities and the propriety of using any or all of the instruments of policy. The maximizing of rationality in the decision process will require everyone who is involved at any stage (intelligence, recommendation, prescription, invocation, application, appraisal, and termination) of policy making to consider the appropriateness of these possible instruments in achieving the objectives (the goal-values) of corporate policy. It is the felicitous combination of all these elements in the policy process that characterizes the successful business leader. And the wisdom of his policies is assessable in these terms.

With the tools of analysis heretofore introduced, it is appropriate to turn now to the major areas of corporate policy, or the great substantive issues that confront the decision maker in the largest business organizations.

CHAPTER IX

Strategic Decision Areas

THE POLICY PROCESS, as it has been described in the preceding chapters, becomes more meaningful when it is analyzed with respect to decision making in the strategic areas of corporate policy. The identification of the strategic areas, however, is a debatable issue. In this chapter we shall consider three different approaches to this problem of priorities for executive management in the large corporation.

Corporate policy may be interpreted primarily as decision making in the management of a competitive business, an entrepreneurial unit in the private sector of the economy. From another point of view, running a business demands "business statesmanship," and this may result in different choices of the strategic decision areas. From still another point of view, all business decisions are public decisions, and the most important issues of corporate policy become quasi-public issues.

Each of these approaches is to some degree subjective. That is to say, each assumes that business and the businessman have certain ideal roles to play in society, and the role assumptions will affect the selection and the priority of strategic decision areas or the problems on which the executive manager will focus his attention. A glance at the accompanying outline of corporate policy areas will suffice to show that some selectivity is required. This list,[1] adapted from studies of the theory of the firm, while not necessarily exhaustive, is at least a fairly complete catalog of issues that arise in establishing and running any large enterprise.

CORPORATE POLICY AREAS

I. Promotion and Initial Organization of the Corporation

A. Setting the corporation's objectives
   (This is a major policy area that is in fact a continuing issue throughout the life of the firm.)

B. Initial organization: problems of initial size, legal organization, financial structure, internal organization, product lines, production and distribution methods, staffing, etc. (elaborated below)

C. Negotiation for the hire of the factors of production, particularly capital

II. Existence of the Corporation as a Going Concern

A. Maintenance and improvement of the organization
   1. Classification of the major functional kinds of work (such as finance, legal, manufacturing, engineering, marketing, research, relations, managing) and allocation of these kinds of work among the various components of the company
   2. Specification of the loci of authority and responsibility, according to selected patterns of centralization or decentralization and selected concepts of the corporate polity
   3. Decision-making process within the firm
      (a) Centralized decision making: setting up the methods by which company-as-a-whole policies are to be made, including services of staff components' functions and methods of securing the participation of subordinate operating components
      (b) Delegation: specification of the degree of autonomy of subsidiary components, and the substantive areas in which they are to make their own decisions
      (c) Relationships with outside advisers, consultants, etc.
   4. Orientation of the internal organization to external conditions and forces

B. Legal: compliance with law, adversary proceedings in judicial and other tribunals, representation in contractual transactions of the corporation, etc.

C. Production
   1. Product selection, product development, and diversification of products

2. Research and engineering
3. Plant and equipment

D. Supply
   1. Purchasing channels
   2. Purchasing areas
   3. Cultivation of sources of supply
   4. Relations with suppliers

E. Marketing
   1. Marketing channels
   2. Marketing areas
   3. Sales promotion: advertising, sales organization and methods
   4. Relations with customers, including dealers and distributors
   5. Pricing
   6. Relations with competitors

F. Finance
   1. Capital structure
      debt vs. equity
      short-term vs. long-term debt
      outside vs. inside sources of equity capital
      rental vs. ownership of capital assets
   2. Payments for services of land and capital
      rent
      interest
      dividends
   3. Composition of current assets
      inventories
      cash, receivables and other current assets
   4. Provision for risk and uncertainty
      insurance
      reserves
   5. Taxation
      incidence of federal and state taxes
      tax consequences of action or inaction

G. Personnel policies (directors, managers and individual contributors)
   1. Wages and salaries
   2. Other compensation: incentives, bonuses, vacations, retirement and other benefits
   3. Working conditions in offices and plants

    4. Communication among personnel

    5. Collective bargaining and union relations

    6. Hours: the work week, leisure time

    7. Recreational, cultural and educational activities

    8. Organizational demands vs. personal freedoms of company personnel

  H. Public Relations

    1. Determination of the public relations function of the firm

    2. Selection of the key publics of significance to the firm

    3. Selection of appropriate media for communication with these publics

    4. Determination of the content of communications

    5. Measuring the results of public relations work

III. *Reorganization or Liquidation*

  A. Transitional issues, in case of reorganization

  B. Terms of liquidation, especially as to distribution of assets

Many of these issues are of tactical, rather than strategic, significance. Let us see how one's view of the purposes of corporate policy can affect one's designation of certain of these issues as strategic rather than tactical.

FIRST APPROACH: CORPORATE POLICY IN TERMS OF COMPETITIVE BUSINESS

Corporate policy, considered from the first approach, is distinguishable from public policy in that it is concerned with business affairs and with entrepreneurial matters, all of which, in our political and economic system, fall within the province of the private sectors of the economy. The focus of our attention is on those policy areas which allow corporations to contribute to the growth of the economy as a whole through aggressive and competitive private enterprise. Under this theory, corporate managers are not makers of public policy in the proper sense of that term, since public policy is the province of government. They may, of course, bring their influence to bear upon the formulation of public policy, acting under the right of petition guaran-

teed to all by the Constitution; but it is misleading to assume that corporate managers have either the right or the duty to engage in public decision making within the frame of reference set out by corporate charters for profit-making institutions.

The corporate manager as an entrepreneur certainly always needs to be guided, among other things, by careful estimates of external forces in the corporate environment, both natural and human, in his attempt to achieve rationality in decision making; and, in this sense, he can never be oblivious to the public aspects of corporate policy. He calculates the most advantageous alternative open to him in terms of optimum yield (economic return) on his investment, not in a social vacuum but in situations which have been likened to a game in which adversaries are engaged in the same kind of calculations.

This, however, is quite different from weighing the public interest as a determinate factor in corporate decisions, or from tempering corporate interest with considerations of abstract economic justice, "the general welfare," or from following some moral imperative stated in altruistic language. When managers allow corporate policy to deviate from the pursuit of the central objectives of the business as a business operation, diffusing their efforts toward a "social" orientation of the enterprise and concerning themselves with public policies at the expense of the company's productive and profit-making activities, they fail, according to this view of the corporation, to serve the true social function of an enterprise. Moreover, they invite public regulation of the business by reason of the quasi-public status they tend to confer upon the company.

The assumption of social responsibilities by industrial corporations, this argument continues, is a misleading and dangerous practice. Any social responsibilities that rest upon the businessman will take care of themselves so long as the business is run at a profit by lawful means, for profit is an adequate index of the social usefulness of the business. Promotion of the public good in this way is all that can be expected of the entrepreneur aside from the ordinary duties of citizenship he shares with his fellow citizens. To foster the idea that corporate managers step into the role of quasi-public policy makers—because their business policies affect the interests of many people—is to dilute their effectiveness as aggressive businessmen in a highly competitive system. They cannot sit on both sides of the table at the same time. Their assignment is that of the protagonist for their company's own interests, not only against competitors but also against the encroachments of government upon the province of private business enterprise.

The modern corporation, from this point of view, is indeed an important social institution, but not because it has become any less private in character than it was before. Its significance lies in the contribution it makes to society by jealously guarding its autonomy as a private sector and in championing the principle that a free society can survive only when there is deliberate protection—as a matter of public policy—of many such autonomous sectors in the economy, each free to make its own decisions. The significant policy areas, then, are areas in which the corporation as an enterprise concerns itself with the central problems of an entrepreneur: how to produce and market salable goods and services through the most efficient use of resources and at a price that will yield optimum profits over the long as well as the short term.

These policy areas fall under headings that correspond to the major functional types of work to be done in order to reach the goal as stated above. In any large, diversified industrial corporation, the major functions will ordinarily include finance, accounting, manufacturing, research and engineering, marketing, legal work, and relations with employees and with various public sectors. All of these functions must be organized—in the fullest sense of the term. Various formulas have been devised to explain the processes involved in organizing. Various verbs are used to describe this essential work: to analyze, organize, deputize, or supervise. Others have suggested the terms: planning, organizing, command, and control. Still others have concluded that in each functional field the work to be done includes planning, organizing, integrating, and measuring. These last four terms have been selected as a convenient nomenclature for this discussion.

Planning necessitates the formulation of policies concerning the flow of business information to managerial levels, including intelligence of the general social, political, economic, and competitive environment in which the business is conducted. It also requires policy decisions in the form of long-range objectives, plans, schedules, and budgets.

Organizational policies will develop a sound and adaptable long-range organization through which the various functional types of work can be carried out efficiently in every component of the company. Policies will also be necessary with respect to staffing: recruitment of personnel, training, compensation, promotions, and retirement.

Integrating human effort and the material resources required to run the business will be reflected in policies that give unity to the whole enterprise: sound policies of finance, procurement of supplies, development of plant and equipment, deployment and concentration of services, basic and applied research and, above all, coordination of all the functions of the company.

Measuring performance in every functional field necessitates policies which set standards of business performance and indicate the ways and means of assessing operating conditions and the efficient utilization of resources.

Planning, organizing, integrating, and measuring are thus the essential aspects of the work of managing. Corporate policy, in this view, should focus upon these matters rather than upon peripheral problems with which the modern corporation sometimes becomes entangled.

To conclude this line of argument: The premise that the modern corporation is primarily a social institution, rather than a business enterprise, has misled some business leaders into overemphasis upon external relations that have only a remote connection with the main job.

The modern corporation is certainly of great social significance; but this is said to be true not so much because it is intent upon serving society, but because of the by-products that result from a well-run and productive business enterprise. Over and above its direct contributions to the market in the form of goods and services, which it can only continue to provide at a profit on the investment, there are plus-values of many kinds that permeate the corporate environment. A well-run company stands as an example of outstanding organizational effort in getting the world's work done. Its staff work in every functional field creates socially useful knowledge applicable beyond the confines of the company's own operations. Its members, from the board level to the individual contributor, become better citizens by reason of developed skills of many kinds and because of their practice of the art of responsibility commensurate with authority.

To sum up the first approach: the significant policy areas in the large corporations are the same policy areas that one would find in any enterprise, large or small. Their significance lies in the fact that sound managerial decisions in these particular areas strengthen the individual enterprise as a productive and profitable *business.*

SECOND APPROACH: "BUSINESS STATESMANSHIP" AS THE KEY

Examine the second position, the view that corporate managers are more than businessmen in the classical sense and that they are expected to be "industrial statesmen" as well. The idea of business statesmanship is urged in many quarters, not least by businessmen themselves. Private advantage, it is emphasized, should be tempered with public interest in corporate decision making.

Corporate policies, when they affect any considerable sectors of the public, become socially significant. Society generally, it is held, has a legitimate interest in both the decision process and the substance of these policies. This is thought to be particularly true of the larger corporations. These have widely dispersed shares of stock, hundreds of thousands of employees, plants in many different communities in this and other countries, resources that may exceed the wealth of a small sovereign state, and influence that has to be reckoned with. These have become "powers" on which certain responsibilities rest. Their policies, it is often insisted, should reflect responsibility commensurate with their authority. They may be "private corporations" in the technical and legal sense, but they are quasi-public institutions in fact.

The softening of the description of the public character of these business institutions with "quasi" is significant. It indicates a prevailing desire, in the United States at least, to preserve the autonomy of business corporations so far as possible, and a general feeling that central planning of the economy is a necessary evil to be tolerated only in times of extreme national emergency. The general principle favors dispersion of the decision-making centers, not only in the economy but in most areas of human activity. Central controls have to be resisted until their absolute necessity becomes established by due process of law, supported by overwhelming public opinion.

To disperse authority and responsibility for decision making, under this approach, however, does not remove the decision-making centers from public view. On the contrary, the elaborate and intricate communication system—press, radio, TV, free assembly, the free market, and so on—continually maintains this visibility. In one way or another, the actions of the corporate decision maker become public. Moreover, the decision process in the corporation is increasingly subjected to the same kind of penetrating analysis as has been applied to governmental processes. There is keen and legitimate public interest in the content of corporate policies. And it is this interest, if a narrow view be taken, that impels business leaders to adopt the role of "business statesmen."

This posture, however, is not merely the result of irresistible public pressures upon the corporate decision maker. The public aspects of corporate policy are insisted upon by business executives themselves, primarily because they have become convinced of the changing role of managers at higher levels of the corporate polity. They no longer look at themselves as mere agents and representatives of the share owners' interests exclusively. Instead, they see themselves as adjusters and balancers of many different interests, of which the stockholders comprise but one important group. Managers, in their important decisions, must necessarily attempt to balance the interests of share owners, employees, customers, suppliers, and the public at large, including the public's official representatives in governmental organs. This century's large business corporation is not simply an enlarged version of the owner-entrepreneur who characterized the business system of the last century. It is the focus of many contributor-claimant interests that have a legitimate claim upon the attention of the corporate decision maker. In this sense, so the argument goes, there are clear social responsibilities for the corporate manager, dealing not with the visionary ideals of a Utopian, but rather with the day-to-day operations of an institution essential to the lives of big sectors of the nation.

The public aspects of corporate policy thus are simply the inevitable result of corporate development and the frank recognition of the external conditions for corporate growth and survival. Whether as a profit maximizer, pure and simple, or as a bearer of social responsibilities, the corporate decision maker must look far beyond the confines of the usual corporate limits to assess the forces that play a determinate part in business policy formation. The probable impact of a policy upon diverse groups of interests will be an important policy consideration.

What weight will be given to one group of interests as against others is a question that may bring into play the value systems of the managers who make the decisions. But even in this weighting process managers are not completely free agents. The alternatives usually represent a parallelogram of forces, some of which are more intense and effective than others. The decision is made at a point where many pressures meet, and a decision is a resolution of these forces.

The continuity in office of a particular management may be taken as a clue to the success with which its members assess these various forces in arriving at important decisions. Failure to take into account the public aspects of corporate policy, as just described, has led to the ouster of one set of managers and the installation of another with better sensing equipment, with antennae attuned to the corporate environment. Business statesmanship, like statesmanship in public governments, is governed in the long run by norms generated by public opinion. And, in a free society, tenure of office depends in the final analysis upon measuring up to those norms.

This line of argument leads to the exploration of somewhat different key policy areas from those previously considered. Under the first approach, the significant policy areas had to do with the conduct of a profitable enterprise. By the second approach, profitability is included as a major objective in the minds of managers and the public generally, but, at the same time, it has to make room for coordinate objectives, such as: the continuity of the firm, its prestige as an institution, its success in harmonizing the many diverse interests among its contributor-claimants, and its stature as a "corporate citizen." The term "corporate citizen" is used increasingly by businessmen themselves to indicate that the corporate entity, quite aside from the real persons who make it go, must be able to meet public expectations about its contributions to the health of the body politic.

National defense, economic growth and stability for the country as a whole, scientific and technological developments, education, the values cherished by a free society—these are the significant areas of corporate policy for those who speak of business statesmanship. These areas of policy would be regarded as peripheral under the first-named approach, based on the theory that corporate managers must keep their sights set on efficient production and profits. These socially dimensioned interests would not be excluded policy areas, to be sure, but they would not be permitted to consume much of the time and energies of corporate managers as business enterprisers. In contrast, the second approach requires much greater managerial attention to the public aspects of corporate policy.

THIRD APPROACH: CORPORATE ENTERPRISE AS PUBLIC BUSINESS

Last to be considered is the position that there are no non-public aspects of corporate policy and that the *large* industrial corporation is, to all intents and purposes, a public institution. Thus it is sometimes argued that by birth, as well as by upbringing, the modern corporation has lost any claim to its "private" character. This is, of course, an extreme position. It is seldom advocated in all of its implications. Yet it may be observed that some well established doctrines of the law and of American political thought point strongly in this direction. One should not be overly certain that what is implicit in this position will not become explicit as time goes on.

The corporation is said, for example, to be nothing but the creature of society. Since it owes its birth to the creative act of the Sovereign, without whose intervention a corporation could not exist as a legal person, it has a public character stamped upon it genetically. This "concession theory" of corporateness is standard doctrine in Anglo-American law, though it should be noted that in the development of American jurisprudence a clear distinction has been drawn between private and public corporations.

The idea of the "private corporation" grew out of constitutional interpretation at the hands of Joseph Story and John Marshall when they developed the rule that Dartmouth College's charter (granted by the Sovereign) not only created a corporation but constituted, as well, a contract which binds the Sovereign. The purpose of this line of reasoning in the Dartmouth College case was to arrive at an important conclusion: that nonpublic corporations, such as privately endowed colleges, are protected against state laws that impair the obligation of contracts, and that the attempt on the part of the New Hampshire legislature to change the governmental system of the college amounted to such an impairment. This case became the precedent for the rule that private corporations, in general, enjoy a degree of autonomy that cannot be assumed for public corporations, such as municipalities or government corporations. Important as this rule was and is, however, it does not disturb the fundamental principle enunciated in the concession theory: that corporateness is conferred by public act, and cannot be generated by private agreements alone.

One might have expected that, on the basis of such a theory, businessmen would shun the corporate form of organization. As it turned out, the rule of the Dartmouth College case provided no adequate protection from extensive public regulation of corporate business, because the Supreme Court held in 1837 that a state may reserve the right to amend, alter and repeal a corporation's charter, the legal basis for its very existence.[2] Under state police power, thus reserved, state regulation of corporate businesses could not effectively be curbed by the contract clause. The great expansion of corporate business came after this decision, a development made possible through ingenious efforts on the part of corporation lawyers to find other cloaks of protection from legislative encroachments upon the private sectors of business in corporate form.

The development of constitutional doctrines to achieve this purpose is a history in itself and will not be recited in detail here. It involved interpretations of the due process and equal protection clauses of the Fourteenth Amendment (1868); the expansion of the meaning of the commerce clause so as to create a nation-wide market place relatively free from the Balkanization of the economy that might otherwise have resulted; and strong assertion of the right of state-created corporations to resort to the federal courts for protection against local restrictions on corporate business. Meanwhile, general incorporation statutes became the rule, and the Sovereign's procreative potentialities were vastly increased so far as business corporations were concerned. The rapid industrialization of the country, together with the need for large aggregations of capital to develop its resources, spurred on the growth of corporate enterprise. In general, up to the reformist era, beginning in the 1890s, the atmosphere was highly favorable to the use of the corporate form of business. But even the antitrust and New Deal movements, although directed in part at some of the alleged abuses of power by Big Business, did not halt the progressive adoption of corporate business organization. Nor did it ever lead to massive state intervention into corporate affairs.

It is fair to conclude, then, that the concession theory of corporateness, though clearly authoritarian in its abstract implications, and in principle a sword of Damocles over the heads of corporate managers, is in practice nothing of the sort. At least it has not been, up to now. Yet there is reason to consider the other side of the picture. The basis for consideration at this moment is, namely, that the business corporation is more than a *quasi*-public institution and that its policies are essentially of a public character.

In juristic theory, the Sovereign—and more realistically the officials in legislatures, executive mansions, commissions, and courts—are in a position to exercise considerable surveillance over corporate affairs, not only by right of parentage, but more especially because of the wide scope of governmental powers, state and federal, as they stand today. That these powers are exercised less extensively than they might be, within present constitutional limitations, does not obscure the fact that they could be brought into play in the future. Regulatory agencies and legislation have multiplied in the business field over the past few decades, and it would require no change in constitutional verbiage for them to be pushed further. The concept of a "business affected with a public interest" no longer applies to a narrowly restricted class of public utilities. The practical effect is to widen indefinitely the field within which legislatures may regulate corporate affairs. The "clash between democratic and business traditions," which Thomas Cochran describes, has precipitated a series of political issues in the nation, some of which could emerge as sweeping statutory reforms of the business system as a whole.[3] Political careers have been made on elaborations of the theme that business decision making has let the country down, that misrule in the private economic sectors has weakened the economy and caused depressions, and that the public aspects of corporate policy are too important to be left in the hands of businessmen.

The opportunities for this line of attack may be increased by the course of domestic and international events. Some future severe depression coinciding with a feeling of general pessimism could revive and amplify the cry for more thoroughgoing public control of business. Nor will the form of this demand necessarily take the shape of outright statutory regulation. It might alternatively or concurrently take the shape of reform measures within the corporate polity, sponsored by groups with immediate interests at stake. Movements for "share owner democracy," pressures from unions upon the domain of "managerial prerogative," dealer and distributor demands upon manufacturers, are cases in point.

Businessmen, as Cochran has said, have justified the nonpublic character of their policies with the idea that business decisions were unalterably based on the requirements of the market. He adds:

No doubt in the old days of small business, low mechanization, and weak market controls the businessman struggling for survival in a competitive economy had little leeway. But the big companies of the mid-twentieth century, the ones that set the tones of business thinking, had considerable control over prices in the market. And . . . such companies had already gone far in the support of community services, education and welfare plans for workers.

The fact remains that the *decisions* to do these good deeds were not generally participated in by their beneficiaries. Aside from dealings with organized labor, there were few democratic procedures in business by which opinion from below could effectively influence the major actions of those on top, or by which changes in policy could be opened to advance discussions. The practical difficulties were great, but if business was to be truly democratic, they had to be overcome.[4]

The criterion of democratic procedure may not, of course, be the controlling one in the demand that business policy making be regarded as public policy making. In the struggle for survival between East and West, men may come to believe that the requirements of the market have to be subordinated to the requirements of national strength, and that the strength of the nation as a protagonist in this epic struggle cannot be measured mainly in terms of maintaining a free market system in which business policy bases itself on the concept of a self-regulating economy. "Consumer sovereignty" may have to bow before State sovereignty.

In the light of such an analysis it is easy to see that there are few, if any, areas of corporate policy that could escape the scrutiny of the public. Problems of capital investment become more than problems of adequate resources to conduct a profitable business. A wartime economy finds it must husband the nation's resources as a whole and cannot permit diversions of capital into uses that impede the national effort. Wage policies, from the national point of view, may be regarded by the president as bearing a direct relation to inflation or deflation. Relations between employer and employee, in corporations engaged in defense production, may have to be governed by rules of industrial security that treat the private enterprise as though it were a government bureau.

Thus, when the large industrial company is regarded as a public enterprise in all but name, the significant areas of corporate policy are as numerous as the demands of national interest upon a business.

OPERATIONAL VS. SUBJECTIVE SELECTION OF KEY POLICY AREAS

Reviewing the three approaches to the definition of significant areas of corporate policy in an attempt to identify the strategic areas of corporate policy making, it becomes evident that each position is based upon a subjective or normative principle. Each position assumes a certain function that the business corporation *ought* to perform in society as shown in the accompanying schema (p. 205).

In the first case, the corporation is expected to act the part only of the entrepreneur in a self-regulating economy, intent upon maximization of profits or like values of concern to itself alone. In the second case, the corporation concedes certain social responsibilities, but these are conceived to be peripheral to the central task and are in large part simply contributory to the accomplishment of this task; business is seen to be a private operation, though set in a socially-dimensioned environment which requires attention as a matter of enlightened self-interest. In the third case, there is insistence upon certain moral imperatives, such as national interest and democratic values, which impel a few observers to conclude that no area of corporate policy can be entirely private in character.

A normative approach distinguishes between what is and what might better be; it emphasizes the "ought." It is an ethical approach and as such has its uses. Certainly, no business policy maker can operate without norms of ethical value. These norms may be implicit, perhaps hidden from his view as he looks at the decision process. But they are always there. And it is probably a requirement of "business statesmanship" that a manager bring to the surface the value system by which he lives, act upon it in specific cases, and defend it when he must.

But the practical significance of a policy area may not be the same as its ethical significance. The attention it really receives may be far less than a manager thinks it deserves.

For purposes of scientific analysis a nonnormative, objective, and naturalistic approach to the definition of significant policy areas is desirable. One objective is to discern the realities of

TYPES OF BUSINESS UNITS: A NORMATIVE CLASSIFICATION

A. The business unit regarded as an exclusively private organ	I. The traditional or austere corporation	The business unit is the private domain of the stockholders *exclusively,* operated on their behalf by board and managers who are responsible only to them.
	II. The metro-corporation	The business unit is a private domain in which a *constellation* of private interests is represented and served.
B. The business unit regarded as a mixed public-private organ	III. Chiefly private *	The business unit serves a complex of private interests primarily, but has certain public responsibilities related to privileges and powers granted by the public.
	IV. Chiefly public *	The business unit serves the public interest primarily, but not to the exclusion of profits to private shareholders (e.g., a public utility).
C. The business unit regarded as an exclusively public organ	V. The public corporation	A semi-autonomous public "business" unit, as in case of T.V.A., Panama Canal; the *corporazioni* and *sindacati* in corporative systems.
	VI. The administrative bureau	A business operation as an arm of public government subject to direct control in totalitarian and constitutional regimes (as in case of a public transport system).

* These types also have characteristics of the metrocorporate pattern.

corporate behavior and to avoid preferential statements about the nobility of an issue. It is easy to pick out a half-dozen policy areas to which "statesmanlike" corporate managers ought to give their major attention; but one might not thereby discover the real focus of their attention. It is important, in scientific inquiry, to develop a true picture of the present role of the modern corporation in terms of the major decisions actually made within it. How can this be done in an objective way?

One way is to begin with the inventory of all the decision areas as they are seen by contemporary students of the theory of the firm. The next step would be an objective inquiry as to the focus of managerial attention, asking which of these areas are today regarded as the most significant by corporate managers themselves and why they think they are significant. Are certain problems important simply because executives spend most of their time on them? Or are these problems considered to be the key to the success of the business, and if so, why? Is the key maximization of profit, growth of the firm, prestige of its leaders, contributions to the nation, or something else? It would be desirable to try to discern trends over a long period of time, say one or two decades. Definitive answers to these questions cannot be attempted here; this would require extended and intensive studies covering many firms.

In the absence of any reliable statistics, it is impossible to say what most corporate executives regard as the strategic decision areas on which they do, or should, focus their attention. In practice it is probable that questions of corporation finance, corporate organization, and public relations stand at the top of the list. But a careful study, extended over a period of years, would probably show that there have been significant changes in the kinds of issues on which boards and executive managers spend most of their time. In recent years, business leaders have undoubtedly been more and more concerned about corporate ecology: the study of environmental conditions [5] which influence the success of the business. Market conditions have always required the careful attention of the successful executive, but recently the scope of the market area has notably widened, and the state of the market is more and more intimately related to the political situation, national and international.

As the size of a firm grows larger, on the other hand, the corporate executive becomes more and more engrossed in the problems of internal organization and questions of corporate polity. The pressures which require attention to such problems are both internal and external: internally, the complexity of the organization demands new types of expertise to achieve the necessary integration of human and material resources; externally, the forces generated by the democratic ethos are strongly felt by managers who wrestle with problems of "human relations" in policies concerning employees and with problems of economic justice in dealing with security-holders, customers, and suppliers.[6]

Corporate Responsibilities

The conflict of responsibilities is a characteristic
of cooperative efforts.

Chester I. Barnard, *California Management Review,*
Fall, 1958.

CHAPTER X

Claimants on the Corporation

MANY CONTRIBUTE, directly or indirectly, their efforts, their time, and their substance, to the establishment and growth of the modern corporation. For this reason many lay claim to the fruits of its productivity. The problem of corporate social responsibilities can best be illuminated by identifying these contributor-claimants. This chapter lists and defines the contributor-claimants on the corporation; the chapters following discuss in detail the corporation's responsibilities to these major groupings.[1]

DIRECT CONTRIBUTOR-CLAIMANTS

Four general categories of contributor-claimants are almost universally recognized in current thought about the business corporation. They are the corporation's security holders, its customers, its employees, and its suppliers. Each of these groups expects the corporation to meet specific kinds of responsibilities, and each in turn owes specific duties to the corporation. Within each group, however, there are subgroups with differentiated rights and duties.

Security Holders
The security holders are those who supply the corporation's capital—the "definite amount of wealth [that] has been segregated and placed at the disposal of the directors to enable them to carry

out the purpose for which the corporation was organized." [2] This capital [3] may be contributed by stockholders or merely loaned to the corporation for a stipulated period by holders of bonds and preferred stock. There is a third type of capital which accumulates through the business activities of the enterprise itself and is distinguishable from the "contributed" capital of stockholders and bond-holders. In the widest sense, of course, capital as "tools of production" and as wealth dedicated to the further production of wealth includes intangible values that are distinguishable from material wealth contributed by security holders.[4] The term "capital" is used here, however, to cover primarily the "permanent liabilities of the corporation—its capital stock and its bonds and notes with maturities in excess of a year," [5] which Dewing refers to as the concept of capitalization in common business usage. The capital of a corporation is held by the corporation which, in effect, owns and controls it.

The term "share owners" has been given wide currency in recent years and much use is made of the phrase "people's capitalism" to symbolize the idea that corporations are ultimately owned by millions of "share owners." What these people own, however, are stock certificates which give them a status clearly distinguishable from that of a partner in a proprietor-managed enterprise. Unlike proprietor-managers of an unincorporated business, their liabilities are limited and so are their claims on the corporation.

The seniority of certain types of securities over others indicates that there are important subcategories of security holders or capital suppliers. The obligations of a corporation toward its security holders vary from subcategory to subcategory; and they vary in time. The content of these obligations depends on many factors, some of which are beyond the control of the individual security holder. Governmental agencies, as well as the corporation acting through its board, have powers to act upon the content of these obligations without necessarily consulting the individual holder of the stock certificate or the bond.[6] Thus, a distinction has to be made between various kinds of corporate responsibilities to various subcategories of security holders.

The precise content of a corporation's responsibility to holders of its common stock is the more difficult to define when attention is turned to the third type of capital referred to above: the "accumulated capital" or "surplus" of the corporation.[7] Should it be reinvested or distributed as dividends? Are there any standards in law, economics, or morals which dictate the responsibilities of a board of directors in determining the disposition of profits? What are the postulates that should be used in accounting for income, in calculating depreciation and obsolescence, in making adjustments to income or surplus for contingencies and reserves, and in balancing long- and short-range planning of the enterprise with due regard for the possibility of industrial booms and depressions?

These questions are raised here, not in the hope that definitive answers can be given—and it is probable that no agreement could be found at all in answer to the last named series of issues —but rather to point up the diversity, as well as the importance, of a corporation's obligations toward its various categories of security holders.

Customers

A corporation's customers include all the purchasers of the commodities and services it offers for sale or exchange. Its responsibilities, however, are not uniform for every subcategory of customers. Distinctions are made, in law and custom, between a firm's relations with its dealers and distributors, and with customers at retail. There are also various categories of ultimate consumers. The national and state governments are now important customers for large corporations; this customer relationship is often treated differently from relations with nongovernment buyers. These and other subcategories of customers raise diverse problems with respect to a corporation's external responsibilities.

Employees

Has a corporation the same responsibilities toward its blue-collar employees as it has toward its white-collar ones? Is there a line to be drawn in this respect between managers and individual contributors, between line and staff, between central and field personnel, between the skilled and the unskilled, between career and noncareer people? Offhand, one might say no, but closer inspection reveals distinctions both in law and by custom.

Suppliers

Aside from suppliers of "contributed capital" (security holders) and suppliers of services within the organization (employees), both of which are treated separately here in accordance with current usage, there are various kinds of suppliers toward whom the corporation recognizes specific types of responsibilities. The most general subclassification distinguishes between suppliers (vendors) of goods and suppliers of services. This distinction is perhaps significant for the purpose of discerning diverse types of responsibility. Pertinent also are classifications by size, organizational character of the vendor firm, degree of independent status of the vendor, and the vendor's relationship with the company.

Small supplier firms and individual vendors may expect from the large corporate buyer certain kinds of services which the large corporate vendor does not expect. Some vendors, whether large or small, are, in effect, satellite firms whose market position, profitability, and perhaps their very existence depend upon the orders placed by the corporate buyer. Dealings with vendor firms may also vary considerably depending upon their organizational structure, whether centralized or decentralized, for example.

INDIRECT CLAIMANTS

Corporate responsibilities toward the four claimant groups mentioned above can be distinguished in some ways from those obligations which arise with groups whose contributions are less direct—though substantial—and whose claims on the corporation are not based primarily on contractual relations.

Of the indirect claimants, the most important are these: competitors and others in the business community, local communities in which a corporation conducts substantial operations, the general public, and governments.

Competitors and Others in the Business Community

Some of the obligations of a corporation toward its competitors are set forth in law; but they are also regulated by custom and codes of business ethics. The same applies to other-than-competitor relationships. It applies to associated firms within the same industry which have common problems, and to the business community generally. However, these obligations are usually thought of as separate and distinct from the broader social responsibilities of businessmen.

Local Communities

The reference here is to those local communities in which a company has installations, or operates to such an extent that it is expected to fulfil the ordinary obligations of citizens of those communities. It is in this sense that the term "corporate citizenship" frequently applies in current usage. That there should be a wider sense of "community" in business circles—national and international in scope—is sometimes urged. But one does not find the same specificity or concreteness of obligation toward national and global communities in contemporary business philosophy. Corporate obligations toward local communities, by contrast, are widely recognized in the public statements of business leaders and in company policies.

Perhaps this indicates a certain parochialism in the businessman's outlook on world affairs, a heritage that may be from times past when political forces in the national and international arenas did not impinge so directly as they now do upon corporate affairs. The largest companies are gradually adapting their public and external relations policies to these forces; here and there one sees the development of internal organizational components, staffed with specialists with training and vision adequate to discern the mutual responsibilities of the corporation and the greater society.

The General Public

The move in this direction can be observed in corporate attention to "the general public" and increasing concern about corporate responsibilities toward this vaguely defined group. The "general public" may mean—in the mind of management—the national community or something less comprehensive though wider than the local communities in which a company operates. It rarely, if ever, means the international community.

If a proper claimant on the corporation is a *contributor*-claimant, it may well be asked how the "general public" contributes to the welfare of a specific company or has any legitimate claims upon it beyond those which people could reasonably make as members of any of the groups already listed above. This is a problem to which some attention will be given later when the nature of public relationships and corporate interests will be analyzed at some length.

Governments

Governments may be regarded as claimants on the corporation for any one of a number of reasons, some of which will be less persuasive than others. As the official representatives of the general public, governments are the grantors of the corporate privilege and as such, they may entertain expectations of corporate behavior in concord with the privilege extended. In other capacities, governments as groups of official persons have many different kinds of relations with corporations. Governments, for example, are customers, suppliers, and competitors of many industrial companies. In these and other capacities, government officialdom, so far as corporate responsibilities are concerned, may possibly be regarded in quite a different light than when it acts in its sovereign role. The vast extension of governmental powers and activities into what were hitherto regarded as the sacred and private precincts of economic sectors has raised some difficult problems for corporate managements desirous of understanding and fulfilling their social responsibilities.

Here, then, are the chief claimants on the modern corporation. It is necessary to get them clearly in view, since the general proposition about the social responsibilities of corporate enterprise takes on little meaning unless one specifies *who* is responsible to *whom* for *what*. Having noted now the second term in this formula, it is time to turn to the "what."

CHAPTER XI

Security Holders and Customers

EARLIER, THE DILEMMA of corporate social responsibility was defined and the historical development of this problem introduced. Implications abound. Some of them have been explored. They cover the whole complex of corporate impact on the life of modern man.

If the modern corporation has certain social responsibilities, it is reasonable to ask who the obligees are in this connection and what the corporation owes to each of them. The various responsibilities toward those who contribute and those who claim—the contributor-claimant group, as outlined in the preceding chapter —have never been fully catalogued. Nor can they be. This is so because the dynamism of social change constantly effects alterations in the list. Nevertheless, in evolving a philosophy of the corporation it becomes necessary to attempt at least a partial survey of the substantive obligations to each particular group.

An analysis of the content of corporate responsibility gives rise to fundamental issues. Are the so-called social responsibilities simply the sum of corporate obligations to the several groups of contributor-claimants? Are they, by contradistinction, only those obligations to such specified groups as the business community, local plant communities, and governments? Are they generalized obligations to the "public"? Or, to take a purely negative position, are they really nonexistent? Is it a basic error to speak of the social responsibilities of a business corporation? In the end, how is the dilemma of corporate social responsibility resolved?

Responsibilities toward Security Holders

Security holders of the corporation are direct claimants. One might assume that corporate responsibilities are so clear-cut and so well-established in this area that the content of this obligation is undebatable. Thus the obligation might easily be contrasted with the vague, alleged, and perhaps nonexistent "social responsibilities" about which so much dispute has arisen. This supposed contrast, however, becomes increasingly doubtful as the subject matter unfolds.

The general character of a corporation's responsibilities toward its security holders, and especially to the holders of its common stock, must be seen in historical perspective. Beginning in 1927 with William Z. Ripley's *Main Street and Wall Street,* a pioneering work in the field of corporate-stockholder relations which to some extent inspired the later work in 1932 by Berle and Means on *The Modern Corporation and Private Property,* there have been many studies of the nature of these responsibilities. There have been legislative investigations and a considerable amount of resultant regulation.

In 1939, Judge Pecora, who had been counsel to the Senate Committee on Banking and Currency (1933–34) during its investigations of stock exchange, banking and security markets practices, wrote these words about the results of the reforms:

The old regime of unlimited license may be said to have definitely come to an end. The testimony had brought to light a shocking corruption in our banking system, a widespread repudiation of old-fashioned standards of honest and fair dealing in the creation and sale of securities, and a merciless exploitation of the vicious possibilities of intricate corporate chicanery. The public had been deeply aroused by the spectacle of cynical disregard of fiduciary duty on the part of many of its most respected leaders; of directors, who conveniently subordinated their official obligations to an avid pursuit of personal gain; of great banks, which combined the functions of a bank with those of a stock jobber, of supposedly impartial public markets for the sale of securities, actually operated as private clubs for the individual benefit of their members.[1]

Pecora cited four statutes as marking "the beginning of a new era in the history of American finance." The Banking Act of 1933 had required commercial banks to divorce their security affiliates. The Securities Act of 1933 had put the "burden of telling the whole truth on the seller." The Securities Exchange Act of 1934 had created the Securities and Exchange Commission and placed stock exchanges under regulation. And the Public Utility Holding Act of 1935 had given the SEC jurisdiction over such companies and aimed ultimately to "eliminate the use of this dangerous device where it served only to further speculative control." Pecora concluded that, while all this marked progress, vigilance was necessary to maintain it. Doubtless his reference was to public vigilance but not to the exclusion of continuous fulfillment by stockholders and corporate managements themselves of their private responsibilities.

More recent events underline this conclusion. The recent emergence of a new doctrine under the title of "people's capitalism," emphasizes the widespread distribution of corporate shareholding and thus the sharing by people generally of ownership in large enterprises. It questions anew the extent of managerial responsibility to this growing corporate constituency. Managements recognize the need to protect themselves and their constituencies from "pirates by proxy." [2] However, it is the structure of the corporate polity that may need revision in order to guard against the "corporate raider."

Currently it is not unusual to hear the argument that professional managers, who have little or no financial investment in the companies they run, cannot be depended upon to guard and fulfill the company's responsibilities to its security holders.[3] In some quarters it has been urged that "corporate democracy" is the answer. Lewis D. Gilbert, a leader of this movement, lays down the major planks of his platform in these terms: [4]

More democratic, better attended, better located regional and annual meetings

Full disclosure of corporate financial affairs through proper annual and postmeeting reports

Strengthening of the SEC's proposal rule

Equitable pensions, option control, and executive compensation with reasonable ceilings and periodic shareholder review

Cumulative voting to give the minority representation and the majority the benefit of the minority's criticism

Preemptive rights to purchase new stock

The elimination of the stagger system of electing board directors

The election of auditors by shareholders

The elimination of the millions of automatic, uninstructed proxy votes cast by fiduciaries for management

The stipulation by SEC order of a maximum sum that can be spent in a proxy contest

The nomination of independent directors through the company proxy statement

Ownership of stock by directors in the companies on whose boards they sit

The election of qualified women to boards of directors

Impartial and factual press reports on corporate affairs

The right of a secret corporate ballot as inviolable in its privacy as a political vote

It is noteworthy that most of these planks in the platform of "corporate democracy" call for reform within the corporate polity —not necessarily through legislative action. The "corporate democrats," as stockholders, demand a voice in "the management of their own property," to see to it that "earnings are not squandered through mismanagement, diverted to improper sources by those who profit by such diversion, or stolen through chicanery." [5]

But this again raises the question about whose property is being managed, when it comes to the capital of a large, widely held business corporation. Do the share holders "own" the corporation's property in the same sense that the proprietor-manager "owns" his business? What is the status of the owners of senior securities [6] as compared with the holders of common stock? Has the risk taker—the common stock owner in the large corporation —become, in effect, the holder of a bond, expecting as he often does certainty and regularity of reasonable dividend payments? Considering the limited obligations and responsibilities of such share owners, can they be regarded as suppliers of venture capital in the older sense of that term, and are they in any way comparable with the entrepreneur of classical doctrine?

In a 1957 analysis by the Federal Reserve Board of the untapped market for corporate securities, it was shown that the great majority of families (nine out of ten) still owned no stock in American industry. [7] Even among those in the highest bracket of incomes (the top three percent), nearly half owned no corporate stock. In their drive for new equity capital, corporations face an interesting situation. There are many people with savings who might invest in corporate shares if only they could be convinced that the risks of stock ownership were worth taking for the benefits to be gained. This conviction is the result of many factors over which corporate managers have no direct control. Recessions inhibit the potential investor and executive management has only indirect means of influencing public policy aimed at the maintenance of general stability for the economy as a whole. Nor can they control the ebb and flow of the securities markets.

But there are elements in the corporate relationship with security holders which do permit direct control by managers. They can analyze with great care the various sectors of the investor public: their own security holders and the groups of potential security owners. They can improve their working relations with the financial community and, in particular, with security analysts and the financial press. They have a responsibility to all these groups to keep them reasonably informed,[8] to elicit their views and to encourage an inflow of intelligence from all competent sources, and to sustain generally an atmosphere of mutual confidence.

Adequate annual reporting is a necessity and for many companies there is much room here for improvement. Some companies may have to use heroic measures to overcome stockholder apathy. The wide dispersion of share ownership may engender a diffusion of responsibility. To some corporate officers this combined diffusion of stock ownership and stockholder responsibility may not seem to be a regrettable trend; it augments the authority of professional managers. But the more democratized basis of corporate ownership under a people's capitalism cannot be expanded indefinitely in this way. The investor public, actual and potential, must sooner or later be brought more actively into the world of corporate affairs as interested participants. All this means a vast educational effort far beyond anything yet attempted or even contemplated by most corporate executives. It is no longer a question of keeping a select group of security analysts and investment bankers informed about the problems of corporation finance, technological innovation, production, selling, managing.

If American industry is to be owned by the people of America in accordance with the tenets of a people's capitalism, the mysteries of the modern corporation will have to be thrown open to a vast and still uneducated public. Some efforts are being made here and there to foster—by corporate subsidy—so-called educational programs on the American free enterprise system. This is hardly the answer to the problem because, in most cases, these programs amount only to ineffective propaganda campaigns with negligible scientific content and superficial pedagogical value. The alleged "educational" programs on the American free enterprise system almost always are designed with the objective of neutralizing attacks on Big Business. Too frequently, the materials produced are resented by the academic community, read almost exclusively by the business community, and have no measurable effect of any kind on the larger community—those key publics on which the life of the enterprise depends.

This negative approach will not satisfy the great untapped investor public and will not answer the questions legitimately put to management by existing security holders. What managements need to do as a matter of regular business procedure is to undertake a long-range program for educating security holders and potential investors in the major problems and policies of their particular corporations. This is quite a different matter from indoctrination of the public in the generalized tenets of economic orthodoxy.

To do the job, corporate executives will invite really penetrating inquiry by the investor public into corporate polities and their affairs, just as statesmanlike political leaders encourage the general citizenry to participate actively in public affairs. They will provide adequate budgeting of corporate funds to establish and maintain a full program of corporate external relations, as distinguished from the more limited scope of public relations. They will enlarge their investor relations staffs and encourage a vigorous two-way stream of communication with the security holders of the corporation.

The end result, many fear, could be the weakening of managerial authority before an onrush of "stockholder democracy." Active and systematic encouragement of stockholder participation in the affairs of corporations, however, will be neither a threat to management's status nor a panacea for overcoming stockholder apathy.[9] The apathy of voters in both public and private elections is notorious. An economic stake in an enterprise—even with universal suffrage and the complete equipment of party machinery, campaigns, and the Australian ballot—gives no guarantee that the adage, *vox populi, vox Dei,* will be realized in fact.[10] The corporate polity presents, of course, no parallel to the democratic state. It will be a long time before the number of actual investors begins to approach their potential number, and even the present corporate constituency will but slowly rise to its electoral responsibilities.

It is indeed doubtful that most corporate managements have any desire to transform the "people's capitalism" into a *democratic* people's capitalism, as Gilbert so earnestly urges. There is desperate need for more equity capital for the future expansion of industry. But it is debatable whether corporate managements will or *should* be willing to bargain away their authority to control corporate affairs as the price of this vast extension of shareholding. The question is perhaps academic, for the security holder is now said to be in an unenviable position in comparison with other contributor-claimant groups, and especially the unions, when it comes to this question of "democratizing" control. The security holder sees progressive concessions to union "demands" and other pressures, some within management itself, which seem to him to undermine his equity.[11] These are well-organized pressures without any counterpart on the side of the security holder.

It is here, precisely, that corporate responsibility toward the security holder emerges with clarity: the responsibility to exert leadership of companies with at least *equal* concern for the interests of this particular contributor-claimant group. Many corporate managers insist that they must balance all the interests equitably; the large corporation, under this view, is not run for the interest of the security holders exclusively. But it is far from certain that investors and potential investors are now convinced that this balancing process is being prosecuted according to the most equitable canons. Until such canons have been clearly articulated and accepted by all the contributor-claimant groups, and *followed in practice* in the distribution of earnings, the modern corporation will have failed in its central responsibility to its security holders.

The formulation of such canons is primarily the duty of executive management, but they cannot solve the problem *in camera*. It is predictable that in the years to come, the whole subject will be ventilated in many quarters; it will be debated not only in the financial and labor press but in the public press generally. Those who now regard such issues as the exclusive province of the financial specialist and the top corporate command will find it difficult to adjust to the new situation. But an analysis of the social responsibilities of the modern corporation focuses on precisely such issues as these. This particular issue surely is fundamental in the broad complex of corporate policy formulation.[12]

Responsibilities toward Customers

"King Customer" should be first on the list of corporate obligees if one were to adopt uncritically the doctrines of many business leaders. The customer is often said to be the "true sovereign" of modern industry, the ultimate source of the real power and authority of the enterpriser. He must be satisfied if there is to be any profitable production at all. The customer's power, moreover, is often decisive. "What the busy housewife does in the split second she stands in front of merchandise displays in food and department stores shapes the operating statements of thousands of corporations" is the way one management consultant states the matter.[13]

The so-called "sovereign" status of customers is not only the result of market forces. It is firmly ingrained in the law as well, especially in view of widening doctrines of the "police power" of the states and the powers of Congress over commerce.[14] *Caveat emptor* is not the rule. The seller must beware of a considerable network of regulations, even though enforcement may be more ritualistic than real when public budgets are trimmed.

Corporate responsibility toward the customer, in the sense of a social responsibility, would never be limited by enlightened business leaders to the mandates of law or custom, however. This responsibility is thought of as a bigger thing, a part of our ethos. It is related to our faith in the necessity of continuing and never-ending economic growth, higher and higher levels of productivity, and a better standard of living for everybody. A company "owes" its customers new, better, and needed products and services year after year, taking full advantage of all technological advances. Innovation is not only a business requirement for survival in a competitive economy; it is the expected contribution of a forward-looking enterpriser to the American way.

For our purposes it is well to distinguish between the social responsibilities of corporate enterprise as a whole to *consumers* and the obligations of a specific company toward its own *customers*—the actual buyers of its products and services.

Customer satisfaction, from the individual corporation's point of view, is simply a means—indeed the indispensable means—to the ends of profitability, market position, prestige, and power. Nor does this exclude the warmer human virtues, the desire on the part of producer and seller to play a significant and even cherished part in the community. We know too little about management and worker motivation to brush aside such considerations as sentimental and unrealistic, the economic interpretation of history to the contrary notwithstanding.

Nevertheless, "customer satisfaction" may be only a shibboleth that really means "innovate or die" in a hard competitive market. It is simply expedient to coddle the reluctant buyer. As the perceptive columnist Malvina Lindsay has put it: When the manufacturers of plumbing fixtures turn belatedly to a Women's Housing Congress to discover what a housewife really wants in her model bathroom; when the "hard selling" commercials on radio and TV finally produce violent explosions of protest from a long-suffering public; when car buyers turn with fury on auto designers and assert their rights to life, limb, and passageway; when office workers begin to raise the roof about noisy, crowded, poorly lighted and ventilated work-space—then the problems of redesign and more palatable distribution show up on the profit-and-loss sheet. The market can be a force that works automatically toward the fulfillment of a company's responsibilities toward its consumers.

Management generally recognizes that there is a responsibility to pass along, to the consumer, the fruits of technological improvement in the form of better values, lower prices, more desirable products. It has been said that profit margins in the United States can be smaller than in most other countries, while adequate return on capital is still maintained, because management assures a rapid flow through the whole sequence of manufacture and distribution. In this country, probably to a greater extent than anywhere else, the wishes of the consumer are consulted with assiduity. Despite the fact that ten percent of all our economic activity goes into purely defense requirements, and an additional ten percent into nontangible channels such as education, cultural institutions, recreation and amusements, medical and hospital facilities, and measures to provide economic security for the mass of workers, consumer goods still comprise fully forty percent of our over-all output; thus, the strong drive for customer preference.[15]

But does this tack get us to the heart of the matter? Perhaps it does if we are talking about a particular company's obligations to its customers. Certainly it does not if we are talking about the generic responsibilities of corporate enterprise toward *consumers*.

A bridge to this wider problem is to be found in a statement by Peter Drucker: "The corporation can only function as the representative social institution of our society if it can fulfill its social functions in a manner which strengthens it as *an efficient producer,* and vice versa." [16] The "purpose of the corporation," he writes, "is to be *economically efficient,*" and the first rule it must follow as an institution is "survival as an efficient organization of human efforts to the common end of most *economical production*." [17] If it fails to play its part in the general operation of a free-enterprise society—in which there must be an allocation of scarce goods, the integration of "individual motives and individual actions into social effectiveness" and "a determinant of the direction of economic activity and a control over mistakes" [18]— the corporation will fail as an efficient producer and, by implication, will not serve the needs of consumers.

Particular corporations may not be efficient producers; and barring any cover of protectionism they are likely to disappear in time from the competitive market. The consumer is thus served, at least according to what has been aptly termed the "central tradition" of economics,[19] by the survival of the more efficient. But there seems to be a growing doubt that this is the whole answer to the question of corporate responsibilities toward consumers as a generic class.

The proper allocation of scarce resources is a further responsibility. Schumpeter once observed that "there is an economic logic that has nothing specifically 'capitalist' about it"; [20] there can likewise be a capitalist logic of resource allocation that has nothing specifically pro-corporation in it. The modern industrial corporation has an enviable record as a magnificent producer of goods and services that consumers want. But goods and service are not necessarily produced most efficiently in an economy in which private corporate enterprise predominates. Nor is it a foregone conclusion that such an economy allocates scarce human and material resources most wisely.

Whether in the long run the modern corporation will be up to the task of chief allocator of scarce resources and chief creator of goods and services that satisfy the whole range of human needs is cast into doubt by critics of the central tradition of economic theory. But this is not to conclude that the modern corporation inherently lacks the ingenuity and wisdom—in short, the capacity —to perform these functions. There is no reason to assume that private enterprise can never perform these tasks of allocation of resources and efficient production of goods and services as effectively as the State. For the modern corporation to forego this kind of responsibility is to pave the way to a centrally planned and controlled society.

Allocation theory, as derived from Marshall's *Principles of Economics* and widely accepted today, is built on assumptions which have been seriously questioned. Gardiner C. Means,[21] for

example, declares flatly that the assumptions of "classical" allocation theory as to flexibility of prices which adjust to equate supply and demand; as to full employment; as to labor as a commodity; and as to ownership and control of representative firms
being combined in a single owner or partnership, do not suffice.
Instead, he would postulate, "the modern corporation with its
vast size and the separation of ownership and control"; labor "not
as a commodity . . . but as a group of human beings"; and "not
flexible prices which equate supply and demand, but administered
prices under which supply and demand can be different." He
proposes an economic model consisting of a few great collectives.
In such a model "we have to deal not only with the determinants
of relative prices which help to guide the flow of resources into
different uses but also with the direction of resources within the
great collectives. . . . The problem of the allocation of resources
through corporate enterprise is both a matter of efficiency in production and importantly a matter of what is produced. A consumer veto over wasteful use of resources is by no means the same
as consumer control over their use." Means declares that "no
coherent theory has been produced which would effectively describe allocation in a model economy of collective capitalism or
for our actual economy, which is so largely composed of big collective corporate enterprises." He suggests that a better allocation theory is needed "if we are to understand our actual economy and make wise decisions in such matters as antitrust policy,
government regulation, and economic planning."

Clearly, the scope of corporate responsibilities toward a nation of consumers will turn out to be a very different charter of
obligations, if Means is correct, from those which one usually encounters in company statements of "customer responsibilities."
Nor can the significance of Means's argument be overlooked in
an age of continual international tension. Consider, for example,
the current search in military circles for better theoretical models
to deal with "nonprice allocators." Efficient priority or allocation
systems become a matter of major importance in national emergencies short of war, when legally imposed priority systems are
not operable.

W. G. Mellon [22] stated recently that "while the solution of the problem of efficient allocation *is* economics in its broadest sense, that science has concentrated a disproportionate share of its attention on the allocating function of the price system." He declared that in many instances, "for example, in the operation of a Socialist or centrally controlled economy, in consumer rationing, in production scheduling, or in the choice between alternative investment plans within the firm—the allocating function of the price system is either ineffective, or—the general case—is not completely superseded but must be performed in conjunction with other factors." For Mellon, "it is the last—the combinatorial case—which provides the greatest theoretical problem, and it is precisely in this case that our knowledge of the theory which underlies the system is most deficient." Mellon noted that not all economists accept the view that the price system is ineffective in certain situations; but past experience had clearly demonstrated that no central authority would rely entirely on the price system in periods of emergency as the only control over distribution. He noted also the view of Oskar Morgenstern that "there exists no real theory of priorities" and that "especially the working of priorities in systems where, also, prices prevail and localized decisions are frequently possible, is only imperfectly understood." [23]

It is significant that Mellon's bibliography, drawn up as it was with the wider considerations of general allocation theory in mind, contains so few items dealing with the broader problem of economic theory—a partial confirmation, at least, of Means's observation about the paucity of work in this area. Given this hiatus in the development of economic theory, it might be expected that corporate decision makers, most of whom have probably been indoctrinated directly or indirectly in Marshallian theory, base their decisions concerning allocation of resources on unrealistic assumptions.

But the difficulty is not entirely one of inadequacy in the theoretical models, serious as this may be. It lies deep in our philosophical assumptions about the purposes of economic production. Berle has recently declared that "great corporate power is exercised in relation to certain obligations" and as one of these he specifies that it should "supply the want in the area of its production. . . . Where the community has come to rely on a corporation for steel, oil, automobiles, or cigarettes, the corporation is obliged reasonably to meet that demand." [24]

But it is not immediately obvious, to take a hypothetical example, why a major tobacco company should continue indefinitely to supply tobacco to the community if its competitor is able to capture the market and drive the former company out of business. People will still be getting their cigarettes; and the first company certainly has no *public obligation* to maintain an unprofitable business for even one day. It is even questionable whether, taking all tobacco manufacturers together, there is any public responsibility at all to keep up the good work, assuming for the nonce that the consuming public wants a steady supply of cigarettes. Maybe the capital assets now used for this particular industry could better be used for other economic purposes. "Better" use of a country's capital assets, it may be objected, is a question to be decided by the consumer public, and, so long as there is a "demand" for the product in terms of purchasing power in the open market, no one should interfere by deliberately diverting that purchasing power to other products. Yet that is what society does all the time, especially in times of national crisis.

Gambling concerns operate profitably and legally in Nevada. Prostitution is still a legitimate business in some foreign jurisdictions. Corporate enterprise is undoubtedly efficient. It can satisfy any consumer demand. But can we be so sure about the "economic harmonies" which classical economists believed would bring about natural contributions to the welfare of society as a whole when each company pursued its own self-interest, serving the single goal of profitability by meeting any and all conceivable customer demands? To ask the question is to answer it.

Corporate policy will always include limitations on the kinds of goods and services it offers customers, whether they demand them or not. To this extent, corporate responsibilities toward customers are negative as well as positive. Nor are these limitations always imposed by external authority. Responsible product selectivity may mean the exclusion of product lines that promise large returns but would require the use of capital for socially dubious purposes. A company may choose among alternatives, none of which will result in socially deleterious products and services, but some of which may contribute more substantially to the upbuilding of the kind of community the responsible executive wants to see.

Product and service selectivity, then, involves a high degree of responsibility to the consumer public. Steady advancement in the standard of living, economic stability, community improvement, the maintenance of a high moral tone in society—all these are practical considerations that will often weigh as heavily in the scales as the mere satisfaction of consumer demands. One may object that all this has a patronizing air about it. "Let the consumer decide what he wants; it's the corporation's job to supply him." But here the "consumer sovereignty" theory breaks down. Corporate managements neither can, nor should, operate on that theory. The alternative is not necessarily a corporate oligarchy dictating to people what they should have in the way of products and services. Corporate enterprise geared to a free society never operates in this way. There is give and take, multilateral communication, consultation—in short, a working market system that is partly free and partly regulated.

Galbraith, in *The Affluent Society,* insists upon a kind of "social balance" as our economic goal, instead of the blind urgency—justified by the "conventional wisdom" and the "central tradition" of economic theory—to satiate the consumer through unimpeded productivity in the open market. The point will not be well received by corporate executives and can certainly not be expected to find its way into statements of corporate policy about responsibilities toward either the customer or the public at large. But his argument has relevance to the matter at hand, however unpalatable it may be to those who hold with the "conventional wisdom"—and these include both liberal and conservative politicians and economists, as he defines the term.

Enshrined in the "conventional wisdom," Galbraith thinks, is the belief that production for production's sake is unalloyed virtue. This sanctifying of production is something that we come by naturally; it reflects the central tradition of economic theory that arose out of the true need of the poorer societies of two centuries ago. We continue to measure progress in crude totals of production, as in the Gross National Product, and are alternately elated and depressed when this grand total rises or falls, as though this were an accurate index of our economic achievement as a nation. In fact, though we are an affluent society, richer by far than any known in history, obsolete economic axioms have led us to a paradoxical position.

While there is an opulent flow of consumer goods in the things that the private sector produces at a profit and forces into the market by "creating consumer demand," there is relative poverty in the things we badly need through action in the public sector— a good school system, slum clearance, city planning, decent provision for our aged, proper medical care, clean and adequate streets, parks, playgrounds, and so on. A foolish frugality in the public sector is more than matched by overproduction in the private sectors. Even military budgets have been kept down by the fear that we shall "defeat ourselves through bankruptcy," with flagrant results to an otherwise opulent society such as the painfully unnecessary frustrations over Korea.

Galbraith's case is pointed against the social imbalance that accompanies the false worship of consumer-sovereignty doctrine, the feeding of an insatiable hunger for more and more private consumption while we starve the public services essential to national vigor and national security. No matter how high the Gross National Product figure becomes, there will always be too little left over for public roads, education, and the rest. Private production and consumption are idolized; but the public services are suspect.

Significantly, Galbraith selects for the fly-leaf this quotation from Alfred Marshall: "The economist, like everyone else, must concern himself with the ultimate aims of man." The economists, in other words, cannot avoid the moral questions involved in the economics of distribution. He cannot assume that "wants" are all of equal value. So to argue, of course, is to fly in the face of the "conventional wisdom" which denies the propriety of the question: "How shall we make sure that there is a balance in the satisfaction of human need across the *entire range* of public and privately administered services?" This view indeed excites the nerve centers of many corporate managers who hold very different views from Galbraith about methods for weighting the relative merits of tailfin and missile production, for example. The method relied upon by corporate enterprise is the market. In the market the consumer decides what corporate enterprise produces. This— in the "conventional wisdom"—is the efficient allocator of scarce resources.

That Galbraith, as an economist, denies the whole tenor of this latter argument is perhaps not so significant for the corporate executive in search of a theory of corporate responsibility toward consumers. His book may indicate a significant trend in public opinion. It is not necessary to conclude, however, that this opinion, if it becomes dominant, will greatly transform the customer policies of individual companies. They will still need to give sober attention to the acceptability of their prices, the reliability and timeliness of their services, the integrity of their advertising, the propriety of their relationships with dealers and distributors. These are the micro-measures of good *customer* relations. They do not reach to the core of the larger issue: the responsibilities of large industrial corporations to the *consumer* public.

The latter area of responsibility is one which makes demands on economic and social theory that cannot, perhaps, be met at this time. We need to know a great deal more than we do about how the large corporation operates as a part of the whole system of production and distribution and what can reasonably be expected of it as an allocator of resources. Moreover, we need to know what value systems it can and should adopt as corporate objectives, given the kind of society we can anticipate.

Summing up the responsibilities of the corporation toward customers and consumers, there are, first, basic issues to be defined as to allocation theory and the role of the large corporation in the kind of allocation system that seems to be desired by the preponderant majority of consumers in our own national community; and secondly, more specific issues as to the direct relations between a specific company and its actual and potential customer group. The latter kind of issues—as to customers of a particular company—are not so difficult to define; most large corporations already have fairly well-established canons of conduct for their customer relations.

It is the former kind of issue that gives trouble. For it involves questions of basic social philosophy, and especially questions about priorities in our value system. Economic growth, pointed toward an ever-increasing flow of consumer goods and services distributed primarily in accordance with the forces of the market, now stands high upon the list of values that are generally accepted. Given the priority of such a value (ever-increasing production to meet consumer demands as defined by the market, and even, perhaps, as determined by what Galbraith calls "created demand"), corporate responsibilities toward the consumer public are clear enough: to provide an opulent flow of goods and services that people want or can be made to want by advertising and salesmanship—new and better and more exciting products at prices that will yield a profit and permit capital expansion for the eventual production of more and more such products.

This can be defended as the sum total of the corporation's responsibility toward consumers. For the industrial corporation is a *business,* it can be argued, and not a theological institution charged with the duty of weighing the ethical and cosmic merits of various kinds of consumer demands. The demands that the corporation has to fulfill are precisely those which market forces indicate, and it is not the function of corporate managements to teach consumers that they ought to want less of some things low on the scale of virtue and to cultivate desire for the higher things of life.

Persuasive as this argument is, it has been countered by a growing sense of doubt about production as an end in itself, or at least about *unselective* economic growth, with inadequate attention to social balance. But not even Galbraith proposes that it is the responsibility of corporations to redress any alleged imbalance. For him it is the responsibility of government, speaking for the consumer public as a whole; it would be expecting too much of the private corporation, however socially responsible, that in normal times it limit voluntarily its productivity in salable consumer goods and services in the national interest.

To insist upon such a self-denying ordinance would be to fly in the face of the injunctions of those who hold that the sole responsibility of the corporation is to its stockholders and to yield profits to them. On the other hand, it is probable that no great corporation today takes so orthodox a view of its responsibilities. On the contrary, there is more and more emphasis upon balanced responsibility to all contributor-claimant groups, including "the public at large." The public at large is perhaps another way of saying the "consumer public." And since the consumer public is one which consumes the products and services of *both* the public and the private sectors, we are thrown back to the question of social balance.

The sum of the reasoning here is that the large corporation does have a social responsibility at least to face this question and to provide some responsible answers. It must establish a rationale in defense of its own autonomy in making decisions about the allocation of its own resources or, better yet, a rationale in defense of a mixed economy in which most of the decisions about the allocation of the nation's resources are left to business units. Such a rationale has yet to be stated to the satisfaction of influential critics of the system as it now operates. Certainly, there is evidence that mere repetition of the "conventional wisdom" from the central tradition of economic theory, with variations on the theme of "freedom of enterprise," will not suffice.

CHAPTER XII

Employees and Suppliers

Responsibilities to Employees

THE EMPLOYEE RELATIONSHIP is fundamentally different from corporate relationships with other groups of contributor-claimants. Employees are internal to the organization; the others are outside. The view adopted here is that employees spend the greater part of their time in close and intimate relation with the command centers of the organization. From them the corporation demands a loyalty that is pervasive. The business is their business in a real sense, even though they may own none of its shares. It is the chief source of their livelihood. The fabric of their lives is woven into patterns that are prescribed by the nature of the enterprise. In this sense, share owners, customers, and suppliers are peripheral to the company's design for living; employees are at the heart of it. This fact alone provides an important clue to the nature of corporate responsibilities toward employees.

Because a corporation has so many kinds of employees, it is difficult to generalize about corporate responsibilities toward all of them. Nevertheless, two broad categories can be distinguished: managerial and nonmanagerial employees. In the first category are the president and his executive group, plus an indeterminate number of supervisory employees whose functions tend to identify them with management. In the second category are nonmanagerial employees—all others.

The line between these two categories is far from clear in specific situations. Foremen, for example, are a vital link between top management and the work force, and for that reason many American companies recently have taken a number of steps to restore the foreman to his true position as a key member of management.[1] Yet in other companies it is doubtful that foremen would be classified with the managerial group at all. Foremen are apt to be regarded as blue-collar employees toward whom management assumes different responsibilities from those they would assume toward the white-collar group. This latter distinction, however, provides no clue to the kinds of responsibilities a corporation can reasonably be expected to assume toward employees. The color of the collar is no index of degree of responsibility and delegated company authority.

An employee's locus in the company power pyramid is, in fact, an indispensable key not only to the responsibility of the corporation toward him but to his own responsibility as well. The structure of authority and command in the corporate polity may be either hierarchical-authoritative or democratic-permissive.[2] In either case, the substance of a company's responsibilities toward its employees will vary considerably with the degree and kind of authority reserved or delegated. Where little authority is delegated down from the president's office, greater responsibility toward all other employees necessarily rests upon the president. Responsibility is diffused as authority is diffused. There is a current trend of thought toward the permissive type of authority structure. But management still insists in most corporations upon the "right to direct the working force" and management in this sense may include everyone down to the foreman. This "right"—which involves correlative duties—has been limited through restrictions written into union agreements; but it is still regarded as a "managerial prerogative."[3]

The right to control the work force derives from managerial obligations toward groups other than employees, notably the company's security holders. Management is bound, moreover, to exercise its own authority over nonmanagerial employees to the exclusion of intrusive pressures from the outside. Thus, the New York Waterfront Commission levied a penalty against a stevedoring firm for submitting to the demands of a shop steward for the International Longshoremen's Association. The shop steward had called a work stoppage to enforce his demands for the discharge of a licensed hiring agent and several dockmen in violation of the Waterfront Compact. Waterfront regulations bar participation by the union in the employment of hiring agents and longshoremen. The Commission found that the company had "surrendered its basic responsibility" under the compact when it ended the strike by conceding to the shop steward's demands. Both the shop steward and the stevedoring company were convicted by the Commission.[4]

The responsibility of managerial employees for the proper exercise of authority over nonmanagerial employees thus becomes a responsibility of the corporation (acting through its board of directors) toward both categories. The corporation is expected to establish and maintain an adequate chain of command in its managerial personnel to meet its corporate obligations. And although one occasionally encounters in loose talk the idea that all personnel of a company must work as "one big team"—as though no distinction were to be drawn between the bosses and the bossed—the facts appear as a matter of necessity to be otherwise. The result is that there are substantial differences between the claims of nonmanagerial and managerial employees upon the corporation.

Managerial employees are seldom unionized whereas nonmanagerial employees frequently are. Corporate responsibilities toward the nonmanagerial are complicated by contractual obligations toward the unions which represent them, while the company's obligation with respect to managerial employees is directly to individuals. Multiemployer bargaining, where it exists, further complicates the corporate-employee relationship so far as company responsibilities are concerned. Even in the absence of such a further complication, the prevalence and scope of grievance procedures—culminating usually in private voluntary arbitration—tend to institutionalize the relationship in a significant way. It moves the mechanism for enforcing corporate responsibilities toward its nonmanagerial employees outside the strict confines of the company.

A new corpus of rights and duties is developing under the joint auspices of union and management representatives, together with outside arbitrators. A complete account of corporate responsibilities toward nonmanagerial employees would include a systematic statement of the rights and duties in this new corpus. Such a systematic statement has never been made, so far as is known, for large corporate enterprises generally, nor even for specific companies. But even a statement of present practice would not necessarily be a good index of an ideal code by which corporate responsibilities toward employees are to be judged. To set forth into the blue speculative yonder with a dreamed-up set of corporate responsibilities in this area would be quite unrealistic. Some "management philosophies" give the impression of having been so formulated. Given the strong trend toward unionization on the one hand and the development of professional management [5] of company relations with unions on the other, with the resultant growth of a large body of law [6] generated by collective bargaining agreements, one should expect to find the substance of corporate responsibilities toward nonmanagerial employees inductively, in this growing corpus, and not by deductive reasoning from subjectively selected premises.

It is often said that through collective bargaining there has been a gradual encroachment of unions upon managerial functions in corporate enterprises. Evidence of this trend appears in the subjects which have been covered in certain collective bargaining agreements.[7] Also there have been "adventures into joint administration (by management and union) of matters which would earlier have been the unquestioned province of management." [8] But, at the same time, there has been an effort made for stiffer management attitudes toward unions, and evidence of "more vigorous efforts to contain the union on substantive matters, or to control the avenues along which the substantive matters would come to rest." [9] Management has attempted to strengthen its arm in dealing with unions as spokesmen for nonmanagerial workers: it has given attention to training of first-line supervisors; it has made labor relations a major functional kind of managerial work; and it has come more and more to take the initiative in collective bargaining negotiations. Two decades ago it might have been predicted that the government of large corporations would eventually evolve into joint union-management forms. This no longer seems to be probable. Managerial employees increasingly take the position that they must balance many different contributor-claimant interests, not just those of the company and the union.

In practice, this means that the corporation, acting through its board as the governing organ, increasingly imposes upon managerial employees the duty of assessing *all* of the contributor-claimant interests and of recommending (through the president) to the board appropriate policies to guard these interests equitably. One result of this trend is the recognition by boards that they owe to the managerial group of employees the responsibility to delegate adequate authority over the nonmanagerial group. To the nonmanagerial employees, the board (technically, the corporation) owes a responsibility for a proper balance between authority and freedom in the governing of the corporate polity. A practical medium must be sought between despotism and anarchy; between excessive delegation of authority to managers, on the one hand, and, on the other, the hampering of their control over personnel so that the major goals of the enterprise as a whole cannot be achieved.

Here we have reached a veritable battleground of corporate policy. It is the scene of struggle over the problem of the Organization Man versus personal freedom. The outcome of this struggle is unpredictable. Perhaps the end result will be the establishment of some form of internal corporate constitutionalism. Or it may be, as Berle believes, the extension of judicial review to the protection of the rights, under the Bill of Rights and other constitutional clauses, of persons against the powers of the corporation. In any case, the crux of the matter is a procedural issue—the development of *processes* of corporate governance that provide practical means of redress against abuses of corporate power. To some extent the trend in this direction is indicated by the grievance procedures under collective bargaining agreements. But this falls far short of what Berle has in mind. He would have the judiciary brought in to enforce private rights against corporate power (in addition to public government's). For Berle, this judicial protection would be available to all persons, within or outside of the corporation, who might claim the right to judicial protection. This would include managerial as well as nonmanagerial employees.

The mere introduction into the debate of such an argument as Berle's, and his prognosis of legal development, may have a profound effect upon future forms of corporate governance. Boards will try to forestall the encroachment of public government into the internal affairs of the corporate polity. They will do this by elaborating new charters of company responsibility toward all classes of employees. Some of these charters will be nonoperational—for public consumption only. Others will be substantial, amounting to enforceable limitations on managerial authority all the way up and down the chain of command.

One effect of such a trend may be to work transformations within the present scheme of managerial tenure and compensation, including perquisites and retirement pay. It is possible that the principles governing tenure and compensation in the public service will gradually be adopted in the larger corporations to cover all employees. Public and private administration have many similarities that have been obscured by dogmatic and uncritical contrasts between government and business. The bureaucracy of the large corporation, though private, bears a strong resemblance to bureaucracy in public government. In both, the necessity of *continuity of service* and *efficiency in operation* precludes any break-up of indispensable large organizations. Large organizations are here to stay. Their internal polities, however, are subject to change as public necessity dictates. And in charting the responsibilities of any large organization toward its personnel, we enter the realm of theory that is both administrative and political.

In public administration we have seen the emergence of issues concerning the personal rights of employees that are not basically different from issues that arise in the large corporation. Loyalty investigations, army discharges, and so on, have lately become the subject of rather stringent judicial review. The competing claims of national interest and personal freedom are belatedly getting an objective hearing, whereas a few years ago the primary emphasis was upon tribal demands. So it is within the corporation. The emphasis has been upon the superior demands of the corporate entity: its survival and growth. A balance may gradually be achieved between this legitimate demand and the counter requirement of human consideration for the individual employee, at whatever level in the chain of command.

The balance will be reflected only in part by the substance of employee rights incorporated in collective bargaining agreements. For managerial employees such contracts will hardly become the instrument of justice in the corporate polity. The approach to their problem will be a very different one. It might conceivably be through statutory and case law. But preferably it could also come through purely internal reforms of the corporate polity, undertaken voluntarily by individual corporations in diverse ways.

A major difficulty with the latter alternative is that a corporation's responsibilities toward its employees already have been largely diluted simply because its authority has been diluted with the rising power of labor unions. From the company's point of view there has been an encroachment by labor unions upon managerial prerogatives in directing the work force and even in selecting it. But there are larger issues arising here from the standpoint of society generally. An employee is a person with many roles. Wage and salary earners alike are bearers of rights and duties in relation to more than one social group. In so far as they are unionized, their principals include not only the corporate employers but also other centers of command in union bureaucracies. The nature and extent of labor union power over millions of corporate employees have never been adequately explored either in political or economic theory.[10] The notion that either corporation or union enjoys a quasi-sovereign authority over employees hardly squares with the facts.[11]

Collective bargaining should not be regarded simply as a method of wage determination nor as an instrument of peace in industrial relations. It is a mechanism by which organized workers attempt to achieve an element of control and exercise it jointly with management.[12] Many analysts see this area of control extending to matters formerly thought to be exclusively the province of management. However, as the scope of union power expands, so will the scope of its responsibility, arguably with corresponding diminution of the responsibility of the corporate employer.

To what extent, then, can the corporation be held responsible toward *unionized* employees? To what extent is it responsible in its relations with *non*unionized employees? This last question raises the issue of the right of an individual employee *not* to join a union, a right which imposes upon the employer some responsibility to protect such an employee against pressure to join. "Employer opposition [to unions] is a bitter memory," writes E. H. Chamberlin, "but only in recent years is it coming to be realized that the pressures used by unions to gain control over laborers may be as vicious as union-busting tactics of employers have ever been." [13] Brown and Myers, reviewing current trends in management's attitudes toward employees and unions, observe that "there seems to have been a diminution in the conviction that management is the best judge of the interests of its employees," but they enter two cautionary notes: "In the first place, we should not exaggerate either the magnitude of the changes in philosophy or the certainty of their permanence"; and, secondly, "While management may not be held to be the best judge of employee interests, *it may regard itself as a better judge than, say, the union.*" [14]

In the light of recent congressional investigations into questionable practices on the sides both of unions and management, the impartial observer is inclined to question whether either the corporation or the union should be permitted to exercise too much power over employees, and to raise the more fundamental issues: To the extent that such power is unavoidable, how can its exercise be made responsible on both sides? And given the pluralistic character of our free society, to what extent should both corporate and union power over a man as employee and union member be limited by the legitimate claims upon him by other societal groups which also demand his loyalty?

A restricted concept of the corporate polity in terms of a management-employee relationship will not be a very useful model to work with in attacking these fundamental issues. The "firm" does not encompass unions. Nor do firms and unions have a right to encompass a man's loyalties. Yet unions participate in certain decisions made within the firm that profoundly affect the total lives of its employees. The conclusion seems inevitable that, sooner or later, the whole problem of a company's responsibilities toward its employees will have to be recast in a larger frame of reference. Moves toward further legislative regulation of the employer-employee relation—with special emphasis upon such items as union finances and pension funds—indicate that this wider frame of reference will involve the public sector as an active agent in the relationship. And as public control always tends to diminish private responsibility, so in the relations of corporations with their employees (nonunion, as well as unionized), one may expect to see the development of more limited managerial claims to total loyalty of the individual employee. Less sweeping generalizations about managerial "prerogatives" and a more carefully defined scope of managerial obligations may be one result. Another may be restrictions on union authority over members.

From the individual worker's point of view—and from the point of view of citizens in a free society—the issue is not the danger of *corporate* tyranny alone, but the danger of autocratic control over a man's life by any organization, whether it be a corporation, a union, or some other group in which membership is "voluntary" only in a Pickwickian sense. Again, the basic issue leads back to problems of social organization and procedural regularities in *all* organizations in which one has "voluntary" membership. Due process in this universal sense can be designed to preserve the dignity and rights of real persons as distinguished from corporate persons and organizational entities. A society in which one must choose between a despotic employer and a despotic union is hardly a free society. It is in this larger frame of reference that corporate responsibilities to employees must be worked out.

Responsibilities to Suppliers

The next group of contributor-claimants associated immediately with the large corporate enterprise is its suppliers. So far as corporate responsibilities are concerned, the most important of these subgroups of suppliers are two: satellite and nonsatellite vendors.

Satellite vendors depend so heavily upon the large corporation that special problems arise in its relationships with them. When a large corporation is a supplier's principal customer, the effect upon the supplier's business—and indeed its very survival—of the corporation's policies can be enormous. Ordering and scheduling practices of the corporation may or may not enable the satellite to maintain an efficient and stable operation. If the supplier's invoices are not paid when they are due and the payments are inordinately delayed, the result can be costly to both parties. The primary company may need, in its own interest, to extend special services to the satellite supplier, as, for example, in aids to its manufacturing, engineering, and research departments.

Nonsatellite vendors, on the other hand, are regarded as businesses that can or should stand on their own feet regardless of the primary company's operations and policies. And this raises the difficult problem of distinguishing between satellite and nonsatellite industries.

In the central tradition of economic theory there seems to be no room for such a distinction and no place for special corporate responsibilities with respect to any suppliers. They are all parts of the competitive system and subject to the discipline of the market place, like the primary company itself. If they fail, other sources of supply must be found. "Artificial" supports of their businesses are not called for.

Despite the prevailing credo of American businessmen along these lines, however, it is more than doubtful that corporate manager's practices in relationships with suppliers actually conform to the dogma. They are concerned about the continuity and economic health of all their suppliers for both practical and sentimental reasons. Established patterns of vendor relations are the line of least resistance; but personalities are involved too. Moreover, there are strong pressures generated in the business community itself to sustain the life of little companies, to say nothing of the general feeling that small businesses must be protected as an article of faith in the free enterprise system.

Thus, there are many forces which converge upon the managements of large corporations to show special consideration for vendors in or near the category of "satellite." In fact, it has now become standard operating procedure in the public relations output of some of the major industrial corporations to publicize their contributions to this vital sector of the economy. Big Business, in short, in defending bigness, seeks to demonstrate that the great and the small are interdependent and that diversity of size is a sign of health in the economy as a whole.[15]

One of the most important stands in this argument is that industrial progress depends heavily upon the contributions made to scientific and technological knowledge by great companies, which alone can mobilize the necessary resources and which then distribute this knowledge as a kind of "plus-value" to other enterprises, competitors as well as suppliers.[16] There is implied in this argument a certain responsibility on the part of the large corporation so to distribute its technological knowledge that its suppliers will benefit therefrom.

Other areas of supplier relationships concern the ethics of purchasing practices. Company representatives who accept gifts from vendors who are trying to curry favor and garner valuable orders obviously violate the best canons of corporate responsibility toward suppliers. Such practices are possibly legion in the world of trade and are not unknown in the sphere of public affairs. Are there not fundamental differences between favoritism in government and favoritism in a freely competitive market? Perhaps these basic differences might provide some clue to the character of corporate responsibility. Officials in government have power which the influence peddlers seek to divert in the direction of their clients. Representatives of large corporations also have power, albeit of a somewhat diluted quality. Corporate power does not have the coercive agencies of the state at its command. Nonetheless, it has the power to decide the allocation of considerable resources among competing suppliers and, moreover, it is a power that is a function of size. Big Government and Big Business have much in common when it comes to the far-reaching influence of their decision makers. Both Big Government and Big Business—along with Big Labor—face the necessity of formulating and enforcing standards of personal behavior upon their purchasing representatives.

We have yet to witness the development of a common body of ethical rules to govern the decisions of men who sit in these strategic positions. In the absence of such a universal code, acceptable to all, every company must draw up its own standards and seek the most appropriate methods for enforcing them. The kind of judicial review of corporate action foreshadowed by Berle to assure "due process" to suppliers and others may not emerge if the business community is able to provide its own standards, procedures, and authority limitations to the general satisfaction of the American public.

CHAPTER XIII

Competitors, Local Communities, the
General Public and Governments

Responsibilities to Competitors

ASK THE PRACTICAL corporate executive where he goes to find guidance on competitor relations. He will say: first, to lawyers; second, to marketing counselors. Or he might reverse this order: first, to the sales components to find out what the competition is and how it must be met; second, to legal counsel to find out what the company dare not do. He is constrained to act within the bounds of public expectations expressed in law and custom. But these are only negative guideposts. The responsibility owed to stockholders to maximize profits generates a positive drive to improve the company's market position—but only up to a certain point. What point? Only that prescribed by law?

Competition is rivalry. But rivalry, even among nations at war, is seldom defended to the extreme of extermination of the adversary. Unconditional surrender is a debatable goal in war and no less so in the struggle for economic survival among business competitors. Rules of the game are presupposed. The institutions of private property and contract, of profit making and freedom of trade are major premises in the rules of the competitive game. They are to be preserved and protected in the continuing struggle. They are also, as Walton Hamilton once observed, the "mechanics of competition."

The lure of profit draws individuals and corporations into industry and impels them to produce and market goods. The openness of an industry to all who care to take its chances prevents monopoly and limits money-making to reasonable gains. The bait of profits is beacon and guide; the freedom of trade is brake and governor. Together they direct industry, keep it orderly and adjust it to a changing social order.[1]

The point beyond which an adversary may not go in business competition is not readily definable by law or business ethics. These codes are men's estimates of the role of business competition in the larger business of a society.

Contemporary societies—and especially that of the United States—are dynamic, however. And the far boundaries of allowable rivalry in any field, not excluding business, are subject to change. Although competition in the market is widely regarded as the *sine qua non* of free enterprise, laissez faire, and capitalism, doubt grows about its centrality in our contemporary economic order, whatever may be its respected status in our economic creed. In the creed, competition is the great natural selector of enterprises that are fit to survive. In practice, competition is hedged. Nor is the hedging necessarily furtive, in the penumbra of illegality; it is openly defended as a civilized way of doing business, an escape from the "law of the jungle." The antitrust principle, embalmed in our written law since the nineties as an undebatable tenet of righteous economic faith in competition, has been progressively honored in the breach.[2] The sovereign sway of value, as defined by the free play of market forces, by supply and demand, by rivalry among many competitors, has gradually given way to other norms.

National security, a higher standard of living for workers, and a place in the sun for industries hard-driven by foreign competition, a charitable regard for the depressed sectors of the economy, a sense of duty toward the small business—these and other considerations have worked inroads upon competition as a universal way of life. Combinations, so suspect by economic theorists of the central tradition, seem no longer to be the exception that proves the rule of competitive efficacy. Economic decisions today, though not so centralized in government here as they are in other economies, are hardly the multitudinous individual decisions imagined in the classical model of competition. Public and private collectivities "compete" alongside individual entrepreneurs in ways that arouse the deepest skepticism among economic theorists. They invent new terms like "oligopoly," "duopoly," and the "mixed economy" to explain the prevailing economic order. At times also, they criticize it severely for having strayed so far from the purity of our faith.

The critics about whom we are here concerned are not those who would extirpate the "evils" of competition and capitalism and replace them with a new order of things along socialistic lines. They are rather the more conservative group that would get us back to pure and undefiled competition and to capitalism with a capital C.[3] It may fairly be asked, where does the modern corporation stand on such issues? And how will the position it takes on these issues affect its responsibilities toward competitors?

Corporate responsibilities toward competitors are, to a great extent, determined by the prevailing sense of justice in the matter. But what is the prevailing expectation regarding competitive behavior? As to farm prices and farm incomes, it is doubtful that people are overwhelmingly in favor of competition. The fair trade laws seem to have diminished in scope and degree of enforceability, but it is also doubtful that for the foreseeable future public policy will prescribe for the retail trade the universal principle of unfettered competition. In coal and oil industries there are elaborate arrangements, under the force of law, to adjust supply-demand relationships without leaving it to price competition alone. Wage rates are competitive only in a very special sense which must take into account the legally protected collective bargaining power of unions and the countervailing powers of employers. In the industrial sector of the economy, it is true, competition is the accepted order of things. But what kind of competition?

There are competing theories of "effective" competition. From which shall the modern corporation choose? Is "workable competition" [4] a question of market structure, or of limitations on market position, or of the scope of action permissible to firms? Does it require a fairly large number of sellers and buyers, no one of whom occupies a large share of the market? Does it mean only the absence of collusion, such as conspiracy to set prices? Does it include complete freedom of entry into the market by new enterprisers? Or is the test of a competitive system the actual performance of firms: product and process improvement, downward adjustment of prices as a result of reduction of costs, concentration of production in units of the most efficient size, efficient adjustment of capacity to output, and waste avoidance in distribution?

Shall society require the corporation to choose the standards of a freely competitive economy from the legal criteria established by legislatures, courts, and administrative agencies; or should such standards be those set up by the economists (and, if so, *which* economists)? Criteria drawn exclusively from legal norms are obviously inadequate. It is not so much that they are difficult to define with accuracy, given the shifts and nuances of statutory interpretation by official agencies. This is a technical question for corporate counsel who must always predict somehow what the courts will do if antitrust laws are invoked, or likely to be invoked, against the corporation. Accurate prediction is hard, perhaps impossible, but management always has to depend in the last analysis upon legal counsel for guidance in the proprieties of competitor relations. Still, counsel may find that there are conflicting rules of law, or that there are several possible interpretations of relevant legal provisions to be pressed upon courts and administrative agencies, or that no legal precedent exists. The choice then becomes more than a legalistic problem. It may require managerial decision on central issues of social policy. Fair trade legislation, for example, clearly interferes with the free play of competition, but in fairness to its distributor-dealers, the large industrial corporation may conclude that it must make every effort to see that such laws are enforced with respect to its own products. In fair trade laws, as in antitrust, there is a conflict of social and economic theories. The corporation cannot always avoid taking a stand on one side or the other. The rules of law may be poor reeds to lean upon.

In seeking guidance from the economists, on the other hand, the corporation finds no consensus. They are not agreed as to the objectives of antimonopoly policy. Edward S. Mason states the problem in this way:

Should [antitrust policy] attempt to bring about a structure of industrial markets and a set of business practices such that the scope of action of individual firms is severely limited by the action of rival firms in the economy?   Or should the objective be efficient use of economic resources, considering elements of market structure only when they can be shown to lead to ineffective business performance? [5]

Mason contends that both these tests have to be used to complement rather than to exclude each other.   He concedes that as to adequate business performance it is very difficult to devise tests that can be administered by a court of law, but argues that "with respect to many industrial markets an informed judgment is possible"—a judgment, that is to say, as to whether the business performance of a particular industry is relatively "good" or "bad," or is "adequate" or "inadequate." [6]

Such judgments are bound to be influenced by preferences that are a part of the operational code [7] of the man who makes them. The corporate executive may have a very different operational code from that of the economist or the jurist.   And within each of these groups there are internal debates about the goals, the standards and the tests of a competitive system.   If the corporation takes as its standard the classical competitive model, holding to the view that monopoly is bad while the "competitive order" of Hayek is good, it will still face the problem Mason has stated. Will it assign greater relative importance, in assessing its own responsibilities toward the business community, to the objective of limiting the scope of action of the firm in the market (e.g., avoiding too great a share of the market) or to the objective of efficient performance in the use of resources (e.g., progressiveness in product and process innovation, a good cost-price relationship, a good capacity-output relationship with the lowest possible investment for a given level of productivity, appropriate profit levels that are not continuously and substantially higher than in comparable industries, minimum selling expenditures with competitive effort chiefly indicated by service and product improvements and price reductions),[8] or to both of these objectives?   Or will it reject either objective and set up one of its own?   And if so, what would be the substance of that independent objective?

Mason observes, interestingly enough, that when it comes to a choice between the two antitrust objectives indicated above, "there are those who are willing to sacrifice a lot in the way of [business] performance to establish market structures which severely limit the power and scope of action of individual firms," while to others this seems less important. He is reflecting the views of students of antitrust problems. It is doubtful that the business-man will choose either objective with alacrity, though presumably this choice is necessary—barring a third objective set up inde-pendently as a firm's own competitive goal—since large corpora-tions can hardly, in the present business climate, deny the virtue of competition as an article of faith. And if he does choose be-tween the two he necessarily makes a basic value judgment about one of the most important issues of public policy. "How much, in fact, would have to be sacrificed in the attainment of one objec-tive to secure a given amount of progress towards the other is the heart of the public policy problem in the area of business organi-zation," Mason continues, adding that, in his opinion, "the choice of one of these objectives, to the exclusion of the other, would make a substantial amount of difference in many industrial markets." [9] Needless to say, it would make a great deal of differ-ence to the corporation that exercises the choice, for it would not only determine its policy with respect to competitors but also its relations with government.

Government agencies are apt to regard the antitrust pro-visions simply as laws that have to be enforced. Corporations view them respectfully as something to be avoided in the breach. But these statutes are not ordinary laws. They reflect a theory of business enterprise, a philosophy of business. In this respect they are, as Chief Justice Hughes observed, of the same order of gener-ality as a constitutional provision. It is not a question of how many cases can be won by either side. The more significant issue is whether, case by case, there is maintenance of competition in accordance with the principles of antitrust provisions which actu-ally benefit the economy as a whole and the American system of relatively free enterprise. This consideration has priority over an attorney general's desire to win the government's suits against alleged violators of the law or the corporation's desire to escape prosecution. Nor is it the case of public *versus* private interests. Presumably the public interest and the interests of the corpora-tion are served simultaneously by enforcement of antitrust laws and the maintenance of a truly competitive system.

Recently, however, there has been a reaction against antitrust and the emergence of pleas for the "new competition." Lilienthal [10] attacks trust-busting as an anachronism. Frederick Lewis Allen, in *The Big Change: America Transforms Itself,* defends the growth of great enterprises. Schumpeter [11] found the "creative destruction" of obsolescent products and processes by large firms, and their replacement with new things and more efficient ways, to be a mark of progress and took a jaundiced view of zealous enforcement of the traditional antitrust policies. Galbraith, no opponent of antitrust, a few years ago [12] seemed to think that better results could be expected in controlling the market power of large firms by relying upon the countervailing power of other groups. In his recent account of *The Affluent Society* his search for a solution of the problem of inflation gives short shrift to the "conventional wisdom" about the virtues of competition as any significant clue. And business leaders, however faithful they may remain to the underlying doctrine of the Sherman Act, have often insisted—and courts have often agreed with them—upon a "rule of reason" in its interpretation. The Attorney General's Committee on Antitrust Policy in 1955 was said—by Louis B. Schwartz, a dissenter to the majority report—to have faced a "powerfully supported proposal to reorient antitrust administration to give greater scope to the 'rule of reason' and, by the same token, to cut down or eliminate the classes of restraint prohibited as illegal 'per se' ".[13] One of the grounds for his objection to giving greater scope to the "rule of reason," as against "per se" prohibitions, was the fear that reliance upon it in enforcement of the law would require "full economic investigation" into the effects of alleged violations. He felt, moreover, that such protracted inquiries would really weaken the law. It is perhaps significant that few of the many distinguished members of the Committee agreed with him on this point.

Yet, as the majority report of the attorney General's Committee clearly stated at the outset of their document: "The general objective of the antitrust laws is promotion of competition in open markets. This policy is a primary feature of private enterprise. Most Americans have long recognized that opportunity for market access and fostering of market rivalry are basic tenets of our faith in competition as a form of economic organization." The Sherman Act was "a charter of economic freedom," and together with the Federal Trade Commission Act and the Clayton Act it made a trinity that was the "core of the present antitrust policy."

The basic problem for the large corporation is not whether it will or will not obey the charter of economic freedom in which the principle of competition is enshrined. Committed as it is to obedience to the law of the land as a more general principle, the modern corporation has its responsibilities cut out for it unless it intends to advocate openly the revision of the basic charter. Such advocacy is entirely within the rights of a corporate citizen, just as it is within the rights of any citizen. But to launch out upon this course is to entail certain obligations. In the main there is an obligation to propose alternatives to antitrust policy. So frontal an attack upon a basic tenet of American economic faith, involving as it would a complete rethinking of the business philosophy that underlies the trinity of statutes, is an awesome assignment for any corporate executive. So sweeping a revision of our business philosophy has not yet been proposed in any responsible quarter of the corporate sector.

What has appeared, nevertheless, is a proposed "reorientation" of antitrust administration. Schwartz attacked this idea in his dissent to the majority report of the Attorney General's Committee. Mason says bluntly that this is the road to an emasculation of the basic antitrust statutes. "The demand for full investigation of the consequences of a market situation or a course of business conduct is a demand for nonenforcement of the antitrust laws." [14] And it would appear from the remarks of the dissenters associated with Schwartz—J. M. Clark, Alfred E. Kahn, Eugene V. Rostow, and George Stigler—that they were in substantial agreement with this dictum.

What the reaction of corporate executives generally may have been to this issue is not clear. But the report of the Business Advisory Council on "Effective Competition," although it gives respectful obeisance to the Sherman Act, does clearly come out for increasing the scope of the "rule of reason." Many businessmen are suspicious, and properly so, of the trend of thought which would read the antitrust laws as a condemnation of bigness in the firm as an evil per se. Business criticism of antitrust policy, as Mason has pointed out, tends to center on the allegation that this policy is an attack on "size" as such. The fear is that government agencies bent upon zealous enforcement of this policy will threaten the very foundations of the economy by tearing down structures that are essential to the growth, prosperity, and security of the United States. While Mason denies [15] that this is a correct reading of the intent of the enforcement agencies—he insists that, instead, they are concerned, and correctly concerned, with overweening *market power* and not with bigness per se—the fear remains. So, short of any radical revision of antitrust policy, it has evidently seemed the course of wisdom on the part of large firms to insist upon better interpretation and administration of antitrust policy. It is possible that corporate management would find Mason's reading as a condemnation of market power quite as unpalatable as condemnation of size. But at least the test of market power opens the door to factual examination of business performance. And it is in this realm of inquiry that the corporation could bring to bear its own guns of economic analysis. Business need not concede that the antitrust division of the Justice Department alone has a monopoly on the knowledge of economic life.

This leads, then, to some conclusions about the content of corporate responsibilities with respect to competitors and the business community generally. We have not here discussed in detail other kinds of statutes that bear upon this problem. There are many. But antitrust is the leading example and will suffice to make the point.

There is, in the first place, a corporate obligation to take a clear position on antitrust (and other broad public policies affecting corporate relations with competitors and the business community)—either for it or against it—and with a well-reasoned case. The jurists and the economists may be right or they may be wrong. The corporation must decide for itself. Or to put it another way, corporate managements have an obligation to all their contributor-claimant groups to think through such basic issues of public policy, affecting as they do so vitally the interests of all these groups, and to arrive at an independent judgment which protects and preserves contributor-claimant interests as they merge in the corporate enterprise.

It will not do simply to take the lawyers' analysis. Legal counsel characteristically takes the position that the corporation must keep out of trouble with the law as it is, or at least press for favorable interpretations of existent statutes. Practicing lawyers rarely have the time to devote their talents and energies to the problem of basic revision of public policies.

Nor can the economists be the chief mentors; they disagree among themselves, and examination of the literature shows clearly enough that what they have in mind is not so much advocacy of the corporate position as the public interest as they see it. Such a point of view is entirely appropriate to academic scientists and philosophers. But it leaves unanswered the specific problem that faces the corporate executive who has his own responsibilities. That these responsibilities *do* embrace a concern for the public interest is unquestionable; but that is not the whole of a corporate executive's responsibilities by any means. The balance-of-interest doctrine, which has generally been adopted in corporate thought, requires that the public interest be taken into account in formulating corporate policy. It does not require that no other interests be taken into account. And it is elementary, in our pluralistic society, that one must look out for his own, albeit with reasonable attention to the interests of the commonweal.

The second major responsibility of the corporation toward its competitors and the business community generally is to implement the philosophical position it takes on issues of public policy. If the position is radical revision of antitrust, for example, the obvious duty of the corporate executive is to put people to work —in the legal department, but also in all research departments of the company where public policy specialists in this area are competent to make a contribution—on the substance of the proposed revision. The alternatives must be backstopped with thorough analysis of the relevant facts, a structure of theory that will stand up in public debate, and drafts of legislation that will command respect from Congressional committees before which hearings will inevitably be held.

If the position is reinterpretation of existent law, much the same process applies, though with reference to courts and administrative agencies and not legislatures. In both cases, however, the danger is that the task will be assigned to legal specialists alone. The results of corporate cogitation on the kind of problems we are dealing with here will have to be communicated to many audiences: juristic, academic, journalistic, and lay. The task of formulating a philosophy of business, implemented by practical proposals, demands all the internal resources of even the largest corporation and, in many instances, outside resources also.

Here, we cannot go beyond these general prescriptions. The details of corporate responsibilities toward competitors depend entirely upon a set of basic premises. Most company statements of such responsibilities deal only with the details, without elaborating the premises. If the premises are made clear, the specific responsibilities that flow from them will become obvious.

Responsibilities to Local Communities

Every well-managed company makes a considerable effort for an effective community relations program.[16] For this is an indispensable function of prudent management. It is that management function, to quote from the Community Relations Manual of one of the largest companies, which "appraises plant community attitudes, identifies and relates company policies with community interests, and initiates programs of action to earn community respect and confidence for the company." The expenditures for such programs are justified, as a rule, as necessary budget items. Ideally, they are a legitimate part of the cost of doing business; they are warranted by reason of the expectation of certain benefits to the company; they represent a good investment of corporate funds; usually the returns justify the outlay.

Benefits to the company, though somewhat intangible, are nevertheless specific enough to make the case: the recruitment of better workers, the reduction of turnover and absenteeism, the improvement of job satisfaction and morale, increased sales, and the creation of a better local understanding and acceptance of the company. Good public relations, it is often said, must begin at the grass roots; and the local communities in which a large company operates are obvious places to do such work.

The case for community relations programs can also be put on the basis of mutual obligation as between company and community. Business firms "expect the schools to provide well-educated employees with good attitudes, skill, and work habits; the churches to contribute persons of good morals and character; the local government to furnish fire, police and sanitary protection, and highway facilities; the public utilities to provide water supply, gas, electricity, and transportation; and the social service organizations to contribute health, hospital, and medical facilities." And in return, the community expects business organizations "to provide regular employment, good working conditions, fair pay, and satisfying work; to purchase goods and services locally and put more money in circulation in the community; to contribute to worthwhile local charitable and cultural projects; to pay its share of taxes to support the local government; and to be a good neighbor keeping a clean and attractive place of business." [17]

This give-and-take argument, however, does not exhaust the resources of business rationale concerning company responsibilities to local communities. "Today's industrial leaders recognize that it no longer is enough just to build a better mousetrap. Good industrial citizenship must go hand in hand with the production end of the business. Good industrial citizenship consists mainly of becoming a part of the community and cultivating genuinely friendly relationships with the people who live in it." So runs the line of reasoning in the *General Motors Plant Visits Plan Book*. And it can be found in numerous statements of businessmen in recent years. William T. Gossett has declared that "we can hope . . . that whether or not there is a 'corporate conscience,' there may at least be 'corporations of conscientious men.' We can base that hope on the vigor and tenacity of the moral principles that underlie our civilization." [18] He then quotes Crawford H. Greenewalt to the effect that there are pressures upon business for the preservation of a moral code, to do things, not because they are required, but because they are right. "Ethical principles," said Greenewalt, "are vibrantly and affirmatively alive. The segment of humanity concerned with business will be no less responsive to these pressures than any other group." [19]

This is hardly the *quid pro quo* argument. One moves here in a very different realm of discourse. The case for community responsibilities becomes the Aristotelian case for *koinonia,* the friendship of neighbors who have the moral virtues requisite to true citizenship.[20] The corporation is a kind of association that is more than a grouping of utilitarian producers. It is more than a common participation in profitable enterprise. It is a smaller community of citizens within the larger community of citizens, all of whom participate in a common life with aims that rise above economic goals alone. The *koinonia* of Aristotle was a partnership or a fellowship of men who, unlike slaves, could know and practice the principles of justice. Such an Aristotelian fellowship "must be a common participation not in mere life but in something higher, especially in thought and conversation," writes McIlwain in a penetrating commentary upon this aspect of Aristotle's political theory. And he quotes from the *Nichomachean Ethics:*

[This is] what we mean when we speak of living together in the case of men . . . not, as in the case of cattle, merely occupying the same feeding ground. . . . Some people are companions in drinking, some in gymnastic exercises, or in the chase or in philosophy, and each class spends its days in that for which it cares more than for anything else in life; for it is their wish to live with their friends, they do the things and participate in the things which seem to them to constitute a common life.

But the fellowship, or *koinonia,* of every association from the household on up to that of the city-state itself, was cemented by the bonds of justice; and "in the household first we have the sources and springs of friendship, of political organization, and of justice" for "man is not a lonely being, but has a tendency to partnership with those to whom he is by nature akin." [21]

It is, then, this kinship in a common sense of justice that presumes to breed the sense of corporate citizenship in the local community. It is more than a mere propinquity—the fact that neighbor should respect the rights of neighbor and that a company's local plant is juxtaposed with the local community—that indicates corporate responsibilities. The corporate neighbor is, in fact, an association of human beings who share with their fellow citizens a conscientious interest in the commonweal.

That these ideas are now widely accepted in corporate managerial circles is perhaps a debatable point. More probably, the manager of community relations work will phrase the rationale in less philosophical language. He might agree with Greenewalt in principle, but in practice he has constantly to resist pressures for outlays of company resources—under the heading of community responsibilities—that seem to him and his colleagues to be little more than raids upon the corporate treasury. And in view of his obligations to groups of other interests, such as those of stockholders, few of which may be represented in the local community in which he operates, his decisions are sometimes likely to appear to the local community as ungenerous in the extreme.

The suspension or discontinuance of operations in a local plant is a case in point. On balance, it may be the only logical and prudent decision in company headquarters possibly thousands of miles away. All the good will that has been built up so painstakingly over the years in fulfilling community responsibilities in smaller details can be swept away by that one decision. The dictum that this is a "corporation of conscientious men" may then be taken by the local community at less than face value. The answer must, of course, be that there are larger issues at stake, that the community to be served by the corporation is wider than the local community, and that the "balanced best interests" of all contributor-claimants in the whole enterprise take precedence over the single claims of the one local community concerned. There can be varying degrees of abruptness in pulling up stakes and ways of softening the blow. But in the last analysis, the company may have no real choice in the matter. It may have to subordinate its community responsibilities to others of a higher order.

The fact is that the largest industrial corporations, with installations in many places throughout the nation and in foreign countries, are not "citizens" in any ordinary sense. Nor are the obligations of corporate citizenship merely the sum of the *local* community obligations it has in the sites of its plants and other installations. The largest corporations are citizens of the world, with customers, stockholders, employees, and suppliers scattered through many nations. To conceptualize the modern corporation as a congeries of separate plants is to belie the facts of modern large-scale enterprise and the role it plays in contemporary society. The colored areas on political maps provide no real clue to the scope of its activities as a living organism. Thus we must widen the perspective for assessing community responsibilities to so wide-ranging a general public as this organism serves and take into account the several political governments that represent this public.

Responsibilities to the General Public and Governments

Our analysis of the social responsibilities of the corporation began with an enumeration of certain specific obligee groups toward which companies have fairly clear and established obligations that are enforceable. These groups included security holders, customers, employees, suppliers, competitors, and others in the business community and local communities. For all of these groups there are enforceable obligations. Some of the obligations are legal and enforceable in courts and administrative agencies of government. Others are enforced by custom and the working of the market system. Still others, while not enforceable by external agencies, public or private, are voluntarily assumed by corporate management. The basis for this voluntary assumption of corporate responsibilities has been variously described. It may be simply "expedient" to assume them or there may be response to the "corporate conscience"—or at least to the sense of duty in conscientious men who manage corporations.

On the narrowest view of the matter, taking the whole range of business philosophies concerning the social responsibilities of the modern corporation, there is only one such responsibility: to make a profit for the owners of the business, namely, the stockholders. All other so-called social responsibilities flow, if they exist at all, from this major obligation of corporate managements. And these peripheral responsibilities are said to be justified only in so far as they are instrumental to the chief aim of a business enterprise: the production of goods and services that are sold on the open market at a profit.

So limited a view of social responsibilities is seldom expressed by corporate leaders today. Rather they take the position, by and large, that the corporation has obligations to many different groups which contribute to the enterprise and therefore have legitimate claims upon it. One of the most important of these groups—important, that is to say, to the minds of many executives and to many contemporary commentators on public affairs—must now be reviewed. That group is often described as "the general public." With this broadly designated group it is possible to link the public's representative, Government. Thus arises the proposition that corporations have a social responsibility to the public and to governments.

There is one virtue in the conservative argument that corporations owe the primary responsibility to stockholders. It permits the analyst to subsume any alleged obligations to other groups as ancillary to this central responsibility and it provides the touchstone for testing the purity of these allegations. But it is a logical virtue without moral dimensions. Certainly this would be the judgment of many practical men, at least, and it could hardly be maintained that their position is merely defensive. It is no doubt true that many business leaders feel that they must avow lofty concern for the public interest in the ambient criticism of Big Business. It is likewise presumptuous to assert that there can be no other cause for their concern. The Big Businessman can also be Man Thinking, in the Emersonian sense. His thoughts partake of the ideas that permeate the community. Some of these ideas, as they relate to corporate obligations, carry a rather high potential. Sitting where they do, corporate managers are keenly aware of the conduct people expect of the corporation and what conduct they will not tolerate.

When one reviews the specific content of corporate obligations toward the several groups of contributor-claimants described in the preceding pages, it becomes obvious that the managerial sense of multiple responsibilities is fully justified. It would be justified alone on the ground that the law governing business relationships defines many different obligees and that there are no clearly stated principles to be derived from this extensive legal corpus which gives one set of obligees undisputed priority.

But there is, in addition to the law, another corpus of obligations created by custom, by business practice, by codes of ethics, by the proponents and the critics of the conventional wisdom, and by the "public philosophy." All of these ideas impinge upon corporate managements. In the minds of business executives they leave a residue of conviction that they do, in fact, stand responsibly at the helm of a major social institution. Its role in modern society is a changing one, but it is already a multidimensional role, whatever may be its delineation in the central tradition of law and economics.

With these considerations in mind we turn to the question of corporate obligations to the general public and to governments which purport to represent the public. As time goes on, the public, acting through governments, shows more and more interest in corporate affairs. Gossett has put it that "the corporation in all its various relationships with other economic interests, with society at large, even with foreign nations, has been increasingly subject to legal control during the past century." And he hastens to add that important as this legal trend is for those who determine the policies and practices of corporations, it is far from the whole story. Managers would err, he thought, in predicting future trends of social control, were they to overemphasize the law as it may be found today in the books. There had been a tendency among lawyers, especially young lawyers, to place too much reliance upon the books. Some of the answers were to be found there; but many were not. "The law necessarily deals with existing situations; it generally does not anticipate new developments. And so it generally does not provide ready solutions of new problems. For these, we must look into the living social, economic, and political environment of our day, which is the real determinant of corporate action." [22]

Gossett goes on to examine the "human factors in the corporate ecology" in order to find the newer dimensions of corporate responsibility. He refers to Berle's comment that "power to deal with other men's property and occupation, however absolute it may be as a matter of technical contract law, is subject to certain limitations" which still lie uncrystallized "in the field of inchoate law." These inchoate areas are of special concern to management, Gossett declared, "lest they become areas of repressive law." Management decisions thus tend to reflect an awareness of public attitudes. The standard of reference "is not alone what the law says, but to the total environment that will give color and character and significance to our acts." The effect of this environment upon the conduct of the corporation, furthermore, "is increased by the fact that the modern-day big business enterprise lives in a world of communication"; it dwells in the constant glare of publicity. And when it is taken for granted that "a fundamental goal of the corporation is to preserve the greatest freedom of action consistent with the public interest, "together with the fact that the law is a delayed reflection of social mores and ideas, "the effort to safeguard corporate freedom requires constant attention to the whole environment and ideological climate of the enterprise." [23]

The tenor of these remarks is that through constant attention to public expectations,[24] and not alone to the law as it stands on the books, corporate autonomy can be preserved. But, one might well ask, is there any social responsibility on the part of the corporation to protect its autonomy? Although the lectures from which these passages are taken were in a series under the title of "Corporate Citizenship," the larger part of the discussion was devoted to practical advice to corporation counsel as a defender of the corporate interests. Warning that the public demands should be *heeded* is not the same as saying that they ought to be *acted* upon. There is implicit in the argument the idea that freedom of corporate action, which in practice means freedom of decision making on the part of corporate management,[25] is a good thing for society generally, that public expectations usually lead to demands for governmental action, and that warding off encroachments on freedom of corporate action is a good thing for everyone —if only everyone knew it.

Accepting these premises, one can conclude that there is a corporate responsibility to society to guard the private sectors of business decision making—whether in the small or the large enterprise—from intervention by public governments.

This, of course, is a special application of pluralistic theory to the case of economic enterprise. Like all groupist doctrine it must be qualified in important respects. Most significant is the qualification that group autonomy should not be bought at the expense of individual liberty or the rights and privileges of natural persons. The *persona ficta* of the corporation has no natural rights that take precedence over the rights of man.

No business leader of repute today asserts the contrary. Rather, there is a strong trend toward the position that the corporation should, and does, have regard for the rights of individuals and that, indeed, one of the most important functions of management is to act as a wise and just arbiter of competing claims. Thus a heavy responsibility is placed upon management to perform this quasi-judicial function to the general satisfaction of society so that corporate autonomy can be preserved.

This line of thought suggests that another major public responsibility of the business corporation may be that of developing an internal polity that meets the tests of fairness and justice. For, otherwise, free corporate enterprise will sooner or later disappear from the scene. The critic of Big Business will demur. Who cares, he will say, whether big business corporations retain their freedom? Let them try, if they will, to set up some semblance of equitable arbitrament within their corporate empires. They will never succeed so long as management "sits in judgment on itself" and doles out "justice," as management sees it, to the other groups with their competing claims, some of them directly counter to the interests of management itself.

Where, indeed, does management presume to have derived this judicial authority, which it has so deftly assumed in place of the primary responsibility it once had, to guard the interests of the stockholders? Let the Big Corporation, with its self-perpetuating oligarchy rationalize this essentially irresponsible power as it will. The facts are plain that the so-called quasi-judicial function is a mere cover for an undemocratic system of private government, surviving as an anachronistic enclave in a constitutional system. So the negative argument might run.

These charges are serious enough to demand the most searching inquiry by corporate managers into the nature of the corporate polity, how it actually operates and whether it can survive in its present form within a free society. We do not pause here to explore the problem. But it needs to be underlined in any discussion of the responsibilities of the corporation to the general public. For the self-examination of corporate polities is in itself a corporate responsibility to society.

Corporate responsibilities toward the public, however, embrace more than responsibilities to a particular community, state, or nation. A company may operate in a number of nations, some of them free and some governed according to authoritarian principles. To which set of principles must it be loyal? Neutrality in politics is a well-understood stance of the businessman who habitually crosses international boundary lines. The corporation on home ground faces a different problem. One may be "neutral for" or "neutral against" a certain party, a certain platform, a set of legislative proposals, a slate of candidates. The problem of corporate-government relations raises special issues of corporate responsibilities to governments. These issues have never been systematically treated. One point may be made here, however, without reservation. The corporate citizen in our own country will be expected to participate in the public affairs of local, state, and national jurisdictions.

The canons of conduct governing such participation have not emerged with clarity. Some of them are foreshadowed in lobbying legislation, but only foreshadowed. For legislators have not themselves yet made up their minds about the allowable limits of functional representation by private groups. If the old air of furtiveness and suspicion no longer surrounds the representation of interests in legislative halls and in other governmental agencies, there is still a large area of doubt as to what the representatives of these interests have a right to do and say. It is at least incumbent upon corporate managements to participate actively in the debate on such issues as these and not to leave the decisions entirely to others. It is likewise a corporate responsibility to invite the active participation of other groups of interests in the debate, to encourage an atmosphere of freedom of inquiry, and to take a firm stand against suppression of unpopular views, within and outside the company.

Here the corporation has a responsibility that is often difficult for managers to sustain either for their subordinates or for their fellow-citizens on the Right and the Left of their own position. Freedom is indivisible. To talk of freedom for corporate enterprise out of context of human liberty is of course to invite derision. But what is more important, it would seem to reflect so narrow a view of the character of a free society as to raise widespread doubts that leaders in business can measure up to the high standards set by themselves for the practice of corporate citizenship. Such doubts, often expressed by the critics of Big Business, are sometimes well grounded. Yet a reminder of the pluralistic character of American society is in order here. There is room for a wide range of views and of practices in both internal arrangements and the external relationships of corporate polities. Fortunately there is no dictatorial public rule over the private sectors. Experimentation within a considerable range is still possible and desirable. In time, out of the give-and-take of public debate on the relative merits of opposing views, an enlightened code of social responsibilities will emerge.

Synthesizing the argument, when the modern corporation is viewed in time and in depth and in relation to other institutions, it exhibits no clearly defined and fixed patterns of social responsibility. This does not imply that social responsibility for the corporation is nonexistent. Moreover, this should not suggest that various theorists have not assigned the business corporation a multiplicity of responsibilities nor that the disparity between corporate practice and theory is necessarily a reflection upon theory making as such. The lack of generally accepted and well-established patterns of social responsibility is traceable to the absence of a viable corporate philosophy.

The lack of such patterns is a warning against too narrow a view of the corporation as an institution. It is also a warning against too much reliance upon some particular brand of corporate theory stemming from a particular discipline. "Business institutions are growing things; they are subject to many more forces—personal, social and intellectual—than are usually conceived to have relevance in theorizing about them." [26]

The modern corporation is undoubtedly an instrument for conducting a profitable business enterprise through the pooling of venture capital. So regarded, its board of directors represents the interests of capitalists—the stockholders—and the board's responsibility is clear: to return a profit on the investment. From this point of view, the corporation's responsibility is simply and singly stated. Any responsibilities toward others besides share owners are purely secondary. To be sure, no corporate enterprise can become, and remain, a going concern without incurring many obligations, for example, to employees whose services it hires, to bondholders whose money it borrows, to suppliers whose products it contracts for, and so on. But it is only through one theory of the corporation that these and other obligations are derivative and not primary.

This elementary theory of the modern corporation has many competitors, as we have seen. It represents a particular view of corporate enterprise that is not universally accepted today. The corporation is more than a business enterprise in this strict sense, according to many thinking persons, both within and without the walls of business. It has taken on institutional dimensions that are not included in the neat models of most economic theorists. From the points of view of the many contributor-claimant groups involved in the corporate constellation, the modern corporation has multiple functions and goals. Each group is inclined to emphasize the function or goal that lies nearest to its own interests. In the composite picture, where all of these points of view are brought together, the modern corporation thus has a multiplicity of responsibilities and opportunities for service.

The past four chapters have been an attempt to canvass these responsibilities from the points of view of all the major contributor-claimant groups. The purpose has not been to present an exhaustive list. Many of the groups and their claims which have been mentioned are debatable from one theoretical position or another. There emerges, as a result, a subject of infinitely greater complexity than one would encounter in simplistic theories of corporate enterprise.

One might be tempted to construct an eclectic theory of the corporation from this analysis of corporate responsibilities. But would this not be premature? Another view might arise from the fact that a corporation is the subject of rights as well as duties, and we have focused our attention here almost exclusively upon its obligations. A different picture might emerge if the focus were upon those things which the corporation might reasonably demand from its contributor-claimant groups. Yet this is not the major obstacle to the formulation of an eclectic theory at this point in the discussion. For not even the most comprehensive and exhaustive synthesis of the corporation, as a right-and-duty-bearing unit, would come near to the realities of the corporation as an institution.

The preoccupation with obligation, in describing any human activity, is misleading so far as scientific understanding is concerned. To make the corporation comprehensible—quite aside from any question of ethical judgment or normative evaluation —one must view it from many angles and look at all aspects of the complex patterns of behavior exhibited by the phenomena we so neatly epitomize in the word "corporation." In preceding chapters, selected approaches to these phenomena have been made in terms, for example, of decision process, policy making, and corporate objectives. Many other approaches are possible, such as the study of corporate polity or a consideration of the impact of the corporation on human freedom and corporate ecology in a global, as well as a national, setting. The most exhaustive discussion of the social responsibilities of the corporation, therefore, would not carry one very far into a true comprehension of the institution from all these other possible avenues of understanding.

The detailed examination of corporate responsibilities, as alleged from the standpoints here reviewed, has its uses. This is especially the case now when the whole problem of social responsibility is being aired. An examination of the problem is merited for many reasons, and particularly in view of the current search for a philosophy of business. The lines are being drawn for what promises to be a full-scale public debate about the nature and content of these responsibilities and, indeed, about whether they exist at all.

It is too easy to conclude that there are corporate social responsibilities simply because so many respectable people say they exist and that the substance of them can be determined simply by adding up all the claims that are made upon the corporation as an institution. There is no validity to such a conclusion beyond the proposition that it is widely and effusively proclaimed. On the other hand, there is no validity to the contrary view— that the corporation has no social responsibilities—beyond the normative judgment of proponents of this view.

The pros and cons of this argument, nevertheless, have probative value to this extent: they help to supply evidence in constructing a comprehensive theory of the corporation. The claims and counterclaims are facts in an important sense, for they symbolize postures of real persons with degrees and kinds of influence in the world of affairs.

When a contemporary observer of business practice such as Theodore Levitt declares earnestly that management's preoccupation with social responsibility is "not an attitudinizing pose" nor merely "a Philistinic form of self-flattery practiced at an occasional Community Chest banquet or at a news conference," but "a deadly serious occupation" which may be "letting the country in for a nightmare return to feudalism" because top executives are "forgetting that they must be businessmen first, last, and almost always," [27] he is engaging in more than a war of words. A prediction is being made that business will diminish its chance of survival unless it leaves off "this nonsense about its goals" and sticks to what he regards as the real job—material gain and long-run profit maximization. In this judgment, Levitt may reflect the posture of a large and possibly important sector of the business community.

The dilemma of social responsibility was set forth earlier in this book. If a corporation's social responsibilities are denied, the expectations of many of its contributor-claimant groups will not be met. And if this denial becomes the general rule, the corporation as a major social institution may disappear from the scene.   If these expectations are fulfilled, on the other hand, it is possible that business corporations may lose their character as private enterprises and evolve into quasi-public institutions, with loss of autonomy, increasingly subject to publicly imposed standards of performance.   This dilemma is not yet sharply defined in the minds of most businessmen, but as time goes on it will doubtless become a major issue for decision.

CHAPTER XIV

Public Relationships and

Corporate Interests

ALL THE FORCES and conditions that impinge upon and shape the modern corporation may be exhibited by analyzing any one of a number of major corporate activities. One of the most illustrative of such activities involves the public relationships of the corporation. These relationships lie near the heart of management and become an extension of the corporate identity and corporate interests.

An examination of the public relations function, in terms of what it is now and, especially, in terms of what it may become in the future, is an illustration—a case study, as it were—of the major issues discussed so far: the dilemma of social responsibility; the real objectives of the organization; the operational codes of the policy makers; the fit of the corporate institution in the greater society; the steps leading to policy formulation; the instruments and plans of action whereby men's goals are realized.

Plans of action are designed to achieve certain goals and will always include careful attention to available instruments of policy. These instruments include economic means, the indirect use of force (through the coercive power of governments), negotiation, and ideological means. While economic and negotiatory means are the predominant instruments of corporate policy, the planned use of other instruments is also important. Invocation of the coercive powers of public agencies (courts, legislatures, administrative and executive organs) is the function of attorneys as specialists in the use of public sanctions. The use of ideological means without the invocation of such sanctions, on the other hand, is peculiarly the province of the public relations specialist, especially in the external relations of a corporation. It is a special kind of managerial responsibility. The study of corporate public relations from this point of view provides one of the most important keys to an understanding of the realities of the modern corporation in action.

THE PUBLIC RELATIONS FUNCTION

Public relations policy in a large company, although it deals with one of the instruments of corporate policy and only indirectly with substantive issues such as finance, manufacturing, and marketing, is of such generally recognized importance today that every large industrial organization has found it necessary to set up specialized staff and operating components within the company to manage this particular functional kind of work.[1] Like other instrumental functions—legal, accounting, and engineering —the public relations function requires definition if only for the purpose of achieving a workable division of labor within the organization.

There are more compelling reasons, however, for thoughtful inquiry into the public relations function. From the point of view of the board and the executive management which must conduct the affairs of the corporation as more than just a profitable business operation, a broad concept of public relationships is indispensable. The institutional character of the concern, its long-range goals, its essential role in the society that nourishes it and which it serves, its contributions to many different groups who in turn make their contribution to the welfare of the corporate institution itself—all these are among the wider considerations that enter into a far-sighted public relations policy for a company.

From the point of view of outsiders, especially those who are concerned with the public philosophy, the public relations policies of large corporations are of equally compelling interest. The use of ideological means by any group, public or private, to achieve its ends cannot be a matter of indifference to the citizens of a free society. Propaganda, however innocent the derivation of the term may be, has come to be a highly colored word; it connotes *advocacy*, rather than judicious balance, and deliberately one-sided statements through mass media of all kinds. Public relations may be euphemized into "publicity" or regarded cynically as mere propaganda to be guarded against by rational men. The tendency to rely heavily on such an instrument of corporate policy and to minimize economic and negotiatory instruments in acceptable market situations always arouses suspicion and defensive reaction. When a corporation, in addition, frequently invokes coercion via government, the reaction may be sharp and bitter.

For these reasons, enlightened business leaders have regarded the public relations function as one of the most important areas of corporate management. But despite a plethora of writing and talking about the essential nature of public relations work, this aspect of the philosophy of business is characterized by a peculiar immaturity. Homilies and platitudes abound, together with shrewd recipes for "selling" a company as an institution to a presumably credulous public. Seldom does one encounter the germ of a theory of corporate public relations in which this special function is related systematically to the broad purposes of the corporate institution, in short, to a philosophy of corporate enterprise.

A realistic theory of corporate public relations—acceptable to scientists as well as practitioners of the art—will eventually emerge as a corollary of some general theorem about communication [2] as a social phenomenon. Until that time arrives, the student of corporate affairs must content himself with the exploration of certain basic policy issues confronting every large company.

How, for example, does the company envisage the central purpose of its public relations? How does it conceive the public or the various "publics" as parties to the relationship? What specific kinds of relations are involved? And at the company end of the relationship who speaks for the corporation? The answers to these questions have a direct bearing upon one's comprehension of the corporate institution and the way in which it is integrated with the flow of events in the world of affairs.

THE CENTRAL PURPOSE

Good will through publicity is the generally accepted goal of public relations work. Publicity means, as a rule, the effective use of mass media—press, television, radio—in which carefully framed messages are directed at selected "target areas" in the general public. This is outward communication of ideas and is certainly one of the more important ways in which the ideological instrument of policy can be used.

In recent years, the concept of the "two-way street" has been introduced. Public relations work, it is said, must be reciprocal. A company should listen as much as it talks. Its messages are beamed outward, but that is not the end of the communication process, for one must measure the response. The listening, moreover, needs to be continuous and systematic since audience characteristics will, to a degree, determine the content of the message to be sent and the media through which it is to be channeled; and both the audience characteristics and the media are changeable as a result of social and technological dynamics. Public relations work is thus sometimes likened to an input-output system.

In this reciprocal system the concern is with far more than public relations output in the conventional sense and with listening to more than the response to public relations efforts. It is an egregious error to assume that communication is successful only when conversion of the listener has been achieved.

In practice, a true balance between input and output is rarely achieved. Two-way communication between the corporation and the public is difficult to establish and maintain, on any systematic basis, through public relations departments. This is only partly due to the fact that the external relationships of a complex organization, many parts of which interrelate with people and groups on the outside for many different purposes, cover far more than communication processes in the strict sense of ideological intercourse. Simultaneously with public relations work, thus defined, others in the company are conducting economic transactions with the outsiders, negotiating agreements of a noneconomic kind, and invoking the coercive powers of government to protect or advance the interests of the corporation. No one knows whether, in the combined use of all these policy instruments, there is any balance between message input and output or whether for all personnel there is, in the net, as much listening as talking.

The two-way-street idea in public relations work does not, of course, embrace company communication with the external world in any such comprehensive sense as this. The public relations specialist is concerned only with limited kinds of communication content and the use of certain types of media for communicating it. Other instruments of policy are likewise specialized as to communicational techniques and contents. Thus the negotiator makes proposals and counterproposals as bases for agreement (as in collective bargaining, where no commodity is involved); the participant in economic transactions communicates offers and counter offers; the attorney pleads the company's case in a court of law. But the public relations man is not a negotiator, nor a bargainer, nor an attorney. His communications are idea exchanges for other purposes, not yet defined here.

But even in the interchange between company and public, conveying the public relations man's special kind of message, there is seldom, in most companies, any input-output balance that is effectively monitored. The public relations function, so far as the listening process is concerned, hardly goes beyond rudimentary techniques of opinion sampling (sometimes given more elaborate labels) about the general reputation of the company or of its products and services. The feedback of such findings may or may not be adequate to have optimum impact upon policy. As far as output and input of messages is concerned, much research is needed in information theory [3] and the theory and measurement of influence,[4] especially as these areas apply to public relations work in the large corporation.

But the application of new techniques, however sophisticated, can never be very useful until agreement has been reached within the organization on the central objectives of the company itself. Public relations, as a concept of communication, is probably a definable function of management—but communication to what ends?

The central purpose of public relations in the modern corporation is more than publicity for enhancing good will, although this is certainly a valid purpose in itself. A more comprehensive view of the communication network which interrelates the organization with its social environs embraces all those corporate objectives that can be attained more efficiently by improved understanding and use of communication processes. So, in order to establish a proper basis for defining the public relations function, it is necessary to delineate a company's public relations objectives in fairly concrete terms.

PUBLIC RELATIONS AND CORPORATE GOALS

The central purpose of public relations can be defined only in terms of two steps: the first, development of a statement of general company objectives in operational form, so that they can be translated into functional objectives for public relations specialists themselves; and, second, translation of these general company objectives into public relations plans, programs, and policies. In the absence of these two steps, taken sequentially, public relations work may proceed haphazardly or in accordance with the preconceived notions of public relations managers. When this discord occurs, the public relations function can scarcely be at harmony with corporate purposes.

Many large companies have adopted a set of general objectives, and public relations goals can be deduced from these. The set of general company objectives should be comprehensive enough to constitute a basic blueprint from which the charters of all kinds of functional work may be derived. The basic blueprint states the major goals of the enterprise; and, if these are fully, though succinctly, stated they should indicate clearly the subpurposes to be kept in mind by policy makers in all the major functional areas of the firm, including the area of public relations.

There are many possible ways [5] to state a company's objectives. When the job is well done, it will include all the major groups with which a company carries on external relations, and all the major purposes of its relationships with those groups. This is the indispensable first step toward a definition of a company's public relations function.

The published objectives of a company will never contain all of its corporate goals. As has been indicated, the goal of influence and strength is never explicitly mentioned. This is a basic objective of every organization, and, if it is not expressly stated, it must be assumed in any realistic public relations policy.

The first step is, thus, more exacting than the task of writing a "company creed" for public consumption. All the real goals must be included and listed, for operational purposes, in order of priority. Ideally, the public relations department will get continuous briefing on the priorities of the day, with clear instructions as to the themes that are to be emphasized in message output. This kind of liaison between top management and the public relations specialist is often not realized in practice. But the intimate tie is indispensable to effective implementation of company policy. For it works both ways. If the public relations specialist is a good "listener," he will inform executive management about trends of opinion and audience characteristics that may affect company policy, which then may be implemented by ideological, as well as other, instruments. Good listening can help to shape good policy objectives.

The second step is the translation of general company objectives into operational goals for the kind of communicational work the public relations man specializes in. At this point he drafts the specific forms of outgoing messages that he must communicate to the appropriate media. He is then ready to follow through with a communication process designed to achieve the policy objectives agreed upon in advance.

To perform this operation successfully, however, he must watch every element in the communication process. He must know the publics with whom the company proposes to establish the communication relationship, the available channels, the situation in which the conversation is to be carried on, and the probable response to the company's message.

There is a familiar and readily understood formula which describes this whole communication process and asks the key questions about it: *Who* says *what* to *whom,* through what *channels,* under what *conditions,* and with what *effects?* The italicized words identify the important elements which enter into usage of the ideological instrument. It may seem that the central purpose of the public relations function in the large corporation is closely tied to two of these terms: *what* is communicated and the *effects* expected. And indeed it is, but the other elements in the formula are equally significant. First to be considered here is the "who"—the subject or the corporate self in the communication process.

WHOSE PUBLIC RELATIONS?

On whose behalf are corporate public relations conducted?

The "corporation," as such, never sends or receives messages; it is always people who do this on behalf of the company. The spokesmen are many, and they are human. The premises on which they make decisions, when they act as company spokesmen, are not all necessarily the same with respect to the meaning of the phrase "the best interests of the company." They may hold quite diverse concepts of the corporation. Their concepts of the corporation and its role in society may change from time to time. In one context, say, with respect to marketing policies, they may regard the corporation as an entrepreneur, essentially seeking to maximize profits. In the context of another policy, say, corporate giving, they may think of the company as a philanthropist, or perhaps as an institution of great prestige in the community, or as a "good corporate citizen."

These varying premises, in turn, will have varying effects upon policy decisions. To speak for the "company" means, for some, to speak for the "owners"—the stockholders; for others it means upholding the prerogatives of "management" against the demands of unions. In decentralized companies where there are many product businesses federated into a more or less well unified enterprise, the "corporation" represents to the managers of each of the separate businesses an adversary interest, to some extent. The man on the assembly line may not think of himself so much a member of the "team" as an antagonist pitted against bosses who represent "the company"; yet in his community he is identified with the company and in many ways speaks and acts on its behalf, even when he is not aware of this.

Two examples will illustrate the problem. The first one is drawn from the advertising activities of a company. The second case deals with stockholder relations.

A running battle may go on in the large corporation between the proponents of institutional and product advertising. Institutional advertising is intended to promote the general reputation of the company as a whole. By its very nature, it minimizes message content that promotes specific products. How will these respective claims be resolved? Will public relations components, acting for the company as a whole, limit their institutional advertising budgets to relatively small proportions, leaving the major part of the advertising costs to be allocated to product advertising? What criteria are to be used in allocating advertising costs?

All advertising costs must ultimately be defrayed from earnings, and it is usual to say that the cost of advertising must be borne by the customers who buy the products. But this is oversimplification. There are many claimants on corporate income. Production costs, including advertising, affect any benefits that customers, as a claimant group, can expect in the form of lower prices. From the customers' point of view, is it sufficient to let market forces determine costs of advertising? But these costs might, in some quarters, also be considered a legitimate subject for public debate or, at least, for managerial weighing of the public interest in institutional and product advertising budgets. It is observable that many corporations today spend considerable sums for the purpose of stating the case, not only for the company as a competitor but, more broadly, for the free enterprise system as a whole. To what extent is it proper to add the cost of such advertising to the price of a company's products or to require other claimant interests within the company to reduce their production costs in favor of large advertising budgets?

Obviously, there are many different interests, not a single "corporate" interest, clamoring to be the spokesmen in the public relations output in the field of advertising. These interests are both internal and external to the company. The task of managers at top levels is to identify who "we" are in such public relations efforts. Their decisions on questions of this kind will be affected by premises about the economic system as a whole and about the structure of the firm, that is, by their private theories of the firm. A good guess would be that these premises are rarely made explicit and that the factors affecting rationality in this decision process are seldom tracked down.

Another example can be found in the area of stockholder relations.[6] Can a company conduct *public* relations with its share owners, as suggested earlier, or, are they a part of the company? In practice, stockholders do not deal directly with corporate policy making. It is their trustees on the board, and the agents of the board in professional management, who make the great majority of decisions for the company. But even the directors assembled, when only they can make decisions on behalf of the corporation, have little opportunity to direct the affairs of the enterprise, nor do they usually attempt to do so except as to broad policy issues. The result is that the real spokesmen for "the company" to the stockholders are to be found in the ranks of the executive managers.

Corporate relations with share owners, then, become in fact relations between managers and stockholders. Yet managers probably do not think of themselves as "the corporation." Increasingly, they seem to look at their role as that of interest-balancers, representing the interests of share owners along with the interests of all other contributor-claimant groups that cluster in and about the enterprise. Although from the legal point of view, with emphasis on the common-law property rights of stockholders, the share owner group is the primary constituency of the corporate polity, decisions with respect to distribution of earnings cannot be their decisions. Alfred Marshall once referred to the corporate income as a composite *quasi-rent,* to be distributed among the different persons in the business by bargaining, supplemented by custom and by notions of fairness;[7] and Hurff suggests that "in many respects the division of the corporate usufruct tends today more and more to resemble the strategies and pressures determining the share of public benefits."[8] In these circumstances, what is "the corporation" as it carries on relationships with its stockholders?

Questions as to the appropriate character of relationships involving share owners also emerge in matters of public policy, as for instance, in the growth, during the past few decades, of legislation governing securities and securities exchanges. Here is evidence that the spokesmen for share-owner interests are not all conceived to be within the "corporation" nor to be found in any part of the corporate polity alone but to include public representatives in Congress as well. Federal legislation has not gone far in attempting to reconstruct the internal arrangement of the corporate polity; but it has moved significantly toward the protection of a major contributor-claimant interest and to that extent it has both broadened and narrowed the concept of the corporation.

The concept has been broadened to the extent that the public interest is concretely represented through federal legislation affecting corporate policy making where share-owner interests are concerned. The concept has been narrowed, on the other hand, in that the necessity for such legislation points up the relative weakness of stockholders as contributor-claimants within the corporate polity. Legislation has placed responsibility upon the Securities and Exchange Commission to assert certain claims upon the corporation, and the corporation to that extent regards the Commission as another external "public" to be dealt with through various public relations strategies.

The two foregoing examples illustrate the practical difficulty of defining "who" does the communicating when public relations are defined as a communicational process. The problem is further complicated by difficulties that arise in perceiving and communicating the "corporate image." [9]

PROBLEM OF PERCEIVING AND COMMUNICATING THE CORPORATE IMAGE

Peter Drucker "sees the essence and purpose of the corporation not in its economic performance or in its formal rules but in the *human relationships* both between the members of the corporation and between the corporation and the citizens outside of it." [10] In examining the corporation as an institution, he is interested in three levels of analysis: (1) its autonomy ("governed by the rules of its own structure and determined by the desire for survival—capable to be judged in terms of its own purposes"); (2) the beliefs and promises of the society it serves; and (3) its relationship to the "functional requirements of the society of which the institution is a part." It is essential, he writes, that "the corporation be organized in such a way as to be able itself to function and to survive as an *institution,* as to enable society to realize its *basic promises and beliefs,* and as to enable *society* to function and survive."

When Drucker turns to what he calls the problem of the "parochialism of the executive imagination" [11]—the inability of managers to project internal relations "against the broad canvas of social beliefs and promises"—and to see themselves and their company as people on the outside see them, he points to the case of General Motors. There, he reports, specific instruments have been developed "to break the imaginative isolation of the corporation executive." In customer relations there was the Customer Research Staff. In dealer relations, there were the Dealer Relations Council and the Motors Holding Division. For community relations, there were plant-city committees. But such devices may not clarify the managerial concept of the corporation and its role in society.

The main problem is to find out how the corporation is conceived of both by the people inside it and by the people outside of it and, especially, how the perception of "the company" as an actor in the public relations process affects policies of the company. It is very doubtful that research, however thorough, that is fractionated into separate categories of functional work within the corporation, and into these separate work relationships with the outside world, will yield the over-all concept of the company that provides a sound basis for policy.

Henry Ford, II, commenting early in 1957 upon the "growing sense of labor-management responsibility toward mutual problems," observed that "labor and management still face each other, but each is *facing itself first."* The "primitive and relatively unstable capitalism of the past [had] given way to a consumer-dominated, self-regulating system that broadly serves the interests of the great mass of our people." The real issue as Ford saw it then was between "those who hold that business should be geared to immediate, short-range social problems and those who believe that the great long-term social gains will come from letting industry respond freely to the natural play of economic drives—subject, of course, to the principles of social justice and Christian charity." [12]

When one asks how a corporate management "is facing itself" and assessing its role in the economic and general social milieu, one gets divergent answers, depending upon a manager's apprehension of reality, or what has been called in a previous chapter his "operational code." "The limit of human understanding in the presence of complex social structures leads human beings to construct simplified maps (i.e., theories or models) of the social system in which they are acting, and to behave as though the maps were the reality." [13]

The complex social structure, of which one's company is a part, cannot be seen or felt directly in all of its implications; one must rely upon the maps, the models, the theories he has inherited and accepted. Some of the maps in the managerial mind are most realistic and usable for short excursions into the immediate corporate environment, and for specific functional tasks, such as marketing a product or recruiting equity capital. For wider-ranging journeys, the maps may be disastrously misleading. Long-term planning for the company and assessment of the social, political, and economic trends of the human environment require models different from those managers are likely to have at their disposal.

Schumpeter's account of Mill's theory of laissez faire is illustrative of the point. In describing the economic thought of the period from 1790 to 1870, he wrote:

Practically all economists *believed*—no matter what they *desired*—that, as J. S. Mill put it, laissez-faire was the general rule for the administration of a nation's economic affairs and that what was significantly called "state interference" was the exception. And, though for different reasons in different countries, this was so in actual practice not only as a matter of fact but also as a matter of practical necessity: no responsible administrator could have held then, and no responsible historian should hold now, that, social and economic conditions and the organs of public administration being what they were, any ambitious ventures in regulation and control could have issued in anything but failure. . . . The top-heavy structure of eighteenth-century bureaucracy . . . was inefficient, wasteful, littered with sinecures, associated with unpopular mercantilist policy, and even with political corruption. . . . Mill realized the superiority, which was in the circumstances simply not open to doubt, of the businessman's administration of the productive resources over what could possibly have been expected from the public official of his day.[14]

These assumptions about the State, Schumpeter adds, were time-bound, and the recommendations and applied economics were dated, even though the theory of the "classic type" which they used for purposes of economic analysis would be useful as long as it remained a question only of regulation and control of private business enterprise.

These models are of debatable utility today. However, many policy makers have inherited time-bound concepts not only of state and government but also of private enterprise itself. Their current road maps will certainly be affected by both the old and the new models of contemporary institutions. Their operational codes will reflect their views of the corporate "self" and its relationship to alter egos.

Current concepts of the nature of the corporation and especially those which posit certain "social responsibilities," indicate that concepts of the company held by managers are not always time-bound and dated; but it is observable that the concept may not be uniform for all policy-making purposes. Mental sets of an insular kind seem to premise certain policy decisions in men who in other policy areas exhibit no such mental isolationism. "No other world but this company" is an attitude that may lead, for example, to company policies opposed to national policies of tariff abatement, even though such a national policy may make for firmer alliances with countries oriented toward the West and with those nations still uncommitted in the world struggle. On the other hand, the same managers may exhibit zeal in undertaking defense contracts that yield little or no profit to the company, on the ground that this is the duty of a good corporate citizen.

Because of these variations in management's point of view, it is not surprising that the corporate image held by key publics may be confused. The image of business is confused because it mirrors inconsistencies in the minds and behavior of the men who manage the business enterprise.

It is a major function of public relations to resolve these confusions and to formulate company policies that clearly set forth an unambiguous concept of the corporate self as a guide to all other policy making concerning the company's external relationships. No company, so far as can be determined now, has undertaken to do this. Nor is it here maintained that it is the duty of any company to identify itself with larger spheres of interest—community-wide, national, or international. On the contrary, in a system such as ours, in which a multiplicity of private decision centers is regarded as a necessary condition for the preservation of a free society, it is difficult to see how a business corporation, no matter how large, can permit its image to become frayed at the edges and fused with the image of society as a whole. The business corporation must maintain a distinct individuality, a high degree of integrity and great flexibility in order to withstand the constant pressures on its growth which, if unrelieved, so frequently and so easily lead to state intervention and, finally, state control.

The point is that managerial premises in matters affecting the role of the corporation in society cannot safely be ambivalent. Accurate knowledge and realism in evaluating the goals, aspirations, needs, and activities of others outside the corporate island are consistent with a forthright stand in favor of corporate self-interest and indeed are essential to an accurate perception of the corporate image. Diffuse and equivocal policy making arises in part from lack of such knowledge.

These considerations lead to the conclusion that public relations policy must be built on a system of corporate intelligence. Most large corporations today are not geared to develop the information area necessary to such policy making.

THE RELATED PUBLICS

In the large corporation there are many "publics" with which communication must be maintained. The scope of the public relations function depends upon the inclusiveness of these publics. However, the public relations managers' perception of "the world out there" is a limitation on the number and character of these publics. A decision on this point is an important element of public relations policy. Too narrow a view of the outer reach of corporate interests in the complex social, political, and economic environment may limit the effectiveness of public relations work. Yet, some lines must be drawn. Occasionally, there may be a tendency to exclude certain publics for budgetary reasons, with the plausible argument that the excluded publics are too remote from the affairs of the business. Or, there may be confusion as to the meaningful categories of "publics" for public relations as distinguished from other kinds of functional work within the organization as a whole.

The "general public" is too ambiguous a term to permit systematic development of appropriate targets for managing public relations work. Yet, if one classifies external groups into such typical categories as employees, unions, customers, share owners, suppliers, competitors, distributors, dealers, and so on—groupings that obviously bear a direct relation to the nature of the enterprise—it is at once apparent that relations with all of these "publics" may encompass too much, so that public relations work duplicates other functional fields. Customer relations, for example, are essentially marketing relationships and are apt to be claimed as the province of marketing components. Share-owner relationships and relations with the financial community generally are logically assignable to components that deal with financial policies. Here there is also the nice question about the locus of stockholders as a group—whether stockholders can properly be treated as an external "public" at all. Employees, too, are hardly external to the company, although the unions that represent them certainly are. Nevertheless, to treat employees and unions primarily as a "public" and the relationship between them and the company as essentially one of public relations is obviously wide of the mark.

A somewhat closer look at the problem of employee and union relations will illustrate the difficulty of determining the list of "publics" for public relations work. A dual role is frequently assigned for employees: they are members of the company "team," but they are also members of an outside organization that bargains collectively with management. In the latter role, they may sometimes be identified in the minds of some managers with an adversary interest. In the former role elaborate efforts are made to identify them with "the company." Does their union constitute a "public" for the purpose of public relations work? And how is this kind of work to be integrated with "union relations"?

Special problems arise, though with wide social implications, when employees are regarded as a part of the internal and formal organization of the company. The company's demands upon them, as a part of the formal organization, may be quite out of line with their needs as well-integrated and healthy persons—as individuals.[15] The formal organization, directive leadership by management—as distinguished from "democratic leadership"—and firm management controls, together with "human relations" programs, are said to be devices that managers use to heighten the employees' feeling that they are a part of the team, in order to increase their productivity. Although the intent of management is to allay the antagonism that sometimes exists between itself and employees on the production line, it is argued that these very devices compound the antagonism.

Case studies seem to show that, by increasing the degree of directive leadership, increasing the degree of management controls, and increasing the number of "pseudo human relations" programs, management fails to achieve that "fusion" of the individual and the organization which is the purpose of these devices. So, it is argued, the identity of managerial and employee interests has to be sought rather through such managerial actions as changing the nature of the formal organizational structure, the establishment of "participative or employee-centered leadership," and enlargement of jobs and roles in the production process, especially in assembly-line operations. A "reality-oriented" or "reality-centered" leadership is required.[16] These are the kinds of things that personnel managers are concerned with. They are not usually regarded as "public relations" at all but as internal employee relations.

In its relations with unions, on the other hand, management hardly seeks identity of interests, at least not in the same sense. It will seek a common ground for determining policies as to wage structures, working conditions, benefits, and the like; but it will resist attempts on the part of a union to encroach upon "management prerogatives" and thus to identify itself with the company as an institution. The union is an outsider, and as such it is a legitimate target for public relations communicational work. As with other publics, the company is vitally interested in the kind of corporate image held in the minds of union leaders and rank-and-file members, but this is hardly the chief end and aim of union relations. Unions, like other power centers, have to be dealt with by the company on many substantive issues that result in specific agreements, and the work of arriving at such agreements is not, properly speaking, public relations work. Public relations work only contributes collaterally to the end result.

This does not mean, of course, that it would be inappropriate to set up within a public relations component a subcomponent for union public relations, but it raises the question whether such work is not better assigned to personnel departments. Counter to this position is the view that, in the very large firm, the employees, though technically an internal group, are in effect a "public" for the purposes of communication through mass media; and the public relations specialist is usually thought of as the company expert in the use of such media, regardless of the audience to be reached. If, alternatively, the work of public relations is regarded more broadly as external relations, with general attention to the integration of company interests with those of all contributor-claimant groups, then one cannot safely assume that union-relations or personnel specialists will take the required over-all view.

The difficulty of defining the "publics" for public relations work has just been illustrated by the special case of employees and unions. The general problem may be indicated in another way, namely, by listing an inventory of these publics. Here is one list that might emerge from such a study:

People as members of the national community
People as citizens, voters, and constituents
People in their roles as customers, share owners, employees, and
    suppliers of the company
People in their roles as members of the press

People in their roles as members of educational groups

People in their roles as leaders and members of religious groups

People in their roles as members of governmental organs

People in their roles as members of the financial community

People in their roles as members of labor organizations

People in their roles as members of industry and trade organizations

People in their roles as members of service organizations

People in their roles as members of professional and scientific societies

People in their roles as members of fraternal, cultural, and ethnic associations

This listing makes the assumption that a company may have a relationship with the same individuals in various ways, through the various roles they play in their life situations. For every person there are multiple roles, and each of these roles carries with it definite attitudes, beliefs, customs, codes, manners, aspirations. A company, in attempting to establish intercommunicational relationships with people in their various roles, has to acquire a working knowledge of these roles in all the aspects just described. It cannot limit its work to relations with the formally organized external organizations exclusively.

A company's contractual relations with such groups are assignable to specific components within the company which have functional kinds of work to do, such as marketing, employee relations, manufacturing, engineering and so on. The public relations specialist is interested in other-than-contractual relationships. In order to project to people as individuals a favorable corporate image, through mass media or other channels, and to elicit a favorable response, one must know their predispositions and these are most readily definable in terms of the roles they assume in society. To be able to listen to people, as well as to speak *to* them through media, one must direct one's attention in a number of directions. The role listing provides a clue to this number of directions. If the listening work is well done, the result will be a sensing of the climate of opinion in which the company operates.[17]

Inventories of publics have been examined in some detail for the purpose of showing one approach to the empirical study of public relations policy making in large companies. As noted, the objective or naturalistic approach to significant areas of corporate policy, as distinguished from the normative or subjective approach, requires one to look at what corporate managers do, in fact, concern themselves with—in other words, what they themselves regard as important decision areas. So the alternatives arise: whether attention is to be given to a comparatively wide range of publics or whether, on the contrary, most large corporations will limit themselves to few and proximate publics.

General observation of corporate public relations work indicates that the work is mainly publicity-oriented. When this is the case, the view of key groups and the roles of people in society becomes limited, and external relations work in the broadest sense of the term is not carried forward. Nor does it appear that corporate public relations, taken as a whole, systematically attempts to sense the business environment, to take the results of comprehensive sensing operations as feedback for premises to policy decisions throughout all functional fields of the company. This conclusion, to be sure, is not based upon exhaustive field surveys, which certainly ought to be made, but rather upon observation of practices in representative companies. The picture might be different if more evidence were available.

THE COMMUNICATIONAL RELATIONSHIP

It should now be evident that one of the difficulties of defining the central purpose of public relations in the large corporation, aside from the tendency to regard this work as publicity chiefly, is the failure to state and translate general company objectives into public relations objectives, and the tendency to restrict unduly the publics involved. In some companies the usual classification of functional types of work specifies "relations" generally as a definite kind of work comparable to accounting, marketing, engineering, finance, and so on. Within the framework of such nomenclature, public relations becomes a subfunction of the total work of carrying on "relations," since other types of relations, such as employee relations, must also be carried forward. This line of reasoning may be faulty and may lead the corporation into aberrant decisions with respect to its role in society.

The term "public relations," though time-honored, seems to be a misnomer. More nearly accurate would be "external relations"—a designation that is universally used (with verbal modifications, such as "foreign affairs") by nation-states to distinguish problems of foreign policy from those of domestic policy. Why would it not be wise for the large corporation to have a "Department of External Affairs"?

A corporation is not, of course, really comparable to a nation-state. It is not sovereign; it is a sovereign's creature and is contained within a nation-state (or one of our states in the federal system). At least that is the legal argument. This is not true in any realistic sense, for state-created corporations "do business" in foreign territories; and within the United States, at least, the "foreign corporation" created in Delaware but doing business in New York is protected as a going concern—an organic entity—by well-developed rules of American constitutional law and by custom.

To a lesser extent, this is true even for American corporations that engage in business abroad. It is not unlikely that, in the decades ahead, we shall see a kind of world law that will protect corporate enterprise in much the same way that it has been able to achieve a continental market area in the United States. Once the bitter international rivalries of our time subside, it may be universally recognized that the world's work cannot be done without the use of widely ranging business corporations operating as highly autonomous organisms with greater viability than many existing States have. The survival value of the corporate form of doing business can hardly be doubted. Would it not, therefore, be reasonable to expect the corporation of the future to be characterized by definite policies of *external relations* through which a balance would be maintained between the autonomy of the entity and the demands of society on a regional or world basis?

The argument is tempting. But it overlooks the hard facts, some of which have been indicated in preceding pages, namely, that external relations are multifunctional. They involve marketing, supply, legal relations, financial relations, and a host of others.   To merge all of these functional kinds of external relations into a single organizational component is manifestly impossible.   Nation-states are not able to do it, as witness the corps of attachés in foreign embassies—each of the attachés being responsible not to the foreign office but to some other department of the home government.   One might add that in this age of pressure toward people-to-people contacts across international frontiers, by-passing state departments and foreign offices with increasing frequency and effectiveness—not least in the realm of international business operations—the attempt by governments to funnel all such contacts through national governmental agencies becomes increasingly impracticable.

Foreign policy, the cynics say, is the art of influencing other nations to your own nation's ends.   Corporation public relations policy, by similar analogy, could be said to be the art of influencing external groups of interests to corporate ends.   Although the ideal aims of states and corporations are higher, and the instruments of policy are not the same in the two cases, they do exhibit striking similarities.   The instruments of foreign policy include arms, economic measures, diplomacy (negotiation and agreement), and communication through mass media and other channels (government-to-people).   The instruments of corporation policy, in its external relations with various groups in the environment include legal measures, economic measures, negotiation and agreement, and communication through mass media and other channels (corporation-to-people).

An overview of the entire range of external relations of the corporation—on which there is practically no literature today— would involve systematic surveys of the ways in which particular companies use all the instruments legitimately at their command. Such surveys would undoubtedly show that some companies make inadequate use of some of these instruments and that few indeed use these instruments coordinately and with singleness of purpose. Like nations, corporations frequently suffer from the lack of well-formulated and considered external relations policies.   Public relations as *communicational* relations requires the correct use of the communicational instrument of corporate policy in coordination with other instruments. The coordinating work itself is a top-management responsibility and can be called the "relations" function in a broad sense. The specialized work of advising and counseling on the use of communicational instruments could logically be assigned to public relations components.

This leaves public relations specialists with a less comprehensive task than many would like to assume, but it also leaves a highly exacting and complex task that they have not yet sufficiently mastered.

That task can be subdivided into manageable subfunctions. A theory of public relations may be built around the communicational formula. In so doing, public relations specialists would concentrate on the separate elements of the communicational process [18] and be prepared to counsel executive management on:

The identity and the characteristics of all the key *publics* toward which company messages are to be directed

The *content* of these messages, with special attention to the things that should be said and done in public view by persons and components acting on behalf of the company

The *corporate image,* not only as it appears in the minds of the key publics toward which company messages are directed, but also as it operates upon the minds of company personnel in their decision making in all kinds of external relations

The most effective *media* or channels to be used for communicating with the key publics, not excluding the possible effect of unintended messages sent out from the company to the external world in the form of activities that are not usually considered to be public relations work

The *effects* of outward-directed messages upon these key publics, measured not only in terms of their verbal responses, their opinions and attitudes, but also their actions with respect to matters of concern to all decision makers in every kind of functional work throughout the company

Public relations specialists, in other words, are properly the specialists on the use of communication as an instrument of corporation policy in all of its many aspects. As such, their task is not only to counsel and advise executive management in the work of coordinating all external relations of the company. In addition, they should serve as consultants to every functional specialist in such fields as marketing, finance, legal work, manufacturing, accounting, and managing.

Public relations policies, then, deal with all the above categories of subfunctional work in the field of corporate communications. While some decisions in public relations obviously deal with highly technical matters (as, e.g., choice of media, content analysis) there is always the danger that public relations policy, for this reason, will be regarded as peripheral to the central issues of business policy. This is far from the truth. The choice of key publics, for instance, may profoundly affect the growth and even the survival of the corporation. To cite a single illustration: to leave governmental officials out of the list of key publics can be a vital error, especially in an age of mounting governmental regulation of business at every level of public government. The restriction of communicational output to "publicity," to take another instance, in effect disarms the company and deprives it of some other effective communicational devices.

BUILDING THE CORPORATE REPUTATION

It is clear, of course, that as a matter of policy a company needs to be favorably known for such things as: its enlightened objectives; the value of its products and services; the worth of its securities; its fair treatment of employees, customers, share owners, suppliers, competitors, and other groups with which it has contacts; its contributions to the advancement of science and technology in all the fields in which it is active; its contribution to improved standard of living and general well-being of the community (local, national, international) in which it operates; and its contribution to the basic institutions of a free society. To be widely and favorably known for these things requires deliberate effort on the part of specialized personnel within the company, who are skilled in communicational techniques. This is what most observers on the outside ordinarily think of when they speak of the "public relations" of a company. They tend to regard it as a large-scale promotional effort. In a sense, this is true; a company is hardly expected to hide its light under a bushel.

But to be known for these things requires more than skillful output of releases through effective channels. A company must also perform so that there is a story to tell. The public relations function thus extends to stimulating managers in all parts of the firm to do the things expected of them by the public. This means doing the things that many different publics expect of the company. It therefore becomes one of the intricate tasks of public relations specialists to develop a comprehensive and detailed view of these publics: to know who and where they are, what they are thinking, what they want, how hazardous it may be to neglect the opinions and attitudes they hold, and how rewarding it might be to take these opinions and attitudes into account in every phase of company policy making.

Public relations work, then, involves input as well as output of information in company external relations, and the input is closely tied in with corporate policy in all functional fields. The input thus assumes particular importance and requires a sophisticated intelligence operation of a special kind. What is required is a sensing operation in which the antennae are delicately attuned to many wave lengths and pointed in many directions. Investors, customers, suppliers, competitors are obvious groups from which incoming messages have to be assessed. But the *potential* suppliers of equity capital, goods and services, the *potential* customers, the *potential* competitors, as well as the "public at large" and especially its representatives in local, state, national, and international governments, are all extremely important sources of intelligence about the reputation of the company and its impact upon social institutions.

The work of public relations, thus broadly considered, does not end with the informational input-output process, for this is only the beginning step. Public relations work must not be weakened by failing to integrate the findings of "sensing operations" with policy making throughout the company. Feedback of opinion polling may be highly useful in developing a new set of premises for future policy decisions in various functional areas. It may be used, of course, for policy making in public relations work with respect to informational output, or "selling" the company. Measures of the effectiveness of an institutional advertisement, for example, may lead to radical revisions of future design and content of institutional ads. But of equal importance is feedback of the same type of information to managers in research and engineering, in finance, in legal departments, in manufacturing. Later, the question arises: To what extent is the information assessed by these managers and then integrated with their own planning?

The "fit" of the corporation into the prevailing social norms of fair dealing, of corporate citizenship, of expectation concerning the role of the company in society depends upon managerial decisions in all functional fields and not alone in the specific work of public relations as a communicational activity. This meshing of corporate activity as a whole with the ideals and aspirations of the public is not accomplished so much by verbal pronouncements as it is through the day-to-day performance by representatives of the company in their regular business dealings with various sectors of the public. The requirement is not a mechanical reaction to feelings widely held by the public, but the meeting of these needs in ways appropriate to a major social institution.

It is the broad function of public relations to keep a watchful eye upon this process and to alert the entire organization to public reaction to deviations from standards of performance set by general company objectives. Some may object that this is too comprehensive a function to require of the public relations specialist. Perhaps it is true that because of the way public relations work is sometimes organized and staffed—and especially in view of the relatively subordinate role the public relations specialist plays in the operations of many firms—it is asking too much. But the answer is simple. The function is of vital importance to the large corporation. If one prefers to attach the public relations label only to those who perform the more modest role of advertising the virtues of the company, then another name must be found for this broader function.

If it is protested that this broader function is the responsibility of the executive head of the company, the question arises whether he is properly staffed to undertake it. Usually, as a matter of fact, he is not. Nor is it a sufficient answer to insist, as is often done, that the necessary staff exists but is distributed among various organizational components and committees. It is undoubtedly true that every functionally specialized component has its own antennae out to the pertinent environmental forces that affect its particular kind of work. What is often lacking, however, is a synthesis. Even in the larger corporation there is no systematic effort made to synthesize public relations intelligence with multiform corporate activities. Such a synthesis would present a unified picture, to executive management, of the *changing role of the company as seen from the outside.* A second step would be a follow-up to determine whether the appropriate policy decisions had been made throughout the company. Instead, there is usually a mass of unrelated reports on external relations of all sorts that are circulated to many desks at various times. These reports are never processed as a whole nor acted upon as a whole, nor indeed are they intended to be acted upon as a whole.

This problem is not peculiar to the corporation. The intelligence operations of governments also appear to fail notoriously in the critical act of integrating the necessary information needed by policy makers at top executive and legislative levels. Failure to solve this problem for any nation could mean a national disaster. Failure to solve it in the corporation could have a direct bearing upon its survival as an institution.

In all large organizations the necessity for a workable, synthesized information theory has become increasingly evident and as time goes on we may expect to see radical revision of decision processes—both in governmental and private organizations—as a result of developments in this branch of knowledge. Simply stated, in order to reach a company's general objectives, this broad "intelligence function," an unexplored aspect of the polity of the corporation, must be performed somewhere in the organization. The organizational structure of the large corporation does not now take this activity into account. Yet, properly conceived, there is hardly a more critical function for insuring the long-range adjustment and survival of the enterprise.

PUBLIC RELATIONSHIPS IN THE FORESEEABLE FUTURE

The social dimensions of the modern corporation become clearer as one explores the potentialities of the public relations function of management. Leaving behind the limited view of this function as mainly a publicity operation and pressing out into newer frontiers of corporate external relationships, one can readily discern fields that are still undeveloped in this relatively new functional kind of managerial work.

Here is an area of corporate policy in which the distorting elements (mentioned in Chapter VII) are clearly evident. Rationality in decision making may be hampered in a number of ways: failure to define the policy area in general and its relationship to the whole problem of company external relations; failure to derive public relations objectives from well-formulated general company objectives; confusion arising from varying operational codes of company personnel, particularly from difficulties in defining what "the company" is in relation to its total environment; failure to conceive of the communicational instrument of corporate policy as a coordinate means for assuring the growth and survival of the company as an institution, and forestalling a lack of harmony with other social institutions.

Public relationships are sometimes thought of as peripheral to the real job of the large firm, the efficient production and distribution of goods and services at a profit. However, there is a growing awareness on the part of management that the organization over which it presides and whose destinies it determines is, in large part, much more than a strictly conceived entrepreneurial firm. As an institution, it is intricately related to many other institutions of society. The nature of these interrelationships, in fact, causes the modern corporation to be regarded as a *social* institution. Public relations policy, conceived with this view in mind, lies near the center of corporate management. It is not merely an instrument of other and "more important" substantive policies. Rather, it is itself one of them.

The public relations policy of a company is of key importance in evaluating its character. What a corporation does in this area provides an index to the true objectives of the organization, to the operational codes of the policy makers, and to their general conception of the role their company plays in the total social structure. For the public relations function is essentially the specialized use of communication as an *ideological* instrument of corporate policy.

An eventual philosophy of corporate enterprise will include among its principles certain ethical rules concerning ideological intercourse. It would be premature to state such rules, even tentatively. Too little is known about the essential nature of the communication process in society and about the role of corporations in this process. For this reason, standards of approval or disapproval would seem to be untimely. Yet, there are some clues to both the metaphysics and the ethics of corporate philosophy, so far as the public relations function is concerned. One place where this link might be made is in the rapidly developing field of cybernetics.

Norbert Wiener has explored the theory of messages in relation to entropy—the general tendency of the world to run down, to approach chaos and de-differentiation. In time's long run, some physicists see the great common purpose of maximum entropy for the universe and all of its parts. And while this may be the most enduring purpose of all, although some would disagree, it is still true that "in the intermediate stages, an organism or a society of organisms will tend to dally longer in those modes of activity in which the different parts work together, according to a more or less meaningful pattern." [19]

Corporations, like organisms, "dally" as long as they can in an entropic universe. That is the meaning of the struggle to survive. The modern corporation is one of the organisms men use to preserve a degree of order in what would otherwise be a chaotic and entropic environment. It is "a local zone of organization in a world whose general tendency is to run down." Even the greatest corporation, despite its immortality in law, lasts but a tick in time. For any organism, its little span is one in which it fights the external forces of disintegration, as it always must.

As an enclave in the general stream of increasing entropy, the modern corporation exhibits certain behavior patterns which may or may not indicate to the cyberneticist a good chance of survival. An important point here is that organization—as an antientropic element—has its correlative in information. The building up of information is vital in the living organism. "Information is a name for the content of what is exchanged with the outer world as we adjust to it, and make our adjustment felt upon it." And "the process of receiving and using information is the process of our adjusting to the contingencies of the outer environment, and of our living effectively within that environment. . . . To live effectively is to live with adequate information." [20]

Could it not be that the public relations function in the modern corporation is suggested in these passages when one regards corporate policy as a whole in terms of corporate ecology? As a communicational process, public relations work has its own implicit standards dictated by the organic nature of the corporation, and its defiance, so to speak, of entropy. To "swim upstream" the corporation must be more than an internally integrated organization; its message-transmitting and receiving mechanisms in relation to the outside world must be in antientropic working order.

Wiener refers to the brilliant idea of W. Ross Ashby in his *Design for a Brain*—that the unpurposeful random mechanism seeks its own purpose through a process of learning—as one of the great philosophical contributions of our age. We can now build purpose into machines, but more than that, "in an overwhelming majority of cases a machine designed to avoid certain pitfalls of breakdown will *look for purposes which it can fulfill.*" [21]

The corporate organism, like all other organisms, displays, as a whole, a certain unpurposeful randomness despite the claims that are often made that it pursues only the coldly rational courses of action laid down by its managers as entrepreneurs in a completely consistent economic model. As a matter of fact, their purposes are usually multifold and partly "irrational." Yet, the corporate organism as a whole can be designed to avoid some of the pitfalls of breakdown and, thus, look for new purposes to fulfill.

The broadly conceived public relations function does not necessarily take as axiomatic the corporate goals envisaged by any decision maker, of whatever status, either within the organization itself or in some center of power on the outside. The objectives of the modern corporation have not been fixed for all time to come. Its "learning processes"—so closely tied to the communicational processes—are vital. In the rapidity of social change so characteristic of our age, the continual reassessment and restatement of corporate goals on the basis of new information may determine the survival of the corporation as an institution.

The future concept of public relations will perhaps be a world apart from the present one of publicity (in all its sophisticated forms), preoccupation with the details of media, and polling techniques. The "know-how" of the communication specialist will be augmented by the "know-why" of the corporate philosopher.

The Future Course

It remains an open question whether men at large can acquire and maintain under stress the attitudes and habits of thought essential to the successful working of a free, open society in a revolutionary world.

Herbert J. Muller, *The Loom of History*

CHAPTER XV

The Well-Tempered Corporation

A TENABLE PHILOSOPHY of business will focus mainly upon the nature and functions of the business corporation of tomorrow. What can we expect of it? What philosophy can guide it?

COUNTERPOSED CORPORATE MODELS

Contemporary thinking about the corporation rests on certain conflicting assumptions which have been set forth in this book in terms of two divergent models of the large incorporated business enterprise. One of these we have called the traditional corporation—an instrument, theoretically, of its stockholders though in practice a hierarchy topped by professional managers who run the business on behalf of its owners. The other model has been designated as the metrocorporation—the instrument of a constellation of interests with an organization that requires professional managers to balance, adjust, and arbitrate the demands of a great variety of claimants.

In the traditional corporation, the property interests of a single group of claimants determine the corporate goals and the course of corporate policy. In the metrocorporation, the "economic man" gives way to the "whole man," and we see in it the proliferation of corporate goals together with a strong tendency to over-mother the brood that clusters about this somewhat pretentious lesser society. This pretentiousness appears not only in the tendency to govern the lives of its Organization Men but also in the theory that its executive managers should seek, through policy making, to balance the interests of groups that lie both within and without the corporate orbit. In its zeal to live up to the social responsibilities increasingly thrust upon it, the metrocorporation even attempts to bring the public interest into the balance.

As we have seen, a reaction has set in against what the traditionalists see as the overweening ambition of the metrocorporation and its allegedly dangerous departure from established norms of the profit-making function of a straight business enterprise. In other quarters, there is apprehension about corporate power and the legitimacy of authority vested in corporate officialdom. As other groups—notably the labor unions—press for a larger voice in the decision process of corporate enterprise, and as pressures mount to widen the concept of a public utility to include businesses that affect the "health and safety" of the economy and the nation, the businessman will begin to search for more tenable models of corporate enterprise.

This search for a better rationale has recently taken the form of varying kinds of doctrine about the social responsibilities of business and the businessman. It is not surprising that this should be so, for the major issues concern the external relationships of the business unit. Yet, as has been shown here, the problem involves more than external relationships and so-called public responsibilities. It also raises the relatively unexplored issue of corporate governance.

The polity of the business corporation is a subject that has been neglected because of the widespread assumption that government is the exclusive business of the state—though of course it has long been recognized that ecclesiastical polity is of great importance to churches, while recently the public has become deeply concerned about the governance of labor unions. It is predictable that there will be growing interest—within and without companies—in the polity of the business corporation. But the reason for this is not so much the question of any abuse of power by corporate governors as it is the larger issue of distributing the authority and responsibility for governing the affairs of men throughout a society characterized by numerous private and voluntary associations.

REQUIREMENTS OF A BETTER CORPORATE MODEL

A corporate model, or heuristic device, for comprehending the actual role of business corporations in the society of today and tomorrow needs to take into account this pervasive governmental process. But before one can construct such a model, one must see the corporation in its more immediately relevant role as a participant in the whole economic process. Finally, one must try to see it in relation to the wider social and cultural functions of a free society.

In this concluding chapter an effort is made to orient the corporation of the future in these respects and to distinguish what we have termed the well-tempered corporation from the dubious traditional and metrocorporate patterns. The distinction will be summarized in terms of the five scientific problems raised in Chapter V.

The requirements of a viable model, with reference to those five problems, are that it state a corporation's goals realistically, set forth the ecological factors that determine in large part its chances for survival and growth, describe the policy process and the areas within which strategic decisions are made by those who govern the corporate polity, and describe that polity adequately in terms of the locus and uses of authority.

But in addition to these scientific requirements, which refer only to the adequacy of the corporate model as an investigative device and a framework for empirical inquiry, there are certain normative requirements. The model should not be at odds with our preferred values. It is unavoidable, then, that in this concluding chapter we shall commingle statements of fact with preferential statements about the kind of corporation one wants in the kind of society one hopes for. Nor is any apology offered for this commingling of what is with what ought to be. The reader can readily separate the one from the other, and it is the intent not to permit our hopes to cloud our judgment of fact.

THE ECONOMIC PROCESS IN A FREE SOCIETY

A capitalist society has been defined as one in which the economic process is entrusted to the private businessman operating under the invisible hand of self-regulating market forces. Can the corporation of tomorrow be regarded as the instrument of the private businessman in managing the economic process in this automatic way? Is a free society, in an age of great organizations, one in which the economic process is entrusted to private organizations like the business corporation?

Some will deny, at the start, that business corporations have or should have any share at all in the control over the economic process for society as a whole. But their role cannot be understood in isolated analysis of their business operations nor out of the organizational context of the whole social structure. It seems undeniable that the great increase in the size, the number, and the power of large organizations of many kinds during the past century—which has been called the Organizational Revolution [1]— was a response to the universal demand for better instruments in men's hands to improve their economic conditions, implemented by greatly improved organizational skills and techniques. This trend has been worldwide: we see it in the rise of powerful organizations among workers, farmers, professional people, and businessmen, as well as in the rise of economically powerful national governments that intervene in that economic process which, under "intact" or "old-style" capitalism, was supposed to be entrusted to a "hidden hand," without state intervention.

The intervention has in fact been an organizational intervention, not confined to legislation but of a more generalized character. The progressive and dangerous statization of one economy after the other throughout the world is thus but one aspect of the transfer of invisible control over the economic process in the self-regulating market, governed by the incremental decisions of countless private businessmen, to deliberate control over the process by public and private organizations. [2] In the West, the transfer is nowhere complete, but the direction of the change is clear enough. If this were not so, antitrust policy would be meaningless, the concern about the power of organized labor would have no foundation in fact, and the dread of statization would be base-less. Large organizations designed to achieve economic purposes would be quite irrational ventures in institution-building if men did not think that they could more effectively control the eco-nomic process by the use of such instruments. It is not only na-tional states that have got into the act; we are witnessing a drama with many kinds of characters.

To understand this drama we need to understand the general outlines of the economic process, for this is what the play is about. For society as a whole, the economic process means more than profitable production; this is the biased view of those who play but one role in the process. The production and the dis-tribution of goods and services—whether profitable or not to the producers and distributors—and their consumption, comes close to the description of the economic process. But not close enough.

The economic process involves the development of the quality and quantity of resources (some of which are allocated to the pro-duction of more resources); the achievement of a certain rate of growth or output from resources as allocated; some method (or methods) of distributing claims on resources, both for production and ultimate consumption purposes; mechanisms for widening or narrowing the field of choice available to the possible users of resources; and the stabilization of the economy in the sense of "reconciling total claims with total resources to be claimed." [3]

Stability in a looser sense means the prevention of intolerable fluctuations in the economy; but this acceptance of the term im-plies a normative view about a "good" economic system, albeit one that we would adopt in our American view of a free society. The economic process, objectively viewed, is one that any society has to concern itself with; and the requirements under each of the elements we have listed will vary according to prevailing ethical standards. So, also, will there be various requirements as to the relative weight to be given to these several elements in the economic process.

Accumulation of capital resources can be stepped up, for ex-ample, at the expense of a "fair" distribution of consumers' goods, and may even be carried so far—as in the Soviet Union—as to annihilate whole populations by starvation. If Galbraith's recent thesis is correct, on the other hand, our own economic process is characterized by inadequate allocation of resources to indispensable public services. The public services that are indispensable in a garrison state preparing for war will be condemned as outrageously wasteful in a welfare state. Decisions on these matters involve important normative judgments that need to be considered apart from the nature of the process itself.

We need go no further here in the analysis of the economic process. Economic theorists will differ as to the listing of its significant elements; but these will do for our purposes. What we need to discover, if we can, are the requirements for good management of this process in a free society and the correlative role of the business corporation. In general, there is a presumption against centralized controls of the process in the United States and in most Western countries; for it is thought that central bureaucratic management of the economic process is inimical to the maximizing of individual choice and thus constitutes a threat to human freedom. A plurality of decision centers in the economic process is required by a free society.

Nor do we need to discourse at length about the more general nature of a free society. As we understand the term in the United States—and indeed in all Western countries—it refers to a civilization founded on the principles of democracy, individual liberty, and the rule of law. It is a condition of human affairs that lies somewhere on a scale that ranges between the anarchistic ideal of freedom from all external restraint on the person and the totalitarian nightmare of complete regimentation under a garrison state. In this wide scale of values, a free society yearns for the anarchistic goal of nonrestraint, knowing that it can never be reached. It is a comparatively free society, with grudging acceptance of such restraints on men as may be demonstrably necessary for the preservation of a community that nourishes other values that men cherish: affection, well-being, rectitude, enlightenment, skill, wealth, respect, power, and, of course, survival. Since a free society deliberately aims toward the maximization of individual freedom of choice, it prescribes no "ideal type" of human being, no conformist Utopia.

Far from being anything like the authoritarian theocracies

and secular despotisms that men have sometimes contrived, a free society looks more like the democracy that Plato delineated with biting sarcasm in *The Republic:* [4] the permissive principle rules; each man arranges his own life to suit himself; it is "distinguished by the wonderful variety of men in it"; and its constitution will be the fairest to look upon "like a garment of many colors of every shade and variety"—in short, a mosaic of public and private governments suited to the multifarious needs and whims of its citizens. It was, for Plato, a "bazaar of commonwealths," splendid in its forebearance and deliberately negative in avoiding encroachments on the private sectors. We reject Plato's sarcastic estimate of democracy if only because of our revulsion for its alternatives—anarchy or tyranny.

CONTROL OF THE ECONOMIC PROCESS IN A FREE SOCIETY

But we do not let everyone do as he pleases, especially with respect to the economic process. There are rational controls; but we fear any sweeping commitment of such controls to the State or to any other organization. If the "hidden hand" of autonomous market forces is unreliable as governor of the economic process, a towering central bureaucracy is equally unacceptable in a free society.

A decade ago it was cogently argued [5] that men turned away from their faith in the "self-regulating market utopia" because of its terrible destructive effects on the fabric and substance of society. Nineteenth century liberalism, with its insistence on laissez faire and noninterventionism of every kind, gave way before a universal but uncoordinated movement toward organized intervention in the economic process. At both public and private levels, nations and private organizations made deliberate efforts to stay the disintegrative force of the older negativism. This is perhaps an additional explanation of the Organizational Revolution. At any rate, the notion that the economic process will govern itself tolerably, if organized intervention is precluded, has been jettisoned.

But from the bazaar of commonwealths that have intruded

into the once-revered atomism of an automatically self-regulating economic system, we have derived what has been described [6] as an "Organizational Economy" that is far from being completely statized. A complete statization of the economy has not been the goal of free societies dedicated to the preservation of human liberty. The Organizational Economy is a transformation of the "old-style" capitalism of laissez faire and individual enterprise into a mixed economy, reserving as much of the price system as possible, while using publicly and privately organized efforts to ameliorate the economic status of the lower-income groups and to keep our modern complex economy functioning without intolerable fluctuations. In this "great transformation" we have striven to avoid an organizational strait jacket along thoroughly collectivistic lines; but we have had to accept radical intervention in the economic process that would have been anathema to the nineteenth-century liberal.

While this transformation has been unavoidable, it poses threats to individual liberty; for we may not be able to stop short of the danger zone where liberty begins seriously to be impaired by progressive statization. Organizational control of the economic process, in some form, is inevitable; but with the postulates of a free society we shall have to develop "forms and processes of economic organization . . . which will not in themselves be inimical to personal liberty and which will relieve the state of the necessity for assuming complete responsibility." [7]

Can we keep the role of the state below "the critical level where the tyrant and his bureaucracy take over"? And having drawn with sharpness the boundaries of the danger zone, will we find the leadership required to keep the state below the critical level? That will depend upon whether those who supply the guidance in the evolution of the institutions of modern capitalism "are endowed with the sometimes contradictory traits of toughmindedness, goodwill, and responsibleness." [8]

The management of the economic process in a free society has thus become a problem of organizational method, and the problem requires us to make choices, not between no-control and control, but rather between completely statized and other forms of organized control. It is not, in other words, a choice between a romantic return to the self-regulating market and an unadminis-tered price system, on the one hand, and a state-dominated econ-omy, on the other. Rather it is a choice between an organiza-tional economy that preserves large areas of human freedom, on the one hand, as against one that seriously threatens individual liberty. The elements of the economic process we listed above are somehow going to be managed, governed, or controlled by more or less rational and effective methods; and the management, governance, or control of these elements of the process will in-evitably be lodged in organizations.

It would be inaccurate to predict that we can never preserve or enlarge the areas in which the price system and the market alone, unimpeded by organizational controls over the economic process, will operate "automatically" to maximize freedom while providing us with the commodities we need and want. We are more and more confronted with collective decisions—for the economy and the political system as a whole—about the combina-tion of political and economic techniques we need to use in order to reach preferred goals. The price system cannot carry the load by itself; and in designing the combined kind of public-private control system for the economic process as a whole, we shall have to be realistic about the techniques available, given the presence of large organizations. There are several possible techniques, with varying degrees of reliance on public and private organiza-tions as co-determiners of public policy, as collective bargainers, and as more or less hierarchical[9] governors of certain private economic sectors, depending upon the roles they are called upon to play in the entire process.

The corporation is essentially a hierarchical system. While it is sometimes contended that there is no place, in a free society, for hierarchical organizations, this position is obviously unten-able. Public government itself, even on democratic principles, cannot dispense with hierarchically constructed bureaucracy in the administrative branches, civil or military. Nor can it success-fully be maintained that the governments of the private sectors must all be nonhierarchical. Most churches and the universities are essentially hierarchical in governmental structure, yet one hears of no great movement to democratize them lest they threaten the foundations of a free society.

In economic organizations such as corporations and labor unions it seems unlikely that there will be any effective movement towards elimination of essentially hierarchical polities for many reasons, among them the requirement that they act as units in bargaining. The traditional corporation, as we have seen, depends upon the hierarchical structure of its internal government to carry out its main function: the maximization of the profits of its owners, for whom all the others in the organization are agents or, even more strictly, fiduciaries and employees. But even with great modifications of the traditional corporation, hierarchical structure will probably remain, especially in view of the fact that heavier social responsibilities will be thrust upon it regardless of its objectives.

To sum up at this point then: the control or management of a considerable part of the economic process—in view of an organizational revolution that is worldwide—is at least partly in the hands of public and private organizations, even in a free society, and that increasingly more so rather than less. In free societies a deliberate effort is required to minimize statization of the economic process; but in practice this cannot mean the transfer of control from a highly centralized public bureaucracy to a completely atomized private sector. It can only mean the assumption by organizations in the private sector of some of the responsibility for governing the economic process. Some of these organizations will be hierarchical in form. This leads to the question: What is the role of the business corporation in this distributed system of control?

COORDINATE ECONOMIC FUNCTIONS OF THE CORPORATION

Because the business corporation is a salient type of economic organization in the organizational economy of capitalist countries, it is bound to have important *coordinate functions in the economic process* in those countries. It operates alongside other important economic institutions, such as banking, labor, and other private organizations, all of which collaborate with varying degrees of effectiveness in the management of the economic process. All of them, moreover, work out various collaborative arrangements with public governmental agencies. There has arisen a new kind of *condominium* [10]—the formal collaboration of representatives from business organizations, labor unions, and public agencies—which, in some Western European countries, is offered as the contemporary solution of this problem. In the United States we have not gone so far. But the coordinate function of these public and private economic organizations is nonetheless clear in all non-Communist countries.

Rationalization of the economic process within the corporation itself is, of course, standard operating procedure in any well-run business. In the allocation and use of its own resources, and in the distribution of resources among various claim holders, the business corporation relies on intricate mechanisms that are not left to chance or the "hidden hand." In coordinating this unit operation with the economic process of the whole organizational economy, however, it is sometimes thought to be heretical to suggest that comparable methods of rational control are appropriate. The heresy is not, properly speaking, in the suggestion but in some of the possible solutions. An utter absence of rationality in the entire process, a complete lack of coordination, is intolerable. Authoritarian planning is equally intolerable in a free society. It is the middle ground that needs exploration, and the exploratory work is the joint responsibility of leaders in both the public and the private sectors of the economy.

How to coordinate the work of all the economic institutions of a free society so that individual choice can be preserved so far as possible is thus a common problem. In practice, the common effort to solve this problem demands the attention of corporate policy makers to specific issues concerning the various elements of the economic process.

The development of adequate resources for the economic system as a whole, for example, is an unavoidable problem for every important decision center, public and private, in a decentralized free economy. In a highly centralized and totalitarian system, this problem is reserved for the agenda of the public bureaucracy. In a well-articulated free system, this problem appears on the agenda of every influential private economic organization. Profligate use of natural resources, relegation of the problem of developing human resources, and dodging of responsibility for balancing capital requirements for the economy as a whole, are examples of uncoordinated functioning of the business corporation in the economic process.

Similar observations are relevant with respect to the other elements in the economic process such as stabilizing and regulating the rate of growth of the economy. For the traditional corporation, efforts in these directions are irrelevant or even irreverent. Veneration for the self-regulating forces of the market, together with persistent dogma about the disparateness of Business and Government, would preclude any attention to such problems within the framework of corporate policy. The metrocorporation, on the other hand, would exhaust its interest in the resolution of claims within the microsystem that defines the scope of its business operations. The viable corporation of the future will find that its very survival depends upon a more ecumenical point of view; it will accept coordinate economic responsibility in the management of the whole economic process.

The coordinate economic function of a particular business corporation will be based on its own managers' theory of the whole economic process and the role of that particular corporation in the process. On this point, however, managers are often zealous advocates rather than seekers after truth. Much of the current effort on the part of businessmen to advance "economic education" of the public, and to show how the free enterprise system works, puts the cart before the horse. One has to know how it works before one can transmit the knowledge. Otherwise "economic education" becomes a thinly veiled propaganda device that fools no one. A sounder knowledge of the economic process and the role of a particular corporation in that process might well lead to the backing of measures calling for far more intervention by public and private organizations in the "self-regulating market" in some spheres, and far less in others. The humility of the scientist before the unknown needs to be coupled with courageous assertion of corporate interests in such a venture. But the courageous assertion of corporate self-interest—which none can deny is a legitimate stance in a free society—has also to be coupled with the common search for formulas that will keep us all this side of the danger zone beyond which the organizational economy swallows up personal liberty.

In this sense there are corporate responsibilities to the community. But the boundaries of the real community have widened so rapidly in recent decades that the coordinate economic function of the large corporation is extremely difficult to fulfill. The community within which it exercises influence and must assume correlative responsibilities often overlaps the established political frontiers. Political boundaries may not be congruent with the real community boundaries as they shift with ethnic, technological, and commercial change. A business corporation is not infrequently required to redraw the boundaries of "community" as defined for its own commercial and technological purposes. But whatever that community, any business corporation has a responsibility to serve that community not merely as a supplier of goods and services for profitable returns to its own factors of production. The corporation also has responsibilities as a co-determiner of the basic economic conditions for its own survival as a business corporation. One of these conditions is the survival of a free society in an economic sense—one in which individual choices are maximized.

COORDINATE POLITICAL FUNCTIONS OF THE CORPORATION

There are two other coordinate functions of the business corporation. These are its political and social (and cultural) functions, both of which are subordinate to its coordinate economic functions. For the viable corporation in a free society, however, they are of such obvious importance that they command increasing attention in every large enterprise.

The coordinate political function of a business corporation is defined by its role in the political process, or the process of government in the community that sustains the corporation. The nature and scope of that community, and the governmental process in that community, are prior considerations that have to be investigated before any particular corporation is in a position to define its own coordinate political functions. The investigation is seldom simple.

A large company normally operates in many political jurisdictions. It crosses numerous frontiers. The pertinent governmental processes which concern it are likewise numerous, embracing the electoral, legislative, administrative, and judicial processes of local, state, national, and international public governments.

But this is not all. Governance, as a distinctive kind of social control, prevails in private as well as public polities. It permeates the social structure. Rule making, rule enforcement, administration, arbitration, and adjudication—these familiar processes of public governance all appear in such private polities as labor unions and business corporations. Even in totalitarian systems, the ambit of public governance cannot possibly cover the multitudinous groupings of society. In a free society a deliberate and systematic effort is made not only to preserve maximal areas for private governance, but also—and more important for the present discussion—to maintain a desirable coordination between the public and private polities.

The tremendous expansion of public governmental activities in the economic process in recent decades has not necessarily reduced the significance of private polities. On the contrary, the "power" of private economic organizations is a matter of great public interest. The use and abuse of the private power is a perennial public issue. That powerful private (or "quasi-public") economic organizations are indispensable is only seldom questioned: Big Business, like Big Labor, is a response to clear needs in a technologically advanced society. That the influence of these "power blocs" can be deleterious to freedom, as well as advantageous as a constructive force is generally assumed as a political truism. They all participate in the governmental process. Thus they all have coordinate political functions.

There are at least two important aspects of this coordinate participation in the governmental process that must be noted in delineating the coordinate political functions of the business corporation. One has to do with the internal polity of the corporation; the other concerns its rights and duties as a comember of the political community.

The corporation as a system of private government is relatively free—up to a point—to determine its own system of governance. The traditional corporate polity is said to be of necessity, if not a "self-perpetuating oligarchy," at least a system of private government that is nondemocratic in theory and practice. Directors choose their own successors, with little or no stockholder control, it is often argued. But the practice varies considerably from company to company; and so far as is known there are numerous types of control: by professional management, by various combinations of managers and directors, by combinations of influential stockholding groups such as financial institutions and pension trusts, and by directors alone.

In theory, a business corporation is the instrument of its stockholders; but not as a rule on a one-man-one-vote basis. Generally, the theoretical constituency is one of private property *interests,* regardless of the number of shareholders. Their votes are weighted with respect to the amount and nature of their capital contributions to the enterprise. The protection of this constituent *property* interest has been a major concern of legislators, but not the prescription of a democratic type of corporate polity.

Other legislative objectives have been the protection of creditors' property interest: the protection of competitors' interests (as in antitrust); and the protection of employees' and consumers' interests by rules of law formulated with the special quality of corporate "power" in mind. Yet as to the internal polity of the business corporation there has been comparatively little legislative intervention once the original charter of corporate governance has been set up by public action. Within its own domain—functionally and not geographically defined—the business corporation, like all private organizations, is comparatively free to carry out its own private governmental process as it pleases within very broad limits.

The impact of this private governmental system on people

within the reach of corporate influence, however, is a matter of more than company concern. All responsible corporate managements recognize this. Indeed, recognition of the fact is the primary cause of increasing attention to a company's so-called social responsibilities. In the technical sense, a corporation thereby undertakes to fulfill one of its coordinate political functions: the function of governing within the corporate domain.

It is a coordinate function because the corporation, like all private organizations, must assume jointly with public organizations the powers and responsibilities inherent in a *shared* governmental process in any free society. Private and public polities, in other words share the burdens of maintaining law and order, establishing justice, and doing all the other things modern political systems are called upon to do. Such private sharing of the responsibility for governing is of course alien to an authoritarian regime.

Corporate Constitutionalism

One aspect of the coordinate political function of a business corporation—the internal structure of its own governmental system—tends to be completely overlooked in the traditional corporation. In the metrocorporation the internal governmental function is dangerously inflated. The metrocorporation becomes, at the worst, a more or less benevolent despotism, or, at best, a small city-state that absorbs unduly the citizenship interests of its constituents. A viable and well-tempered corporate polity must find a middle ground in some form of corporate constitutionalism. The solution is in adequate corporate authority to govern its own affairs, functionally defined, with adequate limitations on that authority to protect the liberties of those whom it governs.

The search throughout the history of freedom for solutions to these two basic issues about government has been the guiding theme of constitutionalism in every country and in every human association, secular or ecclesiastical. What *powers* must be conceded to those who govern in order that they can do what they are supposed to do in the name of the association? What *limita-*

tions on their power must be instituted to see that officials do not exceed their authority?

Recent critics of corporate polity have tended to emphasize the latter question without due attention to the first one. Both are important, of course, but it seems unlikely that the question of restraints on corporate power can be dealt with correctly without first considering the question of adequate corporate authority.

Neither the traditional nor the metrocorporate pattern provides a good answer to the question of adequate authority to govern the corporation. If one accepts the coordinate economic, political, and social functions of a business corporation, the present scope of corporate governance may be too narrowly circumscribed in certain respects and too loosely defined in others. Corrupt practices acts, for example, may deny to corporate governors some political functions which they should not avoid, such as participation in the electoral process of public government. Corporate authority in relation to security holders, on the other hand, may be too broadly defined or inadequately hedged about by needed restraints. In the area of employee relations and the direction of the enterprise, there is, arguably, a serious trend toward the ousting of the management from its legitimate functions of directing the works. These are all debated issues of the day—indicating lack of consensus about the locus and scope of governing authority in the corporate polity.

Yet one hears increasingly—without prior disposition of such basic issues—the demand for restraints on corporate authority by extension of federal constitutional law. The corporation would be constitutionalized by transforming it into a species of public government subject to Fifth and Fourteenth Amendment limitations. The courts would review the actions of corporate officialdom for violations of the due process and equal protection clauses, just as they now review the acts of federal and state agencies for possible encroachments on private rights by public officials.

The argument is that a corporation is a creature of the state and, in effect, an arm of public government. As a recipient of privileges inherent in the corporate form, it has reciprocal obligations that should be enforceable on behalf of private persons pleading constitutional rights as well as rights under common and statutory law rules.

Such an extension of the principles of federal constitutional law to the corporate polity would have far-reaching consequences, not only for the governors of corporate affairs but also for our political and economic system in general. A whole new corpus of constitutional law would have to be developed, mainly through judicial interpretation of the due process and equal protection clauses as applied to corporate power. But that is not all. In delineating the scope of the corporate power to govern, the courts would have to develop also an entirely new area of functional federalism defining the distribution of governmental powers among three kinds of officialdom—federal, state, and corporate.

It is certainly doubtful that the courts have the background to move into such radically new fields of constitutional interpretation. The proper forum for working out norms of corporate constitutionalism is the corporation itself, though this is not to say that statutory guidance should be precluded. In the case of labor union governments, the Landrum-Griffin Act (the Labor-Management Reporting and Disclosure Act of 1959) indicates one way in which Congress has attempted to provide guidelines for the reform of private polities. But it is to be noted that even here Congress has moved slowly, since the so-called Bill of Rights in that law sets up no *constitutional* guarantees of union members' rights as against their union governments. Nor are the enumerated rights enforceable by the procedures used to enforce civil rights against state and federal authorities.

We have yet to see how this Congressional move toward the reform of private government will work out in practice. But surely the governors of corporate polities will not take the Bill of Rights in this Act as an approved pattern for the development of corporate constitutionalism.

The Landrum-Griffin Act may nevertheless be a harbinger of federal statutory intervention in the internal government of all powerful economic associations. Its enactment should spur corporate managements toward systematic efforts to review their own polities.

Thus, corporate internal affairs raise issues that go far beyond the coordinate economic function of the business enterprise. This constitutional aspect of the corporate polity touches the co-ordinate political functions of any large corporation.

Corporate Citizenship

The other aspect of a business corporation's coordinate polit-ical functions concerns "corporate citizenship" in a wider sense: the role of a company in its relations with organizations, public and private, in the governance of the entire community.   Cor-porate external affairs are both political in the narrower sense of "corporate-government" relations, and in the broader sense of co-existence with a multitude of other decision (hence, power) cen-ters in the private sector.

Seldom does one find a corporation whose theory of external political relations suffices for all these coordinate political func-tions.   This inadequacy is only partly owing to narrowly archaic views of the nature of the governmental process, though this is a contributory cause traceable in some degree to the failure of polit-ical scientists to shake off sectarian approaches to the study of politics.[11]   A more direct cause is the fear of entanglement in the involved business of "political action" and a sense of danger in any move that may undermine corporate autonomy or freedom of action.

Sporadic forays of companies into the political arena, for ex-ample, frequently betray a poverty of grand strategy.   Corporate political action is sometimes suspect as a thinly-disguised one-party promotional scheme or an attack on unionism.   In a free society, a corporation, like any other legitimate organization, should be expected to exert its influence in the political arena as well as the market place.   Its views about the "public interest" are neither more nor less worthy of attention in the political arena than those of any other group.   But the grand strategy can be more soundly based on a realistic theory of the governmental process as a whole; business corporations have an indispensable part in that process—as do other private organizations—and it is a role they cannot shirk.   Government, in a free society, is emphatically not the exclusive business of public polities; the burden has to be shared with all legitimate private systems.

The coordinate function in the governmental process is thus far more extensive than is ordinarily assumed in most corporate management circles. The internal and external affairs of the corporation are deeply involved in the process. As to external affairs, one needs more than a director of civic affairs or a government relations specialist to advise on the interplay of business-related organizations or on pressure tactics. The viable corporation of the future is more likely to have a corporate version of the foreign office, with numerous specialized attachés competent to guide external affairs policy in diverse fields: union relations; plant-community relations; relations with the financial community; relations with specialized consumer groups including dealers and distributors); and relations with a variety of business, professional, education, scientific, and cultural organizations, as well as public governments at home and abroad.

In sum, coordinate political functions of a corporation are needed because we live in a pluralistic society characterized by numerous decision centers, all of which must somehow act in concord to carry on the governmental process of that kind of a free society.

COORDINATE SOCIAL AND CULTURAL FUNCTIONS OF THE CORPORATION

We have considered the economic and political functions of the business corporations as a coordinate institution of society: its functions, that is to say, as a co-member of a free society concerned about widely shared responsibility for carrying out the economic and political processes satisfactorily. One must also consider the more general social and cultural processes and the resultant coordinate social functions of the business corporation.

In the advancement of science, in education, in the arts, in the religious life of the community, and with respect to all those processes which are not primarily economic or political, the business corporation, like all other private associations, has coordinate functions. We have seen how the traditional corporation resists every effort to enlist its resources in these general social functions, regarding them as alien to its narrowly specialized purpose. The metrocorporation by contrast embraces all these social functions with respect to its constituents, for it sees itself as a microcosm of the greater society. But the corporation of the future must find a *via media* between these two extreme positions.

What are the social functions that can reasonably be expected of a business corporation that is primarily an economic institution but still accepts a coordinate social and cultural role in a highly interdependent organizational society?

The metrocorporation develops a unique ethos of its own—a way of life to which people within its sphere of influence are expected to conform. It has the special culture of a contained society. The traditional corporation, on the other hand, expects no more than on-the-job performance from its employees and deals with others contractually, impersonally, and calculatedly.

Some qualities of both models will be found in any type of business corporation that has long-range survival value; and, by the very nature of organizational life, it is bound to create a certain cultural existence of its own. But any organization, however large, is part of a larger community to which it contributes and from which it receives support not measurable in economic or political terms.

The business corporation has in this way a coordinate social and cultural function which, in many companies today, is at least partially fulfilled by such programs as plant-community activities, corporate giving, and "human relations" projects in dealing with employees. These programs, while sometimes justified on hard-boiled principles of calculated self-interest, are not in fact always —or, perhaps, generally—so motivated.

Many corporate executives are sensitive about charges of irresponsibility, excessive materialism, and cynicism that have been made in attacks on Big Business. Some of them have retorted indignantly that businessmen are as much interested in cultural equilibrium as are those who abuse them. The caricature of the giant corporation as a stronghold of the tycoon and the robber baron is distressing to them. Philanthropic and active community work provides one avenue for demonstrating that businesses are cultural and social as well as economic assets to the community.

The coordinate social and cultural role of the business corporation, however, is not carried out by proving that businessmen are altruistic, cultured, and high-minded people determined to transform the competitive enterprise unit of "old-style" capitalism into a social welfare agency. A business unit in a competitive economy is, after all, primarily an instrument of the economic process. There are, nevertheless, important by-products of corporate enterprise that can make immense contributions towards strengthening the social fabric of a free society. There are values that can accrue from big business operations that can, by careful planning, be diverted into socially desirable channels.

One of these values is an intellectual product. Large-scale enterprise requires research and development in manufacturing, engineering, marketing, finance, public relations, and management. The research product in these fields is customarily retained for corporate use exclusively and often far more restrictively than could reasonably be required to satisfy immediate proprietary interests. Public and private bureaucracies both are inclined to sit on the new knowledge they produce and to keep it out of circulation. Secrecy in government has its counterpart in industrial secrecy. There are reasonable limits to both. One effective alternative to the generous outright grants of money to education might well be systematic efforts on the part of corporations to distribute much larger increments of their intellectual product. These benefits could accrue eventually to the store of corporate knowledge, inasmuch as scientific advance depends upon the communication of research results throughout the scientific community. This argument can, of course, be extended to the field of the social sciences.

The corporation today is one of the major producers of scientific knowledge, but it is notorious that freedom of publication does not prevail in most companies. Personnel are usually strictly limited in the right of publication. The result is to withdraw the corporate community from the free interchange of ideas that is so essential to a free society.

Another value of large-scale enterprise is the spiritual energy generated by highly rational and organized communities of men who are drawn together around their productive tools. In the metrocorporation this energy is entirely consumed by the organization itself. A coordinate social institution, however, must contribute something to the whole social process. The release of corporate personnel—on protracted leaves of absence if necessary —for political, social, cultural, and educational activities in the surrounding community is one way of diverting some of the spiritual energy generated by large organizations to the upbuilding of other institutions of a free society. Some continuous contact with the needs of the greater society is a necessity; it is essential to the scientist's or scholar's continuity of purpose, once he has cast his lot with the corporation. It may be objected that a competitive company cannot afford this kind of diversion of its energies to "unrelated activities"; but its old concept of relatedness is undergoing marked changes.

There are far too many sectors of society in the corporate environment that are languishing for want of more than material sustenance, with ultimate dangers to the autonomy of the corporate enterprise itself. The independent college is but one case in point. In the fields of science, the arts, recreational opportunities for youth, the development of meaningful careers for our rapidly increasing aged population, the rehabilitation of the mentally ill, and, in general, the development of healthful patterns of living outside the work place, it is possible for the corporation to be effective and active in collaboration with other organizations without depending on grants of money. Extending organizational know-how to these other private groups might achieve better results faster though it would demand considerable revision of employment policies in most companies with respect to leaves, continuity of pension rights, and so on. But more than this is the need for revision of intracompany job descriptions, with a view to integrating socially useful work with the work a man does for the immediate purposes of short-range productivity.

TOWARD A MORE TENABLE MODEL

What we have called the coordinate economic, political, and social functions of the corporation are presumably the indispensable characteristics of a viable form of corporate enterprise in the foreseeable future of a free society. To survive in such a society, the business corporation must progress beyond the traditional model of performance. Equally, it will have to avoid the metrocorporate pattern. Neither suffices as a recipe for social adaptation. One appears to be already outmoded; the other could destroy itself by becoming a socioeconomic collective.

The corporation that is tempered to its times, and more specifically to the requirements of a pluralistic society grounded on the principles of democracy, individual liberty, and the rule of law as a safeguard to freedom, is what we have called the well-tempered corporation. Its viability as an institution will depend upon its ability to maintain a certain equilibrium within a complex social and supranational environment.

ECOLOGY OF THE WELL-TEMPERED CORPORATION

Until recently, much of the policy thinking in large business corporations has been in terms of the "rational model" of organizations, with emphasis on internal structure and processes more narrowly considered as problems of business administration and scientific management. Now there is increasing emphasis on what has been called the "natural-system model of organizational analysis" [12] wherein the emphasis is on the business organization in relation to its total environment. To understand its functions in this environment—or what we have called its coordinate functions —one must try to envisage the business corporation as part of a total "social ecosystem." From an ecological point of view, organizations such as the business corporation maintain a state of equilibrium for shorter or longer periods in relation to a complex of physical, biological, and social ecosystems, depending upon their adaptation to the milieu and the state of equilibrium in the ecosystems as a whole.

The science of ecology—dealing with the mutual relations among organisms, and between them and their physical, biological, and social environment—can thus be extended profitably to the study of long-range adaptation of the business corporation to the conditions prevailing in a free society. The well-tempered corporation is one that is viable in a free society and adapts successfully to the conditions of such a society. The well-tempered corporation not only depends on its interrelationships with other organizations and with the biological and physical environment prevailing in such a society; it is a contributory element in the maintenance of equilibrium in that ecosystem.

We do not know enough about the structure of the ecosystem of a free society to describe the conditions of equilibrium in such a system; but this we do know: human societies, like biological species, are likely to be in a state of constant change rather than one of permanent and unchangeable equilibrium. The organizations, institutions, ideas, and techniques of one period are likely to be displaced by those of a following period in a natural order of ecological succession.

In this long process of ecological change, moving sometimes with great rapidity and sometimes with glacial leisure, one may trace the rise and demise of the business corporation. The critical variables in the ecosystems of the business corporation, on which its viability depends, are not well understood. The physical ecosystem has to be considered, in an age of rapidly changing science and technology, as applied to the derivation of energy sources by man and the possible effect of these new discoveries on the face of the earth and the atmosphere that envelops it; but we leave this fascinating question aside. The biological ecosystem, too, is important, particularly with respect to nonhuman species, like bacteria and the insects, which might win out eventually in the long struggle for survival if any living thing does. But of more immediate importance are demographic movements. One might well inquire whether the business corporation would be a viable institution in a world overwhelmed with its human population, pressing disastrously on its limited resources. We leave this question aside also. Enough for our purpose here is the question of corporate viability in relation to the social ecosystem.

One might posit any number of alternative types of social ecosystems that the business corporation could conceivably encounter in the foreseeable future—say, the next fifty to a hundred years. As a people, we choose to posit the free society; but it is possible that in the immense process of ecological succession we may be moving—despite our best hopes—away from a social ecosystem characterized by a relatively wide scope for individual liberty, toward a closed and unfree society. Assuming the viability of the business corporation as an institution in an unfree society—a highly questionable assumption—one would have to conclude that corporations adaptable to that milieu would have quite different coordinate functions than those we have been describing.

Politically, the now relatively autonomous business corporation could conceivably degenerate into a mere administrative arm of the state or its ecological successor. Economically, it might still be a major instrument for those economic processes we have considered earlier, though not as an autonomous entity operating in a price system. Socially, it would conceivably be saddled with an enormous variety of guildlike functions. All these changes could occur under the conditions of a closed society, with organizational interdependence far beyond what we now have even in our system of transformed capitalism.

On the other hand, one might posit a protracted countermovement to the organizational economy we now have, in the direction of disorganization and atomizing of political, social, and economic institutions. The combined forces of the physical, biological, and social environment could conceivably precipitate a reversal of the trend toward Bigness everywhere. The business corporation would hardly escape the forces of dissolution. Those who see in the business corporation of today the forerunner of social organization in a new age, the basic form of organization around which the new society will be formed, a replacement of the moribund sovereign state—they have an argument not lightly to be dismissed. But if that happens, we shall see a basic transformation in the primary as well as the coordinate function of the corporation. It will no longer be a business corporation but a political instrument primarily.

In America we reject these alternatives to the free society because we believe there is room for the exercise of the will and human imagination in shaping the kind of society we want to live in. Those who preside over the destinies of the business corporation—shaping corporate policy from within its four walls as well as public policy as it impinges on the future of the corporation—have some freedom of choice. But like all other contemporary institutions, the business corporation will have to make progressive adaptations to the changing needs of the men and the societies of which it is a specialized and indispensable instrument.

CORPORATE ADAPTATION TO A GLOBAL ECOSYSTEM

The major opportunity for corporate contribution to its global environment has perhaps never been consistently emphasized, though both Mary Parker Follett and Lyndall Urwick pointed out that if business has nothing else to offer society it would still be a model of productive, cooperative human organization. And perhaps the dilemma in which the modern corporation finds itself rises out of its very success at large-scale, efficient organization. When the traditional corporation appeared to be growing at the expense of society, the State intervened. Now that its economic drive is under control, the looming metrocorporation seems to offer a threat to social freedom, and sociologists, psychologists, and others are concerned. Part of today's fear of the large corporation, however, is the fear of its demonstrated ability to handle a legion of disparate problems and still operate a business for profit. Yet this is no threat to society but only a threat to a philosophy of totalitarianism.

In national emergencies business leaders are called to Washington to help resolve and expedite matters that could, in normal times, be handled with speed and efficiency through ordinary agencies of government. And our economic effort to rehabilitate war-torn or underdeveloped nations has been notably more successful than some of our political gambits abroad. It has in fact been so successful as to generate for American business a new kind of competition that challenges our products in areas where they had not been challenged before. The ecosystem of business, accordingly, has widened.

The economic basis for an orderly global system now begins to be perceptible in the movements toward common markets that transcend political demarcations. Cautious optimism leads to the hope, if not the immediate expectation, that the older diplomatic and military rivalries may eventually recede in favor of peaceful economic coexistence among nation-states that have been at each other's throats for generations. Some degree of order is gradually being brought out of the trade chaos that prevailed before Bretton Woods and before the institution of the General Agreement on Tariffs and Trade (GATT). In these and other international movements toward an orderly market place of world-wide dimensions, the business corporation will be called upon to play an important part.

The ecosystem of the corporation is, as a result, now global rather than purely national. Whatever the corporation's present nature and function, plainly many business companies will have to reorganize completely [13] to regard the world as their market, and to resolve strategic questions not merely on a local level but in the light of opportunities all over the globe.

If the ecosystem of the corporation is now global, the question it raises for a particular company is not merely, *What* ought we to be doing? but also, *Where* should we be doing what we are best geared to do in a world market? Will the answer radically alter the nature of corporate goals? Will the environment of the corporation be so changed as to change the nature of its organization? It is impossible to say, but it is imperative that every company face the problem squarely.

The challenge is enormous and demands an enormous flexibility. One is dealing at the global level with mind-sets quite different from ours. A company must be prepared to operate under social conditions that differ radically from those which prevail in its home environment. But it is not only the great cultural and economic differentials that challenge the corporate policy maker as he moves into the world arena. In the epic struggle between ideologies, will it be possible for the business corporation to move outside the orbit of freedom and to make its contribution in uncommitted areas where all warring forces are suspect? Or should it sever all ideological ties under the banner of complete neutralism?

There is a sense in which the corporation tempered to these

times cannot be neutral. Moving in the world arena, it must subscribe a kind of economic brotherhood of man. This is only remotely an ideological alignment, however, and it has nothing to do with religious and political crusades. Still, the revolutionary force of secular business enterprise on a global scale does find some common ground with two kinds of historic revolutionary movements: the unifying force of the universal religions and, at another level, of the more recent proletarian movement. They all have sought new and wider concepts of community; yet may it not be that the present moves toward economic integration—in which corporate enterprise will figure prominently—will be more effective means of establishing a world community than the cross, the sword, the clenched fist, and the hammer and sickle?

The stage is being set for crusading in the more prosaic terms of the production and distribution of goods and services for a global market, and on a businesslike basis familiar to those who conduct large corporate enterprises. This is the opportunity for the emergence of what we may call the well-tempered corporation.

THE WELL-TEMPERED CORPORATION

The salient elements in such a corporate instrument can be summarized in the model of the well-tempered corporation.

(1) *Corporate goals.* The corporation aims at profitable long-run return on investments in the enterprise, with basic concern for those who have committed their property and their careers to the company, and full consideration of the commitments their enterprise has made to society.

(2) *Corporate ecology.* The corporation, though it is chiefly an instrument of those who invest their property and their careers in the enterprise, is also inseparably linked with the total economic, political, and cultural environment; and as an entity it has commitments that require it to sustain the social processes of the entire ecosystem, specifically the economic and political processes.

(3) *The policy process.* The decision making within the corporation takes into account the multiplicity of corporate goals,

with emphasis upon its profit-making function but not to the exclusion of other commitments, and with optimum use of all the instruments of corporate policy.

(4) *The strategic decisions* in the well-tempered corporation, though primarily economic in character and related directly to the profit-making purpose of the enterprise, will also include the decisions required to meet other commitments arising from the ecological factors that determine the rate of growth, the social acceptance, and the survival of the organization.

(5) *Corporate polity*. The well-tempered corporation is a system of private government with *self-generated* principles of constitutionalism that match corporate authority to corporate responsibilities and impose restraints upon corporate officialdom for the protection of the rights of persons and property against abuse of corporate power.

With these elements in mind, it is not difficult to derive at least tentative answers to the question of social responsibilities of the well-tempered corporation. The focus, in the first place, should be on some specific persons or groups of persons within the corporate structure and not upon the corporation as an entity. For the present, a primary obligation rests upon corporate directors and executive managers to formulate the goals of their own companies for the foreseeable future, and then to design the corporate polity and the decision process in such a way as to make the achievement of these goals possible.

Insofar as the polity remains, as it usually is today, hierarchical and highly centralized in form, the responsibilities of the corporation are in effect the moral obligations of the directors and their agents. In a more decentralized polity, with some elements of a federative and representative system of corporate governance, the responsibilities of the corporation will become correspondingly diffused among relatively numerous decision centers.

To whom are these corporate governors responsible? Certainly in the first instance, they have an obligation to run an enterprise that produces salable goods and services with profitable return to those who put up the risk capital. And increasingly it is urged that the risk is shared by employees as well as stockholders, though the correlative obligation (on the part of both these classes of investors in the enterprise) to sustain losses as well as to share in earnings has no definitive formulation as yet. There are also commitments, once an enterprise is launched, to other groups which depend in varying degrees on the *continuity* of the enterprise. Customers, suppliers, plant communities, and often much larger sectors of society have expectations that have to be met. But no definitive list of obligees can be drawn up today.

The substance of the obligations involved in the commitments to these obligees is not definable in any universally valid terms. This is true even of the primary obligation of management toward investors of risk capital. In a federative and representative corporate polity one need not assume that the shareholders as a class constitute the basic or exclusive constituency whose claims have priority over expectations that arise in other quarters of the corporate complex. It seems clear, for example, that there are many legitimate claims on the fruits of the enterprise; and one insistent claim is that it maintain its viability and growth as an institution, quite aside from rate of return or productivity. A further responsibility, in the case of certain well-established companies, is to participate *continuously* in the coordinate economic, political, and social processes of a free society. They are no longer free to act as though they were just small, private businessmen operating in a classical market situation.

The emergence of this kind of corporate social responsibility is especially marked when a company is in a position to influence the equilibrium of the total ecosystem, whether in its economic or its political aspects. Corporate executives understandably recoil at the more extreme implications of this responsibility; but it is an unavoidable consequence of the influence which their organizations have in the community.

We can only dimly perceive what coming generations will expect of their institutions. Will there be a race that will have left behind it the disastrous parochial and intercontinental conflicts that now absorb so much of men's energies? Will our descendants have so mastered the age-old problems of human ecology that they can harness science to spiritual goals, no longer grubbing about in eternal conflict with material limitations, under the shadow of Malthusian fear? Will they have found such radically different dimensions of time and space that the "good life" for them will be a way of life that we could not have dreamed of? In a society possessed of science and technology adequate to maintaining an incredibly high and universal standard of living within the oxygen envelope that surrounds our own planet, and to supporting the inquiring mind in pursuit of nuclear and spatial secrets still closed to us, it is altogether probable that the corporation may be transformed into a radically different instrument of man's will. If the traditional corporation and the metrocorporation recede into the limbo of discarded social institutions, could not the same prediction be made for the well-tempered corporation?

Perhaps we shall then have no "business' corporation at all, as we now conceive the business function. What seems less likely is that the *organizational instrument* represented by corporate forms will have outlived its usefulness. The corporation is a superb instrument. And for a long time to come many men will be challenged, as explorers of human affairs, to scale the heights of meaning in so towering an institution; for, like Sir Edmund Hillary's mountain, it is there. And it is likely to be there for generations. The challenge to corporate policy makers today is to transfer its uses to the requirements of a materially, intellectually, and spiritually ambitious race.

Notes

Notes

INTRODUCTION

1. Frank Pierson and others, *The Education of American Businessmen: a study of University-College Programs in Business Administration* (New York: McGraw-Hill, 1959).

2. Robert Aaron Gordon and James Edwin Howell, *Higher Education for Business* (New York: Columbia University Press, 1959).

I. THE SEARCH FOR A PHILOSOPHY OF BUSINESS

1. "Philosophy" is a word with several referents. It is used here with the meaning given in Webster: "The body of principles or general conceptions underlying a given branch of learning, or major discipline, a religious system, a human activity, or the like, and the application of it; as the *philosophy* of history, Christianity, or of business."

2. The term "the modern corporation" as used in this book refers primarily to the large business corporation in the United States, and especially to "corporations of such magnitude, or performing such essential economic services, as to make their existence and administration matters of public concern." A. S. Dewing, *The Financial Policy of Corporations* (5th ed., New York: Ronald Press, 1953), I, 33.

As to magnitude, *The Fortune Directory*, August, 1959, lists the 500 largest U.S. industrial corporations (ranked by sales), the 50 largest commercial banks (ranked by assets), the 50 largest life-insurance companies (ranked by assets), the 50 largest merchandising firms (ranked by sales), the 50 largest transportation companies (ranked by operating revenues), and the 50 largest utilities (ranked by assets). These lists provide useful clues to what one means in the concrete by the abstract term "the modern corporation" although they do not necessarily constitute the only possible statistical universe for all generalizations about it. Relatively small companies have considerable social and economic significance in certain environments.

In 1957, the "Billion Dollar Club" (corporations having assets of a billion dollars or more) had 90 "members," according to United Press reports by Robert G. Shortal, on April 22 and 23, 1958. The Bureau of Labor Statistics, U. S. Department of Labor, reported in *Employment and Earnings, 1956,* that almost 1,000 American companies were earnings more than $5 million annually, and more than 500 earned more than $10 million. Those which showed sales volume of a billion dollars or more numbered 48 in the same year. These figures do not, of course, provide any clue as to the total impact of these large companies upon the population as a whole, and they leave unrevealed the great extent to which economic enterprise is still carried on by small and unincorporated businesses. Only 23 of the 90 corporations in the billion-dollar-asset group in 1957 were industrial firms. Of the remainder, 23 were banks, 16 insurance companies, 10 public utilities, 7 railroads, 3 credit firms, 2 investment companies (mutual funds), and one a mail-order house. Standard Oil (New Jersey), the leading industrial firm on this assets scale, was outranked by Bell Telephone System, Metropolitan Life, Prudential Insurance, Bank of America, and Equitable Life. General Motors was the second ranking industrial firm on this scale, but it was outranked by Chase Manhattan Bank and First National City Bank. The largest industrial corporations in terms of stockholders were General Motors, Standard Oil (New Jersey), Ford Motor Co., General Electric, and U. S. Steel. Sears, Roebuck, with over 200,000 employees, ranked along with these five as top hirers of personnel.

It has been estimated that "about two-thirds of the economically productive assets of the United States, excluding agriculture, are owned by a group of [probably] not more than 500 corporations." Adolf A. Berle, *Economic Power and the Free Society* (New York: Fund for the Republic, 1957), p. 14. Yet magnitude is not the only key to the socially significant corporation. A relatively small company, in a certain environment, may dominate the scene and set both the economic and cultural patterns for a community or an industry. Nor is it safe to assume that the industrial corporation is the only significant kind of corporate enterprise. The corporate form is used in agriculture and in other nonindustrial types of business enterprise. But it is the large industrial corporation that sets the tone for corporate business, generally speaking.

Many kinds of "regulated" enterprises come under the general heading of business corporations; and, while all enterprise in corporate form is to some extent regulable by government, this book is concerned mainly with industrial companies that buy their materials in the competitive market and not with public utilities, banks, and insurance companies.

3. These characteristics were noted by Herbert von Beckerath, *Modern Industrial Organization: an Economic Interpretation,* tr. by Robinson Newcomb and Franziska Krebs (New York: McGraw-Hill, 1933), Chap. II, p. 37.

Although, as Schumpeter has pointed out, there was large-scale enterprise in the commercial and financial spheres as early as the fourteenth century in Italy, in the fifteenth in Germany, and in the sixteenth in England, followed eventually by large units in the manufacturing industry as a result of the Industrial Revolution, it is remarkable how slow the economists were to recognize the significance of it. "No author, not even A. Smith, had any very clear idea of what the processes really meant that led to what economic historians have dubbed the Industrial Revolution. A. Smith felt that the corporate form of industry was an anomaly except in such cases as canals and the like. To him and his contemporaries big business still meant commercial and financial big business—colonial enterprise particularly. And they looked upon it . . . with feelings of resentful distrust." J. A. Schumpeter, *History of Economic Analysis* (New York: Oxford University Press, 1955), p. 150.

4. Walton H. Hamilton, *The Pattern of Competition* (New York: Columbia Press, 1940), p. 22. "Industry cannot be set down as the great antithesis between competition and monopoly. It holds far too much of detail and drama, of color and variety, to be crowded into a few simple molds." *Ibid.,* p. 25. Recently Hamilton declared in *The Politicis of Industry* (New York: Knopf, 1957), p. 25, that free enterprise "in law, in common sense, and in classical economics . . . has long been employed as a synonym for the competitive system" and (p. 169) that while it was not "important that the arrangements which currently are set down as the competitive system will endure" it *was* "important that the spirit of competition shall be enhanced and not impaired" as an "outlet for the creative urge, free play for the dynamic drive."

5. Oswald Knauth, *Managerial Enterprise: Its Growth and Methods of Operation* (New York: Norton, 1948).

6. *Ibid.*, pp. 198, 209–10.

Knauth proposed at this point some questions that had to be faced in evolving a "philosophy of managerial enterprise":

To what degree is competition in prices desirable? Can competition be forced to a point that is ruinous?

Should production be regulated to coincide with consumption?

Is division into smaller units desirable? Even if output will be sacrificed?

Are the policies that lead to balance also those that make for the greatest output?

Is there a practical difference between actual agreement and a tacit trade understanding, such as "follow the leader"?

How can the power of management be controlled? How should management be selected?

How may prices be equally adjusted at the points where free and managerial enterprise overlap?

The solution of these questions, he added, required clarification of:

The standards by which industries should be classified as belonging to the free-enterprise, collectivist, or managerial form of economy, and the interpretation of borderline cases

The standards adapted to each form of economy

The duties, rights and responsibilities of employees

The duties, rights and responsibilities of directors and managers

Safeguards to permit individuals to move as freely as possible among the different forms of economy

Points at which the interest of the managerial enterprise and the national welfare are identical or antagonistic

7. Oswald Knauth, *Business Practices, Trade Position and Competition* (New York: Columbia University Press, 1956), p. 5. He added that "the problems, policies, and methods of today's industrialists and businessmen have been determined by efforts to meet today's necessities" and that "they do not correspond to present legal theory, which is based on the classical economic ideology of a century ago" (p. 8). He estimated that two-thirds of our "mixed economy" falls under the heading of "mass production and distribution, continuous flow of goods and dynamic change"; about one-sixth operated by government, "with methods inconsistently conforming to socialism"; the

rest being "small business" which "more nearly conforms to the assumptions of classical analysis" (p. 12).

8. See Reinhard Bendix, *Work and Authority in Industry* (New York: John Wiley, 1956), Chap. 5, and *A Study of Managerial Ideologies* (Berkeley: Institute of Industrial Relations, University of California, 1957).

9. Francis X. Sutton, Seymour E. Harris, Carl Kaysen, and James Tobin, *The American Business Creed* (Cambridge, Mass.: Harvard University Press, 1956), p. 385. See Chap. VII, note 16, below.

10. *Ibid.,* especially Chap. 17 and 18. The "conventional wisdom" of American businessmen, among others, draws in part upon the "central tradition" (the main current of economic ideas in descent from Adam Smith) and in part upon the doctrines of Herbert Spencer and William Graham Sumner ("survival of the fittest"), to produce a strong strain of Social Darwinism, according to John Kenneth Galbraith, *The Affluent Society* (Boston: Houghton Mifflin, 1958), pp. 55–60.

11. Sutton and others, *The American Business Creed,* p. 358.

12. "Not surprisingly, the [managerial] ideology's conception of competitive behavior is extremely catholic. It contrasts with the economist's narrow definition of pure competition, assumed in the classical argument on which business ideology lays so much stress. But economists' notions of competition are dismissed as impractical, with a unison and an impatience of external moral criticism which again are symptomatic of a solidarity protecting internal moral standards of which the group is none too sure." *Ibid.,* p. 368.

13. *Ibid.,* p. 58.

14. "Business Holds Key to U. S. Future: Why Corporate Management Must Assume Increasing Responsibility to the Public," an interview with Dean Courtney C. Brown, *Nation's Business,* XLV, No. 7 (July, 1957), 32 ff.

15. Courtney C. Brown, "Business in Cap and Gown: the New Higher Education of Executives," *Saturday Review,* January 19, 1957, pp. 16 ff. See also his editorial, "Knowledge of What?" *Saturday Review,* January 17, 1959, pp. 52 ff.

16. The reference is especially to F. W. Maitland's brilliant and influential "Introduction" to his translation of a section of the third volume of Otto von Gierke's monumental historical study of the German law of associations from its medieval beginnings, *Das Deutsche Genossenschaftsrecht* (4 vols., Berlin: 1868–1913, Vol. IV unfinished). Maitland's translation, under the title, *Political Theories of the Mid-*

dle Age, was published in 1900 (Cambridge, Eng.), and in the succeeding decades his "Introduction" stimulated the development of
pluralistic political theory both in England and in America, emphasizing as it does Gierke's concept of the *Genossenschaft* (fellowship or
cooperative association) as distinguished from *Herrschaft* (sovereignty), its antithesis, in the evolution of Germanic law.   Gierke's
work was permeated by "the central idea of real group personality"
as contrasted with the theory that a corporation is the artificial creation of the sovereign, a fictitious person.   "Apart from its theoretical
implications the greatness of Gierke's work lies in the firmness with
which it is rooted in the past of German legal history," writes C. J.
Friedrich in a biographical note (*Encyclopaedia of the Social Sciences,*
VI, 655); and he "profoundly influenced branches of law which are
of particular importance at present, such as the law of joint stock
companies, the law of cooperative associations and industrial laws."
Friedrich adds that "whoever wishes to do either theoretical or practical work in these fields must go back to Gierke."   Most of *Das
Deutsche Genossenschaftsrecht* remains untranslated into English.   In
1934 Ernest Barker published in England his translation of certain
sections of the last volume of this work under the title of *Natural
Law and the Theory of Society, 1500 to 1800,* together with an illuminating introduction of his own that throws much light for the
British reader on the history of corporation theory. (A paperback edition of Barker's translation was published by the Beacon Press, Boston, 1957.)   In the sections there translated, Gierke treats at length,
and with copious notes, the natural-law theory of associations, the
general theory of the group, and the natural-law theory of corporations, as these ideas were developed by the major writers of Europe
and England from 1500 to 1800.   See also the chapter on "The Whole
Church as a Corporation," in Brian Tierney, *Foundations of the Conciliar Theory; the Contribution of the Medieval Canonists from
Gratian to the Great Schism* (Cambridge, Eng.: The University Press,
1955).

17. A concise review, with special reference to business corporations, is in Dewing, *The Financial Policy of Corporations,* Chap. I,
"The Corporation."

18. Some examples are: William Robert Scott, *The Constitution
and Finance of English, Scottish and Irish Joint-Stock Companies to
1720* (3 vols., Cambridge, Eng.: The University Press, 1910–12), C. T.
Carr, "Early Forms of Corporateness," in *Select Essays in Anglo-
American Legal History* (Boston: Little, Brown, 1909); Joseph S.

Davis, *Essays in the Earlier History of American Corporations* (Cambridge, Mass.: Harvard University Press, 1917); Shaw Livermore, *Early American Land Companies; Their Influence on Corporate Development* (New York: The Commonwealth Fund, 1939); Simeon E. Baldwin, "Private Corporations, 1701–1901," in *Select Essays in Anglo-American Legal History,* cited above; George Wharton Pepper, "An Introduction to the Study of the Law of Associations," *American Law Register,* XL (1901), pp. 255 ff.; Samuel Williston, "History of the Law of Business Corporations Before 1800," in *Select Essays in Anglo-American Legal History,* cited above.

19. Adolf A. Berle, Jr., and Gardiner C. Means, *The Modern Corporation and Private Property* (New York: Macmillan, 1933). Antecedents to their thinking will be found in the works of Thorstein Veblen and W. Z. Ripley.

20. Walter Rathenau, *In Days To Come,* tr. by E. & C. Paul (London: Allen & Unwin, 1921), cited by Berle and Means, *The Modern Corporation and Private Property,* p. 352.

21. Berle and Means, *The Modern Corporation and Private Property,* p. 357.

22. Adolf A. Berle, Jr., "The Developing Law of Corporate Concentration," *University of Chicago Law Review,* XIX, No. 4 (Summer, 1952), 639–61, esp. 656 and 661.

23. Peter F. Drucker, *The Concept of The Corporation* (New York: John Day, 1946), Chap. I, p. 14.

24. Carl Kaysen, "The Social Significance of the Modern Corporation," *American Economic Review,* XLVII, No. 2 (May, 1957), 311–19.

25. Compare Raymond A. Bauer, "Our Big Advantage: the Social Sciences," *Harvard Business Review,* XXXVI, No. 3 (May-June, 1958), 125–36; the rapidly growing literature in the field of operations research as applied to corporate management, such as *Operations Research* (Journal of the Operations Research Society of America), *Naval Research Logistics Quarterly* (Office of Naval Research, Department of the Navy), and *Management Science;* and more generally the quantitative and interdisciplinary approaches to business enterprise research indicated in Mary Jean Bowman, ed., *Expectations, Uncertainty, and Business Behavior* (New York: Social Science Research Council, 1958) and in Howard R. Bowen, *The Business Enterprise as a Subject for Research* (New York: Social Science Research Council, 1955).

26. "The rationale of the market is applicable to a process in which inputs and outputs are distinguishable, and inputs are viewed

as potentially transferable among alternative outputs, which, in turn, are competing salable products. But if inputs and outputs are tied together in an indissoluble bundle, so that the one is not transferable and the other not salable, we are dealing with a way of life, not a production process. . . . We classically contrast favorably the operation of business with that of a government department aimed at promoting the public welfare. But the soulful corporation becomes less and less distinguishable, except in the matter of formal control and management responsibility, from the socialist enterprise if the latter operates under instructions to serve the public welfare but not to rely on the public treasury. They share common structural features: market power and a very long decision horizon—although typically the socialist enterprise as observable to date excels in both directions." Kaysen, "The Social Significance of The Modern Corporation," *American Economic Review,* XLVII, 318.

27. "Economic theory is relatively incompetent to analyze the major dimensions of the corporation that Mr. Kaysen has identified," according to Charles E. Lindblom, commenting at the sixty-ninth annual meeting of the American Economic Association upon Mr. Kaysen's paper referred to above (p. 325). Deriding the usual narrow approaches to the corporation in terms of the monopoly problem, and questioning whether the major focus for economic analysis upon this problem was not now obsolete, Lindblom nevertheless doubted that Kaysen's "multidimension corporation" would have much significance for the development of new theory. "It appears to be one more in the long line of provocative essays and books that have failed to shake theorists much in their disposition to treat the corporation simply as a maximizing individual" and Lindblom mentioned Veblen, Berle, Rothschild, Gordon, Neil Chamberlain "to indicate the variety." "Our present concept of the corporation is less troublesome than [Kaysen's]" and "makes this unfamiliar giant in our midst an ordinary creature like everyone else, requiring no special developments in theory" however badly these were needed for accurate analysis. Kaysen had made the point, Lindblom continued, that the modern corporation has changed the character of economic calculation: in a world in which tastes are substantially formed and rapidly changed by sellers, concepts of efficiency which rest on satisfying given consumer preferences lose their sharpness; but then Kaysen had gone on to show that institutional developments gave this criticism of theory new relevance. "I think this point hits where it hurts," commented Lindblom. "Our theoretical insights might gain enormously if we

set to work on the assumption that *the pattern of production is the major influence on the pattern of consumer choice,* as is more obviously true in music and the arts. But having fought the dependence on production as less than a fatal objection to theory for all these years, we would invite confusion by accepting the objection now." (Italics added.) Lindblom concluded: "In all seriousness it is no doubt true that if we as economists were to take account of the many dimensions of the corporation in our theory, we would take on a very great burden. It would mean that we would lose some of our professional distinctiveness and that we would become social scientists with specialization in economics rather than economists." *American Economic Review,* XLVII, No. 2 (May, 1957), 324–26.

28. Summarized in John Desmond Glover, *The Attack on Big Business* (Boston: Graduate School of Business Administration, Harvard University, 1954).

29. Margaret Mead, *And Keep Your Powder Dry* (New York: Morrow, 1942), Chapter XI.

30. Geoffrey Gorer, *The American People; a Study in National Character* (New York: Norton, 1948), pp. 39–40.

31. *Ibid.,* Gorer thought that our respect and awe were reserved for abstract symbols like the Constitution, the Flag, Liberty Bell, the Lincoln Memorial, and the Alamo.

32. *Ibid.,* p. 41. He gave as an illustration of our antiauthority feeling the high glee of the public with the widely-circulated press photograph of J. P. Morgan—powerful, austere, withdrawn—as he sat in a Senate committee room, with a smuggled midget thrust ludicrously upon his knee. The picture "had not reduced by one jot or tittle Mr. Morgan's financial power, which many people had considered dangerous; but it had at least momentarily made Mr. Morgan look ridiculous; it had lessened his resemblance to a figure of authority; a surprised looking man with an elderly midget on his knee is no figure to inspire respect and awe." Authority over people, he goes on to say, "is looked on as a sin, and those who seek authority as sinners."

"The typical American attitudes toward authority have remained substantially the same as those manifested by the framers of the American Constitution: authority is inherently bad and dangerous; the survival and growth of the state make it inevitable that some individuals must be endowed with authority; but this authority must be as circumscribed and limited as legal ingenuity can devise; and the holders of these positions should be under constant scrutiny, should be watched as potential enemies. . . . People, or institutions, who 'push other people around' are bad, repugnant to decent feelings, thoroughly reprehensible. . . . Thus the least respected and most suspect professions are those which, by their nature, involve the exercise of authority over other people—politics, and, in peacetime, military service. People who enter these professions for any other reason except to improve their social position or to make money are deeply suspect. . . . Politicians are not suspect if it is believed that they have gone into politics for their own personal advantage, to make money or to improve their position. . . . [Otherwise] he is perhaps secretly lusting after authority, and the greatest vigilance must be exercised to see that he does not gratify this sinful craving. . . . The government itself must necessarily have some authority, and the people in the higher positions must therefore be tainted with this sin." *Ibid.*, pp. 27–36.

33. Some economists may deny that it is the function of their discipline to state the role of the corporation in these terms. But economic analysts can hardly dodge this issue, though to be sure the corporation cannot be understood through economic analysis alone.

34. Sigmund Timberg, "The Corporation as a Technique of International Administration," *University of Chicago Law Review*, XIX, No. 4 (Summer, 1952), 739–59.

35. Louis D. Brandeis, *Business—a Profession* (Boston: Small, Maynard, 1914), p. 12.

36. Reinhold Niebuhr, *Pious and Secular America* (New York: Scribner, 1958).

37. Alfred North Whitehead, "Foresight," the introduction to Wallace B. Donham, *Business Adrift* (New York: McGraw-Hill, 1931), p. xxvii.

38. "It is not the communist revolution but the machine age, the mass-consumption economy, and the managerial revolution that are destined to inherit the earth." William C. Bober, "Thinking Ahead," *Harvard Business Review*, XXV, No. 4 (July-August, 1957), 32.

39. The reference is to a remark by Earl Latham in commenting critically upon the theories of Galbraith, Mills, and Berle in "Anthropomorphic Corporations, Elites, and Monopoly Power," *American Economic Review*, XLVII, No. 2 (May, 1957), 303–10. A revised edition of this paper was published in 1957 in pamphlet form by the Bureau of Governmental Research, University of Maryland, as *Political Theories of Monopoly Power*.

II. THE TRADITIONAL CORPORATION

1. The use of F. H. Bradley's form of words should not be taken to mean that I adopt Bradley's brand of ethical idealism. His essay, "My Station and Its Duties," in *Ethical Studies* (Oxford: Clarendon Press, 1876; 2d ed. 1927), pp. 160–206, takes a Hegelian position on the ethical relationship between the individual and the community. His criticisms of the "administrative nihilism" of Herbert Spencer and of hedonistic utilitarianism as a defense of the factory system and unbridled competition in nineteenth-century England were penetrating. But when he talks in true Hegelian fashion about "the realization of ourselves" in the "will which is above ourselves . . . 'objective' . . . and 'universal' . . . not abstract but a concrete universal," and goes on to say that "in its affirmation I affirm myself, for I am but a 'heartbeat in its system,' " Bradley is a philosophical harbinger of that hateful totalitarian theory of the State which was a component of Nazism and Fascism. Compare William M. McGovern, *From Luther to Hitler* (Boston: Houghton Mifflin, 1941). Today, we find it increasingly difficult to believe that the State or any social institution is that "realized idea which, superior to me," as Bradley put it, "and yet here and now in and by me, affirms itself in a continuous process," and that here "we have found the end . . . the self-realization, duty, and happiness in one; yes, we have found ourselves, when we have found our station and its duties, our function as an organ in the social organism." *Ethical Studies,* pp. 147–48.

2. In "The Philosophy of Midcentury Corporation Statutes," *Law and Contemporary Problems,* XXIII, No. 2 (Spring, 1958), Wilber G. Katz, professor of law at the University of Chicago, distinguishes four "philosophies" of corporate statutes which reflect divergent answers to the question faced by legislatures: "whether there are special threats to irresponsibility inherent in the corporate form which require special restraints on the freedom (of management) to allocate risk, control, and profit." These philosophies are, briefly: (1) that a corporation statute should be merely an "enabling act" making limited liability freely available, leaving the promoters relatively free to define the scope of the enterprise and to allocate risk, control, and profit through the corporation's security structure; (2) that this allocative authority, while still very broad, should be modified in certain respects because the common-law doctrines of contracts, torts, and agency are not eough to assure responsible individual decision in the corporate setting as compared with unincorporated business organiza-

tions; (3) that the legislature needs to prescribe definite restrictions on the freedom of the parties to allocate risk, control, and profit by contract (e.g., such restrictions as the outlawing of nonvoting stock, the prescription of a specified margin of safety for creditors, the requirement of a simple majority vote for various corporate adjustments); and (4) that corporate managers have a "social responsibility" to exercise corporate powers not only—or even mainly—in the interest of stockholders, but also in the interest of employees, customers, and the "general public."

Katz regards the second and third of these theories as protective primarily of the interests of investors and creditors, but the proponents of these theories also want "to reduce the likelihood of financial catastrophes which might destroy the climate of reasonable confidence which business enterprise requires." The writings of Jerome N. Frank and William O. Douglas are cited as examples of this position. Katz thinks the third theory is one of "paternal responsibility" because it attempts to protect the interests of investors and creditors by limiting the area of permissible arrangements made by corporate managers. The first theory, by contrast, "calls for no limitations of size [of the incorporated business], duration, purposes, or general powers," and would make the enabling act sufficiently detailed to leave no doubt about these matters.

Katz is describing, in the main, the theories that underlie current statutory rules and not the theories that might be found in the general literature on corporations, but he does say that the fourth theory, though much discussed by philosophers of corporation law (e.g., Berle and Dodd), "has almost no reflection in the actual statutes." He thinks the recent statutes reflect an "enabling act" theory—the first one mentioned above, "more or less modified by the theory that corporation statutes, while assuring freedom of conract, should reinforce in various ways the responsibility of individual decisions; and that the freedom of the parties should be limited in order that the results of responsible freedom may more nearly be approximated." Had he elaborated upon the more general literature, he might have mentioned writers like Friedman, Kelso, and Adler, whose views (see Chapter IV, above) are comparable with the third theory listed by Katz. He regards Peter F. Drucker as a proponent of the fourth theory, since Drucker has advocated the abolition of shareholder voting rights and the vesting of voting power in perpetuity to the board of directors, who would elect to their number "representatives" of investors, management, and the "plant community." See Peter Ferdinand Drucker, *The New Society* (New York: Harper, 1950), pp. 340, 342.

For our present purposes, Katz's first, or "enabling act" theory stands in contrast to the second, third, and fourth, since all of these latter theories insist upon varying degrees of managerial responsibility enforceable by statute. The latter theories are, in a sense, all "social responsibility" theories, but the second and the third are concerned almost exclusively with investors and creditors of the corporation, whereas the fourth theory extends the list to other social segments.

3. See the reference to Katz, note 2 above. The one exception he finds to the general rule that the actual corporation statutes reflect the "enabling act" theory is "the wide adoption of provisions authorizing corporate gifts to charity." He does not agree with Berle that these statutes show the direction of a "20th Century Capitalist Revolution." Responsible management in the interests of the stockholder, he holds, is the objective of most of the recent corporation statutes, including those in Delaware and North Carolina, and even of the Model Business Corporation Act of the American Bar Association, which has been credited as the principal source of six new statutes in Wisconsin, Oregon, the District of Columbia, Texas, Virginia, and North Dakota, and an influential factor in the statutory revisions made in Maryland, Ohio, North Carolina, and Pennsylvania. "Aside from [the] provisions for charitable contributions," he writes, "the new concept of social responsibility has had almost no elaboration. It is not merely that the theory has had no further influence on the actual statutes, but in a quarter of a century, neither the originators of this philosophy nor their disciples have sketched with any detail or persuasiveness the lines of possible practical application. And the few suggestions which have been made justify skepticism as to the seminal quality of the new theory."

Nor does Katz agree with the view of some critics that the Model Act is "a seductive invitation to irresponsibility." One commentator declares that the Model Act substantially restricts "the rights of shareholders democratically to participate in corporate affairs" at a time "when management power is widely regarded as becoming increasingly dominant." Frank D. Emerson, "The Roles of Management and Shareholders in Corporate Government," *Law and Contemporary Problems,* XXIII, No. 2 (Spring, 1958), 238. Others see progress in the Model Act precisely because it enables the corporation to be more flexible in making changes in its capital structure, with only such limits on its powers as may be "reasonably protective" of security holders' interests. See William D. Ford, "Share Characteristics under the New Corporation Statutes," *Law and Contemporary Problems,* XXIII, No. 2 (Spring, 1958), 282.

One gathers from the favorable comments on the new statutes that it is not any move they make in the direction of social responsibility that draws approval but rather the stronger position they give to management in corporate governance. In an article by George D. Gibson from the journal cited, entitled "How Fixed Are Class Shareholder Rights?," the conclusion is reached that "the class shareholder rights are not fixed, but relative, and it is better in the public interest that this be so." He expounds "the modern view" as "securely established that a two-thirds majority of the affected class will bind the minority, as under the Model Act." Gibson concedes that the resulting responsibilities for management are considerable but says that "there are massive sanctions to enforce these new responsibilities, though for the most part they are beyond the processes of a court and not utilizable in ordinary litigation." Most directly, he adds, these responsibilities are to the shareholders. "But that is not all. With great new size and power, there also come great new responsibilities toward all the groups who are affected by the corporate undertaking." Remedies for enforcing the responsibilities of the corporation to the other groups are not discussed, however, in Gibson's article.

4. "Under the accepted canons of business enterprise, businessmen are *supposed* to act only in terms of monetary considerations. . . . Actually, they seldom carry out literally the injunctions of their official creed. As with workers, owners and managers have never acted strictly in terms of narrow self-interest ascribed to them by economic theory. There has always been a system of *human* relations as well as a system of *economic* relations. The two systems function in terms of two different and sometimes conflicting sets of values, with the result that there is often confusion as to the role the businessman is actually playing at any particular time. It is amusing to observe the extent to which the businessman will sometimes go in his efforts to explain in terms of self-interest an action which he wants to take for perhaps quite different reasons, some of which may be definitely generous and unselfish. But because generosity and unselfishness are explicitly outside the frame of reference within which the businessman, *as a businessman,* is supposed to operate, he feels it necessary to explain himself in other terms. One such term is likely to be 'enlightened self-interest.' One suspects that the frequency with which *enlightened* self-interest is appealed to, reflects the difficulty of relating certain acts

to self-interest at all and that the adjective 'enlightened' serves merely to suggest a relationship that might be exceedingly difficult to trace out in detail." James C. Worthy, "Religion and Its Role in the World of Business," *The Journal of Business,* XXXI, No. 4 (October, 1958), 300. The author makes a plea for "a set of norms which will not serve as a cloak behind which sinful selfishness can hide but a standard which will highlight deviations from the Christian mode of conduct" (p. 301).

That there are other motives than monetary self-interest which impel the corporate manager is the thesis of Chapter VI of the present book . The traditional corporation underwrites no other motive, though its proponents would concede that managers sometimes deviate from the norm. "Enlightened self-interest" is, of course, still ego-oriented and not basically altruistic. If it identifies "outside" interests with those of the corporation and its owners, priority is still given to the interests of the latter. The "socially responsible" corporation, on the other hand, has norms that go well beyond even "enlightened" self-interest. It is notable that self-interest is not necessarily excludable as a Christian doctrine, as R. H. Tawney explained in *Religion and the Rise of Capitalism* (New ed., New York: Harcourt, Brace, 1947).

On the complexity of the problem of managerial motivation, see Chapters VI and VII above. Chester I. Barnard urges (in "Elementary Conditions of Business Morals," *California Management Review,* I, No. 1 [Spring, 1958]) that business behavior is motivated far more by moral considerations than is generally recognized, but that we know too little about "the number and character of the moral problems that are faced by those who do the world's work," and too little about the "conflicts of responsibility" they face because of conflicting moral codes.

5. Bertrand de Jouvenel, "Wage Restraint," a letter published in *The Economist* (London), August 10, 1957. De Jouvenel was directing his attention mainly to the question of inflation and the responsibility of labor unions and business leaders to exercise voluntary restraint to hold the wage-price spiral in check. In the August 3d issue of *The Economist,* M. Ionides, to whom he replies, had objected that when leaders of special interest act with an eye to the public interest they would "be used as administrative extensions of the machinery of government."

6. "Let us quit talking of our work in the far countries, close to the peril of Communism. Let us put the focus on our own lives and

on our own communities." This is the argument of F. S. Cornell, executive vice-president, A. O. Smith Corporation, in a letter to the editor (*Harvard Business Review,* XXXVII, No. 1 [January-February, 1959], 20 f. and 164) criticizing the article by Theodore Levitt (see Chap. IV, note 22, above). Mr. Cornell attempts to make the case *for* corporate social responsibilities, while denying any substantial responsibilities beyond those in the immediate community. In his limited view of the relevant corporate environment he exhibits the qualities of the manager of an austere corporation, despite his insistence upon the ideology of the civic corporation.

7. The contrasting elements of the liberal tradition referred to here are well analyzed by George H. Sabine, *A History of Political Theory* (Rev. ed., New York: Holt, 1950), Chaps. 31 and 32: "Liberalism: Philosophical Radicalism" and "Liberalism Modernized."

8. Theodore O. Yntema, "Our Long-Run Internal Problems," *Saturday Review,* January 17, 1959, pp. 18–24.

9. Dr. Yntema thought the major hazards of a severe depression lay in "the rapidly mounting level and deteriorating quality of private debt"; the "attempts to deal with cost-inflation by monetary and fiscal means"; and "political failure to translate our economic knowledge into appropriate action in the area of fiscal policy." *Ibid.,* p. 20.

10. The law of entropy applies to closed systems which are running down, i.e., gradually becoming disorganized into an eventual state of thermodynamic equilibrium or death. Life, from this point of view, is the entropy-reducing capacity of an organism or system. A society that is highly organized and has within it the capacity to reduce entropy for the system as a whole has greater survival value, presumably, than one which has no such resources. It is arguable that the corporation, as a superb organizational device, supplies a kind of "Maxwell demon" (Norbert Wiener, *The Human Use of Human Beings* [Boston: Houghton Mifflin, 1954], pp. 28–30) that energizes society and introduces an element of "negative entropy" essential to human survival; further, that this contribution to civilization would be impossible were the corporation to be regarded as an integral part of the "closed system" in which entropic tendencies are inevitable—in other words, if it were to be treated as no more than a cell in the social organism with strictly limited functions. The austere corporation, despite the austerity of its qualifying adjective, has to be more "playful" than that, with much more freedom of choice and venturesomeness than the social corporation, and not knit too closely into the social fabric. (Wiener refers to J. Huizinga, *Homo*

Ludens; a Study of the Play-Element in Culture [Boston: Beacon Press, 1950], on the greater "seriousness" of contemporary industrial civilization as compared with earlier centuries.) Only in this way can it become the *external* source of life-giving and energizing value to an entropic system—the larger society. The assignment of a narrowly specific functional role to business corporations, like the role of a cell in an organism, is repugnant to many business leaders because of the implication of totalitarian authoritarianism with resultant narrowing of autonomy in corporate decision making. The view that governmental organizations are not creative of wealth, as are private business organizations, is related to this point of view; and many would also deny that wealth production is the sole function of business corporations. They are thought to be counter-entropic in many other ways and independent of the effects of other social institutions.

III. THE METROCORPORATION

1. Neil W. Chamberlain, Frank C. Pierson, and Theresa Wolfson, eds., *A Decade of Industrial Relations Research, 1946–1956* (New York: Harper, 1958).

2. John R. Commons, "Labor Movement," in *Encyclopaedia of the Social Sciences,* VIII, 682–96. Commons added that capitalism is not a single or static concept but evolutionary in three historic stages—merchant capitalism, employer capitalism, and banker capitalism. He also pointed out that two different goals had divided the labor movement: displacement of capitalism and bargaining with capitalism. Writing this article in the early thirties and before the New Deal, he was of the opinion that "diffusion of corporate ownership, labor legislation and voluntary concessions by giant corporations have apparently rendered unionism unnecessary to many of the workers," and that "large scale business has been forestalling unionism by providing for labor as much or more than the unions offer." Promotion of workers up and out of the working class was also, he thought, a bar to the development of class feeling.

3. Selig Perlman, *A History of Trade Unionism in the United States* (New York: Augustus M. Kelly, 1950) and *A Theory of the Labor Movement* (New York: Macmillan, 1928).

4. Selig Perlman, *A Theory of the Labor Movement,* p. 199.

5. Selig Perlman, "The Principle of Collective Bargaining," *Annals of the Academy of Political and Social Science,* CLXXXIV (1936), 154. For analyses of Perlman's influential theory see Mark Perlman, *Labor Union Theories in America: Background and Development*

(Evanston, Ill.: Row, Peterson, 1958), and Jack Ellenbogen, The Development of Labor Movement Theory, Unpublished doctoral dissertation, University of Wisconsin, 1954.

6. Mark Perlman, *Labor Union Theories in America,* distinguishes
five major labor union theories: unionism as a moral institution
(Richard Ely, John Ryan); unionism as a revolutionary institution
(right- and lift-wing Marxists, Gorman Ware); unionism as a psychological reaction (Veblen, Carleton Parker, Robert Hoxie, Frank Tannenbaum); unionism as a welfare institution (the Webbs, George E.
Barnett); and unionism as a part of the democratic process (Commons, Henry C. Adams, Selig Perlman). The best summing up of
recent research in the field of labor relations is in Chamberlain, Pierson, and Wolfson, *A Decade of Industrial Relations Research.*

7. Frank Tannenbaum, *A Philosophy of Labor* (New York: Knopf,
1952), pp. 7–8.

8. Tannenbaum regards the trade-union movement as "an unconscious effort to harness the drift of our time and reorganize it around
the cohesive identity that men working together always achieve."
Ibid., p. 10.   It is "an unconscious rebellion against the atomization
of industrial society" (p. 14), and a repudiation of both Marxism—
because its ends are moral rather than economic—and the older liberalism with its emphasis upon individualism.

9. *Ibid.,* pp. 105–6.

10. *Ibid.,* pp. 168–69.

11. Richard A. Lester ("Revolution in Industrial Employment,"
Labor Law Journal, IX, No. 6 [June, 1958], 439–46) contrasts the
older "commodity concept" of employment with the more recent and
prevalent "welfare concept." Until the First World War, he says,
corporate management regarded labor as a commodity in line with
classical theory and this view of the matter underlay the philosophy
of "scientific management" (Taylor). Employment was a short-run
business transaction. As a result both of union activities and the
growth of socially responsible professional management, there has developed the idea of "employment as a work-life attachment to a firm.
. . . Between a particular employer and employee, employment builds
up a strengthening network of relationships, rights and benefits
geared to length of service. . . . Less and less does labor 'flow' like commodities: more and more it is developing a single work-life attachment to a company, which tie extends into the period of retirement of
the employee." He asks whether this "welfare concept" of employment may not have profound implications for the future of American

capitalism. "Is the drive to remove distinctions in industry and to make labor more like management serving to transform American capitalism into some new kind of 'Middle Way' that it not socialism, not codetermination and not industry planning?" he asks. He observes that we have arrived at "the kind of welfare employment and welfare capitalism that socialist writers of the past century said was impossible"; but we have not yet comprehended the meaning of the enormous changes that have occurred in industrial employment relationships because we have not sufficiently revised our theoretical constructs or freed our thinking from the old mental ruts.

12. See Walter Gellhorn, *Individual Freedom and Government Restraints* (Baton Rouge: Louisiana State University Press, 1956), pp. 105–151, on the delegation of licensing power by state legislatures to "private" associations. The medieval craft guilds were privileged groups of artisans endowed with the exclusive right to practice a certain profession in accordance with regulations laid down by public authorities.

IV. THE DILEMMA OF CORPORATE RESPONSIBILITY

1. As, for example, in Wesley Newcomb Hohfeld's scheme of "jural correlatives" and "jural opposites" in *Fundamental Legal Conceptions* (New Haven: Yale University Press, 1923), edited by Walter Wheeler Cook. *Right* and *duty* are jural correlatives, in his analysis, whereas *privilege* and *duty* are jural opposites. A jural privilege is the exact opposite, or negation, of a jural duty, he asserts. If one equates corporate responsibilities with jural duties, then these responsibilities become the exact opposite of corporate privileges; and one might possibly work out a systematic list of the jural responsibilities of the corporation that would balance its jural privileges. But these would not necessarily be the same as the jural duties that correlate with corporate jural rights. The *legal* responsibilities of the corporation, in other words, are translatable into either the opposites of its own privileges or the correlatives of others' rights, if one follows Hohfeld's analysis. Perhaps both should be explored comprehensively in an exhaustive review of the social responsibilities of the corporation. The other parties whose rights correlate with the duties, or social responsibilities, of the corporation, would include all the contributor-claimant groups discussed in Chapter X above. But quite independently of this method of arriving at a list of the legal responsibilities of the corporation through analysis of the jural correlatives, one might

construct a different list by specifying those duties which arise because of the absence of certain corporate privileges.

2. The social responsibilities of the modern corporation include, of course, both legal and nonlegal obligations. Some of the obligations, that is to say, are enforceable by public agencies, others by informal means. Legally enforceable social responsibilities are the province of legal counsel of the corporation; nonlegal obligations are generally referred to other components of the corporate organization, e.g., public relations and marketing components. In practice, however, no such firm lines are drawn in the well-run company. The external relations of a company cannot be too mechanically specialized.

3. Pertinent titles are Marquis W. Childs and Douglass Cater, *Ethics in A Business Society* (New York: New American Library, 1954); John K. Galbraith, *American Capitalism* (Boston: Houghton Mifflin, 1952); Wayne A. R. Leys, *Ethics for Policy Decisions* (New York: Prentice-Hall, 1952); and John Desmond Glover, *The Attack on Big Business* (Boston: Graduate School of Business Administration, Harvard University, 1954).

4. Expediency, in the sense that what the corporation undertakes to do under the heading of "social responsibilities" really amounts to a kind of enlightened self-interest and is thus ego-oriented. The line between egoism and altruism is not always so easy to draw, however. Thus, W. T. Gossett, vice-president and general counsel for the Ford Motor Company, in a lecture on "Corporate Citizenship," observed that it was "necessary for modern management to consider how the facts and realities in a corporation's affairs will square with the public philosophy, with the values of the total national community, and its sense of where it is headed. This is not just a matter of what is legal or illegal or doubtful today; it is at the very root of the problem of the *area of freedom that the corporation will have tomorrow.*" *The John Randolph Tucker Lectures, 1953–1956* (Lexington, Va.: Washington and Lee University, 1957), II, 207. (Italics added.) Elsewhere in this lecture he said that "the corporation that is aware of the opportunities, and not merely the obligations, of citizenship wants to go beyond what it is required to do, legally or by other pressures, because corporations cannot live on a day-to-day basis. Any major corporation needs a reservoir of good will. A reservoir of good will is created when [there is] a sufficient body of people who will resent unjust attacks on the corporation because they know something of, and approve, the direction in which it is moving. Consequently,

modern management is watchful of any reasonable opportunity to extend the responsibility of the corporation as a citizen." (*Ibid.*, II, 205). It is fair to interpret these remarks as an expression of the philosophy of enlightened self-interest, and an advocacy of "corporate citizenship" because it pays off in the long run. Compare Ralph J. Cordiner's statement concerning General Electric's educational and charitable contributions: "To the degree that education and other community activities contribute to the success of the Company and the society in which it operates, they should and do receive a share of the proceeds [of the company]." Ralph J. Cordiner, *New Frontiers for Professional Managers* (New York: McGraw-Hill, 1956), p. 19.

5. Frank Tannenbaum, "Man and His Institutions," *Miscelánea de estúdios dedicados á Fernando Ortiz por sus Discípulos, Colegas y Amigos,* (Havana, Privately published, 1957), III, 1411.

6. See the comments and literature cited by Albert Lauterbach, "Social Factors in Business Uncertainty," in Mary Jean Bowman, *Expectations, Uncertainty, and Business Behavior* (New York: Social Science Research Council, 1958), pp. 94–105.

7. Morrell Heald, "Management's Responsibility to Society: the Growth of an Idea," *The Business History Review,* XXXI, No. 4 (Winter, 1957), 375–84.

8. Remarks of Professor Milton Friedman, University of Chicago, as reported in the Social Science Reporter's *Eighth Social Science Seminar on "Three Major Factors in Business Management: Leadership, Decision-making and Social Responsibility"* (San Francisco, March 19, 1958), pp. 4–5. Compare the comments of Frank H. Knight, *Freedom and Reform* (New York: Harper, 1947), rejecting the doctrine of broad social responsibility for business and affirming the ethical dualism embodied in the phrase "business is business": "the dualistic principle must be accepted wholeheartedly . . . if the kind of civilization we call free is to exist. Business must be separated from 'charity,' meaning all personal considerations. The principle of business-is-business is on a par with that of justice-is-blind, though both must be sometimes seasoned with mercy. Moral obligations to persons in consequence of special relationships is the general principle of feudalism, and is anachronistic and disruptive in a commercial and enterprise economy" (pp. 60–61). These and similar points of view are discussed critically by Henry M. Oliver, "Trends Toward a New Moral Philosophy for Business," *Business Horizons,* I, No. 2 (Spring, 1958), 33–43.

9. "In a completely capitalist economy, the division would be made on the basis of the relative contributions made to production by the owners of capital and the owners of labor. . . . The truth that capital is the major producer of wealth would correct the illusion that labor is the major producer of wealth." Louis D. Kelso and Mortimer J. Adler, *The Capitalist Manifesto* (New York: Random House, 1958), pp. 204–7.

10. "A *laborist* economy [is] one in which human labor is the sole or chief productive force, entitling the owners of labor (their own or that of chattel slaves) to shares in the distribution of the wealth produced." *Ibid.*, p. 90. "The capitalist revolution . . . by seeking to make all men capitalists . . . strives to make effective their right to live on what they can earn by their capital property as well as by their labor, as men should be able to live in a society where capital instruments produce most of the wealth." *Ibid.*, p. 103. See also their appendix on "The Concealment of the Declining Productivity of Labor in Our Present Economy."

11. *Ibid.*, p. 206.   12. *Ibid.*, p. 157.

13. *Ibid.*, pp. 207–9.   The Kelso-Adler plan would not work, obviously, under our present tax structure, and the possibility of substantial changes in the near future seem to be remote.

14. *Ibid.*, p. 210.   15. *Ibid.*, Italics added.

16. *Ibid.*, p. 211.   17. *Ibid.*, p. 211

18. J. A. Livingston, *The American Stockholder* (New York: Lippincott, 1958), p. 218.

19. *Ibid.*, pp. 218–19.   20. *Ibid.*, pp. 219–221.

21. *Ibid.*, pp. 222, 241.

22. Theodore Levitt, "The Dangers of Social Responsibility," *Harvard Business Review,* XXXVI, No. 5 (September–October, 1958), 41–60.   For critical comment on this article, and its author's replies, see *Advertising Age,* October 6, and 27, and November 17, 1958; and *Harvard Business Review,* XXXVII, No. 1 (January–February, 1959), 22 ff.

23. See Chapter II, notes 2, 3 and 4, referring to trends in corporation law as reflected in recent corporation statutes.   Wilber G. Katz, there cited, denies that there is any general trend toward a "social responsibility" theory in these statutes, affirming rather that they reflect an "enabling act" theory looking primarily to the interests of security holders.

24. Adolf A. Berle, Jr., *The 20th Century Capitalist Revolution* (New York: Harcourt Brace, 1954) p. 169.

25. E. Merrick Dodd, Jr., "For Whom Are Corporate Managers Trustees?" *Harvard Law Review,* XLV (May, 1932), 1145–63.

V. FIVE SCIENTIFIC PROBLEMS

1. There are three principal factors in a nation's economy, according to Dr. Fritz Machlup, professor of economics at the Johns Hopkins University, that compete for its human resources: production of consumers' goods, production of capital goods, and the production of knowledge. In the last category are three subcategories: basic research (the acquisition of new fundamental knowledge), education (the dissemination of established knowledge), and applied research (the acquisition of new applied knowledge) or IRAD (industrial research and development). The production of basic research does not encroach heavily upon the other economic factors, he says, but the allocation of human resources to education and IRAD does. Education and IRAD, moreover, compete with each other for talent, and the poor showing made by education recently suggests that IRAD may be getting more than its share of the nation's human resources. Any lack of balance among the three competing factors he regards as a matter for collective decision by government. "Different groups try to promote increased outlays for capital investment, increased expenditures for education, increased disbursements for IRAD, and increased consumer spending, all at once . . . . Since these compete with one another we should first make up our collective minds regarding the comparative advantages." *Science,* CXXVIII, No. 3335, (November 28, 1958), 1320–25.

The research done under the category of IRAD is almost entirely technological, and it may be assumed that it will never include fundamental corporate theory as we are discussing it here. The human resources for the production of such knowledge will be allocated to basic research, if it is allocated at all.

2. Harold F. Smiddy, "Managerial Decision-Making," *Advanced Management,* XXIII, No. 11, (November, 1958), 7.

3. *Ibid.,* 9.

4. John M. Clark, *Economic Institutions and Human Welfare* (New York: Knopf, 1957), Chap. 10, "The Interpenetration of Politics and Economics," pp. 226–44. An interesting example of the interdisciplinary approach is *Politics, Economics and Welfare* (New York: Harper, 1953), by Robert A. Dahl and Charles E. Lindblom.

VI. CORPORATE GOALS

1. Note on corporate policy as a working concept:

"Policy," as R. A. Gordon has observed, "is a highly ambiguous term, meaning different things to different men. To some, policies are . . . decisions of the highest degree, setting forth the aims and objectives of an organization. To others, policies include also some lower-ranking decisions provided they set a guide or criterion for meeting future situations. In the latter sense, policies are of varying degrees, the lower ones providing guides to action as a means of implementing the higher or broader policies. As most commonly used by businessmen themselves, policy seems to mean any important decision, whether or not it sets a precedent or furnishes a guide for the future." In his discussion of business leadership he avoids the term except for occasional reference to "any decision which has a time-dimension, that sets up a guide or criterion for future action." Robert A. Gordon, *Business Leadership in the Large Corporation* (Washington: Brookings Institution, 1945), pp. 51–52.

In ordinary business usage, however, the term is widely used to indicate general courses of action pointed toward certain goals of business operations. Policies, then, determine particular actions. Thus Knauth, in commenting upon managerial enterprise, has stated that: "The policies under which business operates are much more significant than their acts, for the latter always depend upon some judgment of an executive in the interpretation of conflicting policies. While an individual act appears more important at any one time, its effect usually ends with it. By way of contrast, the effect of policies is continuous and the consequent trends are susceptible to analysis. It is possible that they may even be traced statistically. A combination of policies might be made the test. Low price, for example, or large output and progressive improvement of quality, or high wages and good working conditions, or again dividends sufficient to attract additional capital, and a surplus sufficient to assure continuity. From many sides there are signs that such policies and standards are emerging. As always, custom, concept, and law lag behind practice." Oswald Knauth, *Managerial Enterprise, Its Growth and Methods of Operation* (New York: Norton, 1948), p. 211.

What the outside might call "policy" may not be so designated by the executives of a given company. In a recent study (A. D. H. Kaplan, Joel B. Dirlam, and Robert F. Lanzillotti, *Pricing in Big Business: a Case Approach* [Washington: Brookings Institution, 1958]) of pricing policies and practices in large corporations, for example, interviewers of company officials found that executives on the whole were reluctant to discuss pricing decisions in terms of price "policy." These officials usually regarded pricing decisions as part of the general strategy for achieving broadly defined goals for their companies. They "tended to minimize price policy as such, or to discuss it in such broad terms that interviewers initially found it difficult to apply the explanation to particular pricing situations." The authors of this study, however, were focusing upon pricing specifically and were not willing to "bury the pricing process in a general study of each company." They believed that "however strongly the firm may insist that pricing is not a major area of decision, or a separable one, price is nevertheless one of the most important outward manifestations of the policy of a large corporation." The difficulties of investigating pricing processes were considerable. Strategic memoranda by the officials involved, detailing in logical fashion competitors' prices, cost factors, and profit margins, and "summarizing the considerations at an important conference leading to a price decision" were rarely to be found. "Perhaps the presumed formal conference was never held. Even where the people doing the pricing tended to have certain staff information placed before them while making up their minds, whether and just how that information was taken into consideration often remained obscure. There was no document tracing the steps by which the staff information could be said to account for the price decision. Repeatedly, reference was made to the 'art' or 'feel' of pricing rather than observance of a formula." Reticence due to fear of revealing information valuable to a competitor also entered the picture. The authors, despite these and other obstacles, nevertheless were able to make some generalization about certain discrepancies between "formal" and "actual" policy. (Quotation from pp. 3–9).

"Policy" is defined by Lasswell and Kaplan as "a projected program of *goal values* and *practices*" that concern the policy maker's relations with others, whether few or many. Harold D. Lasswell and Abraham Kaplan, *Power and Society: a Framework for Political Inquiry* (New Haven: Yale University Press, 1950), p. 71. (Italics added.) In their analysis, "goal values" and "practices" are carefully defined. A definition of policy that lays emphasis upon *both* a plan of action and specific objectives is necessary in examining corporation policy. Lasswell and Kaplan define a decision as "an *effective* determination of policy" and thus it "involves the total process of bringing about a specified course of action." "Those whose acts are affected also participate in decision making: by conformity to or disregard of the policy they help to determine whether it is or is not, in fact, a decision," i.e., "a policy involving severe sanctions (deprivations)." *Ibid.*, pp. 74–75.

Policy, for these authors, involves "the adoption of any perspective —identification, demand, expectation—of the interpersonal relations of the self." *Ibid.*, p. 71, note 18. A corporate policy maker "identifies" himself with some aggregate or group, thus creating a corporate "we." There is thus a "demand aggregate" in the corporation in which a number of persons identify with one another in expressing collectively a desired "goal event," or series of goal events, in a policy statement. For example: Z Company makes high quality goods to sell at fair prices in order to yield optimum return to its stockholders. The "perspective" is a pattern of such identifications and demands, together with certain "expectations." An expectation statement [such as usually occurs in a statement of corporate policy] is one symbolizing the (past, present, or future) occurrence of a state of affairs without demands or identifications." *Ibid.*, p. 21. Thus a company policy may include a statement that investor capital can be attracted and retained only if the returns on investments are attractive to potential stockholders. This is an "expectation statement" which is usually linked to a "demand statement" concerning company intentions with respect to distribution of earnings. The distinction introduced by Lasswell and Kaplan between "demand" and "expectation" statements is important in analyzing corporate policy. Demand statements refer to *desired* goal events; expectation statements to conditions that affect policy making, whether one likes them or not, and must be taken into account in projecting goals and practices over which the policy maker presumably has some control.

The significance of such expectations in shaping corporate policy is considered in the chapters on decision process in the present book (Chapters VII and IX). The immediate chapter is concerned primarily with what Lasswell and Kaplan call "demand statements," which involve values, i.e., "the goal-events of acts of valuation." *Ibid.*, p. 55. Policy is goal-directed, but the policy process includes "the formulation, promulgation, and application of identifications, demands, and expectations concerning" the future interrelations between the corporate self and others. *Ibid.*, p. 71.

"Corporate decisions involve discretion," writes Walton Hamilton in *Politics of Industry* (New York: Knopf, 1957), "and where there is discretion there is the making of policy, and *policy is a political phe-*

nomenon." (Italics added.) The capability one has, whether as a private individual, a corporation executive, or a government official, to project a plan of action designed to bring about desired goal events may be regarded, of course, as a "political" capacity by definition. An advantage of the Lasswell-Kaplan conceptual approach is that it does not necessarily make "politics" the point of departure. It is essentially a theoretical framework for discussing all kinds of "interpersonal" relations, regardless of the identity of the "self." Corporate policy is thus not to be regarded as "like" public or political policy. Both are species of the same genus. Nor, as Lasswell and Kaplan correctly assert, is "policy" to be interpreted as restricted to expediency rather than principle. *Ibid.,* p. 71, note 18. The word, as they use it, and as we use it here, has no ethical coloration.

A distinction is sometimes made between policies, on the one hand, and rules and regulations, on the other. "Policies . . . change more slowly." A. E. Benn, *The Management Dictionary* (New York: Exposition Press, 1952), p. 257. No such distinction is made in the present book, at least in terms of durability over time. Corporate policy may change more rapidly than rules and regulations which inhibit the change.

A distinction, however, can be made between minor and major decisions. We are concerned here only with major decisions that involve what Lasswell and Kaplan refer to as "severe sanctions (deprivations)," the severity being measured in terms of the values prevailing in the culture concerned. *Power and Society*, p. 74. Lasswell and Kaplan define "decision" as a "policy" involving severe sanctions. "Corporate policy," in our usage here, refers to projected plans of action designed to achieve the major goal values of a firm. Under corporate policy, decisions in the Lasswell and Kaplan sense will frequently involve severe sanctions, both in terms of rewards and deprivations of various groups of interests.

Policy, finally, is a term used in some companies with decentralized organization to refer exclusively to company-as-a-whole plans of action which define common purposes that have been mutually agreed upon and accepted by all components and interests concerned for the protection and preservation of defined common interests. The term, so used, is intended to denote mutual agreement as the guiding principle of organization, as distinguished from command. "Authority of knowledge," as this knowledge of common interests and common purposes is set forth explicitly in "policy," becomes the basis for unity of action rather than "authority of command." This is a highly specialized usage of the term policy, and it is not adopted in the present book, though there is truth in Lyndall Urwick's observation that "the effect of a common body of principles is a Policy or Policies to which the varied efforts of all those in any enterprise are oriented and by which they are guided and unified." *The Pattern of Management* (Minneapolis: University of Minnesota Press, 1956), p. 81. The generality of the statement about "a common body of principles," however, is to be contrasted with Lasswell and Kaplan's detailed analysis of the *processes* involved and the elements that enter into decision.

For the purposes of this book it has seemed best to adhere to the definition of corporate policy as the projecting of *plans of action* that are designed to achieve the *major objectives* of the corporate enterprise as a whole. The plans of action include projected uses of certain instruments of policies discussed in Chapter VIII, above.

2. C. Addison Hickman and Manford H. Kuhn, *Individuals, Groups, and Economic Behavior* (New York: Dryden Press, 1956), p. 49. Managerial motivation, according to the authors, is a function of the roles the manager plays. The managerial role is defined by describing "the over-all societal context of the firm"; by delineating the corporation "both as a formal and as an informal social system of roles and statuses"; and by an account of "the roles the executive plays in his community, in his neighborhood, in his club, and in his home." *Ibid.*, p. 139. The role is held to be "antecedent to the individual who adopts it," and in adopting the role "he takes over as his own the socially approved plans of action which it comprises"; these plans of action then become his motives. *Ibid.*, p. 85. In view of the complexity of the process of goal-setting for the large corporation, the exploration of managerial motivation suggested by these authors should, of course, be extended well below the top echelon of executive officers who do not single-handedly formulate the objectives of a company.

3. Edward C. Lindeman, ed., *Basic Selections from Emerson* (New York: New American Library, 1954), p. 104. In "The American Scholar," an oration delivered before the Phi Beta Kappa Society at Cambridge, Massachusetts, August 31, 1837, Emerson alluded to "one of those fables which out of an unknown antiquity convey an unlooked-for wisdom, that the gods, in the beginning, divided Man into men, that he might be more helpful to himself; just as the hand was divided into fingers, the better to answer its end."

"The old fable covers a doctrine ever new and sublime; that there is One Man—present to all particular man only partially, or through one faculty; and that you must take the whole society to find the whole man. Man is not a farmer, or a professor, or an engineer, but he is all. Man is priest, and scholar, and statesman, and producer, and soldier. In the *divided* or social state these functions are parceled out to individuals, each of whom aims to do his stint of the joint work, whilst each other performs his. The fable implies that the individual, to possess himself, must sometimes return from his own labor to embrace all the other laborers. But, unfortunately, this original unit, this fountain of power, has been so distributed to multitudes, has been so minutely subdivided and peddled out, that it is spilled into drops and cannot be gathered. The state of society is one in which the members have suffered amputation from the trunk and strut about as so many walking monsters—a good finger, a neck, a stomach, an elbow—but never as a man.

"Man is thus metamorphosed into a thing, into many things. The planter, who is Man sent out into the field to gather food, is seldom cheered by an idea of the true dignity of his ministry. He sees his bushel and his cart, and nothing beyond, and sinks into the farmer, instead of Man on the farm. The tradesman scarcely ever gives an ideal worth to his work but is ridden by the routine of his craft, and the soul is subject to dollars."

4. See George B. Hurff, *Social Aspects of Enterprise in the Large Corporation* (Philadelphia: University of Pennsylvania Press, 1950), Chap. III, "The Social Functions of Enterprise," from which, together with Joseph A. Schumpeter's *History of Economic Analysis* (New York: Oxford University Press, 1954), the analysis here is primarily drawn.

5. Richard Cantillon, *Essai sur la nature du commerce* (1775).

6. Jean-Baptiste Say, *Traité d'économie politique* (Paris: Deterville, 1803).

7. "While executives and directors of large corporations bear some risks, the major risks fall on the suppliers of capital and on wage earners." Hurff, *Social Aspects of Enterprise,* p. 26. Critics of this view point to the fact that large established companies are under the practical necessity of maintaining a fairly constant rate of return on corporate securities, and to the "laboristic" trend of our political economy, as a counterargument.

8. Francis A. Walker, *The Wages Question* (New York: Holt, 1876).

9. Joseph A. Schumpeter, *The Theory of Economic Development,* tr. by Redvers Opie (Cambridge: Harvard University Press, 1934), p. 64 ff. The original German version of this book appeared in 1911.

Schumpeter rejected "management" as a term that could properly be equated with the entrepreneurial function "because it does not bring out what we consider to be the salient point and the only one which distinguishes entrepreneurial from other activities." *Ibid.*, p. 77.

10. Joseph A. Schumpeter, *History of Economic Analysis* (New York: Oxford University Press, 1954), pp. 893–98, and 1150–52.

11. *Ibid.*, pp. 895–96. "Any functional theory must be under the suspicion of ideological bias . . . [and] must sooner or later be met by equally suspicious opposing theories, the burden of which is to establish that the entrepreneur fills no 'productive' function at all but merely preys upon the productive activity of others." Such "depredation theory of entrepreneurial gain," he added, "enjoy[s] wide currency in the popular economics of our time"; but he had "difficulty in finding any accredited exponents" of the "depredation" theory, even among Marxists.

12. *Ibid.* (italics added).   13. *Ibid.*, p. 894.

14. "Entrepreneur," in *Encyclopaedia Britannica,* 14th ed., VIII, 629. Other authorities would insist upon the assumption of risk as one of the responsibilities of entrepreneurship.

15. Hurff, *Social Aspects of Enterprise,* p. 34.

16. Frank H. Knight, *Risk, Uncertainty, and Profit* (Boston: Houghton Mifflin, 1921, and his article on "Profit," in *Encyclopaedia of the Social Sciences,* XII, 484, cited by Hurff, *Social Aspects of Enterprise,* p. 28.

17. Oswald Knauth, *Business Practices, Trade Position, and Competition* (New York: Columbia University Press, 1956), p. 163.

18. *Ibid.*, pp. 164, 167.

19. *Ibid.*, p. 170 and pp. 164–65.

20. See also Oswald Knauth, *Managerial Enterprise.* In both this earlier book and in the work cited above his plea is for a more realistic approach to antitrust policy.

21. See Knauth, *Business Practices, Trade Position, and Competition,* pp. 170–74. Here are some of the objectives in current theories of business practice that Knauth questions: (*a*) adaptation to "natural automatic forces" in the market (which he says are often thought erroneously to "operate with speed and inevitability to maintain the welfare of the economy"); (*b*) conformity to some allegedly ideal criterion of business practice (such as the ideal structure of a particular industry, which he regards as irrelevant since "the proper test of an industry is how it functions in regard to productivity, distribution, and rate of progress"); (*c*) resistance to all governmental intervention

in the economic sphere ("government plays a necessary, ineluctable, and positive role in stabilizing the economy as a whole and in effecting compromises among industries and groups"); (*d*) resistance to compromises with other groups of interests in the economy ("the leaders of each group—industry, labor, finance, agriculture, government—are under a double obligation to serve their group and the economy as a whole. . . . There is no single criterion of right or wrong. It is the responsibility of leaders not to abuse the trade position which is the lifeblood of their inherent strength"); (*e*) specified goals of productivity ("the notion that each industry and the general economy must increase at a rate of 2.9 percent a year is an *ad hoc* judgment based on questionable historic estimates"); (*f*) innovation without regard for stability (each company needs to maintain a balance between innovation and stability, for "failure to keep the balance leads to deterioration and the loss of trade position").

22. "As monopoly stands at the center of the new economics, so status is the heart of its appropriate social outlook. The two are complementary products of that modernized system of 'granted privilege,' 'special concession,' 'neo-mercantilism,' 'generalized protection,' and 'feudalistic capitalism' being brought about by growing centralization of policy-forming power which is so common a feature of all major capitalistic economies." Robert A. Brady, *Business as a System of Power* (New York: Columbia University Press, 1943), p. 259.

23. *Ibid.,* Chap. VIII and IX. Brady's study was international in scope and did not deal with American business exclusively.

24. C. Wright Mills, *The Power Elite* (New York: Oxford University Press, 1956). He argues that the "corporate rich" are part of "the newer status system of the incorporated economy of the United States." Mills regards this "corporate elite" as a set of governing groups, "a hierarchy developed and run from the economic top down." The executive heads govern a "corporate world, which in turn is a world of economic sovereignty within the nation's politically sovereign area." But he thinks it erroneous "to believe that the political apparatus is merely an extension of the corporate world, or that it has been taken over by the representatives of the corporate rich. The American government is not . . . a committee of the 'ruling class.' It is a network of 'committees,' and other men from other hierarchies . . . sit upon these committees." *Ibid.,* Chap. 7, pp. 157, 165, 170.

25. This list of values is adapted from the analysis of "Values and Value Position" by Lasswell and Kaplan, *Power and Society,* Chaps. IV and V.

26. See Stewart Thompson, *Management Creeds and Philosophies* (New York: American Management Association, 1958), for statements of twenty-eight "company creeds." The examples cited in the text, however, were not drawn from this source.

27. Ralph J. Cordiner, *New Frontiers for Professional Managers* (New York: McGraw-Hill, 1956), pp. 16–17, 40.

28. Richard Henry Tawney, *Equality* (New York: Harcourt, Brace, 1931), p. 230. The Hobbesian maxim is from *Leviathan,* Chap. 10.

29. Lasswell and Kaplan, *Power and Society,* p. 77. They define power is a kind of *influence;* and "influence" as "value position and potential" including more values than power, e.g., deference, security, affection, etc. "Power is participation in the making of decisions." *Ibid.,* p. 75. "The *weight* of power is the degree of participation in the making of decisions; the *scope* consists of the values whose shaping and enjoyment are controlled; the *domain* of power consists of the persons over whom power is exercised." *Ibid.,* p. 77. (Italics added.) Compare Robert A. Dahl, "The Concept of Power," *Behavioral Science,* July, 1957, pp. 201–15: "Scientists have not yet formulated a statement of the concept of power that is rigorous enough to be of use in the systematic study of this important social phenomenon."

30. An important source for empirical investigation of the *operational* objectives (as distinguished from nominal and declared aims) of a corporation would be its actual expenditures for selected purposes for a period of years. Budgets—of an individual or a corporation—are far more revealing than formal declarations of purpose. A comparative study of corporate expenditures for say twenty-five leading industrial companies for a five-year period would throw much light on the operational objectives of these companies. Classification of expenditures for this purpose would be difficult because accounting practices vary and they are not usually designed to show whether a company is reaching its announced objective. What, for example, goes into research, on products, on managing, on public relations, on legal work, etc.? What goes toward the "good corporate citizen" goal? How much is spent to improve relations with customers, stockholders, suppliers, etc.? So far as is known, no company has ever published such an audit of its total operation in terms of goal achievement. The usual annual reports cover but a small segment of the subject.

VII. RATIONALITY AND REALITY
IN DECISION MAKING

1. See Daniel Lerner and Harold D. Lasswell, eds., *The Policy Sciences: Recent Developments in Scope and Methods* (Stanford, Calif.: Stanford University Press, 1951).

2. Harold D. Lasswell, *The Decision Process; Seven Categories of Functional Analysis* (College Park, Md.: Bureau of Governmental Research, College of Business and Public Administration, University of Maryland, 1956).

3. See the discussion of areas of overt actions in Chapter VIII, "Policy Steps and Policy Instruments."

4. Adam Smith, *The Theory of Moral Sentiments* (London: Bell, 1907).

5. Max Weber, "Politics as a Vocation," in *From Max Weber: Essays in Sociology* (New York: Oxford University Press, 1946); *The Protestant Ethic and the Spirit of Capitalism* (New York: Scribner, 1930); Economy and Society, partly translated as *The Theory of Social and Economic Organization,* ed. by Talcott Parsons (London: William Hodge, 1947).

6. John von Neumann and Oskar Morgenstern, *Theory of Games and Economic Behavior* (Princeton: Princeton University Press, 1944). For further elementary references one might mention John Davis Williams, *The Compleat Strategyst* (New York: McGraw-Hill, 1954), or John MacDonald,*Strategy in Poker, Business and War* (New York: Norton, 1950); at a slightly more advanced level, S. Vajda, *The Theory of Games and Linear Programming* (New York: Wiley, 1956), and still more advanced, J. C. McKinsey, *Introduction to the Theory of Games* (New York: McGraw-Hill, 1952). A recent, comprehensive and critical evaluation of the subject can be found in R. Duncan Luce and Howard Raiffa, *Games and Decisions: Introduction and Critical Survey* (New York: Wiley, 1957). Some games (zero-sum two persons with finite number of strategies) have their equivalent linear programing formulation which permits a less cumbersome computational solution than that characteristic of complicated games. It should furthermore be noted that linear, nonlinear, and dynamic programming have become singularly powerful techniques in the solution of optimization problems, thus constituting another powerful decision-making tool for management. See Vera Riley and Saul I. Gass, *Linear Programming and Associatel Techniques; a Comprehensive Bibliography on Linear, Nonlinear, and Dynamic Programming* (Baltimore: The

Johns Hopkins University Press, 1958); for works on the theory of games, see pp. 185–209. Other important progress toward more scientific decision processes has been made in such areas as organization theory, systems analysis, activity and process analysis, etc. For a systematic compilation of pertinent literature, see, *A Comprehensive Bibliography on Operations Research* (Cleveland: Operations Research Group, Case Institute of Technology, 1958); and *Decision-Making: an Annotated Bibliography* by Paul Wasserman and Fred S. Silander (Ithaca, N.Y.: Graduate School of Business and Public Administration, Cornell University, 1958).

7. Note on the assumptions of game theory:

To understand the application of game theory to corporate decision making, it is worthwhile to examine the elements of game theory methodology. As with any mathematical procedure, the strict assumptions of game theory need to be stated. An optimum strategy is identified by the operations of the theory, but only given that the following conditions prevail:

(1) Each player (manager, individual, team or corporation) has a certain number of specific alternative strategies which he can use.

(2) Each player knows what these strategies are for himself and for every other player.

(3) In some respects, at least, the interests of the different players are in conflict so that a combination of strategies that would produce the optimum outcome for one would produce other than the optimum outcome for another.

(4) Each player plays in such a way as to secure for himself as much as he can without risk of greater losses than he need suffer. If each player assumes this, each is assuming that the other players are also rational and will play their optimum strategies, optimum as defined above.

(5) In cases where a player has an alternative of rational moves, the other players do not know what his act will be. In short, perfect knowledge is assumed as to what the alternatives are, but zero knowledge is assumed as to which alternative will be taken.

It can be proved that if there is a conflict situation (i.e., in a game) which meets these simplified assumptions, then it can be solved or at least an approximation of the solution can be made. This means it can be proven that there is a correct strategy and that one can identify to some degree what it is. Since this can be done for each player, it can also be stated within limits what the relative advantage of the players will be at the outcome. These are precisely the things that one wants to do in any conflict situation but which can seldom be done with any degree of certainty. This leads us to the realization that in most conflict siuations in which managers, players, and generals fail, the assumptions listed above do not obtain.

8. Lewis Dexter, "What Do Congressmen Hear: the Mail," *Public Opinion Quarterly,* XX, No. 1 (Spring, 1956), 16–27, and "The Representative and His District," *Human Organization,* XVI, No. 1 (Spring, 1951), 2–13.

Congressmen and the People They Listen To (MS), a report for the Center for International Studies, Massachusetts Institute of Technology; Ph. D. dissertation, Columbia University. A condensation will appear as Part V of Raymond A. Bauer, Ithiel de Sola Pool, and Lewis Dexter, *Business and Public Policy: the Reciprocal Trade Act, 1953–55* (provisional title) forthcoming.

9. Sune Carlson, *Executive Behaviour* (Stockholm: Strömberg, 1951); a study of the work load and the working methods of managing directors.

10. Tom Burns, "Management in Action," *Operations Research Quarterly,* VIII, No. 2 (June, 1957), 45–60; see also, Carroll L. Shartle, *Executive Performance and Leadership* (Englewood Cliffs, N.J.: Prentice-Hall, 1956), p. 82 ff.

11. We might add that the bottom limit of serious planning is in part determined by the practice of keeping records on an annual basis. Many decisions are influenced by the desire that the annual balance sheet should have certain characteristics in every year's, e.g., growth, or a certain percentage return. We might ask ourselves how our business life would differ if the standard accounting period were a season on the one hand or five years on the other. The effects on our ways of investing and planning and thus on our whole society would be profound. It would take a science-fiction writer to imagine what these effects might be. The one-year cycle determined by nature for agricultural production is clearly arbitrary as the record keeping unit for industry.

12. Ruth Benedict, *The Chrysanthemum and the Sword,* (New York: Houghton Mifflin, 1947), presents the conclusions of the wartime studies of the Japanese. Alexander Leighton's *The Governing of Men* (Princeton: Princeton University Press, 1945), shows how these theories were used in arriving at a policy for dealing with the Emperor and with Japanese in relocation centers. Margaret Mead's *And Keep Your Powder Dry* (New York: Morrow, 1942), is a similar study of Britain and of the United States.

13. Geoffrey Gorer, *The People of Great Russia* (New York: Chanticleer Press, 1950).

14. Nathan Leites, *Study of Bolshevism* (Glencoe, Ill.: Free Press, 1953). A shorter form is his *Operational Code of the Politburo* (New York: McGraw-Hill, 1951).

15. Other studies, along these lines have been made regarding contemporary German politicians, Hans Speier, *German Rearmament and Atomic War* (Evanston, Ill.: Row, Peterson, 1957).

16. *The American Business Creed* by Francis X. Sutton, Seymour E. Harris, Carl Kaysen, and James Tobin (Cambridge, Mass.: Harvard University Press, 1956), does not negate this statement, for it is not a study of the current ideology of American business; it examines those elements of the ideology of some earlier businessmen, long since dead, which have survived in the *pro forma* statements of trade association publications and ceremonial speakers.

17. This aspect of American codes and even American business codes has been rather extensively commented on, e.g., by Tocqueville, Kluckhohn, Lynd, Riesman.

18. Compare Ithiel de Sola Pool and Irwin Shulman, "Newsmen's Fantasies, Audiences, and Newswriting," *Public Opinion Quarterly*, XXIII (1959), 145–58. Claire Zimmerman and Raymond A. Bauer, "The Effect of An Audience on What is Remembered," *Public Opinion Quarterly*, XX (1956), 238–48. Raymond A. Bauer, "The Communicator and the Audience," *Journal of Conflict Resolution*, II (1958), 67–77. Ithiel de Sola Pool, *Research Program in International Communication: Second Progress Report* (Cambridge, Mass.: Center for International Studies, Massachusetts Institute of Technology, October, 1955).

19. See Morris I. Stein, Jean N. MacKenzie, Robert R. Rodgers, and Bernard Meer, "A Case Study of a Scientist," in Arthur Burton and Robert E. Harris, *Clinical Studies in Personality* (New York: Harper, 1955).

20. Despite the fact that the very nature of biographical studies makes it difficult to develop a systematic body of knowledge from such sources, analysis of biographies of industrial giants of the past is useful in shedding light on their operational codes and goal values. Considerable attention could well be given to entrepreneurial history in business by all business schools.

21. This illustration and some of the concepts here stem from Raymond A. Bauer, Ithiel de Sola Pool, and Lewis A. Dexter, *Busi-*

ness and Public Policy: The Reciprocal Trade Act 1953–55 (see note 8, above).

22. The mathematical theory of information of Shannon (Claude E. Shannon and Warren Weaver, *The Mathematical Theory of Communication* [Urbana: University of Illinois Press, 1949]) or Wiener deals with a concept of information from which all relevance to meanings has been drained, and it is therefore too abstract to be useful in this connection, although some persons believe that there are helpful analogies in the concepts of cybernetics, e.g., the notion of feedback. Flow studies of the administrative management kind deal, as has been noted above, only with the most trivial kinds of business information, e.g., the flow of orders and billings. There are interesting studies of rumor in nonbusiness contexts, e.g., Leon Festinger, Stanley Schachter, and Kurt Back, *Social Pressures in Informal Groups* (New York: Harper, 1950), and of word-of-mouth communication among the public, see Elihu Katz and Paul F. Lazarsfeld, *Personal Influence* (Glencoe, Ill.: Free Press, 1955). But none of these research approaches have been fruitfully applied to the business world.

VIII. POLICY STEPS AND POLICY INSTRUMENTS

1. "Model" is a synonym for "theory." Models are often set up in terms of interrelationships among identifiable variables. Thus the corporation is partly describable as a complex of *relationships* rather than a thing in itself. One great value of economic and juristic models is, of course, that they focus upon certain of the relationships that are relevant to the particular realm of discourse selected by the economist or the lawyer. Thus the corporation can usefully be examined primarily as "a relationship between those who manage it and those who contribute its capital" (E. Merrick Dodd, Jr., "The Modern Corporation, Private Property, and Recent Federal Legislation," *Harvard Law Review,* LIV, No. 6 (April, 1941), 917–48); or variously as a legal entity (artificial person) or an "enterprise entity" (Adolf A. Berle, Jr., "The Theory of Enterprise Entity," *Columbia Law Review,* XLVII, No. 3 [April, 1947], 343–58). For the economist, other relationships are important, as between the corporation and its competitors as firms; or between the corporation, as represented by management, and its employees, its suppliers, and its customers. Other types of relationships appear in the models of sociologists and political scientists.

A model (or theory) of the corporation in terms of relationships alone, however, even if all possible relationships were to be included in an eclectic model, would not by any means picture completely the complex phenomena it models. See Herbert A. Simon and Allen Newell, "Models: Their Uses and Limitations," in Leonard D. White, *The State of the Social Sciences* (Chicago: University of Chicago Press, 1956), pp. 66–83. Economists, like other social scientists, necessarily abstract out of the whole complex of corporate behavior, the specific behavior functions, e.g., as to "commodities", to which their particular skills apply (as pointed out by Kenneth E. Boulding, *The Skills of the Economist* [Cleveland: Howard Allen, 1958]); and their models may be defective for want of adequate empirical work even within this limited range. See Sidney Schoeffler, *The Failures of Economics: a Diagnostic Study* (Cambridge, Mass.: Harvard University Press, 1955). Similarly the jurist abstracts the elements in corporate behavior that are manipulable as legal concepts. Psychological and sociological approaches likewise yield different models or theories of selected aspects of corporate behavior. All these models are necessarily much simpler than the corporate-institution-in-action as it would be conceived by an omniscient observer—of which there is none, of course. The point here, however, is that even the economic and legal specialist is apt to cling anachronistically to models that no longer present the situation as it exists today.

2. See Harold D. Lasswell, *The Decision Process; Seven Categories of Functional Analysis* (College Park, Md.: Bureau of Governmental Research, College of Business and Public Administration, University of Maryland, 1956); Harold D. Lasswell and Abraham Kaplan, *Power and Society* (New Haven: Yale University Press, 1950), pp. 75–82, and 198; Harold D. Lasswell, "Current Studies of the Decision Process: Automation versus Creativity," *Western Political Quarterly*, VIII, No. 3 (September, 1955), 381–99; and Myres S. McDougal, "The Comparative Study of Law: Value Classification as an Instrument of Democratic World Order," *Yale Law Journal*, LXI (1955), 915–46. Others who have analyzed the decision process include Herbert A. Simon, *Administrative Behavior; a Study of Decision-Making Processes in Administrative Organization* (2d ed., New York: Macmillan, 1957), and his "The Role of Expectations in an Adaptive or Behavioristic Model," in Mary Jean Bowman, ed., *Expectations, Uncertainty, and Business Behavior* (New York: Social Science Research Council, 1958), pp. 49–58; Chester I. Barnard, *The Functions of the Executive* (Cambridge, Mass.: Harvard University Press, 1938); Edwin O. Stene, "An

Approach to a Science of Administration," *American Political Science Review,* XXXIV, No. 6 (December, 1940), 1124–37; Ward Edwards, "The Theory of Decision Making," *Psychological Bulletin,* LI (July, 1954), 380–417; Robert Thrall, and others, ed., *Decision Processes* (New York: Wiley, 1954); George Katona, "Business Expectations in the Framework of Psychological Economics (Toward a Theory of Expectations)," in Mary Jean Bowman, ed., *Expectations, Uncertainty, and Business Behavior.*

3. Arthur Stone Dewing, *The Financial Policy of Corporations* (5th ed., New York: Ronald Press, 1953), I, 743–57.

4. The need, however, for reexamination of basic accounting assumptions and the development of authoritative statements of accounting principles for the guidance of industry and the accounting profession, has been emphasized by Alvin R. Jennings, "Present-Day Challenges in Financial Reporting," *The Journal of Accountancy,* January, 1958, p. 28; Marquis G. Eaton, *Financial Reporting in a Changing Society* (New York: American Institute of Certified Public Accountants, 1957); and Leonard Spacek, "Challenge to Public Accounting," *Harvard Business Review,* XXXVI, No. 3 (May-June, 1958), 115–24. Perusal of these authors' views leaves one with the impression that the intelligence function of the accounting specialist is quite inadequately fulfilled at the present time, so far as corporate policy making is concerned.

5. Dewing, *The Financial Policy of Corporations,* I, 752.

6. *Ibid.,* I, 755–56.

7. As quoted in the New York *Times,* January 14, 1958.

8. A. H. Raskin in the New York *Times,* January 15, 1958.

9. A study of the comparative government of business corporations has yet to be made in the same way that political scientists have made comparative studies of public governments. See Gunnar Heckscher, *The Study of Comparative Government and Politics,* with a preface by W. A. Robson, (London: Allen & Unwin, 1957). Many recent writers have referred to the "private governments" of corporations, labor unions, churches, universities, and other groups ordinarily classified as "nongovernmental," with some attention to the parallels between public and private governmental processes, but no systematic treatise on the whole subject has appeared. The study of church polity is, of course one which has received scholarly as well as polemical treatment for centuries. Academic governments have long interested people in the teaching profession, and a number of articles on the subject have appeared in the *Bulletin* of the American Association

of University Professors. Lately, the public concern about union governments has grown, and political scientists have begun to probe the politics of various professional and trade associations. Scientific inquiry into the corporate polity has been delayed, partly because of the barriers of thought arising out of the limited corporate models of legal and economic theory. Businessmen, on their part, shy away from concepts of power and authority in any political sense as applied to the large enterprise, and do not—with exceptions—welcome the kind of empirical observation that would be indispensable to a mature science of corporate polity.

10. See the list of representative values, and their application to corporations, in Chapter VI, "Corporate Goals."

11. The literature on the practice of invocation of the state's coercive powers is to be found mainly in the corpus of corporation law. On the theoretical side, an early treatment of the subject, still a classic, is John R. Common's *Legal Foundations of Capitalism* (New York: Macmillan, 1924). Much of the long-standing debate about the proper scope of free enterprise and the merits of collectivism centers about this issue of the proper uses of state sanctions, i.e., force applied by the agencies of public government. Liberalism, in the older usage of the term (compare George H. Sabine, *A History of Political Theory* (Rev. ed., New York: Holt, 1950), Chap. 31, "Liberalism") aimed at minimization of such sanctions, not only in the economic sector but everywhere. The newer "liberals" often urge wider use of such sanctions on the ground that the net effect is to maximize the general welfare and human freedom at the same time. Only the philosophical anarchists deny completely the legitimacy of the use of force in any public or private sector; they would rely entirely upon voluntary cooperation. Businessmen are seldom anarchists, even in this benign sense.

IX. STRATEGIC DECISION AREAS

1. This list has been adapted from Robert A. Gordon's *Business Leadership in the Large Corporation* (Washington: Brookings Institution, 1945), pp. 53–55, and Howard R. Bowen's *The Business Enterprise as a Subject for Research,* a report prepared for the Social Science Research Council's Committee on Business Enterprise Research (New York: Social Science Research Council, 1955), pp. 29–39.

The Bowen study was concerned with the formulation of a general framework for a "theory of the firm." ("Firm" is a comprehensive term as it is used here, and does not refer, as in some usages, to partnerships alone. Theories of the firm would cover both partnerships and corporations.) A tentative structuring of such a theory was indicated by classifying into three separate groups the important variables that seem to account for a firm's behavior. One group of variables comprised the "overt actions" of the firm, or those aspects of firm behavior that are ordinarily considered as the objects of the decision-making process within the firm. The second group of variables, at a different level, listed two types of conditions that explain these overt actions: environmental conditions and internal conditions. The third group of variables, at a still different level, consisted of the basic physical, biological, psychological, sociological, political, and historical factors that explain the environmental and internal conditions.

It is the first group of variables—the "overt actions" of a firm—that commands immediate attention in the search for a comprehensive listing of corporate policy areas. The Bowen report listed eighteen kinds of "overt actions." These included actions with respect to turnover of business firms (initiation, dissolution, sale, purchase, merger, etc.), products, location, plant and equipment, composition of current assets, output in the short run, methods of production, vertical integration, research and development, marketing, purchasing, price policies, capital structure, provision for risk and uncertainty, personnel policies, payments for services of land and capital, relations with competitors, and community activities.

Under community activities were subheadings for general public relations; participation in public and community activities; participation in activities and organizations of the business community; compliance with law, regulation, and custom; and "social values created and social costs avoided."

The Committee had before it, among other materials, the earlier study made by Robert A. Gordon in 1945, which set forth in some detail what he considered the more important types of business decisions confronting corporate leaders. Gordon's classification was three-fold, corresponding to "the three stages in the life of the firm." First, were decisions concerning its promotion and initial organization. Second, were decisions relating to its existence as a going concern. Third, were decisions relating to reorganization or liquidation.

The Gordon and Bowen listings can be combined in a way that provides a comprehensive overview of all types of policy areas in the large corporation. This has been done in the outline "Corporate

Policy Areas" (see pp. 190–92, above). Gordon's three-fold classification is followed, and it can be seen that the day-to-day decision areas in most companies will fall into the second category, namely, decisions regarding the corporation as a going concern. Considerable social significance nevertheless attaches to decisions in all three of these categories. In a given company, more emphasis will be given by managers to certain policy areas than others, and over a period of time the emphasis will probably change.

A comprehensive listing of policy areas for large corporations generally cannot serve as a completely accurate guide to the strategic decision areas in particular firms. Yet it does serve the purpose of providing yet one more tool for research into the nature of the modern corporation as a social institution. Taken together with other approaches it can help to overcome the biases which creep into the observer's mind when he draws too hasty conclusions on the basis of narrowly drawn models.

Still another approach, derivable from the Bowen report, is through its suggestive survey of "the internal and environmental conditions" that presumably explain the "overt actions" of a firm. These "conditions" are distinguishable from the "overt actions" which are the objects of the decision process within the firm. Taken by themselves the environmental or external conditions cannot as a rule explain the outcome of the corporate decision process, although the response in corporate policy to some changes in the environment may be highly predictable. But in many cases "the psychical links in the chain of causation" (Bowen, p. 32), i.e., the variables of managerial perception, interpretations and expectations, have to be considered in explaining and predicting corporate behavior. Such variables were listed by Bowen among the "internal conditions" that influence corporate action.

For our purposes, in seeking a comprehensive list of decision areas, the catalog of internal and environmental conditions is helpful because it suggests some of the more important types of strategic decisions that every executive will face sooner or later as a steersman in troubled seas.

Among the more significant external influences that surround and impinge upon the firm, Bowen lists cost and demand conditions, governmental controls, and various social pressures.

Cost conditions include the physical conditions of production; technical knowledge as available to the firm and other firms; and a variety of other conditions operative in markets where the firm is a buyer, borrower, or renter. The latter type of cost conditions cover availability, prices and terms of sale of labor, land and natural resources, material supplies, and capital.

Demand conditions operate as influences upon the firm as a seller. The extent, elasticity, and steadiness of demand were mentioned in the report as the significant factors to be noted in this connection, together with the extent of competition both actual and potential, and the behavior of competitors in the same and other industries.

Under the heading of governmental controls, significant external influences include governmental regulatory measures and taxation, to which might be added the influence of foreign policy and the policies of governments abroad as well as international agencies.

Informal social pressure in the form of accepted traditions, practices, values, and definitions of roles in the local community, in the business community and in the general social milieu were mentioned by the Bowen report as other significant external forces impinging upon the firm, which must be taken into account in any sound theory. In addition, there are pressures exerted by other firms who are bankers, suppliers, and customers.

Turning to the "internal conditions" arising within the firm itself, the Bowen report listed four general categories: the formal and informal organization of the corporation; its decision-making process; its component characteristics and obligations; and the over-all results of operations, or business performance. Since these captions are not fully self-explanatory some further details are in order.

Conditioning elements in the firm's organization would include: locus of the central sources of authority; the definition of positions (roles) and the locus of detailed responsibilities and comparable authority; the communication system both within the firm, and from and to the outside; and methods of controlling operations.

Relevant factors in the decision process are these: the functioning of various authorities in decision making; the degree of participation in central decisions by subordinate staff and operating personnel; internal politics, i.e., the locus of internal sources of advice and centers of influence and modes of influence; delegation, i.e., the degree of autonomy of subsidiary persons and divisional components; and relationships with outside advisers.

By component characteristics and obligations, the Bowen report meant such things as these: sunk capital investment of the firm which has determined its present size, products, location, composition of assets, methods of production, facilities for research, and the like; the

firm's present capital structure; its established marketing and purchasing channels and areas; its unexpired contracts, the vested interests
created, and expectations which it has aroused and which prudence
would require the firm to meet; its established reputation; the characteristics of its personnel as individuals (cultural origins, experiences,
personalities, motives, values, attitudes, intelligence, mental and physical skills, inventiveness, habits, morale, perception, interpretations, and
expectations); and the group characteristics of its personnel (traditions, behavior patterns, symbols, values, attitudes, and roles) which
have come to be accepted throughout all or parts of the organization.

The internal conditions under the heading of business performance, or over-all results of operation include: profitability, productivity, market position, product leadership, personnel development,
and employee attitudes.

It should be noted that the Bowen analysis was made for the purpose of opening up new frontiers of scientific investigation on the
whole theory of the firm; it was not pointed specifically to the object
of our present inquiry into the strategic decision areas. It is, however,
an indispensable introduction to such an inquiry and is suggestive of
lines of investigation which might be followed in distinguishing tactical from strategic decision areas.

2. In *Charles River Bridge v. Warren Bridge,* 11 Peters 420 (1837),
Chief Justice Taney carried into action his strong views of concession
theory, asserting that the grant of peculiar privileges in the charters of
corporations must be presumed to rest on some public interest. His
influence on the development of American corporation law is discussed
at length by Carl Brent Swisher, *Roger B. Taney* (New York: Macmillan, 1935), pp. 361 ff. and in his *American Constitutional Development* 2d ed., Boston, Houghton Mifflin, 1954), Chap. 11.

3. Thomas C. Cochran, *The American Business System: a Historical Perspective, 1900–1955* (Cambridge, Mass.: Harvard University
Press, 1957).

4. *Ibid.,* pp. 200–1.

5. Note 1, above, discusses the environment and internal conditions which influence policy decisions.

6. The interrelation between significant *corporate* policy areas
and *public* policy areas, as these pertain to economic matters, could
be developed systematically from several points of view. One is suggested from comments made by William A. Robson at a recent international conference of political scientists. (See the references to his
remarks in Gunnar Heckscher, *The Study of Comparative Govern-*

ment and Politics (London: Allen & Unwin, 1957), pp. 57–58.) Professor Robson was speaking of ways of evaluating nationalized industry, and the points he made as to defining the criterion of *efficiency* in such an industry are highly suggestive. They included: "(a) output, both aggregate and *per capita,* over a series of years; (b) the state of labor relations and of morale; (c) the effect of nationalization on the distribution of wealth; (d) the degree of public accountability of the undertaking; (e) the price and quality of the commodity or service; (f) development policy; (g) financial results; (h) consumer opinions about the undertaking; (i) its effects on the total economy." If these points are significant in evaluating the policies of a nationalized industry, it is reasonable to assume that they are of equal significance in evaluating—from the public point of view—the policies of a *privately-owned* industry. Thus this list of points of departure for considering the socially significant areas of corporate policy.

X. CLAIMANTS ON THE CORPORATION

1. Corporate responsibility is sometimes differently analyzed than it is here. Thus, Chester I. Barnard distinguishes two kinds of corporate responsibilities, aside from legal obligations: "(1) those which may be called internal, relating to the equitable interests of stockholders, creditors, directors, officers, and employees; and (2) those relating to the interests of competitors, communities, government, and society in general." Chester I. Barnard, "Elementary Conditions of Business Morals," *California Management Review,* 1, No. 1 (Fall, 1958), 7. It seems doubtful that the most meaningful division, at least at the start of an inquiry on corporate responsibilities toward various groups, can be in terms of internal and external relations of the corporation. The boundaries of "the corporation" are not easy to define. In practice, stockholders and creditors are external to the organization operated by directors, officers, and empleyees. The "official organizational morality" is reflected, as Barnard rightly points out, in the concrete action of trustees, officers, and employees. It is the "coordinate activities" of these particular groups, rather than the legal corporate entity, that produce the organization to which moral responsibility is usually imputed, according to Barnard. This is undoubtedly true. But then we are talking about *organizational* and not *corporate* responsibilities in the strictest sense. In this chapter it is assumed that the claimants on the corporation are claimants on the

corporate entity and the property it holds as well as on the beneficent use of the powers it exercises under law.

2. Dewing, *The Financial Policy of Corporations* (5th ed. New York: Ronald Press, 1953), I, 46.

3. The term "capital" is used here in what Dewing refers to as "the businessman's conception of a corporation's capital," as distinguished from the accountant's and the lawyer's conception of it. "It connotes the tools of production; it comprises the objective—in contrast to the human or subjective—resources of the corporation. From the point of view of this fundamental meaning of capital, it makes no difference whether all the capital is owned permanently by the corporation, or is in part owned and in part borrowed. The distinction between owned and borrowed, although very important from the point of view of financial policy, is in the end legal and not economic. The corporation uses its capital as a single fund, whatever the sources or the obligation involved in getting it and in holding it." *Ibid.*, I, 50.

4. E.g., trademarks, patent rights, copyrights, plant sites that have increased in value by reason of fortunate location, advantageous licensing or selling contracts, and able personnel integrated into a productive working organization. The *suppliers* of capital, in the widest sense, include besides security holders, the entire personnel of the corporate enterprise from the lowest-ranking employee to the highest-ranking officer, the external suppliers of goods and services, and even the society which contributes indirectly to all the favorable conditions under which the enterprise prospers. The term "suppliers," as a contributor-claimant group, is used in this book in a more restricted sense, as explained later on.

5. Dewing, *The Financial Policy of Corporations*, I, 53.

6. As to corporate bonds, the decision in *Norman v. Baltimore and Ohio Railroad Company*, 294, U.S. 240 (1935) sustained the power of Congress to abrogate the "gold clauses" of corporate bonds, resulting in substantial alterations of the obligation of the corporation to its bondholders. The powers conferred by legislative acts of states upon corporate boards are sometimes so broad as to permit unilateral action on the part of the corporation in restructuring its financial obligations to various categories of security holders. The power to amend a corporate charter is usually lodged in the majority of the stockholders and, in the case of amendments changing the voting rights or other special rights of a particular class of shares, the affirmative vote of at least a majority of the class of shares affected is generally re-

quired. Pressures "are often successfully brought to bear on preferred shareholders to induce them to consent to an inequitable modification of their rights" (E. M. Dodd, Jr., "Company and Corporation Law," *Encyclopaedia Britannica,* 14th ed., VI, 144–53) however, and the ease with which charter amendments and changes in bylaws can sometimes be put through has led to demands for more extensive federal and state statutory regulation of capital readjustments.

7. W. A. Paton, ed., *Accountants' Handbook* (3d ed., New York: Ronald Press, 1943), p. 43, prefers the use of the terms "contributed capital" and "accumulated capital" to the terms "capital" and "surplus." See also Dewing, *The Financial Policy of Corporations,* Chap. 22.

XI. SECURITY HOLDERS AND CUSTOMERS

1. Ferdinand Pecora, *Wall Street under Oath* (New York: Simon and Schuster, 1939), pp. 283–84.

2. James P. Selvage, "Pirates by Proxy: Guarding against the Corporate Raider," *Management Review,* December, 1957, pp. 17–21.

3. See, e.g., "Keeping the Company Reins in the Owners' Hands," *Business Week,* April 13, 1957, pp. 173 ff.

4. Lewis D. Gilbert, *Dividends and Democracy* (Larchmont, N.Y.: American Research Council, 1956), p. 220.

5. *Ibid.,* p. 221.

6. See E. R. Latty, "Exploration of Legislative Remedy for Prejudicial Changes in Senior Shares," *University of Chicago Law Review,* XIX, No. 4 (Summer, 1952), 759–77.

7. "Who Has Stock: A New Survey," *U.S. News and World Report,* September 13, 1957, pp. 118 ff.: "About 2.8 million families enjoy incomes of $10,000 to $15,000. . . . Many of these families have managed to put aside substantial savings. About 1 in 5 can show $10,000 or more in financial assets. More than a third have at least $5,000 to invest. Yet 1.8 million—or nearly 2 out of 3 with incomes of $10,000 to $15,000—hold no common stock. And only about 1 in 6 owns as much as $5,000 in shares. Few of these people have become convinced that ownership of a share in industry is the best way to invest savings. The number preferring savings accounts or savings bonds outnumbers those preferring stock by 2 to 1." The figures were approximations based on survey methods used in many earlier consumer-finance studies by Federal Reserve Board in cooperation with the Survey Research Center at the University of Michigan.

8. E.g., with respect to management's intentions as to future operations and as to retention and reinvestment of profits, what stockholders may reasonably expect in terms of dividend rates, projections of probable growth of the company in relation to national economic growth.

9. Note, e.g., the panacea suggested by Gilbert: "Millions of average Americans . . . could and would supply additional billions of venture capital *if only* they could have a voice in its use and democratic guarantees against its misuse." L. D. Gilbert, *Dividends and Democracy*, p. 15 (italics added). It seems doubtful that this is the necessary and sufficient condition for corporate capital formation through stocks sales to the millions of Americans who have savings to invest in this way. "Increasing the number of public shareholders," continues Gilbert, "and their democratic control over the nation's business is the way to salvation, the check to communism, the cure for socialism. . . ." He wants "a people's democratic capitalism in which 70 million Americans, instead of the present 7.5 million, will own and operate American business as its stockholders, supplying both capital and brains through the functioning of corporate democracy." *Ibid.,* p. 16.

10. "Representative Brooks Hays (D., Ark.) tells the story of an Arkansas taxpayer who came to Washington to see the sights. 'He drifted down to the Navy Yard and was admiring a great battleship, but found himself in a prohibited zone,' Hays said. 'One of the officers motioned him back with—Get Out of Here. Who do you think you are anyway? Whereupon the visitor from our state replied: Nobody. Nobody much. Just one of the owners.'" Washington *Post and Times-Herald,* May 15, 1956.

11. J. A. Livingston writes in *The American Stockholder* (Philadelphia: Lippincott, 1958) that the 8,600,000 owners of corporate America are "scattered, unorganized, indifferent, and ineffective." They do not wish to be bothered except by dividends. "They cast their vote when something is wrong, not in the ballot box, but in the market place." Of the 3,000-odd companies whose stock is traded on registered exchanges, only twenty-four experienced proxy fights in 1956, a peak year, and only twelve in 1957 up to June 30. Like many other commentators, Livingston deplores the apathy of the security holders in asserting their rights as the basic constituency of the corporate polity. But he also aims his criticism at others for this condition of affairs: (1) "institutional investors, who fail to use their great collective strength and inside information to compel manage-

ment to toe the line"; (2) "corporate executives, whose corporate mores and practices permit high salaries, stock options and pensions"; (3) "the financial press, which 'has a responsibility for lifting the moral tone of industry and finance,' a responsibility that 'it has not always discharged with distinction"; (4) "the New York Stock Exchange, which winked at one of its own strict rules and permitted the listing of Ford Motor stock through a technical device."

The work of the Securities and Exchange Commission, though salutary, does not go far enough to protect the ordinary share holder's equity, according to a widely syndicated conservative commentator:

"Certain investment underwriters in Wall Street, favorably known for their stability, have moved into the field of stock market manipulation with a view to raiding and taking over well-established companies that are attending to their own business. . . .

" 'Strike suit' lawyers, who used to read balance sheets to discover whether there was not a profitable lawsuit in an error of management or a smaller dividend, now look forward to the organization of raiding syndicates. Management suddenly finds itself with new partners, men of uncertain status and probity, men who are even known to have criminal records. . . .

"And there is nothing that can be done about it under the present laws, so far as one can judge from what is being done by either SEC or by the Attorney General's office." George E. Sokolsky, "These Days; Proxy Fights and Stock Raids," Washington *Post and Times-Herald,* April 1, 1957. Compare David Karr, *Fight for Control* (New York: Ballantine Books, 1956); and Edward Ross Aranow and Herbert A. Einhorn, *Proxy Contests for Corporate Control* (New York: Columbia University Press, 1957).

12. Compare Arthur M. Kriedmann, "Dividends—Changing Patterns," *Columbia Law Review,* LVII, No. 3 (March, 1957), 372–85, outlining some of the purposes of recent state statutes concerning dividend policy: to strengthen protection of creditors; to preserve equities among different classes of stockholders *inter se;* to specify the kind of dividend (cash, property, or stock) which may be paid from a particular kind of surplus or other source; to treat certain kinds of surplus similarly to capital and thereby restrict dividends payable from such source; to prohibit the use of revaluation or reappraisal surplus as a dividend source, subject to permissive uses thereof within prescribed narrow limits; to clarify ambiguities in older statutes; to furnish lawyers and accountants with guides. Kriedmann says that traditionally the statutes relating to dividends were designed to pro-

tect creditors; the new laws have extended "a protective arm to the benefit of stockholders and the investing public."

13. What a family does with its money is an all-important question to the businessman; yet inadequate factual information is available to him concerning disposable consumer income. In December, 1957, a grant of $295,000 from the Ford Foundation was made to the Inter-University Committee for Research on Consumer Behavior for a four-year study covering consumer assets, savings, debts, and spending through the period 1957–61. *Business Week,* December 7, 1957, p. 52.

14. "The Munn Case [1876] decided that the power of property might be restrained [by state legislatures] in dealings with customers," wrote John R. Commons, *Legal Foundations of Capitalism* (New York: Macmillan, 1924), p. 62. *Munn v. Illinois* involved a public utility; but since *Nebbia v. New York* (1934), it is clear that there is no closed category of "business affected with a public interest" and "that the State by virtue of its police power may regulate prices whenever it is 'reasonably ncessary' for it to do so in the public interest"; E. S. Corwin, *The Constitution and What It Means Today* (12th ed., Princeton: Princeton University Press, 1958), p. 255. With the broader interpretation of federal powers and the development of "cooperative federalism" (see *Ibid.,* pp. 42–43, 85–88), the authority now available to public governments in the United States to intervene in the operations of the market on behalf of customers is now very extensive. That these powers are used discriminately to favor some kinds of customers over others is arguable, but the fact remains that both state and federal powers are now available through which the consuming public can exert pressures upon corporate policy that were unheard of even for a long time after the *Munn* case was decided.

15. Compare Theodore V. Houser, *Big Business and Human Values,* "Management and Its Publics," (1957 McKinsey Foundation Lectures, Columbia University Graduate School of Business; New York: McGraw-Hill, 1957).

16. Peter F. Drucker, *The Concept of the Corporation* (New York: John Day, 1946), p. 140 (italics added). He adds, however, that the corporation's "social function as a community is as important as its economic function as an efficient producer," and emphasizes the "need for status and function of the individual" (*Ibid.,* p. 152) in accordance with the American creed. The qualification is significant. Compare the remarks of Axel Iveroth, head of the Federation of

Swedish Industries, who recently declared that European management executives "usually maintain that they contribute most to the social welfare by *creating the very resources* on which it is based through the best possible management of their own enterprises. Since good management is undeniably their first duty, they have easily persuaded themselves that they have discharged their full obligations to society by looking out for the narrow interest of their own concerns." (Italics added.) He then put the question: "What part and what responsibility will private enterprise take in the building of the kind of society we want to help create?" Free enterprise, he continued, "does not bestow the right to act as you please; it is not an end that justifies every kind of means. It is in the first place *a system, a method, to assure an efficient production. But the system should not be mistaken for the purpose, which is to assure the greatest possible liberty and satisfaction for all citizens,* whether they are consumers, workers, or owners of capital." Quoted in Holgar J. Johnson, "The Emerging Pattern of Corporate Citizenship," address at Annual Meeting of the Institute of Life Insurance, New York, December 10, 1957 (mimeographed).

Johnson, who was president of the Institute, indicated that American employers had already assumed the responsibilities that Iveroth was urging upon European employers, adding that "the consumer as a part of the general public now has an interest in how management runs its business—not only toward the end of efficiency, but also as to the corporation's share of the social responsibility toward the community. . . . Even though a corporation may—because of its size or management efficiency—be able to produce a product of such consumer value and at such a price that it tends to eliminate its competitors, it dare not do so because of its impact upon the life of the nation. For what is in the best interest of the whole must govern management's decisions, as a citizen of the community. . . . We have come to know that it is good business to conduct one's affairs so that they conform to the public desire. The change is one of first magnitude for public interest and for the long-term interest of the corporation itself, for we now have a working partnership between business and the public that is of vital importance."

All of this commentary adds up to a good deal more than the simple proposition that the aim of enterprise is efficient production per se.

17. Drucker, *The Concept of the Corporation*, pp. 39–40. Italics added.

18. *Ibid.*, p. 245.

19. John K. Galbraith, *The Affluent Society* (Boston: Houghton Mifflin, 1958), p. 24, n. 3. He refers to "the main current of ideas in descent from [Adam] Smith," ruling out the term "classical tradition" because of differences among economists as to whether the line of classical economists ended with J. S. Mill or J. E. Cairnes. Similarly he rules out the term "orthodox tradition" which by implication excludes writers like Keynes, "who, though working in the same current of ideas [as those in the central tradition], have taken sharp issue with accepted conclusions." Galbraith's term "the central tradition" will be used hereafter to refer to economic theory as he delineates it in his book at Chaps. III–V, inc.

20. Joseph A. Schumpeter, *History of Economic Analysis* (New York: Oxford University Press, 1955), p. 1159.

21. Gardiner C. Means, "Collective Capitalism and Economic Theory," *Science,* CXXVI, No. 3268 (August 16, 1957), 287–93 esp. pp. 292 f.

22. W. G. Mellon, in the prefatory comments to his "Selected, Descriptive Bibliography of References on Priority Systems and Related, Nonprice Allocators," *Naval Research Logistics Quarterly,* V, No. 1 (March, 1958), 17–27. Compare Tjalling C. Koopmans, "Allocation of Resources and the Price System," in his *Three Essays on the State of Economic Science* (New York: McGraw-Hill, 1957); and A. C. Harberger, "Monopoly and Resource Allocation," *American Economic Review,* XLIV, No. 2 (May, 1954), 77–87.

23. Oskar Morganstern, "Consistency Problems in the Military Supply System," *Naval Research Logistics Quarterly,* I, No. 4 (December, 1954), 265–81.

24. Adolf A. Berle, Jr., *Economic Power and the Free Society* (New York: Fund for the Republic, 1957).

XII. EMPLOYEES AND SUPPLIERS

1. Charles A. Myers, *Industrial Relations in Sweden: Some Comparisons with American Experience* (Cambridge: Technology Press, Massachusetts Institute of Technology, 1951), p. 73. Compare American Management Association, *The Development of Foremen in Management* (New York, 1945).

2. See Robert N. McMurry, "The Case for Benevolent Autocracy," *Harvard Business Review,* XXXVI, No. 1 (January-February, 1958), 82–90; and Bennett E. Kline and Norman H. Martin, "Freedom, Au-

thority, and Decentralization," *Harvard Business Review*, XXXVI, No. 3 (May-June, 1958), 69–75.

3. Marked changes in management philosophy with respect to managerial prerogatives have occurred in the past few decades. "Put briefly, the changes reflect a shift from the concept that management's decisions are unchallengeable simply because they are management's decisions. The shift permits discussions of matters which had to be at least discussable if the needs of the unions were to be met." Douglass V. Brown and Charles A. Myers, "Management's Attitudes toward Employees and Unions," *Monthly Labor Review*, LXXX, No. 2 (February, 1957), 159. That there is any such thing as a "management philosophy" is questioned by Peter Seitz in a paper on "Management's Adoption of New Labor Relations Methods" in the same issue of the *Monthly Labor Review*. "American management is pluralistic and eclectic in its approach to its role and in its relations with labor unions. . . . The various management philosophies, so-called, are no more than programs of action of particular managements adopted to cope with the specific problems they face this day, this year, this decade. . . . These 'philosophies' do not penetrate beyond the aspirations and compulsions of all institutions in our civilization, namely, assurance of survival and attainment and preservation of power and prestige. . . . The fact is that management policy, like the foreign policy of a nation, or for that matter, the policy of a trade union, has little validity except in the context of and in relationship to the strength of the institution, the correlative strength of the challenger, and a host of other conditions, economic and political, not the least of which is the personality of the representatives on both sides." *Ibid.*, pp. 155–56. Compare Milton Derber, W. Ellison Chalmers, and Ross Stagner, "Collective Bargaining and Management Functions: an Empirical Study," *Journal of Business*, XXXI, No. 2 (April, 1958), 107–19; and Frank Tannenbaum, *A Philosophy of Labor* (New York: Knopf, 1952).

4. The New York *Times*, March 28, 1958, p. 44 M.

5. "Separation of ownership and management, and the growth of a professional managerial group," has been cited by Brown and Myers, "Management's Attitudes toward Employees and Unions," p. 160, as one of the forces impelling companies to restructure their labor relations policies and organizational components. "This separation has led to the development of a professional, rather than family-oriented management, with fewer emotional reactions to the challenge to managerial prerogatives."

6. "If law is by definition the command of the sovereign, it cannot be at the same time an agreement; the two terms are mutually exclusive." Leon Duguit, *Law in the Modern State,* tr. by F. and H. Laski (New York: Huebsch, 1919), p. 119. On these grounds Austinian jurists will protest the use of the word "law" in describing the substance of collective contracts. But as Duguit pointed out the facts have made havoc of what he called the "imperialist theory" of law: "Already our law has ceased to be based on the idea of a unified and indivisible sovereignty. It is and will be an objective law of government; but it is the law of government that does not command. It is the law of a government which serves the public need and secures the coordination of the modern corporate life." *Ibid.,* p. 118. The rapid development of a great body of collective contract law to govern labor relations, mainly through private instruments of government was traced in James J. Robbins, *The Government of Labor Relations in Sweden* (Chapel Hill: University of North Carolina Press, 1942), and with implications for the United States by Neil W. Chamberlain, "The Organized Business in America," *Journal of Political Economy,* LII, No. 2 (June, 1944), 97–111.

7. E.g., extension or contraction of the plant or the industry, location of plant or industry, general organization of the plant, determination of the type of personnel, types of machinery and equipment to be used, the nature and quality of the product or service to be produced, fixing the price of the product or service, quantity of production, advertising methods, sales and distribution policy. Neil Chamberlain, "The Organized Business in America," pp. 105–6. Compare Derber, Chalmers, and Stagner, "Collective Bargaining and Management Functions."

8. Brown and Myers, "Management's Attitudes toward Employees and Unions," p. 160.

9. *Ibid.,* p. 159.

10. See Edward H. Chamberlin, *The Economic Analysis of Labor Union Power* (Washington, D.C.: American Enterprise Association, 1958), which points to the need for an "overhauling" of the "received theory of wages, and in particular the role of unions in the theory." *Ibid.,* p. 45. Chamberlin believes "that unions, like business corporations are 'here to stay,'" but that "like business corporations, they can be subjected to social control," and that "the public interest requires that steps be taken to reduce" their power. *Ibid.,* p. 46. On other aspects of labor union power, see Roscoe Pound, *Legal Immunities of Labor Unions* (Washington, D.C.: American Enterprise

Association, 1957) and Philip D. Bradley, *Involuntary Participation in Unionism* (Washington, D.C.: American Enterprise Association, 1956).

11. Clark Kerr, in "The Balkanization of Labor Markets," in his *Labor Mobility and Economic Opportunity* (New York: Wiley, 1954), has stressed the myriad "institutional rules" by which unions seek to protect and increase job sovereignty both of the union and groups within it, a development at variance with the classical notion of a single labor market. E. H. Chamberlin declares that there are many "noncompeting groups" in the labor market and a further breakdown within each group "until we seem to arrive at a network of interrelated markets quite like the 'chain relationship' so characteristic of product markets. . . . In this 'enclosure movement,' fraternity triumphs over liberty as No Trespassing signs are posted in more and more job markets." E. H. Chamberlin, *The Economic Analysis of Labor Union Power,* p. 14. He argues that this Balkanization of labor markets increases the monopoly elements in the system and restricts the opportunities open to the individual worker. The result of such developments is to leave us far indeed from the simple model of "managerial prerogatives" as a quasi-sovereign concept.

12. Neil W. Chamberlain, *The Union Challenge to Management Control* (New York: Harper, 1948), p. 105.

13. E. H. Chamberlin, *The Economic Analysis of Labor Union Power,* p. 21.

14. *Monthly Labor Review,* LXXX, No. 2 (February, 1957), 158. Italics added.

15. Theodore V. Houser, *Big Business and Human Values* (New York: McGraw-Hill, 1957), pp. 41–46; and Ralph J. Cordiner, *New Frontiers for Professional Managers* (New York: McGraw-Hill, 1956), pp. 25–26, are concise statements of this position.

16. For the other side of this argument see Walton H. Hamilton, *The Pattern of Competition* (New York: Columbia University Press, 1940), and his *The Politics of Industry* (New York: Knopf, 1957), especially Chap. III, "Return of the Honorable Company," and "The Patent System in Action," pp. 78 ff. "In our time access to or denial of technology has become a factor of consequence in international as well as domestic commerce. . . . The dominant instrument for the control of technology is the letter patent." *The Politics of Industry,* p. 116. "A large corporation seeks to blanket as much as possible of its technological processes with letters patent." *Ibid.,* p. 76.

XIII. COMPETITORS, LOCAL COMMUNITIES, THE GENERAL PUBLIC AND GOVERNMENTS

1. Walton H. Hamilton, "Competition," *Encyclopaedia of Social Sciences,* IV, 132.

2. The history of this trend is described in Thomas C. Cochran, *The American Business System: a Historical Perspective, 1900–1955* (Cambridge, Mass.: Harvard University Press, 1957), especially pp. 61 f., 164 f., and 188 f. It is treated systematically in A. R. Burns, *The Decline of Competition* (New York: McGraw-Hill, 1936); George W. Stocking and Myron W. Watkins, *Monopoly and Free Enterprise* (New York: Twentieth Century Fund, 1951); Corwin D. Edwards, *Maintaining Competition: Requisites of a Government of Policy* (New York: McGraw-Hill, 1949); Edward H. Chamberlin, *The Theory of Monopolistic Competition* (Cambridge, Mass.: Harvard University Press, 1933); A. D. H. Kaplan, *Big Enterprise in a Competitive System* (Washington, D.C.: Brookings Institution, 1954); Walton Hamilton, *The Politics of Industry* (New York: Knopf, 1957); Harold Koontz and Richard W. Gable, *Public Control of Economic Enterprise* (New York: McGraw-Hill, 1956), Part IV, "Maintaining Competition."

3. As in *The Capitalist Manifesto* (New York: Random House, 1958) by Louis O. Kelso and Mortimer J. Adler: "What has been acclaimed as *American Capitalism, Modern Capitalism,* or *People's Capitalism* is a mixture of capitalism and socialism" (p. 10). They plead for a "capitalistic revolution" that would bring a "mature," a "fully developed," "pure," and "private property" Capitalism (p. 107), as contrasted with primitive and presently "mixed" capitalism. In Capitalism, "competition is the instrument of just evaluation and, hence of justice in the distribution of wealth" and "the most assiduous efforts of government to regulate the economy are required to preserve free competition in all markets against the inherent propensity of free competition to destroy itself" (p. 153). But "free competition does not and cannot provide full employment . . . [which] is an undesirable objective . . . the means of achieving it are equally undesirable" (p. 152).

Friedrich A. Hayek wrote in 1947 that "what I mean by 'competitive order' is almost the opposite of what is often called 'ordered competition.' The purpose of a competitive order is to make competition work; that of so-called 'ordered competition,' almost always to restrict the effectiveness of competition. Thus understood, this description of our subject at once distinguishes our approach as much from that of the conservative planners as from that of the socialists." Among his proposals were laws so designed "as to impede the indefinite growth of individual corporations" and avoidance of "a slavish application of the concept of property as it has been developed for material things" to such rights and privileges as patents, copyrights and trade-marks, thus fostering the growth of monopoly. Hayek, *Individualism and The Economic Order* (Chicago: University of Chicago Press, 1948), pp. 111–16.

4. See Edward S. Mason, "The Current Status of the Monopoly Problem," *Harvard Law Review,* LXII, No. 8 (June, 1949), also reprinted in his *Economic Concentration and the Monopoly Problem* (Cambridge, Mass.: Harvard University Press, 1957), pp. 351–70.

5. Mason, *Economic Concentration and the Monopoly Problem,* p. 366.

6. *Ibid.,* p. 368. In this article on "The Apologetics of 'Managerialism,'" *Journal of Business,* XXXI, No. 1 (January, 1958), Mason is critical of those who are too ready to jettison classical economic theory, with its reliance on competition, in favor of the newer "managerial" theories of enterprise.

7. See Chapter IV above.

8. These specifications are listed by Mason, *Economic Concentration and the Monopoly Problem,* as illustrative of tests suggested in the literature on monopoly problems.

9. *Ibid.,* p. 369.

10. David Lilienthal, *Big Business: a New Era* (New York: Harper, 1953).

11. Joseph A. Schumpeter, *Capitalism, Socialism, and Democracy* (New York: Harper, 1942), Chap. VII.

12. John K. Galbraith, *American Capitalism* (Boston: Houghton Mifflin, 1952).

13. Louis B. Schwartz, "General Dissent," in *Report of the Attorney-General's National Committee to Study the Antitrust Laws* (Washington, D.C.: U.S. Government Printing Office, 1955), pp. 390–91.

14. Mason, *Economic Concentration and the Monopoly Problem,* p. 398.

15. *Ibid.,* pp. 372 f.

16. It appears from a reliable survey that in the *smaller* communities the great majority of business firms engage in full-scale community relations programs, while such programs are of more limited scope in the larger cities. *Community Relations,* Survey No. 18 of

BNA's Personnel Policies Forum (Washington, D.C.: Bureau of National Affairs, 1953).

17. Bertrand R. Canfield, *Public Relations Principles, Cases and Problems* (Rev. ed., Homewood, Ill.: Richard D. Irwin, 1956).

18. William T. Gossett, "Corporate Citizenship," in *The John Randolph Tucker Lectures, 1953–1956* (Lexington, Va.: Washington and Lee University, 1957), II, 189. Mr. Gossett is vice-president and general counsel of the Ford Motor Co.

19. C. H. Greenewalt, "Key to Progress—the Uncommon Man," speech before American Newspaper Publishers' Association, April 25, 1956, quoted by Gossett, p. 189. Mr. Greenewalt is president of E. I. duPont de Nemours & Co.

20. Aristotle, *Ethica Nicomachea,* IX.xii. The important role of *koinonia* (variously rendered also as "fellowship," a "participation," a "reciprocity," a "community" or "communion," a "partnership," a "share holding") in Aristotle's conception of citizenship is discussed by C. H. McIlwain, *The Growth of Political Thought in the West* (New York: Macmillan, 1932), pp. 59 ff., and W. L. Newman, ed., *The Politics of Aristotle* (Oxford: Clarendon Press, 1887–1902), I, 41–44.

21. McIlwain, *The Growth of Political Thought in the West,* pp. 64–65.

22. Gossett, "Corporate Citizenship," p. 176.

23. *Ibid.,* pp. 177, 178, 184, 185.

24. Corporation counsel, according to Gossett, needs to be alert to three major means through which restraints on corporate freedom may be threatened: the introduction of new legislation, the addition of new restrictions or new areas to contractual relationships, and "the elusive process by which unorganized public opinion, while taking no formal expression, nevertheless effectively stigmatizes a corporation as not being allied with the public interest." *Ibid.,* p. 198.

25. "The trend of the law has been to increase, rather than decrease, the area of discretion given to corporate management in dealing with the substantive interests of stockholders in the conduct of business and the distribution of profits." *Ibid.,* p. 173.

26. Arthur H. Cole, "Transcendental Aspects of Business," *Harvard Business Review,* XXXVI, No. 5 (September-October, 1958), 60.

27. Theodore Levitt, "The Dangers of Social Responsibility," *Harvard Business Review,* XXXVI, No. 5 (September-October, 1958), 41.

XIV. PUBLIC RELATIONSHIPS AND
CORPORATE INTERESTS

1. The recognition of public relations as a major function of management, along with such well-established functions as engineering, manufacturing, marketing, finance, and accounting, is a fairly recent development. As a unique functional kind of work it has thus become specialized both as to personnel and as to major staff and operating organizational components. Unlike specialists in other functions, the functional specialists in public relations have no exclusive claim to the kind of work they do. Public relationships are the responsibility of everybody in a company in some way or other. But the functional specialist nevertheless has determinate responsibilities that focus upon the subject of the present chapter. These responsibilities cover, likewise, a determinate area or discipline comparable to finance, engineering, and marketing. It is only in recent years that the discipline has begun to be defined, with a special literature, special theories, and special skills and techniques peculiar to it. This development is in the process of rapid change with changes in technology and the social and behavioral sciences. Therefore the points of view expressed in this chapter are necessarily tentative. Any company's public relations theory and policy needs periodic overhauling at frequent intervals.

2. An ingenious treatment of communcation is by Norbert Wiener, *The Human Use of Human Beings: Cybernetics and Society* (Boston: Houghton Mifflin, 1954), in his theory of messages; though without specific application in any detail to corporate structures it is highly suggestive for corporate theory. Compare A. J. Ayer, "What is Communication?" in A. J. Ayer, J. B. S. Haldane, and others, *Studies in Communication* (London: Secker & Warburg, 1955), pp. 11–28, where communication is referred to as "the transference of information" and "all deliberate uses of language by human beings as well as by voluntary or involuntary exclamations, movements, gestures, singing, crying, laughing, dancing, in so far as they are informative." But J. B. S. Haldane, "Communication in Biology," in the same volume, declares that "a great deal of communication is still at the animal level" and that "its function is to evoke certain actions in the recipients by altering their mood, and not to communicate information." Sir Geoffrey Vickers, writing on "Communication in Economic Systems" in this volume, says that "in the literature of business management 'Communications' has virtually ceased to imply the exchange of informa-

tion as such"; it "has become a term of art to include every form of human contact which may help to get cooperation within the organisation and a good Press outside"; to him it has other important purposes, including the formation of collective decisions, rendering them acceptable and moving people to action. See also references in note 3, below.

3. See James G. Miller, "Toward a General Theory for the Behavioral Sciences," in Leonard D. White, ed., *The State of the Social Sciences* (Chicago: University of Chicago Press, 1956), pp. 29–65, on the "diffusion function" and "information transfer"; Colin Cherry, " 'Communication Theory'—and Human Behavior," in A. J. Ayer, J. B. S. Haldane, and others, *Studies in Communication;* Bruce Lannes Smith, Harold D. Lasswell, and Ralph D. Casey, eds., *Propaganda, Communication and Public Opinion: a Comprehensive Reference Guide* (Princeton: Princeton University Press, 1946), with four essays on the science of mass communication; and Warren Weaver, "Recent Contributions to the Mathematical Theory of Communication," in Claude E. Shannon and Warren Weaver, *The Mathematical Theory of Communication* (Urbana, Ill.: University of Illinois Press, 1949).

4. James G. March, "An Introduction to the Theory and Measurement of Influence," in Heinz Eulau, Samuel J. Eldersveld, and Morris Janowitz, eds., *Political Behavior* (Glencoe,Ill.: The Free Press, 1956), pp. 385–97, and his biblographical references are suggestive. Earl Latham, *Political Theories of Monopoly Power* (College Park, Md.: Bureau of Governmental Research, University of Maryland, 1957), has a critique of the "amateur political theories" of Galbraith, Berle, and C. Wright Mills. Robert A. Dahl, "The Concept of Power," *Behavioral Science,* July, 1957, pp. 201–15, uses a symbolic notation to express power in terms of a relation between people.

5. See Stewart Thompson, *Management Creeds and Philosophies* (New York: American Management Association, 1958).

6. See Chapters II and IX, above, for further discussion of corporate relations with stockholders.

7. Alfred Marshall, *Principles of Economics* (8th ed., London: Macmillan, 1920), pp. 625–26.

8. George B. Hurff, *Social Aspects of Enterprise in the Large Corporation* (Philadelphia: University of Pennsylvania Press, 1950), pp. 120–21.

9. "For the most part," wrote Walter Lippmann, in his classic statement about stereotypes, "we do not first see and then define, we define first and then see. In the great blooming, buzzing confusion

of the outer world we pick out what our culture has already defined for us, and we tend to perceive that which we have picked out in the form stereotyped for us by our culture"; we filter out the information at our disposal, for "the accepted types, the current patterns, the standard versions, intercept information on its way to the consciousness." *Public Opinion* (New York: Harcourt, Brace, 1922), p. 81. Kenneth E. Boulding, in *The Image* (Ann Arbor: University of Michigan Press, 1956), has presented an illuminating account of the way in which patterns of subjective knowledge and value mediate between ourselves and the world, pointing out that the images we have —what we *believe* to be true—and not information as such, control our behavior. The significance of stereotypes for corporate policy is discussed by Pierre Martineau, "Sharper Focus for the Corporate Image," *Harvard Business Review*, XXXVI, No. 6 (November-December, 1958), 49–58, and in literature there cited.

10. Peter F. Drucker, *Concept of the Corporation* (New York: John Day, 1946), pp. 12–14. Italics added.

11. *Ibid.,* p. 89.

12. The New York *Times,* March 25, 1957.

13. Herbert A. Simon, "Comments on the Theory of Organizations," *American Political Science Review,* XLVI, No. 4 (December, 1952), 1135.

14. Joseph A. Schumpeter, *History of Economic Analysis* (New York: Oxford University Press, 1955), pp. 548–49.

15. See Chris Argyris, *Personality and Organization* (New York: Harper, 1957), p. 233.

16. *Ibid.,* pp. 236–37.

17. Such sensing, when it is done systematically, involves further classifications of each of the publics: into significant groups by age, geography, ethnics, sex, and income; and into leader and follower types.

18. The literature of this field is growing rapidly, as indicated in the bibliographical works: Smith, Lasswell, and Casey, eds., *Propaganda, Communication and Public Opinion,* and Bruce Lannes Smith and Chitra M. Smith, *International Communication and Political Opinion: a Guide to the Literature* (Princeton, N.J.: Princeton University Press, 1956). A concise diagrammatic statement of the elements in the communication process by W. Phillips Davison and Alexander L. George is available in "An Outline for the Study of International Political Communication," in Wilbur Schramm, ed., *The Process and Effects of Mass Communication* (Urbana, Ill.: University

of Illinois Press, 1954), pp. 433–43, applying the general principles expounded by Schramm in his article on "How Communication Works" in the same volume, pp. 3–26.

19. Wiener, *The Human Use of Human Beings,* p. 38.

To put the matter this way, as Wiener observes, is to take the Manichaean rather than the Augustinian view of the forces at work. *Ibid.,* pp. 11, 34, 35, 190–92. It is not the willful malice of nature that one struggles against to decrease entropy, but "the devil of confusion," the weakness in man's own nature or in the organisms he contrives, which debilitate him in the struggle to survive.

The process by which an organism resists the general stream of corruption and decay, seeking continuity of life in "an island here and now in a dying world" is homeostasis—reconstituting the *pattern* of the organism faster than it decays. The *pattern* is the essence, and not the materials that come and go. "Certain kinds of machines," Wiener thinks, "and some living organisms—particularly the higher living organisms—can . . . modify their patterns of behavior on the basis of past experience so as to achieve specific anti-entropic ends" (*ibid.,* p. 49); and "the structure of the machine or of the organism is an index of the performance that may be expected from it" (*ibid.,* p. 57).

20. *Ibid.,* pp. 17–18.   21. *Ibid.,* p. 38.

XV. THE WELL-TEMPERED CORPORATION

1. Kenneth E. Boulding, *The Organizational Revolution* (New York: Harper, 1953).

2. Calvin B. Hoover, *The Economy, Liberty, and the State* (New York: Twentieth Century Fund, 1959).

3. Robert A. Dahl and Charles E. Lindblom, *Politics, Economics, and Welfare* (New York: Harper, 1953), p. 129.

4. Passages cited are from the translations of Plato's *Republic* VIII.555B–562A, by Davies and Vaughn, and F. M. Cornford.

5. Karl Polanyi, *The Great Transformation* (New York: Rinehart, 1947).

6. Hoover, *The Economy, Liberty, and the State,* p. 284.

7. *Ibid.,* p. 394.   8. *Ibid.*

9. See Dahl and Lindblom, *Politics, Economics, and Welfare,* for a systematic treatment of the basic "social processes for economizing" and extensive separate discussion of the four separate processes of the price system, hierarchy, polyarchy, and bargaining. Hierarchy is a

system of "control by leaders" as distinguished from "control of leaders" in polyarchy. "Roughly, a hierarchical process of organization is one in which leaders exercise a very high degree of unilateral control over non-leaders." *Ibid.*, p. 227.

10. Hoover, *The Economy, Liberty, and the State,* pp. 305, 310–11, 313–15, 322–24, and 412–16.

11. Compare Robert A. Dahl, "Business and Politics: A Critical Appraisal of Political Science," *American Political Science Review,* LIII, No. 1 (March, 1959), 1–34, and literature there cited.

12. Alvin W. Gouldner, "Organizational Analysis," in Robert K. Merton, Leonard Broom and Leonard S. Cottrell, Jr., eds., *Sociology Today: Problems and Prospects* (New York: Basic Books, 1959). Compare J. G. March and H. A. Simon, *Organizations* (New York: Wiley, 1958).

13. Gilbert H. Clee and Alfred di Scipio, "Creating a *World* Enterprise," *Harvard Business Review,* XXXVII, No. 6 (November-December, 1959), 77–89.

Index

Academic governments, 379; hierarchical structure, 315 f.

Accounting, 168; area of corporate intelligence, 170; period, length of, 375; need for studies re, 379

Acknowledgments, vi

Action, plans of, 141, 273; overt, 141, 381 ff.

Adams, H. C., 358

Adaptation, corporate, to global ecosystem, 333–35

Administration, public, and personal rights of employees, 241 f.

Administrative bureau, defined, 205

Administrative nihilism, 351

Advertising, purpose and direction of, 281; institutional and product, 281 f.

Agreement, mutual, principle of organization, 367

Allen, F. L., *The Big Change: America Transforms Itself*, 254

Alliances, political, 101

Allocation, theory of, 227 f.; non-price, 228; *see also* Resources, allocation of

Allocative authority, 352

Alternatives, future, in concept of corporation, 35–37; in decision making, 139, 198; policy, 173 ff., 179 f.; in choice of products, 231

Altruism, 71, 90; traditional view of, 40; and egoism, 360

American Association of University Professors, 379 f.

American Bar Association, Model Business Corporation Act, 353

American Economic Association, 348

American Federation of Labor, ideology, 59

American Management Association, *The Development of Foremen in Management*, 392

Americans, attitudes re power and authority, 31, 349 f.; attitude toward affection, 131; planning for middle-range future, 151; symbols, 349

Amity, as goal-value, 130–32

Analysis, financial, 171

Anarchists, philosophical, and use of force, 380

Agencies, governmental, power to act, 212; attitude toward antitrust laws, 253

Annual records, and planning, 375

Annual reports, 221, 372

Antitrust, 370; policy, 121, 251 f.; principle, 249; administration, proposed "reorientation," 255

Application, of policy rules, 140, 182

Appraisal, of policy success or failure, 140, 182–84

Approval, public, as desideratum, 73

Aranow, E. R., and H. A. Einhorn, *Proxy Contests for Corporate Control*, 389

Arbitration, labor-management, 238

Argyris, Chris, *Personality and Organization*, 401

Aristotle, *koinonia*, 260, 398; *Nichomachean Ethics*, 398; quoted, 260

Arkansas taxpayer, comment of, 388

Army, 3

Association, freedom of, 8, 63; cooperative, 346; voluntary, 61; German law of, 345; professional and trade, 380

Attorney General, Committee on Antitrust Policy, 254 ff.

Audiences, imaginary, of the decision maker, 155–57; characteristics of, and selection of communications media, 277

Austere corporation, *see* Traditional corporation

Authoritarianism, 312 f.

Authority, 367; and power, 11; and freedom, 26; over people and things, 30–35; American attitude toward, 31, 349 f.; allocative, 39; managerial, 91, 223; and responsibility, 103, 182, 196 f., 237 f.; concentration of, 110; in corporate polity, 237 f.; corporate, freedom and limitations of, 322 f.; concept of, 380

Automobile manufacturers, and Reuther's proposals, 174–80

Autonomy, corporate, 50, 105, 109, 194, 200; metrocorporate, 51; group, and individual liberty, 266

"Average man," image of, in decision making, 156 f.

Ayer, A. J., "What Is Communication?" 399

— J. B. S. Haldane, and others, *Studies in Communication*, 399, 400

Back, Kurt, *see* Festinger, Leon

Baldwin, S. E., "Private Corporations," 347

Balkanization, of the economy, 201; of labor markets, 395

Banking Act of 1933, 218 f.

Banking system, Pecora re, 218

Bank of America, 342

Bargaining, multiemployer, 238; *see also* Collective bargaining

Barker, Ernest, *Natural Law and the Theory of Society, 1500 to 1880*, 346

Barnard, C. L., quoted, 209; "Elementary Conditions of Business Morals," 355, 385 f.; *The Functions of the Executive*, 378

Barnett, G. E., 358

Bauer, R. A., "Our Big Advantage: the Social Sciences," 347; *see also* Zimmerman, Claire

— Ithiel de Sola Pool, and L. A. Dexter, *Business and Public Policy: the Reciprocal Trade Act 1953–55*, 376 f.

Bavelas, Alexander, 163

Behavior, corporate, 17, 301 f., 378; operational code of, 153

Behavioral sciences, 129, 270, 400

Bell Telephone System, 342

Bendix, Reinhard, *A Study of Managerial Ideologies*, 345; *Work and Authority in Industry*, 345

Benedict, Ruth, *The Chrysanthemum and the Sword*, 375

Benn, A. E., *The Management Dictionary*, 367

Berle, A. A., Jr., 247, 350, 352; "The Developing Law of Corporate Concentration," 28, 347; plea for "Lords Spiritual," 30; on corporate obligations, 229 f.; protection of private rights against corporate power, 240 f.; on limitations of power, 265; *Economic Power and the Free Society*, 342, 392; *The 20th Century Capitalist Revolution*, 362, quoted, 92 f.; Capitalist Revolution, 353; "The Theory of Enterprise Entity," 377

— and G. C. Means, *The Modern Corporation and Private Property*, 218, 347, quoted, 27

Big Business, 122, 246, 263, 327; hostility toward, 73, 132, 266 f.; and "educational" programs, 222; as response to need, 320

Big Labor, 320

Bigness, problem of, 25; attitude toward, 29; and power, 32, 52 f.; effect of, on individual integrity, 71; defense of, 246; influence of, 246; antitrust as condemnation of, 256; reversal of trend toward, 332

"Billion Dollar Club," 342

Bill of Rights, 240

Biographies, analysis of, 376

Board of directors, *see* Directors

Bober, W. C., "Thinking Ahead," quoted, 350

"Body corporate and politic," 70

Bondholders, contributors of capital, 212

Bonds, corporate, 386 f.

Boulding, K. E., *The Skills of the Economist*, 378; *The Image*, 401; *The Organizational Revolution*, 402

Bowen, H. R., *The Business Enterprise as a Subject for Research*, 347, 380 ff.

Bowman, M. J., ed., *Expectations, Uncertainty, and Business Behavior*, 347, 361, 378, 379

Bradley, F. H., "My Station and Its Duties," quoted, 351

Bradley, P. D., *Involuntary Participation in Unionism*, 395

Brady, R. A., *Business as a System of Power*, quoted, 371

Brandeis, L. D., *Business—a Profession*, 35, 350

Breech, E. R., 179

Bretton Woods, 334

Broom, Leonard, *see* Merton, R. K.

Brown, Courtney C., vi, 25 f.; "Business Holds Key to U. S. Future," 26, 345; "Business in Cap and Gown," 26, 345; "Knowledge of What?" 26, 345

Brown, D. V., and C. A. Myers, "Management's Attitudes toward Employees and Unions," 393, 394, quoted, 243

Bureaucracy, hierarchical organization, 1; and a free society, 313 f.

Bureau of Labor Statistics, *Employment and Earnings*, 342

Burke, Edmund, 63

Burns, A. R., *The Decline of Competition*, 396

Burns, Tom, 146; "Management in Action," 375

Burton, Arthur, and Harris, R. E., *Clinical Studies in Personality*, 376

Business: primary principle, 4; dynamic force, 8; as a social system, 24; public governments as customers of, 57; metrocorporate meaning of, 66; function of, 88 f.; as private enterprise (*q.v.*), 93; competitive, corporate policy in terms of, 192–96; *see also* Firm; Regulation of business

Business, philosophy of: need for, 5, 13, 17–37; focus of, 11; search for, 26, 271; normative side, 36; and purposes of economic production, 229 f.; and public relations, 275 f.

Business Advisory Council, report on "Effective Competition," 255 f.

Business behavior, 355; as economic statesmanship, 27; norms of, 94; rationality of, 97; variables in causation of, 381

Business education, need for new professorships, 25 f.

Business enterprise, vs. social institution, 195 f.; *see also* Enterprise; Private enterprise

"Business is business," concept of, 5, 7, 40, 361

Businessman, moral responsibilities, 23; public and social responsibilities, 33 f.; motivation, 40; and attacks on business morality, 87 f.; "sensible welfare obligations," 89; rationally calculating, 141, 158; defense of, 142; roles of, and priority of strategic decision areas, 189 ff.; competitive goals, 252 f.; "conventional wisdom," 345; motivations beyond self-interest, 354 f.

Business performance, *see* Performance

Business statesmanship, 196–99; and strategic decisions, 107; and areas of corporate policy, 199

Business units, normative classification, outline, 205

Cairnes, J. E., 392

Canfield, B. R., *Public Relations Principles, Cases and Problems*, 398

Cantillon, Richard, 119; *Essai sur la Nature du Commerce*, 369

Capital, ownership of, 80 ff.; as liabilities of the corporation, 211 f.; equity, drive for, 221; assets, use of, in competitive market, 230; resources, accumulation of, 311 f.; structure, changes in, 353; suppliers of, 386 (*see also* Security holders); term, 386; venture, and stockholder decision re disposition of, 388

Capital gains, vs. dividends, 169

Capitalism, 396; and the economic process, 11; intact or old-style, 39 f., 310, 314; labor movement and, 58 f.; mixed, 80 f.; Kelso-Adler theory, 81 ff.; social and economic ills of, 90; logic of resource allocation, 227; and competition, 250; Commons re, 357; welfare, 359; democratic, 388

Capitalist, and entrepreneur, 119

Capitalist Revolution, 80 ff.

Capitalist society, defined, 310

Carlson, Sune, *Executive Behavior*, 146, 375

Carnegie Corporation, 13

Carr, C. T., "Early Forms of Corporateness," 346

Casey, R. D., *see* Smith, B. L.

Cater, Douglass, *see* Childs, M. W.

Center for International Studies, Massachusetts Institute of Technology, 376

Chalmers, W. E., *see* Derber, Milton

Chamberlain, N. W., "The Organized Business in America," 394; *The Union Challenge to Management Control*, 395

— F. C. Pierson, and Theresa Wolfson, eds., *A Decade of Industrial Relations Research, 1946–1956*, 357, 358

Chamberlin, E. H., quoted, 243; *The Economic Analysis of Labor Union Power*, 394 f.; *The Theory of Monopolistic Competition*, 396

Change, factor of, in economic concepts, 10; corporate, 99; adaptation to, 331

Chapple, Eliot, 146

Charles River Bridge v. Warren Bridge, 384

Charter, corporation, 384, 386

Chase Manhattan Bank, 342

Cherry, Colin, "'Communication Theory'—and Human Behavior," 400

Childs, M. W., and Douglass Cater, *Ethics in a Business Society*, 360

Choice, managerial power of, 105; in decision making, 139; in allocation of time, 149 f.; and pressure of time, 160; freedom of, 312; *see also* Alternatives

Christianity, and mode of conduct, 355

Chrysler Motor Company, reply to Reuther, 177 ff.

Church, the, involvement in the whole of life, 3, 17, 18, 27; polity, 379

Churchill, Winston, 153

Citizenship, corporate, *see* Corporate citizenship

Citizenship, industrial, 259; Aristotle's view of, 398

Civilizations, survival of, 2

Civil rights, business and, 90

Claimants, 76, 211–16, 337; balance of interests of, 6; indirect, 214; direct, 218; enforceable obligations to, 262; *see also* Contributor-claimant groups

Clark, J. M., 120, 255; *Economic Institutions and Human Welfare*, 363; quoted, 110

Classical economic theory, 22, 36, 45, 97 f., 141; "economic harmonies," 230

Classification, of public documents, 130

Clayton Act, 255

Clee, G. H., and Alfred di Scipio, "Creating a World Enterprise," 403

Coal and Steel Community, European, 100

Cochran, T. C., *The American Business System: a Historical Perspective, 1900–1955*, 384, 396; quoted, 202 f.

Coercion, minimization of, in free competitive society, 186; *see also under* Power

Colbert, L. L., 179

Cole, A. H., "Transcendental Aspects of Business," 398

Collective bargaining, 9, 59, 239 f.; transfer of appraisal function to, 184; and corporate policy, 186 f.; grievance procedures, 240; employee rights and, 242

Collective contract law, 394

Collectives, corporate, model of, 228

Collectivism, 79, 380

Collectivities, and contracts, 10; public and private, 249 f.

Command, authority of, 182 f., 367; chain of, in managerial personnel, 238

Committee on Economic Development, list of national issues, 46 f.

Common markets, 333 f.; European, 100

Commons, J. R., 58, 358; "Labor Movement," 357; *Legal Foundations of Capitalism*, 380, 390

Commonwealths, bazaar of, 313 f.

Communication, 399 f.; reciprocity in, 276 ff.; process, 279 ff.; role in public relations policy, 292–96; categories of subfunctional work, 295 f.; of research results, 328

Community, scope of, 7 f.; claims on the corporation, 28; corporate responsibility to, 43, 74, 215, 230, 258–62, 319, 327 f.; corporation as part of, 131; local, mutual obligations between firm and, 259

Community Relations, 397 f.

Community Relations Manual, quoted, 258 f.

Community relations programs, 397

Company, individual: customer relations, 233; and a world market, 334

Competition, and managerial conduct, 24; economic, and social responsibility, 90; economic vs. political, 186; and continuance of unprofitable business, 230; economic creed of, 249; limits on scope of, 250; effective, theories of, 250 f.; legal criteria, 251; maintenance of, 253; economists re, 345

Competitive enterprise, 44

Competitive system, importance of, 64

Competitors, obligations to, 214 f.; corporate responsibilities to, 248 ff.

Comprehensive Bibliography on Operations Research, A, 374

Concession theory of corporateness, 200 f., 384

Condominium, 317

Conflict situation, solution of, 374 f.

Conformity, 32, 370

Congress, investigations, 90, 243; pressures on, 146; power over commerce, 224 f.; power to abrogate "gold clauses" of corporate bonds, 386

"Congressmen and the People They Listen To," 375

Consent of the governed, 83

Conservative wisdom, 39

Consociation, 51

Constitutionalism, principles of, 8 f.; roots of, 10; and ecclesiastical polity, 20; in study of the corporation, 28; corporate, 54 f., 322–25; and labor movement, 59; principles of, in well-tempered corporation, 336 f.

Constitution of the United States, restraints on power, 33; doctrines re protection of private corporations, 201; Fourteenth Amendment, 201; attitude of framers toward authority, 349 f.

Constitutions, limitations on power, 63

Consumer, choices, 44, 46, 349; responsibility toward, 226 f., 233 f.; sovereignty of, 232 ff.

Consumer goods, proportion of national production, 226

Contract, 10; relationship by, 22 f.; state laws and, 200

Contributor-claimant groups, 19, 66, 72, 82 f., 198, 211–16, 269, 359; obligations to, 77 f., 263 f.; pressures of, 223; balance of responsibility toward, 235; equitable treatment of, 240

Control, right of, over work force, 237 f.; over economic process, 310 f.; centralized, 312; economic, public-private system, 315 f.; corporate, 321; governmental, 383 (*see also* Regulation); of and by leaders, 403

"Conventional wisdom," 231 f., 254, 345

Cooperation, voluntary, 380

Coordination, of economic functions, 316 ff.

Cordiner, R. J., *New Frontiers for Professional Managers*, 361, 372, 395

Cornell, F. S., 356

Corporate behavior, approaches to, 270; *see also* Business behavior

Corporate citizenship, 10, 56, 67, 86 f., 130 f., 199, 215, 325 f., 360 f., 391; rights and duties, 51; quasi-judicial function, 82; within local community, 260 f.; and participation in public affairs, 267 f.

Corporate conscience, 40

Corporate democracy, 219

"Corporate Democrats," 109

Corporate giving, 40 f., 353; traditional attitude, 42; and legal sanction, 54; motivation for, 72; Friedman re, 79; and fiduciary responsibility, 92; appraisal of, 183

Corporate identity, perception of, 154 f.

Corporateness, studies of, 27; "concession theory" of, 200 f.

Corporate person, 38, 74, 123–25, 266; authority of, 32; manager as agent of, 98 f.

Corporate theory, lag in, 20–22

Corporation, and society, 3, 35; as system of government, 4, 84, 109; models of, 6 (*see also* Models); as a lesser society, 7 f., 67 f.; and private property, 10, 28, 75; elements in philosophy of, 17 f.; multifunctional institution, 18, 36 f., 118, 123, 136 f., 138, 187, 269, 348; influence of, 20; concepts of, 26–28, 35–37, 283 ff.; as voluntary and democratic organization, 26; as social organization, 27, 194 ff., 226 f.; historical roots, 27; and power (*q.v.*), 27, 32 f.; roles of, 35, 99, 264; derivative, 36 f.; as quasi-public instrumentality, 39; independent life, 42; transformation into nontraditional institution, 48; moral role, 60 (*see also* Ethics); legal duties and liabilities, 70 f.; private institution, 75; continuity of, 75, 85, 120, 337; changing nature, 78; plan for reform and reconstitution of, 81 f.; peripheral activities, 88, 91; theory of, 96 ff., 348; multiple goals, 91 (*see also* Goals); future participation in political action, 102 ff.; contest with competitors, 107; hierarchical structure, 109 (*see also* Hierarchy); economic conceptions, 115; as association of men, 117; economic functions, social and private, 120; as an enterprise, 120 f.; empirical study, 136 f.; time-perspective in, 152; concern with human motivations, 155; promotion and initial organization, outline, 190; as a going concern, outline, 190–92; organization of functions of, 194 f.; British-owned, stand on protectionism, 160; orientation toward rationality and reality, 164 f.; as public institution, 199 ff.; distinction between pri-

Corporation (*Continued*)
vate and public, 200 ff.; ruling re charter, 200 f.; liabilities of, 212; as efficient producer, 226; and antitrust, 255 f.; identity of, 280 ff.; analysis of, as an institution, 284; business abroad, 293 f.; future, nature and functions, 307 ff.; coordinate economic functions, 316–19; rationalization of the economic process, 317; and community boundaries, 319; coordinated political functions of, 319–22, 325 f.; coordinate social and cultural functions, 326–29; in social ecosystems, 331 f.; in a closed society, 332; as organizational instrument, 338; modern, term, 341; largest U. S., 342 f.; security structure, 352; and "negative entropy," 356; community activities, 381 (*see also* Community); component characteristics and obligations, 383 f.; boundaries of, 385; social function, 390

Corporation counsel, and coercive sanctions, 186; areas of alertness, 398

Corporation law, 27, 39, 92, 199 ff.; community requirements, 28; public opinion and, 92 f.; and responsibilities, 264; philosophies of, 351 f.; and charter amendment, 386; *see also* Statutes

Corrupt practices acts, 323

Corwin, E. S., *The Constitution and What It Means Today*, 390

Cost-of-living escalator clause, 175

Costs, and distribution of earnings, 42; allocation of, 44; and policy alternatives, 174; reduction in, and decision processes, 181; claimants on company income, 281; conditions, 382 f.

Cottrell, L. S. *see* Merton, R. K.

Cournot, A. A., 185

Credit, role of, 10

Creed, business, 22–25

Curtice, H. H., 178

Customers, attitude toward, of traditional corporation, 42; responsibility toward, 74, 213, 224–35; priority of interests of, 83, 224

Cybernetics, 377, 399

Dahl, R. A., "The Concept of Power," 400; quoted, 372; "Business and Politics," 403

— and C. E. Lindblom, *Politics, Economics and Welfare*, 363, 402

Dartmouth College case, 200

Davis, J. S., *Essays in the Earlier History of American Corporations*, 346 f.

Davison, W. P., and A. L. George, "An Outline for the Study of International Political Communication," 401

Decision making, 138–65; transferred to management, 38; statization of, 50; social values in, 73; process, 78, 138–41; decentralization of, 105; guiding principles, 115 ff.; influenced by amity as goal, 131; imaginary audiences, 155–57; stages in, 167 ff.; and assessment of policy, 182 f.; elements in, 185; freedom of, 265; autonomy in, 357; literature, 374

— centers, 197; multiplicity of, 105, 312; regulation of, 120; need for reality and rationality in, 164 f.; private, multiplicity of, 287

Decisions, time and, 2 (*see also* Time); moral, of businessmen, 23; areas, academic science and, 29 (*see also* Strategic decision areas); strategic, 97, 106–8; responsibility for, 103; judgment in, 171 f.; and the requirements of the market, 202 f.; union participation in, 244; affected by company spokesmen, 280; well-tempered corporation, 336; defined, 365; classification of types of, 381 ff.; external and internal influences on, 382 f.

Deference values, 124, 185

De Jouvenel, Bertrand, 43; "Wage Restraint," 355

Delaware, 293, 353

Demand, consumer, corporate responsibility in regard to, 230 ff.; "demand aggregate," 366; conditions, 383

Democratic-permissive structure of authority and command, 237

Depression, hazards of, 356

Derber, Milton, W. E. Chalmers, and Ross Stagner, "Collective Bargaining and Management Functions," 393 f.

De Sola Pool, Ithiel, *Research Program in International Communication*, 376; *see also* Bauer, R. A.

— and Irwin Shulman, "Newsmen's Fantasies, Audiences, and Newswriting," 376

Dewing, A. S., *The Financial Policy of Corporations*, 341, 346, 379, 387, quoted, 168 f., 171 f., 386

Dexter, L. A., "What Do Congressmen Hear?" 146, 375; "The Representative and His District," 375; *see also* Bauer, R. A.

Diffusion function, 400

Directors, share owner's *alter ego*, 42; decision making, 75, 116; and corporate giving, 92; oligarchies, 109; distribution of profits, 168 f.; as representatives of stockholders, 169; balance of responsibilities, 172; prescription of rules, 181; and corporate polity, 240 f.; obligation re goals, 336; powers, 352

Dirlam, J. B., *see* Kaplan, A. D. H.

Di Scipio, Alfred, *see* Clee, G. H.

Discretion, in corporate decisions, 367; managerial, 398

Dividends, distribution of net income as, 83, 168 f.; and reinvestment, 170 f.; regularity of payment, 171; state statutes re, 389 f.

Dobbs, Maurice, 120

Dodd, E. M., Jr., 92, 352; "For Whom Are Corporate Managers Trustees?" 363; "The Modern Corporation, Private Property, and Recent Federal Legislation," 377; "Company and Corporation Law," 387

Dodge plan, 84

Douglas, W. O., 352

Drucker, P. F., *Concept of the Corporation*, 85, 347, 390, 391, 401, quoted, 28, 226 f., 283 f.; *The New Society*, 352 f.

Due process of law, 323; within the corporation, 54; and individual rights, 244

Duguit, Leon, *Law in the Modern State*, 394

Duopoly, 250

Dynamism, of society, 35; corporate, 120

Earnings, allocation from, 42; stockholders' right to, 83; statement of, 169 f.; net, computation of, 170 f.; of American companies, 342
— distribution of, 9, 42, 44, 72, 282; and the intelligence function, 168; and balance of interests, 223 f.; *see also* Dividends

Eaton, M. G., *Financial Reporting in a Changing Society*, 379

Ecology, corporate, 99–103, 302; human factors in, 264 f.; of well-tempered corporation, 330–33, 335

Economic analysis, shortcomings of, 34 f.

Economic behavior, 110

Economic democracy, 109

Economic development, issues of, 46 f.

"Economic education," 318 f.

Economic liberalism, 39

Economic man, 6, 117, 307

Economic process, rationalization of, 30, 317; role of corporation in, 309 ff.; transfer of control over, 310 f.; analysis of, 311 f.

Economics, theory, 20–22, 229 ff.; classical theory, 97 f., 141, 286; and rationality, 141; central tradition, 227, 245

Economic system, regulation by, 24; unplanned, 49

Economists, tools of corporate analysis, 95 f.; advocacy of public vs. corporate interest, 257; corporate model, 377

Economy, organizational, 11; controlled, 46; governance of, 47; private sectors, 51, 192; global, metrocorporation in, 69 ff.; "natural," 121; Socialist or centrally controlled, 229; satisfaction of private vs. public demands, 232; hierarchical system, 315 f.; national, principal factors, 363

"Ecosystem, social," 330 f.; global, corporate adaptation to, 333–35

Education, public, and supply of manpower, 57; economic, of the public, 222 f., 318 f.; and IRAD, 363

Edwards, C. D., *Maintaining Competition: Requisites of a Government of Policy*, 396

Edwards, Ward, "The Theory of Decision Making," 379

Efficiency, economic, 226 f.; in operation, 241; criterion of, 385; *see also* Performance

Einhorn, H. A., *see* Aranow, E. R.

Eisenhower, Dwight D., plea for voluntary restraint, 79 f., 175 f.

Eldersveld, S. J., *see* Eulau, Heinz

Ellenbogen, Jack, "The Development of Labor Movement Theory," 358

Ely, Richard, 358

Emergencies, national, business leaders and, 333

Emerson, F. D., "The Roles of Management and Shareholders in Corporate Government," quoted, 353

Emerson, R. W., concept of the whole man, 98, 118; "The American Scholar," quoted, 368 f.

Emotions, appeals to, 168

Employees, benefits, 41; lifetime, 52, 66, 134, 158; goals, 59 f., 62; as share-

Employees (*Continued*)
holders, 61; of traditional corporation, 65; stock purchase, 89; welfare programs, 89 f.; appraisal of satisfactions of, 183; responsibilities to, 213 f., 236–44; managerial and nonmanagerial, 236 ff.; unionized and nonunionized, responsibilities toward, 243 f.; dual role of, 280, 288 f.; risk sharing, 336 f.

Employment, industrial, change in conception of, 62; commodity concept, 358; work-life attachment, 358; welfare concept, 358 f.

Enabling act, 351

England, 343; revised liberalism, 46; status of merchant and manufacturer, 142

Enterprise, large-scale, characteristics of, 20 f.; free, competitive, 21; development of idea of, 119 f.; defined, 120; corporate, as public business, 199–203, 343; mixed, 205; proprietor-owned, 212; *see also* Private enterprise
— free, legal theory, 343; scope of, 380; defined, 391

Entrepreneur, 370; as industrial organizer, 120; manager as, 193; *see also* Owner-entrepreneur

Entrepreneurial functions of corporation, early definitions, 118 f.

Entropy, 48, 301 f.; law of, 356; process of, 402

Environment, man and, 1 f.; adjustment to, 8; of decisions, 143; external and internal conditions, 381
— corporate, 99 ff., 141; traditional view, 45; critical events in, 172 f.; plus-values, 195 f.; total, 265, 330 f.

Equilibrium, in ecosystem, 330 f.

Equitable Life, 342

Equity capital, 42

Ethics, traditional corporation, 45–49; metrocorporate, 52, 67; issue of responsibility, 69 ff.; corporation, 86; business, 87, 355; norms of, 94; values, 204; of purchasing practices, 246; relationship between individual and community, 351
— standards, 30, 33, 126 ff., 259 f.; company statements of, 127; need for universal code of, 247; and the economic process, 311

Eulau, Heinz, S. J. Eldersveld, and Morris Janowitz, eds., *Political Behavior*, 400

Europe, political patterns and the market, 100; Western, *condominium* in, 317

Events, critical, in corporate environment, effect of, 172 f.

Executives, station and duties, 38, 149; of traditional corporation, 46; fiduciary, 70; goal of, 85, 336; Livingston re, 86 f.; and corporate theory, 96 ff.; important policy issues, 106 f.; identification with their organization, 132; decision making (*q.v.*), 116; pressure of time on, 145 ff., 156; responsibilities and duties, 149; time-perspective, 152; operational codes, 154 f.; assessment of motives, 158 f.; perceptions of instruments of policy, 159; view of themselves, 159–62, 197; pressures created by, 160; focus of attention, 206; and questions of the investor public, 222 f.; and formulation of canons re balance of interests, 224; and public relations function, 298 f.; reactions to criticisms of Big Business, 327 f.

Expansion, and pressure of time, 148 f.; *see also* Growth

Expectations, public, corporation and, 265; fulfillment of, 271 f.; "expectation statement," 366

Expediency, and responsibility, 71, 76; in social responsibility, 360

Expenditures, and corporate giving, 41; corporate, suggested study of, 372; *see also* Costs

External groups, classification of, 288

External influences, 382 f.

External relationships, corporate, 276 f.; multifunctional, 293 ff.; as sources of intelligence, 297 f.

Families, American, ownership of corporate stock, 220 f., 387; disposable income, 390

Fascism, 351

Federal Reserve Board, analysis of corporate ownership, 220 f.; "Who Has Stock?" quoted, 387

Federal Trade Commission Act, 255

Feedback, 377; of opinion polling, 297 f.

Fellowship (*koinonia*), 260 f.

Festinger, Leon, Stanley Schachter and Kurt Back, *Social Pressures in Informal Groups*, 377

Feudalism, metrocorporate, 62 f.; principle of. 361; *see also* Neofeudalism

Fiduciary responsibility, 92; Pecora re, 218

Finance, areas of corporate policy, 191

Firm, theory of, 13, 68, 75, 116, 136, 165, 380 f.

First National City Bank, 342

Flow, studies of, 377

Follett, Mary Parker, 333

Force, use of, 106, 380; theories, 140; as instrument of corporate policy, 185 f.

Ford, Henry, II, 167; reply to Reuther, 178; quoted, 284 f.

Ford, W. D., "Share Characteristics under the New Corporation Statutes," 353

Ford Foundation, 13, 390

Ford Motor Company, 342; sale of stock, 85, 389; reply to Reuther, 176 ff.

Foreign aid, economic, 333

Foreign office, corporate version of, 326

Foreign policy, instruments of, 294

Foremen, 236 f.

Fortune Directory, The, 341 f.

Frank, J. N., 352

Freedom, constitutional and philosophical background, 11; preservation of, 20, 265; and authority, 26; and security, 63; from state intervention, 78; individual vs. organization man, 240; economic, charter of, 255; individual, and threat of statization, 314; corporate area of, 360

Friedman, Milton, 352, 361; on social responsibility of business, 79 f.

Friedrich, C. J., re Gierke, 346

Frost, Robert, 96

Future, alternatives in corporation concept, 35–37, 305–38

Gable, R. W., *see* Koontz, Harold

Galbraith, J. K., 311 f., 350; *The Affluent Society,* 231 ff., 254, 345, 392; *American Capitalism,* 360, 397

Game, competitive, rules of, 248 f.

— theory, 141, 162 f.; and business policy, 143–45; and decision process, 166; elements of methodology, 374 f.

Gass, S. I., *see* Riley, Vera

GATT, 334

Gellhorn, Walter, *Individual Freedom and Government Restraints,* 359

General Agreement on Tariffs and Trade, 334

General Electric, 342; corporate giving, 361

General Motors, 342; reply to Reuther, 177 f.; *General Motors Plant Visits Plan Book,* quoted, 259; projection of relationships, 284

Genossenschaft, 346

George, A. L., *see* Davison, W. P.

Germany, 343

Gibson, G. D., "How Fixed Are Class Shareholders Rights?" 354

Gilbert, L. D., program of corporate democracy, 219 f., 223; *Dividends and Democracy,* 387, 388; "Keeping the Company Reins in the Owners' Hands," 387

Gierke, Otto von, *Das Deutsche Genossenschaftsrecht,* 345 f.

Glover, J. D., *The Attack on Big Business,* 349, 360

Goals, corporate, 18 f., 96–99, 115–37; noneconomic, 52, 99 f., 117, 122 f.; political, of metrocorporation, 56 f.; of employees, 62; social, 75 f.; normative, 103; range of, 116; reality vs. hypothesis, 135–38; in the public interest, 198 f.; economic, social balance as, 231; value system in, 233 ff.; antitrust, 252 f.; public relations, 275 ff., 278–80; operational, 279 ff., 372; and social change, 302 f.; proliferation of, 307; of well-tempered corporation, 335; and management philosophies, 393

Goal-values, need for a system of, 115–17; range of, 125 ff.; noneconomic, 136 f.

"Good Citizen, Inc.," 86

Goods, suppliers of, 214

Good will, as goal of public relations work, 276, 360

Gordon, R. A., *Business Leadership in the Large Corporation,* 380, 381, quoted, 364

— and J. E. Howell, *Higher Education for Business,* 341

Gorer, Geoffrey, *The American People,* quoted, 31, 349 f.; *The People of Great Russia,* 153, 376

Gossett, W. T., on corporate citizenship, 82, 264 f., 398; quoted, 259 f., 360

Gouldner, A. W. "Organizational Analysis," 403

Governance, corporate, *see* Polity

Government, private sectors, 108 ff.; and power, 33; and public governments, 379

Government, public: power of, 33; effect of market mechanism on, 39; fear of expansion of, 45; restraint on corporate power, 53; accountability of public servants, 54; and corporate polity, 56 f.; functions of, 57; similarities with corporate polities, 241; integration of information 299; corporation and, 319 ff.

Government regulation, *see* Regulation

Governments, organizational, 32; expansion of functions, 102; coercive powers of, 186; corporate relations with, 215

Greenewalt, C. H., "Key to Progress—the Uncommon Man," 398; quoted, 259 f.

Gross National Product, 232

Group personality, 346

Growth, economic, 125; goal of, 133; time pressures and, 148; problems of, 207; economic, questions re, 234 f.

Guilds, 60, 359

Haldane, J. B. S. "Communication in Biology," 399; *see also* Ayer, A. J.

Hamilton, W. H., *The Politics of Industry*, 366 f., 396, quoted, 343, 395; "Competition," 396, quoted, 248 f.; *The Pattern of Competition*, 395, 396, quoted, 21, 343

Harberger, A. C., "Monopoly and Resource Allocation," 392

Harris, R. R., *see* Burton, Arthur

Harris, S. E., *see* Sutton, Francis X.

Hayek, F. A., "competitive order," 252; *Individualism and the Economic Order*, quoted, 396 f.

Hays, Brooks, story of Arkansas taxpayer, 388

Heald, Morell, "Management's Responsibility to Society," 361

Heckscher, Gunnar, *The Study of Comparative Government and Politics*, 379, 384 f.

Hegel, G. W. F., 351

Herrschaft, 346

Hickman, C. A., and M. H. Kuhn, *Individuals, Groups and Economic Behavior*, 368, quoted, 117

Hierarchy, organizational, 402 f.; and decision making, 105; locus of appraisal function, 184; employee's locus in, 237; structural system, 237, 315 f.

Hillary, Sir Edmund, 338

Historical perspective, 10 f.

Hobbes, Thomas, on power, 132; *Leviathan*, 372

Hohfeld, W. N., *Fundamental Legal Conceptions*, 359

Hoover, C. B., *The Economy, Liberty, and the State*, 402, 403

Houser, T. V., *Big Business and Human Values*, 390, 395

Hoxie, Robert, 358

Howell, J. E., *see* Gordon, R. A.

Hughes, Charles E., re antitrust laws, 253

Huizinga, J., *Homo Ludens*, 356 f.

Human relations, 40; problem of power in, 32; corporate, 283 f.; values in, 354

Hurff, G. B., *Social Aspects of Enterprise in the Large Corporation*, 400, quoted, 282, 369

Identification, with company, 289; with group, 366

Ideology, of American business, 22 ff.; elements in use of, 140, 280; instrument of policy, 187, 273; and economic integration, 334; and global ecosystem, 334 f.

Image, corporate, 283–87; projection of, 291

Imperialist theory, of law, 394

Income, corporate, *see* Earnings

Income, family, and stock ownership, 221

Income tax, upper brackets, and dividends, 169

Incorporation, with limited liability, 38 f.; act of, 70

Individual(s), power and authority over, 30–35; freedom of, vs. corporate power, 52; and the corporation, 71; impact on the organization, 72; private and property rights, 111; control over, 244; rights of, 266; as corporate publics, 290 f.; and the community, 351; need for status and function, 390

Industrial relations research, 58

Industrial research and development (IRAD), 363

Industrial Revolution, 59 f., 343

Industry, nationalized, criterion of efficiency of, 384

Inflation, wages and prices and, 175 ff.; and voluntary restraint, 355

Influence, as corporate goal, 132 f., 279; theory and measurement of, 277; defined, 372

Information, part of policy process, 105; in decision making, 144; flow of, 163; theory, need for research in, 277; input and output, 297; integration of, 299 f.; importance of, 302; mathematical theory of, 377; transfer, 400

Innovation, 371; pressure of time and, 148 f.; as obligation to customer, 225

Input and output, of public relations, 276 ff.; theory of, 348

Institutional economists, search for corporate realities, 118

Institution(s), survival of, 1, 134 f.; as lesser society, 18; human, role of, 72; quasi-public, 197; business, as growing organisms, 269; atomizing of, 332; future expectations re, 337 f.

Insurance, national mass, 89 f.

Integrity, goal-value, 126–28

Intelligence, operations, 128; in policy making, 140, 167–73; and choice of strategy, 162 f.; interrelations between governmental and corporate, 173; inflow of, 221; and public relations policy, 287; public relations, synthesis of corporate activities, 299; function, of accounting specialist, 379

Interest groups, representation of, 61; metrocorporate, 67 f.

Interests, balance of, 6, 42, 76, 83 f., 197 ff., 223 f., 257, 308; representation of, 61, 280 f.; managerial and employee, 289

Internal conditions, and decision process, 383

International Longshoremen's Association, 237 f.

Interrelationships, business, 7; corporate, 75; *see also* Relationships

Inter-University Committee for Research on Consumer Behavior, 390

Intervention, in economic process, 314, 318 f.; governmental, 370 f., 390; *see also* Regulation

Investment, corporate, 30; involuntary, 81, 83; *see also* Reinvestment

Investor public, 221 f.

Invocation of rules, 140, 181 f.; of coercive powers, 273 f.

Ionides, Michael, 355

Italy, 343

Iveroth, Axel, on social responsibilities of European employers, 390 f.

Janowitz, Morris, *see* Eulau, Heinz

Japanese, operational code, 153

Jennings, A. R., "Present-Day Challenges in Financial Reporting," 379

Jevons, W. S., "perfect market," 185

Job, time priorities and, 147 f.; descriptions, intracompany, 329; sovereignty, 395; *see also* Employment; Work

Job-consciousness, in unionism, 59

Johnson, J. J., "The Emerging Pattern of Corporate Citizenship," quoted, 391

Judaeo-Christian traditions, 33, 34

Judgments, normative, 98 f., 107; *see also* Values

Judicial review, 323; of protection of rights, 240 f.; of personal rights of employees, 241

Jural correlations and opposites, 359

Jurisprudence, and studies of the corporation, 26

Juristic theory, of the Sovereign, 201 f.

Jurists, tools of corporate analysis, 95 f.

Justice Department, antitrust division, 256

Kahn, A. E., 255

Kaplan, Abraham, *see* Lasswell, H. D.

Kaplan, A. D. H., *Big Enterprise in a Competitive System*, 396

— J. B. Dirlam, and R. F. Lanzillotti, *Pricing in Big Business*, 364 f.

Karr, David, *Fight for Control*, 389

Katona, George, "Business Expectations in the Framework of Psychological Economics (Toward a Theory of Expectations)," 379

Katz, Elihu, and P. F. Lazarsfeld, *Personal Influence*, 377

Katz, W. G., 362; "The Philosophy of Midcentury Corporation Statutes," 351; quoted, 352

Kaysen, Carl, "The Social Significance of the Modern Corporation," 29, 347, quoted, 348; *see also* Sutton, Francis X.

Kefauver, Estes, investigations of "administered pricing," 177

Kelso, L. D., and Adler, M. J., 352; *The Capitalist Manifesto*, 80–84, quoted, 83, 362, 396

Kerr, Clark, "The Balkanization of Labor Markets," 395; *Labor Mobility and Economic Opportunity*, 395

Kline, B. E., and N. H. Martin, "Freedom, Authority, and Decentralization," 392 f.

Knauth, Oswald, 21 f., 121, 122; *Business Practices, Trade Position and Competition,* quoted, 344 f., 370; *Managerial Enterprise: Its Growth and Methods of Operation,* 370, quoted, 344, 364

Knight, F. H., "Profit," 370; *Freedom and Reform,* 361; *Risk, Uncertainty, and Profit,* 370

Knowledge, as goal-value, 128–30; sharing of, 129, 328; authority of, 182, 367; production of, 363; subjective, and images, 401

Koinonia, 260, 398

Koontz, Harold, and R. W. Gable, *Public Control of Economic Enterprise,* 396

Koopmans, T. C., *Three Essays on the State of Economic Science,* 392

Kriedmann, A. M., "Dividends—Changing Patterns," 389

Kuhn, M. H., *see* Hickman, C. A.

Labor, role of, 8 f.; leaders, power of, 33; commodity concept of, 62, 228, 358; diversion of corporate earnings to, 81; costs, 174 ff.

Labor laws, 239

Labor-management, relations, 43, 59, 238 f.; dispute re wages and prices, 175 ff.; Ford re, 284 f.; and question of authority, 323

Labor-Management Reporting and Disclosure Act of 1959, 324

Labor markets, Balkanization of, 395

Labor movement, theory of, 58 f.; goals, 357; *see also* Union, labor

Labor relations, metrocorporation and, 57–62; orderly government of, 102

Labor union, *see* Union, labor

Laissez aller, 90

Laissez-faire, 142, 314; theory of, 285 f.

Landrum-Griffin Act, 324

Lanzillotti, R. F., *see* Kaplan, A. D. H.

Lasswell, H. D., *The Decision Process,* 373, 378; "Current Studies of the Decision Process: Automation versus Creativity," 378; *see also* Lerner, Daniel; Smith, B. L.

— and Abraham Kaplan, *Power and Society,* 132, 365, 366, 367, 368, 371, 378

Latham, Earl, "Anthropomorphic Corporations, Elites, and Monopoly Power," 350; *Political Theories of Monopoly Power,* 350, 400

Latty, E. R., "Exploration of Legislative Remedy for Prejudicial Changes in Senior Shares," 387

Lauterbach, Albert, "Social Factors in Business Uncertainty," 361

Law, economic, 22; status of customer in, 224 f.; re competition, 250; antitrust, attitudes toward, 253; inchoate areas, 265; and agreement, 394; *see also* Corporation law; Legislation; Statutes

Law and order, of the market, 100; global, 101

Lawyers, "strike suit," 389

Lazarsfeld, P. F., *see* Katz, Elihu

Leaders, business, altruism, 71; overexpansion of interests, 88; voluntary restraint, 355; double obligation, 371

Leadership, social, of business, 73; as goal-value, 125 f.; directive, 289

Legal areas of corporate policy, 190, 359 f.

Legal counselor, corporate, 71; in competitor relations, 251; and issues of public policy, 257

Legal theory, of free enterprise, 344

Legislation, and economic power, 53; regulative, 283; securities and exchanges, 283; protection of interests through, 321

Legislatures, state, police power, 390

Leighton, Alexander, *The Governing of Men,* 375

Leites, Nathan, 153 f.; *Operational Code of the Politburo,* 376; *Study of Bolshevism,* 376

Lerner, Daniel, and H. D. Lasswell, eds., *The Policy Sciences,* 373

Lester, R. A., "Revolution in Industrial Employment," quoted, 358

Letters patent, control of technology, 395

Levitt, Theodore, 356; on corporate preoccupation with social responsibility, 87–91, 271; "The Dangers of Social Responsibility," 362, 398

Leys, W. A. R., *Ethics for Policy Decisions,* 360

Liberalism, 356, 380; theory of power, 63 ff.

Liberal-utilitarian tradition, 45 f.

Liberty, *see* Freedom

Licensing power, delegation of, 359

Life, entropy-reducing capacity of, 356

Lilienthal, David, 254; *Big Business: a New Era,* 397

Limited liability, 39, 351

Lindblom, C. E., quoted, 348; *see also* Dahl, R. A.

Lindeman, E. L., ed., *Basic Selections from Emerson*, 368

Lindsay, Malvina, on effective customer protests, 225

Lippmann, Walter, on stereotypes, quoted, 400 f.

Listening, role of, in public relations policy, 291

Literature, polemical and apologetic, 104 ff., 122

Livermore, Shaw, *Early American Land Companies: Their Influence on Corporate Development*, 347

Livingston, J. A., *The American Stockholder*, 84–87, 362; quoted, 85 f., 388 f.

Lobbying, 56, 267

Longshoremen, work stoppage, 237 f.

Love and war, decision process, 139

Luce, R. D., and Howard Raiffa, *Games and Decisions*, 373

MacDonald, John, *Strategy in Poker, Business or War*, 373

McDougal, M. S., "The Comparative Study of Law: Value Classification as an Instrument of Democratic World Order," 378

McGovern, W. M., *From Luther to Hitler*, 351

Machlup, Fritz, quoted, on industrial research and development, 363

McIlwain, C. H., 260; *The Growth of Political Thought in the West*, 398

MacKenzie, J. N., *see* Stein, M. I.

McKinsey, J. C., *Introduction to the Theory of Games*, 373

McMurry, R. N., "The Case for Benevolent Autocracy," 392

Maintenance, corporate, and improvement, policy areas of, 190

Maitland, F. W., 27; tr., *Political Theories of the Middle Age*, 345 f.

Management, metrocorporate, 53 f.; professionalization of, 72; encroachment on role of, 73 f.; as *alter ego* of owner, 82; and balance of interests, 82 f.; responsibility to owners, 84; goals, 98 ff.; hierarchy, decision making, 116 f.; motivation, 117–21, 166; early definitions of, 118 f.; aspects of, 195; continuity of, 198; authority of managerial employees over nonmanagerial, 238;

quasi-judicial function, 266 f.; public relations as function of, 274 ff.; corporate statutes and, 354; and entrepreneurial function, 370; changes in philosophy of, 393; separation from ownership, 393; functions of, 399; *see also* Executives; Labor-management relations

Management Science, 347

Managerial creed, 36

Managerial enterprise, 21 f., 344

Manager(s), and stockholders' property rights, 23; balance of interests, 24, 77 f., 197 f.; power, 24, 86 f.; role of, 24 f., 123 f., 318, 368; responsibility, 28, 29, 78; and unauthoritarian behavior, 31; of traditional corporation 39 f., 44; of metrocorporation, 51; as representatives of stockholders' interest, 54; station and duties, 66 f.; adaptation to social change, 74; accountability of, 82; problems occupying attention of, 107; motivation, 117–21, 166, 354 f., 368; goal-values, 124 f.; group environment of decision making, 143; roles and responsibilities, 166; perception of competing interests, 184 f.; and public policy, 192 f.; as quasi-public policy makers, 193 f.; elements of economic control, 221 f.; and "stockholder democracy," 223; tenure and compensation, 241; relations with suppliers, 245; of community relations, 261; as stockholders' spokesmen, 282; "parochialism of imagination," 284; social responsibility, 352

— professional, 9, 23, 393; and claimants, 6; dedication, 127; identification with organization, 135; recommendations of, 173 ff.; and the prescription of rules, 181; and responsibilities to security holders, 219

Managerial prerogatives, 393; encroachment on, 60, 242 f., 290; of control over work force, 237 f.

Managerial revolution, 8 f.

Mandeville, Bernard, *The Fable of the Bees*, 142

Manipulation, symbolic, 106

Maps, theories or models as, 285

March, J. G., "An Introduction to the Theory and Measurement of Influence," 400

Market, concept of, 11; forces, regulation by, 24; traditional corporation

Market (*Continued*)
and, 69 f.; concern with, 99; geographical boundaries, 100; protection against fluctuation, 121; discipline of, 140; requirements of, and business decisions, 202 f.; position, and customer satisfaction, 225 f.; as allocator of scarce resources, "conventional wisdom," 232; competitive share of, 252; open, and competition, 254; power, antitrust policy and, 256; self-regulating, 310, 313; rationale, 347 f.; automatic forces, 370
Marketing, areas of corporate policy, 191
Market mechanism, freedom of operation, 39; and preservation of freedom, 49
Market operations, 11; and public interest, 43; as restraint on power, 53; and government intervention, 390
Market system, and the balance of power, 64; and economic responsibilities, 71; partly free, partly regulated, 231
Marshall, Alfred, 282; *Principles of Economics,* 227, 400; theory, 229, 232
Marshall, John, 200
Martin, N. H., *see* Kline, B. E.
Martineau, Pierre, "Sharper Focus for the Corporate Image," 401
Marxists, 59, 358
Mason, E. S., 255, 256; quoted, 251 f.; "The Apologetics of Managerialism," 397; "The Current Status of the Monopoly Problem," 397; *Economic Concentration and the Monopoly Problem,* 397
Massachusetts Institute of Technology, study of values and perspectives, 150 f.; Center for International Studies, 376
Mass production, 121
Mathematicians, use of game theory, 144
Mathematics, theory and communication, 400
"Maxwell demon," 356
Mead, Margaret, *And Keep Your Powder Dry,* 349, 375, quoted, 30
Means, G. C., 227; quoted, 228; "Collective Capitalism and Economic Theory," 392; *see also* Berle, A. A., Jr.
Meer, Bernard, *see* Stein, M. I.
Mellon, W. G., on allocation, 228 f.; "Selected, Descriptive Bibliography of References on Priority Systems and Related, Nonprice Allocators," 392

Merton, R. K., Leonard Broom and L. S. Cottrell, Jr., eds., *Sociology Today,* 403
Messages, theory of, 301
Metrocorporation, 6 f., 50–68, 307 f.; model of, 12; multiplicity of interests and purposes, 36 f.; acceptance of social responsibility, 50 ff.; polity vs. traditional polity, 52–55; multiple responsibilities, 54; alternative to, 65 f.; pattern of, 66–68; and private property, 111; defined, 205; limit of responsibility, 318; nature of, 322; attitude toward social functions, 327; fear of, 333
Metropolitan Life, 342
Michigan, University of, Survey Research Center, 387
Mill, J. S., 350, 392; Schumpeter re, 285 f.
Miller, J. G., "Toward a General Theory for the Behavioral Sciences," 400
Mills, C. W., *The Power Elite,* quoted, 371
Misceláneos de estúdios dedicados á Fernando Ortiz por sus Discípulos, Colegas y Amigos, 361
Mixed capitalism, 80 f.
Mixed economy, 250, 314, 344; regulation of decision centers, 120; basic issues, 120 f.; rationale of, 235; individual freedom and transformation to, 314
Mixed enterprise, defined, 205
Model Business Corporation Act, 353
Models, study of business in terms of, 11 f.; corporation, 37, 91 f., 102 f.; heuristic, 40, 50, 68, 309; of economic and legal theory, 75, 116, 166; of corporate collectives, 228; of management-employee relationship, 243 f.; classical competitive, 252; counterposed corporate, 307–9; scientific requirements of, 309; tenable, 329 f.; economic and juristic, 377; defined, 377; of legal and economic theory, 380; *see also* Metrocorporation; Traditional corporation; Well-tempered corporation
Molière, *Bourgeois Gentilhomme,* 142
Money, role of, 10
Monopoly, advantageous trade position, 122; competitive view of, 252; focus on problem of, 348; and status, 371
Morality, organizational, 385
Moral standards, and power, 33

Morgan, J. P., effect of photograph of, 349

Morgenstern, Oskar, on theory of priorities, 229; "Consistency Problems in the Military Supply System," 392

Motives, executive assessment of, 158 f.; *see also* Goals

Muller, H. J., *The Loom of History,* quoted, 305

Munn v. Illinois, 390

Myers, C. A., *Industrial Relations in Sweden: Some Comparisons with American Experience,* 392; *see also* Brown, D. V.

National character, 153

National issues, listed by Committee on Economic Development, 46 f.

Nation-state, law and order in, 100; economic coexistence, 334

Natural law, and social theories, 346

Natural sciences, 129

Nature, scientific exploration of, 2; and policy maker, 143

Naval Research Logistics Quarterly, 347

Nazism, 351

Nebbia v. New York, 390

Needs, human, satisfaction of, 158 f., 183, 232 f.

Negotiation, 140, 277; in labor relations, 61; quasi-diplomatic, 106; as instrument of corporate policy, 186 f.

Neofascism, 91

Neofeudalism, 9, 88; in labor-management relations, 62

Neutrality, 267; corporate, in global ecosystem, 335

Newell, Allen, *see* Simon, H. A.

New Hampshire, legislature and Dartmouth College charter, 200 f.

Newman, W. L., ed., *The Politics of Aristotle,* 398

New York Stock Exchange, 85, 389

New York *Times,* 379, 393, 401

New York Waterfront Commission, 237

Niebuhr, Reinhold, 35; *Pious and Secular America,* 350

Nonmanagerial employees, corporate responsibilities to, 238 f.

Norman v. Baltimore and Ohio Railroad Company, 386

Norms, ethical, 26, 104 ff.; qualitative, 171; governing business statesmanship, 198; in applying policy, 181 f.; social, corporation and, 298

North Carolina, 353

Objectives, *see* Goals

Obligations, responsibility and, 70 f.; legal, 74; to contributor-claimants (*q.v.*), 77 f.; corporate, and obligees, 337

Obligee groups, *see* Claimants; Contributor-claimants

Oligarchy, corporate, 27 f.; self-perpetuating, 321

Oligopoly, 250

Oliver, H. M., "Trends toward a New Moral Philosophy for Business," 361

Operational approach, to policy making, 107

Operational codes, 152–55; study of, 150 f.; irrationality in, 163; determinants of corporate function, 166; and decisions, 168; elements of, 172; and policy, 182; individual preferences and, 252

Operational task, effect of time pressures on, 147 f.

Operations, business, span of, 141

Operations research procedures, 144

Operations Research, 347

"Organizational Economy," 314

"Organizational Revolution," 7, 310, 313

Organization man, 32, 57, 64, 67, 72, 98, 118, 308; vs. personal freedom, 240

Organizations, large, hierarchical structure, 1; large, development of, 2 f.; traditional, rationale, 3; as contemporary monuments, 14; interruptions imposed by administrative functioning, 147 f.; dynamic, building of, 161 f.; "natural-system model of analysis," 330; decentralized, policy in, 367; conditioning elements in, 383

Owner-entrepreneur, 74 f., 166, 198; effect of time pressure on, 148

Ownership, corporate, 5, 13, 27 f., 388 f.; by management and unions, 61; by labor-management, 66; and control, 83; of corporate property, 220 f.; separation from management, 393

Parker, Carleton, 358

Paternalism, corporate, 61

"Paternal responsibility," 352

Paton, W. A., ed., *Accountants' Handbook,* 387

Pay-off, in game theory, 144; time factor in, 150

Pecora, Ferdinand, quoted, on banking reforms, 218 f.; *Wall Street under Oath*, 387

People, *see* Individuals

People's Capitalism, 109, 219, 223, 396

Pepper, G. W., "An Introduction to the Study of the Law of Associations," 347

Perceptions, operational code and, 154 ff.; of corporate image, 283 ff.; *see also* Sensing

Performance, measurement of, 124, 183 f., 195; evaluation of, 252; standards of, 298; internal conditions of, 384

Perlman, Mark, *Labor Union Theories in America*, 358

Perlman, Selig, *A History of Trade Unionism in the United States*, 357; "The Principle of Collective Bargaining," 357; *A Theory of the Labor Movement*, 357, quoted, 59

Personnel, training, 128; policies, areas of corporate policy, 191 f.; contributions to community, 328 f.; and right of publication, 328; characteristics and attitudes, 384

Philosophy, 5; of corporation law, 39; social, issues of, 234; corporate, 268, 301; defined, 341; of management, 393; business, *see* Business, philosophy of

Pierson, F. C., and others, *The Education of American Businessmen*, 341; *see also* Chamberlain, N. W.

"Pirates by proxy," 219

Planning, 194 f.; time and, 2; economic, traditionalist and, 46; long-range, and time pressures, 148; long-range, test, 151; and annual records, 375

Plant, local, suspension or discontinuance of operations, 261

Plato, *The Republic*, 313, 402

Pluralism, in private associations, 51; application of theory to economic enterprise, 266

Polanyi, Karl, *The Great Transformation*, 402

Police power, 390; of the states, 224

Policy, term, 364

Policy, corporate, 19; instruments of, 7, 105 f., 137, 140, 159, 185–88, 273 f., 294 f.; inherent values, 30; traditional, 46; metrocorporate, 51; and public government, 53; relationship with external polities, 58; labor, formulation of, 61; process, 103–6, 164 f., 366; guiding principles, 113 ff.; social aspects, 140; tradition of economic analysis, 143; as a symbol, 162; assessment of success or failure, 182–84; economic means of implementation, 185 f.; and public policy, 192 ff., 384; public aspects, 194, 197 f.; limitations on goods and services, 230 f.; problem of organization man and personal freedom, 240; and public interest, 257; distorting elements, 300; impact of global ecosystem on, 334 f.; well-tempered corporation, 335 f.; effect of, 364; plan of action and specific goals, 365; defined, 365 f., 367 f.; as a political phenomenon, 366 f.; in decentralized organization, 367; plans of action and major objectives, 368

— areas: list of, 107, 190–92, 381 ff.; of public scrutiny, 203; key, operational vs. subjective selection of, 204–7; significant, approaches to, 292; and public policy areas, 384; socially significant, 385; *see also* Strategic decision areas

Policy making, corporate, and the corporate environment, 99 ff.; deviating influences on, 104; complexity of, 116 f.; realism and rationality in, 137, 164 f.; stages of, 139 f., 184 f.; time as element in, 146 f.; steps and instruments, 166–88; democratic procedure in, 203; and concept of corporation, 286; pricing processes, 365; centralization of power of, 371

Political action, corporate, 56 f., 102 f., 267 f., 325 f.

Political behavior, operational code, 152

Political directorate, 122

Political economy, metrocorporate, 69 ff.; laboristic trend, 369

Political environment, of corporation, 100

Political process, functions of the corporation, 319–22

Political science, studies of the corporation, 26

Political scientists, sectarian approach, 325

Political theory, and private sectors, 108; pluralistic, 346

Politicians, and authority, 350

Polity (governance), corporate, 19 f., 36, 108–11, 308 f.; and public and private polity, 47 f.; and market operations, 48; quasi-public, of metrocorporation, 51; traditional vs. metrocorporate, 52–

55; and constitutionalism, 53 f.; and public governments, 56 f.; problems of, 95–111; science of, 109 f.; processes to reduce abuse of corporate power, 240 f.; future forms, 241; voluntary reform of, 242; fairness and justice in, 266; self-examination of, 267; freedom of, 321; of well-tempered corporation, 322 ff., 336; extension of constitutional law to, 323 f.; statutes and, 354; study of, 379

Polity, ecclesiastical, 20

Polity, private, 320

Polyarchy, 402 f.

Pound, Roscoe, *Legal Immunities of Labor Unions*, 394

Power, balance of, 8, 89; elite, 9, 371; and authority, 11, 30–35; ethical issues of, 52 f.; dispersion of, 110 f.; balance in public and private centers, 111; coercive, 140, 185 f., 274, 380; private, as public issue, 320 f., freedom and limitations of, 322 f.; defined, 372; concept of, 380

Power, corporate, 71, 122, 308; restraints on, 52 f.; uses of, 63–66, 73, 109; and decision, 104; shift in center of, 105; as goal, 132 f.; polity processes vs. abuses of, 240 f.; exercise of, 352

Power figures, influence on decision making, 156

Powers, governmental, separation of, 63 f., 89; state and federal, 202

Prescription, of rules governing policy, 140, 180 f.

Pressures on corporations, 78; groups, 44 (*see also* Claimants; Contributor-claimants); external, 110; decision making and, 145 ff.; created by executive, 161; social, 383

Prestige, and customer satisfaction, 225

Price policy, and voluntary restraint, 44; appraisal of, 183

Prices, voluntary restraint re rise in, 79 f.; and wages, in automobile industry, 175 ff.; administered, 177; flexible, 228; competition and, 240 f.; study of, 364 f.

Price system, allocating function of, 228 f.; administration of, 315

Priorities, on executive's time, 147; in decision making, approaches to, 189 ff.; in national emergency, 228 f.; in value system, 234 f.

"Private corporation," 200, 205

Private enterprise, in open vs. closed society, 5; vs. public instrumentality, 39; and public funds, 57; and tasks of allocation and production, 227

Private government, *see* Government, private

Private property, factor of production, 9; corporation and, 10, 28, 75

Private rights, safeguards of, 63

Privatization, 50

Privilege and duty, as jural opposites, 359

Product, corporate selectivity re, 230 f.

Production, factors of, 9; costs, 174; areas of corporate policy, 190 f.; capital as tool of, 212; national, 226; philosophic assumptions re purposes of, 229 f.; for production's sake, 231; distribution, moral questions in economics of, 232 f.; pattern of, and consumer choice, 349

Productive process, function of entrepreneur, 120

Productivity, corporate concern with, 67; goals of, 371

Professions, authoritative, 350

Profitability, 125; as corporate goal, 117, 199; as goal-value, 123 f.; and customer satisfaction, 225

Profit motive, and general welfare, 40

Profits, and losses, shared, 9, 336 f.; excess, 23, 179; and cheap goods, 28; maximization of, 29, 36; as sole or primary function, 41 f., 88, 90 f.; as test of worth, 89; and social service, 93; distribution of, 212; lure of, 248 f.

Programming, linear, 373

Promoters, freedom of, 39

Propaganda, 275

Property, corporate, maintenance of, 169

Property interests, legal protection of, 39; managers as guardians of, 66 f.

Property rights, in business creed, 22 f.; alienation of, 81; corporate, 84

Proprietor-manager, 220

Proprietor-owner, 212

Proxy control, fight for, 389

Prudential Insurance, 342

Public, the: traditional corporation and, 43–49; effective protests re products, 225 f.; responsibilties to, 215 f., 262 ff., 391; *see also* Public interest

Publication, freedom of, 328

Public business, corporate enterprise as, 199–203
Public corporation, term, 51, 205
Public interest, industrial contributions to, 173; antitrust laws and, 253; corporate policy and, 257; representation of, 283; business and, 390
Publicity, vs. propaganda, 275; orientation of public relations, 292
Public opinion, and law of corporations, 92 f.; company polls of, 131
Public policy, credit and money in, 10; and privatization and statization, 50 f.; union-corporate relations and, 102; and corporate policy, 192 f.; corporation and issues of, 256 f.; corporate responsibility re, 257 f.; public-private determination of, 315
Public relations, counselor, 71; as factor in corporate ideology, 187; areas of corporate policy, 192, 287; and corporate interests, 273–303; as function of management, 274–76, 399; specialist, 277, 399; liaison between management and specialist, 279; context and addressees of, 280 ff.; as communicational relations, 294; task of specialists in, 295 f.; and corporate reputation, 296–99; future, 300–303; literature, 401 f.
Publics, corporate, 286–92, 295 f.; list of, 290 f.
Public services, financing of, 102; allocation of resources to, 312
Public Utility Holding Act of 1935, 219
Public welfare, and traditional corporation, 39; business and, 348
Purchasing practices, 246

Raiffa, Howard, *see* Luce, R. D.
Raskin, A. H., 379
Rathenau, Walter, *In Days to Come,* 27, 347
Rationality, in decision making, 103, 138–65, 188; concept of, 141–43; corporate and individual, 152; information and, 163; corporate orientation, 164 f.; deforming of, 166 f.; in stages of policy, 184; in the economic process, 317
"Rational model" of organizations, 330
Reality, corporate, search for, 118 ff.; in decision making, 138–65; deforming aspects, 145 ff., 156, 162 ff.; corporate orientation, 164 f.
Reason, rule of, in antitrust policy, 254 f.

Recessions, and investment, 221
Recommendation, 140; as decision making, 116 f., 173–80
Reference groups, in decision making, 155 f.
Reform, business, 201 f.
Regulated enterprises, 343
Regulation of business, 3, 76 f., 82, 200 f., 202, 212, 283, 343; legislative, of employer-employee relations, 244
Rehabilitation, economic, 333
Reinvestment in the business, 81, 83, 170 ff.
Relationships, contractual, 22 f., 57 f., 291; transitory and permanent, 86; economic, system of, 354; *see also* Interrelationships
— corporate, 73 f., 377; and polity, 95–111; and empathy, 156 f.; with employees, 236 ff.; and community, 258 ff.; internal and external, 385
Reorganization or liquidation, areas of corporate policy, 192
Representation of interests, 54, 61, 267, 280 f., 282, 283
Reputation, through leadership, 126; corporate, 296–99
Research, corporate, need for, 96 ff., 173; basic and applied, 96 ff., 129, 363; contributions of, 328; operations, 347; listing of policy areas as tool of, 382 f.
Research laboratories, audience sensitivity, 159; pressures created by, 161
Reserves, calculation of, 170 f.
Resources, allocation of, 30, 227, 311; efficient use of, 39, 67, 252 f.; development of, 46, 311, 317 f.; natural, traditional corporation and, 48 f.; integration of, 195
Respect and awe, American attitude toward, 31
Responsibility, corporate, 209–338; managerial, 23 f.; moral, 31; and power, 32; development of, 69–97; nature of, 70–72; economic, 71; eclectic theory of, 270; of well-tempered corporation, 336; corporate statutes and, 354; legal, 359 f.; *see also* Social responsibilities
Restraint, voluntary, 44, 79 f.
Reuther, Walter, proposals re wages and costs, 174–80
Ricardo, David, 22, 117, 118, 142
Riesman, David, on directedness of society, 158

Right and duty, as jural correlatives, 359

Right of control over employees, 237 f.

Rights, of person and property, 111; and duties, labor-management, 238 f.; private, enforcement of, 240 f.

Riley, Vera, and S. I. Gass, *Linear Programming and Associated Techniques*, 373 f.

Ripley, W. Z., 84 f., 347; *Main Street and Wall Street*, 218

Risk, bearing, 117, 369; sharing, 176; taking, 220

Risk capital, and profitability, 44

Rivalry, 248

Robbins, J. J., *The Government of Labor Relations*, 394

Robson, W. A., ways of evaluating nationalized industry, 385

Rodgers, R. R., *see* Stein, M. I.

Rostow, E. V., 255

Rule of reason, and antitrust policy, 254 f.

Rules, policy, prescription of, 180 f.; and regulations, corporate, and policy, 367

Ruml, Beardsley, *Tomorrow's Business*, 110

Rumor, studies of, 377

Russians, character, 153; diplomatic behavior, 153

Ryan, John, 358

Sabine, G. H., *A History of Political Theory*, 356, 380

Sales promotion, and annual report, 170

Sanctions, state, 186 f., 380; severe, 367

Say, J. B., 119; *Traité d'économie politique*, 369

Sayles, Leonard, 146

Schachter, Stanley, *see* Festinger, Leon

Schlichter, S. H., "The Power Holders in the American Economy," quoted, 113

Schoeffler, Sidney, *The Failures of Economics*, 378

Schramm, Wilbur, "How Communication Works," 402; ed., *The Process and Effect of Mass Communication*, 401 f.

Schumpeter, J. A., 119, 254; "creative destruction," 8; on economic logic, 227; quoted re Mill, 285 f.; *The Theory of Economic Development*, 369; *History of Economic Analysis*, 369, 370, 392, 401; quoted, 343; *Capitalism*, 397

Schwartz, L. B., 255; re Attorney General's Committee on Antitrust Policy, 254 f.; "General Dissent," 397

Scientific management, 4, 29, 358

Scientific problems, 95–111

Scientific research, statements re, as goal-value, 128 f.

Scientist, as "lock-picker," 96 ff.

Scott, W. R., *The Constitution and Finance of English, Scottish, and Irish Joint-Stock Companies in 1720*, 346

Sears, Roebuck, 342

Secrecy, vs. sharing of knowledge, 130; and security regulations, governmental, 173

Securities, laws re, 85; senior, 212

Securities Act of 1933, 219

Securities and Exchange Commission, 283, 389

Securities Exchange Act of 1934, 219

Security, of employees, 62; physical, and welfare, types of values, 124

Security holders, corporate responsibility to, 211–13; 218–24; *see also* Stockholders

Security markets, federal regulations of, 76

Seitz, Peter, "Management's Adoption of New Labor Relations Methods," 393

Selectivity, corporate, re products, 230 f.

Self-interest, enlightened, 33 f., 71, 354 f., 360

Self-reliance, doctrine of, 22 f.

Selvage, J. P., "Pirates by Proxy," 387

Senate Committee on Banking and Currency, 218 f.

Sensing operations, 401; and company policy, 292; in public relations work, 297

Service, suppliers of, 214; continuity of, 241

Shannon, C. E., and Warren Weaver, *The Mathematical Theory of Communication*, 377, 400

Share owners, defined, 212; *see also* Security holders; Stockholders

Shartle, C. L., *Executive Performance and Leadership*, 375

Sherman Act, 254

Shortal, Robert G., 342

Short run, time pressure and emphasis on, 148

Shulman, Irwin, *see* De Sola Pool, Ithiel

Silander, F. A., *see* Wasserman, Paul

Simon, H. A., *Administrative Behavior*, 378; "The Role of Expectations in an

Simon, H. A. (*Continued*)
  Adaptive or Behavioristic Model," 378;
  "Comments on the Theory of Organi-
  zations," 401
— and Allen Newell, "Models: Their
  Uses and Limitations," 378
Skills, functional, 126; as goal-value,
  128 ff.
Sloan, Alfred P., Foundation, vii
Small business, protection of, 245; role
  of, 342 f.
Smiddy, H. F., "Managerial Decision-
  Making," 363; quoted, 105, 107
Smith, Adam, 22, 142, 343, 345, 392; *The
  Wealth of Nations,* 143 f.; *The Theory
  of Moral Sentiments,* 373
Smith, B. L., and C. M. Smith, *Interna-
  tional Communication and Political
  Opinion: a Guide to the Literature,*
  401
— H. D. Lasswell, and R. D. Casey, eds.,
  *Propaganda, Communication and Pub-
  lic Opinion,* 400, 401
Smith, C. M., *see* Smith, B. L.
Social and political structures, weak-
  nesses in, 34
Social corporation, *see* Metrocorporation
Social Darwinism, 45, 103, 345
"Social ecosystem," 330 f.
Social institutions, use of ideologies,
  187 f.
Socialism, 11
Social relationships, changing patterns, 8
Social responsibility, corporate, 7, 12 f.,
  18, 27, 33 ff., 326–29; of private governments, 10 f.; traditional corporation and, 38 ff., 46, 63 ff.; theory of,
  40 f.; debate re, 48; case for, 48, 356;
  metrocorpate, 50 ff., 66; traditional vs.
  metrocorporate attitudes toward, 69–
  97; case against, 77 f., 193 f., 361; Kelso
  and Adler re, 82 f.; as dangerous goal,
  98; to contributor-claimants, 211–16;
  analysis of, 217; and balanced economic growth, 234 f.; narrowest view
  of, 262; toward an enlightened code
  of, 268 f.; dilemma re, 271 f.; and coordinated political functions, 322; of
  well-tempered corporation, 336 f.; legal
  and non-legal, 360
Social science, 129; study of decision
  making, 145; studies of Bolshevik behavior, 153
Social Science Reporter, *Eighth Social
  Science Seminar on "Three Major*

Factors in Business Management," 361
Social significance of the corporation,
  29 f.
Society, open vs. closed, 5, 356; greater,
  business and businessman in framework of, 7 f., 18, 67 f.; interdependence
  of sectors of, 19; and the corporation,
  28 ff.; private sectors, 33; dynamic, 35,
  249; and the "whole man" (*q.v.*), 64;
  claims on corporation, 70 f.; climate
  of social responsibility, 72–75; monolithic, 88; as corporate environment,
  99; role of corporation in, 123; interest in corporate policies, 196 f.; corporate contributions to, 329; entropy-
  reducing capacity, 356
— pluralistic: structure, 78; function of
  business in, 88; decision-making sectors, 105; American, 268; managerial
  understanding of, 285
Society, free: corporation as instrument
  of, 35; liberals' defense of, 44; and
  neofeudalism, 62 f.; preservation of,
  70; corporation in, 91 f., 337; nature
  of, 312; economic process in, 310–13;
  control of the economic process, 313–
  16; alternatives to, 331 f.
Sociologists, search for corporate realities,
  118; re business policy, 143
Sokolsky, G. E., "These Days: Proxy
  Fights and Stock Raids," quoted, 389
Sovereign, concept of, 200 f.; in juristic
  theory, 201 f.
Soviet Union, 311
Spacek, Leonard, "Challenge to Public
  Accounting," 379
Specialization, to public relations, 399
Speier, Hans, *German Rearmament and
  Atomic War,* 376
Spencer, Herbert, 345; *Social Statics,* 90;
  "administrative nihilism," 351
Spokesmen, company, 280 f.
Stability, political, 101 f.; economic, 311
Stagner, Ross, *see* Derber, Milton
Standardization, 187
Standard Oil (N.J.), 85, 342
State, the, 3, 17, 27; involvement in the
  whole of life, 18; authority of, 32;
  Mill re, 285 f.; and control of the
  economic process, 313 f.; totalitarian
  theory of, 351; corporation statutes,
  353; invocation of coercive powers of,
  380
Statism, 11

Statization, 50, 310

Status, 371; as goal-value, 15 f.

Statutes, corporate, 54, 351 ff.; incorporation, 201; banking reform, 219; state, re dividend policy, 389 f.

Stein, M. I., J. N. MacKenzie, R. R. Rodgers, and Bernard Meer, "A Case Study of a Scientist," 376

Stene, E. O., "An Approach to a Science of Administration," 378 f.

Stereotypes, Lippmann quoted re, 400 f.

Stevenson, R. L., 150

Stigler, George, 255

Stock, certificates, 212; nonvoting, 352

Stockholders, traditional corporation and, 6, 36, 41–43; as corporate owner, 13; protection of interests of, 38, 84 ff.; dispersion of, in traditional corporation, 51; government protection of, 76 f.; and corporate giving, 79; involuntary investment by, 81; responsibility to, 82, 248, 263, 269, 282; right to corporate earnings, 83; erosion of power of, 86; exclusivity of claims, 93; attitude toward corporate power, 133; interests of, and decision making, 160; and dividends, 169 f.; contributors of capital, 212; wide distribution of, 219; in corporate democracy, 220; and corporate goal of profit making, 262; public relations and, 282 f.; protection of interests of, 321; corporation law and, 353; rights of, 353; power to amend charter, 386; expectations, 388; *see also* Security holders

Stocking, G. W., and M. W. Watkins, *Monopoly and Free Enterprise,* 396

Story, Joseph, 200

Strategic decision areas, 7 f., 45, 106–8, 189–207; metrocorporate, 51; normative approach to definition of, 204; objective approach to definition of, 204 ff.

Strategy, and tactics, corporate, 106; competitive, in decision making, 144; in game theory, under given conditions, 374 f.

Strength, as corporate goal, 279

Student, business, 8; time-perspective test of, 150 f.

Study, need for, 25 f.

Summer, W. G., 345

Suppliers, claims of, 42; responsibilities to, 214, 244–47

Supply, areas of corporate policy, 191

Supreme Court, ruling re corporation charter, 200 f.

Survival, corporate, 88, 100 ff.; as institutional goal, 134 f.; and social responsibilities, 271; responsibility for, 337

Survival of the fittest, 345

Sutton, F. X., S. E. Harris, Carl Kaysen, and James Tobin, *The American Business Creed,* 22, 345, 376; quoted, 23, 25, 345

Swisher, C. B., *American Constitutional Development,* 384; *Roger B. Taney,* 384

Syndicates, raiding, 389

Taney, Roger B., concession theory, 384

Tannenbaum, Frank, 66; view of unionism, 59 f.; quoted, 60; "Man and His Institutions," 361, quoted, 72; *A Philosophy of Labor,* 393, quoted, 358

Tariff, policy, 160; corporate vs. national policy, 286

Tawney, R. H., on power as goal, 132; *Religion and the Rise of Capitalism,* 355; *Equality,* 372

Taylor, F. W., 4, 358

Technology, aid to research, 2; organizational, 3; sharing of fruits of, 225; contributions by corporations to, 246; access or denial to, 395

Tenure and compensation, managerial, 241

Termination, 140; of corporation, 134; of policy, 183, 184

Theory, economic, 21; corporate, studies of, 96 ff., 348

Things, power over, 31

Thompson, Stewart, *Management Creeds and Philosophies,* 372, 400

Thrall, Robert, *et al., Decision Processes,* 379

Tierney, Brian, *Foundations of Conciliar Theory,* 346

Timberg, Sigmund, "The Corporation as a Technique of International Administration," 350

Time, man's perception of, 2; and motion study, 4, 146; decision making and, 145–52; pressure of, and freedom of choice, 160 (*se also* Pressures)

Time-discount, 150 f.

Time-perspective, 150

Time-span, and technological change, 21

Tobin, James, *see* Sutton, Francis X.

Totalitarian authoritarianism, 357

Totalitarianism, 312

Trade, advantageous position, 121; associations, 187; freedom of, and competition, 249, 250

Traditional corporation, 6 f., 36 f., 38–49, 50, 307 f.; model of, 12; owned by security holders, 27; austerity, 41 f., 45; public policy of, 46; as response to ecological stimuli, 48; powers of, 52 f.; transition to metrocorporation, 55; labor relations, 61 f.; view of proponents, 63 ff.; modification of, 65 f.; attitude toward social goals, 76, 327 (*see also under* Social responsibility); and personal values and private needs, 111; defined, 205; hierarchical structure, 316; economic responsibility, 318; and state intervention, 333

"Two-way street," concept of, 276 f.

Union, labor, as system of private government, 4; authority of, 32; special interests, 43; invocation and application of policy, 182; as contributor-claimant, 223; and management, 238; encroachment on managerial functions, 239 f., 242 f.; participation in corporate decisions, 244; corporate relations with, 289 f.; Landrum-Griffin Act, 324; voluntary restraint, 355; theories, 358; governments, 380; power and control of, 394

Unionism, principle of, 8

United Automobile Workers, 174–80

United States, growth of managerial enterprise, 21; political ecology, 101; attitude toward business autonomy and planned economy, 197; profit margins in, 226; corporate ownership, 388 f.

United States Steel, 342

Urwick, Lyndall, *Pattern of Management*, 368, 333

Utilitarianism, 45; hedonistic, 351

Vajda, S., *The Theory of Games and Linear Programming*, 373

Value-goals, achievement of, 187; *see also* Goal-values

Value-judgments, 109; and competitive goals, 253

Values, human, analysis of, 4; social, 5; social, and policy decisions, 73; normative, 94; and decisions, 172; democratic, and appraisal function, 184; conflicting, in human and economic relations, 354 f.

Vanderbilt, Cornelius, 161

Veblen, Thorstein, 347, 358

Vendors, satellite and nonsatellite, 245

Vickers, Sir Geoffrey, "Communication in Economic Systems," 399 f.

Visibility, of decision-making centers, 197

Von Beckerath, Herbert, *Modern Industrial Organization: an Economic Interpretation*, 343

Von Neumann, John, 143; and O. Morgenstern, *The Theory of Games and Economic Behavior*, 373

Voters, apathy of, 223

Voting, apathy of stockholders, 388

Wage earners, percentage in corporations, 13

Wages, voluntary restraint and, 44; and prices, in automobile industry, 175 ff.; received theory of, 394

Walker, F. A., 119; *The Wages Question*, 369

Wall Street, investment underwriters, 389

War, decision making, 139

Ware, Gorman, 358

Wasserman, Paul, and F. S. Silander, *Decision-Making: an Annotated Bibliography*, 374

Watkins, M. W., *see* Stocking, G. W.

Wealth, "laboristic distribution of," 80 f.; accumulation of, as goal, 98; as goal-value, 125; production of, 212

Weaver, Warren, "Recent Contributions to the Mathematical Theory of Communications," 400; *see also* Shannon, C. E.

Webb, Beatrice, and Sidney Webb, 358

Weber, Max, 143; "Politics as a Vocation," 373; *The Protestant Ethic and the Spirit of Capitalism*, 373; *The Theory of Social and Economic Organization*, 373

Welfare, concept of employment, 62; functions, traditional model view of, 65; state, 88; government responsibility, 90; concept of labor, 358

Well-tempered corporation, 12, 37, 307–38; polity and constitutionalism, 322 ff.;

defined, 330; ecology, 330–33; salient elements in model of, 335–38

Western hemisphere, political ecology, 101

White, L. D., ed., *The State of the Social Sciences*, 378, 400

Whitehead, A. N., "Foresight," 350, quoted, 15

"Whole man," Emersonian concept, 6, 64, 98, 118, 307, 368 f.; metrocorporation and, 52; concern with, 88

Whyte, W. H., organization man, 30

Wiener, Norbert, 301; *The Human Use of Human Beings*, 356 f., 399, 402; Mathematical Theory, 377

Williams, J. D., *The Compleat Strategyst*, 373

Williston, Samuel, "History of the Law of Business Corporations before 1800," 347

Wolfson, Theresa, *see* Chamberlain, N. W.

Work, role of, 60; *see also* Labor

Workers, goals of, 59 f., 62; *see also* Employees; Labor

World market, 334

Worthy, J. C., "Religion and Its Role in the World of Business," quoted, 354 f.

Yntema, T. O., "Our Long-Run Internal Problems," quoted, 356

Zimmerman, Claire, and R. A. Bauer, "The Effect of an Audience on What Is Remembered," 376